Minds of Our Own

MINDS OF OUR OWN

Inventing Feminist Scholarship
and Women's Studies in Canada
and Québec, 1966–76

edited by
Wendy Robbins, Meg Luxton,
Margrit Eichler, Francine Descarries

Wilfrid Laurier University Press
WLU

We acknowledge the financial support of the Government of Canada through the Book Publishing Industry Development Program for our publishing activities.

The editors wish gratefully to acknowledge the assistance of the Social Sciences and Humanities Research Council of Canada. A SSHRC Strategic Research Grant, made under the former Women and Change Program, facilitated a portion of the work on this book, as did monies from the Department of English, Faculty of Arts (Busteed Foundation), and Vice-President Research at the University of New Brunswick, Fredericton.

Proceeds from all royalties will go to support the work of advancing women's equality—with men, and with one another—through donation to an equity-seeking group such as the Canadian Research Institute for the Advancement of Women/Institute canadien de recherches sur les femmes (CRIAW/ICREF), or to projects reclaiming the history of the recent women's movement.

Library and Archives Canada Cataloguing in Publication

Minds of our own : inventing feminist scholarship and women's studies in Canada and Quebec, 1966–76 / Wendy Robbins ... [et al.], editors.

Includes bibliographical references and index.
ISBN 978-1-55458-037-8

1. Women's studies—Canada—History. 2. Women scholars—Canada—History. 3. Feminism and education—Canada. 4. Discrimination in higher education—Canada. I. Robbins, Wendy, 1948–

HQ1453.M56 2008   305.4071'171   C2007-906850-2

Cover image: *Promethean Dreams* (2005), handwoven tapestry, 16.5" × 21", by Linda Wallace, from the collection of the artist. Cover design by David Drummond. Text design by C. Bonas-Taylor.

This book is printed on Ancient Forest Friendly paper (100% post-consumer recycled).

Printed in Canada

Published by Wilfrid Laurier University Press
Waterloo, Ontario, Canada
www.wlupress.wlu.ca

Contents

Preface

LIKE WOMEN'S STUDIES, this book has multiple origins and includes many voices. It is the result of the confluence of three research streams springing from a common source: a passionate commitment to documenting women's lives and the development of feminism across Canada, and to ensuring that the historical record includes as many perspectives as possible.

The book brings together three distinct projects. Wendy Robbins, at her home, at the University of New Brunswick (UNB), and nationally in the Canadian Federation for the Humanities and Social Sciences (CFHSS), was closely monitoring the situation of women in Canadian universities and was actively involved in various campaigns to improve women's status. She read *The Politics of Women's Studies: Testimony from 30 Founding Mothers* (2000), a collection of autobiographical essays edited by Florence Howe; the American collection, she recognized, "might serve as a wake-up call to founding mothers of Women's Studies programs across Canada, for our stories, too, are in need of integration, analysis, and articulation" (Robbins 2001). Her commitment to this project was confirmed at the annual meeting of coordinators of women's studies at Dalhousie University in the spring of 2002, where the notion of creating a comparable Canadian collection was generally welcomed as an excellent idea. By then, Wendy had started to supervise an undergraduate student at UNB, Laurie McLaughlan, in the compilation of "A Chronology of the Development of Women's Studies in Canada," which they posted on the PAR-L website for comments and corrections. Entries were written in either English or French, and many of the items concerning Québec were contributed by Francine Descarries. Inspired by the enthusiasm evoked by her various initiatives, Wendy delved further into the development of women's studies during her subsequent year as visiting scholar at the Canadian Association of University Teachers (CAUT).

Another project started with discussions between Margrit Eichler and Meg Luxton, both directors of women's studies programs in Toronto at the time. Recognizing that some of the leading activists involved in setting up women's studies were past retirement, they decided to interview them to make sure that their stories would not be forgotten. They were impressed by the depth of knowledge and the complexity of the issues revealed by the interviews. They were also struck by the contrast between the accounts presented by the pioneers and the assumptions widespread among students and younger faculty about the women's movement of the 1960s and 1970s, and specifically about the origins of women's studies.

Too often, it was claimed, women's studies failed to deal with issues of class inequality, racialization and racism, and other forms of oppression and domination. Noting that much of the material published about that period came from the United States and that too often American accounts were accepted as valid for Canada as well, Eichler and Luxton wondered what sources junior colleagues and students could draw on for the history of the women's movement and women's studies in Canada. They also wondered whether younger women would be able to imagine the difficult intellectual, social, and political circumstances under which the early pioneers conducted their work.

They decided to start documenting the beginnings of women's studies in Canada. As a first step, they organized a workshop with a number of other feminist scholars who had been involved in women's studies early on to consult them on how to approach this issue. The results of this part of the undertaking are reported in *Atlantis* (Eichler and Luxton 2006), and the present book owes its genesis in considerable measure to the impetus provided by this consultation.

It quickly became apparent that for the project, whatever form it took, to meet its objective of tracing the origins and early development of women's studies in Canada, a significant place needed to be accorded to the evolution of feminist studies and the experiences of francophone feminists in Québec, in order to understand the particular social and political nexus in which these studies were conceived. For Francine Descarries, it was self-evident that she would participate in such a venture. She was convinced of the importance of documenting women's history, particularly after having completed, with colleagues at the Université du Québec à Montréal (UQAM), a major project on the history of Montréal women (Darsigny et al. 1994). She agreed to join in, not only to assure the visibility of the Québec experience and to draw attention to its similarities and its distinctiveness, but also because she recognized that collecting first-person narratives by pioneers of Québec feminist studies is part of a much-needed process to remedy the paucity of archival resources on this subject. As feminist historian Nadia Fahmy-Eid wrote to the editors, "This concerns studies which, in Québec as in the rest of Canada, have not always left clear tracks in institutional archives, and which thus risk being more and more difficult to retrace in the future. In these circumstances, the labour of recording falls on the first generation, a labour which becomes *un devoir de mémoire* (a duty to remember) when we think of the generations—of women and of men—who will follow us."

In the fall of 2004, the four editors decided to join forces to produce a book on the first decade of women's studies, from 1966 to 1976—that is, from the founding of the Committee for the Equality of Women in Canada (CEWC) through to the end of the academic year that included the final months of International Women's Year. We set this as the cut-off date since, we reasoned, International Women's Year in 1975 marked a turning point: by then, women's consciousness-raising and political organizing had begun to have a widespread public impact, and a decade of scholarship had produced new resources for classrooms. Using, among other sources, the *Canadian Newsletter of Research on Women*, we identified those who had taught courses in these early years. We sent out an open call for papers on PAR-L and other feminist listservs, in individual emails and letters, and in some cases by telephone.

We invited people who were involved in developing feminist scholarship and/or creating women's studies in universities in Canada up to and including the academic year 1975–76, the earliest pioneers, to send us short papers addressing some or all of the following questions:

1. What brought you into feminist studies, personally and professionally?
2. Who were your allies or mentors?
3. What were the major challenges you faced—personal, intellectual, institutional, political?
4. What was the scholarship you challenged?
5. What helped you mount the challenge?
6. What were the central issues debated?
7. What do you think the major impact of feminism on scholarship has been?

8. What feminist organizations or other relevant political groups were you associated with at the time?

9. What did your early involvement in the field lead to? What are you doing now?

10. Which feminist authors, at the outset, influenced your theoretical position or orientation and your feminist praxis?

11. Which feminist authors or theorists today are the most important in your understanding of feminism as a mode of thought and of action?

12. How were issues of anti-capitalism, imperialism, colonialism, class, racialization, sexual orientation, and ability dealt with in the early period?

The response was far beyond our expectations. Rather than the two dozen essays we had anticipated, we ended up with more than forty. Some people decided to collaborate, and many submissions were initially longer than the 2,500 words we had requested. Evidently, these were stories that wanted to be told.

The essays, written in the first person, tell stories of personal engagement in the creation of feminist scholarship and women's studies, and they also provide nuanced observations and commentaries on the complexities of the times. Thus they are an important form of testimony, and they challenge some of the current preconceptions about feminist academics of the 1970s. Each of the stories is different, none is complete, but together they provide the background for an analysis of the emergence of women's studies as a new way of understanding women, men, and society.

Clearly, not all the people who are amongst the earliest pioneers are to be found in this collection. Some people whose stories we would have valued were not able to make a contribution because of illness or competing commitments; and, sadly, some of the early "founding mothers" have passed away. Some institutions that mounted early feminist courses are not included because no one responded to our call for papers. Others who are also to be counted amongst the founders of feminist scholarship in many disciplines and at many more institutions did not mount their courses or programs prior to the academic year 1975–76 and thus do not fit within the parameters of this book. We are aware that some very important experiences are not included in this volume because they fall outside our time limits. All this and much more will constitute very interesting material for further studies. We hope that this collection will stimulate others so that one day we will be able to map out the full progress of women's studies and the field's branching out into gender studies, cultural studies, sexuality studies, and more.

The book can be read in several different ways. While the essays speak for themselves, we have provided a contextualizing essay by way of introduction to the sixties and seventies, with some reference also to the evolution of feminism in Canada and Québec. It need not be read first. We have presented the essays next, in roughly chronological order, by the age of the author (in the case of multiple authors, we took the oldest one for our ordering). The birth dates range from 1919 to 1951—spanning two generations—but everyone is a pioneer. Chronological age and academic age are, of course, not the same; some people who were born earlier came to women's studies later than others who were born later. Nevertheless, chronological age is important because it locates people within a socio-political structure. The social context within which women lived in Canada changed considerably over the past half century, and age made a difference in the degree to which women were affected by various sexist social structures. Timing, or "academic age," is also very important. Whether a person started teaching women's studies in 1970 or in 1975, for instance, made a difference. By 1975, new means of communication were in place, some important books had been published, and several important conferences had been held. Some of our authors were actually students of other authors.

Another way of reading the essays, rather than chronologically by author, is by discipline. To facilitate these alternatives, we provide an alphabetical list of the authors' names in appendix A and a list of the authors' disciplinary affiliations in appendix B. Because people move from institution to institution and from province to province, we have not included a list by university or by region. The final chapter, "Personal and Intellectual Revolutions: Some Reflections," highlights recurring themes or motifs that weave the essays' narrative threads, however loosely, together. Along with the index, it provides a thematic entry to the collection. Thus, material can be found arranged in roughly chronological order, alphabetically by author, by discipline, or by thematic grouping. There are many ways of reading the book, including simply starting with the people you are most interested in.

The essays are based on memories, and memories, as we know, change with time and circumstances. Many entries describe vivid memories of events etched forever in the minds of those who lived through them. This includes examples of atrocious sexism, which many of the writers experienced. For all, participation in inventing women's studies was a life-transforming experience, with extraordinary highs and lows. We offer this anthology of memoirs as a contribution to the ongoing story of feminism in Canada, and we hope that it will stimulate others to reflect on our collective past.

A word about us, the editors. Three of us, Margrit, Meg, and Wendy, have contributed individual essays of our own. Francine's pioneering research into women's "pink-collar" work and her teaching started just after our 1976 limit. We come from three different disciplinary backgrounds (sociology, anthropology, English)—in four universities (UQAM, Ontario Institute for Studies in Education at the University of Toronto [OISE/UT], York, UNB), located in three provinces (Québec, Ontario, New Brunswick). We include one allophone immigrant (Margrit), one francophone (Francine), and two anglophones (Meg and Wendy); we live in a variety of household and family configurations. Although we share certain things in common, being White academic women, for example, we often do not see eye to eye. Again, we consider this a strength rather than a weakness, for each of us has learned from the others while making the compromises and adjustments necessary in any genuinely collaborative feminist project. We all contributed in different but equivalent ways to the book. We wondered in what order to present ourselves in the list of editors, and finally decided to reverse the hegemony of an ascending alphabetical order by using a descending alphabetical order.

Finally, we would like to express our sincere thanks to all the contributors for sharing their stories with us; to the many people—colleagues, family, and friends—who have generously offered us encouragement and assistance with many facets of our work and our lives; to Katherine Side, who has the distinction of being the first woman to graduate with a free-standing PhD in women's studies in Canada and who provided helpful comments on an early draft of our contextualizing essay; to Nicole Kennedy, who translated the essays written originally in French; to Bill Schipper and James MacKenzie, who tracked down countless hard-to-verify references; and especially to the two graduate students who worked assiduously with us on the bibliography, statistics, and copy-editing, transforming painstaking technical work into a labour of love—Victoria Kannen, Department of Sociology and Equity Studies in Education, OISE/UT, and Vicky Simpson, Department of English, UNB.

◉ Changing Times

In 1965 in Canada there were few women's organizations, no women's bookstores (because there were almost no books about women), and no women's studies courses in schools and universities.

—Adamson, Briskin, and McPhail (1988, 5)

ONE OF THE ENDEARING features of the stories told about feminist scholarship in the period between 1965 and 1976 is how many claim to be the "first." There are many first women's studies courses, and the point is that each claim is largely correct. The women curious about what we now call feminist scholarship and eager to teach it, the students critical of the formal knowledge available to them who pressured faculty to offer alternative courses, the activists from women's liberation keen to bring their politics into the classroom—all were for the most part isolated, alone, or with small groups of friends or colleagues, struggling with few resources in the face of resistant institutions and sometimes fierce opposition. There were no antecedents, no institutional structures, no organizations, no journals, few books, and, of course, no mentors. There was no field—just a desire to correct this situation that was prejudicial, and still is, to half of humankind. As each person designed a course, fought to get it offered (challenging university structures to get formal approval, funding, faculty, an institutional location, and scholarly legitimacy), and celebrated its first appearance, each was inventing a "first."

With hindsight, we can now see how many firsts there were. The essays we have collected document many turning points in the ongoing story of women, formal knowledge creation, and post-secondary education in Canada and Québec, and they also offer us compelling insights into both the people and the climate that produced them. In order to put the experiences described by the essays into context, we outline here some of the main features of that climate.[1]

Women's Organizations (before 1960)

Feminist scholarship and women's studies developed as the academic wing of the women's movement of the 1960s and 1970s, and are an integral part of the feminism of that period.[2] In the years leading up to the 1966 founding of the Committee for the Equality of Women in Canada (CEWC), many women in Canada and Québec, as well as internationally, were engaged in a wide range of efforts to bring women together, to obtain citizenship and educational rights, to provide services, to protect their rights as workers, and to improve their everyday lives. Some of these women's groups dated back to the nineteenth-century women's movement: the Women's Christian Temperance Union (1874), the National Council of Women (1893), and the National Council of Jewish Women (1897). Many more groups were formed in the first half of the twentieth century: the Fédération nationale Saint-Jean-Baptiste (1907), the Montréal Suffrage Association (1912), les Cercles des fermières (1915), the Federated Women's Institutes (1919), the Canadian Federation of University Women (1919), le Comité provincial pour le suffrage féminin (1920), the Canadian Federation of Business and Professional Women (1930), and the Canadian Negro Women's Association (1951). While the Second World War years gave women some new opportunities, especially in the paid labour force, the 1950s was a decade of strong reaction against feminism, women's equality, and women's participation in the paid labour force—the strongest opposition probably coming from the leaders of Catholic Québec. However, women and their organizations, including socialist women such as Idola St-Jean, an activist in the Québec suffrage movement of the 1930s and 1940s,[3] and union leaders, such as Yvette Charpentier, Madeleine Parent, Léa Roback, Grace Hartman, and Evelyn Armstrong, all worked for women's rights (Collectif Clio 1992; Luxton 2001b).

Politically, women's groups ranged from deeply conservative to socialist, but all of them brought women together and provided opportunities for them to develop collective knowledge about their experiences, sharpen their political skills, and create strategies to advance their concerns. Some of these groups were national branches of international organizations; through those ties, they were actively involved in international activities and organizations, particularly the United Nations (UN) and its Status of Women Commission. As representatives to UN committees with formal participatory status, they both influenced debates there and brought back home new ideas and international connections. In Canada and Québec, women met to discuss their own concerns; to develop demands of their governments, their communities, and their workplaces; and to strategize about how to make progress. For them and their allies, democracy meant equal rights, equal access for women and men, and greater social justice. These women and their organizations focussed public attention on women and many sustained a women's rights perspective, laying a foundation for the mobilizations to come. Their political sophistication and their experiences of working collectively contributed to the emergence of social conditions favourable to the resurgence of the women's movement in the mid-1960s.

Women's Changing Social Position

The generation that came of age during or just after the Second World War, and their daughters of the "baby boom" generation, lived through major changes in the position of women in Canada and Québec. The typical experiences of women in terms of education, sexuality, marriage, parenting, employment, and citizenship meant that, by the 1970s, women's lives and the options available to them started to be increasingly different from those of previous generations and their ways of life more diverse (Jones, Marsden, and Tepperman 1990). However, it is always important to distinguish between measures based on statistical surveys that show national trends and the actual variations within the population.[4] For example, statistics for the Canadian population show that there was a steady increase through the twentieth century in women's paid labour force participation. However, in Québec, as in Canada as a whole, women's participation declined after the war—from 26.9% and 31.0% respectively in 1944, to 20.5% and 21.9% in 1947—rising again to the 1944 rate only in 1965 for Québec and in 1968 for Canada (Travail Canada 1973; Women's Bureau 1973). Throughout the period, Black women had much higher paid labour force participation rates than the national average, and Aboriginal women continued to have much lower rates. While respecting major differences within and among specific groups of women, here we sketch some of the overall trends in women's changing social position that contributed to the re-emergence of the activist women's movement in the 1960s, and with it the development of feminist scholarship and women's studies.

Changing Demographics

In the 1960s, the population in Canada and Québec was predominantly White and of Euro–North American descent. Other sectors of the population, subject to discrimination on the basis of language, national origin, religion, and "race," tended to be clustered in small communities or urban neighbourhoods across the country. Aboriginal peoples were a small minority, mostly isolated in rural and remote areas, although increasing numbers lived in urban centres (Bourgeault 1983). Various immigrant populations formed and settled according to the changing immigration laws, existing labour markets, and legal and social regulations. In the late 1960s, the federal government changed the laws in order to encourage greater numbers of immigrants and thus meet growing labour demands (Simmons 1990). As a result, waves of new immigrants from the Caribbean, Africa, and Asia arrived, settling primarily in the major cities. They brought their own political traditions and new political mobilizing energy, especially around issues of immigration, citizenship rights, and anti-racism (Stasiulis 1997). Their presence both strengthened the women's movement and posed serious challenges to existing women's politics just at the moment that the women's movement was going through major changes, significantly in response to changing patterns of work and family life for most women (Carty 1993).

Immediately after the end of the Second World War, there was a substantial increase in the numbers of women getting married. At the same time, the age at which they both married and had children dropped, resulting in the baby boom. The majority of women married and lived as married women for most of their adult lives. Most also had children. For the large majority of them, no love life, sexuality, or maternity was realistically possible outside of marriage, and having children was essential to marriage. Children born "out of wedlock" were identified as illegitimate children, *bâtard* (bastard) in French—a concept that, fortunately, no longer carries any meaning. They were legally discriminated against and were mostly given up for adoption, a social status that was often marginal and shameful.

However, after 1957, the Canadian birth rate decreased as women had fewer children and stopped child-bearing at an earlier age than previous generations had. By 1971, the average number of births was 16.8 per 1,000 of the total population. The average number of children per family decreased from 1.9 in 1961 to 1.7 in 1971, even though women in rural communities and most Native women maintained higher rates (Statistics Canada 1977, 171). During 1961–71 the birth rate in Québec dropped by almost half to become the lowest in the country—after Québec's renowned *revanche des berceaux* (revenge of the cradle)—dropping during this period from 26.6 to 15.3 per 1,000 (Institut de la statistique du Québec 2007a).

The adoption of the Divorce Act in 1968, Canada's first unified divorce law, made it easier for couples in all provinces and territories to be released from the constraints of an unsatisfactory union. Divorce was possible on two grounds: matrimonial offences or marriage breakdown. However, the grounds for establishing the latter were still quite restrictive: a person could petition for divorce if the couple lived separately and apart for at least three years, or five years when the deserting party petitioned for divorce (Eichler 1988, 360). Before the liberalization of the law, it is estimated that one marriage out of ten was likely to end in a matrimonial dissolution (Descarries and Corbeil 1989). Following its adoption, the annual rate of divorce multiplied more than five times between 1968 and 1980, increasing from 54.8 to 280 per 100,000 inhabitants (Dumas and Péron 1992), whereas it is estimated that one out of three couples that got married in 1975 in Québec are now divorced (Institut de la statistique du Québec 2007b).

Another important change was that women's life-expectancy rates increased more than men's, rising from 63 years for men and 66 years for women in 1940–42, to 69 and 76 in 1970–72 (Statistics Canada 2000). As a result, growing numbers of women were single and were without child-care responsibilities for longer periods. Between 1966 and 1971, for example, the total number of households in Canada increased by 17%; the number of households of single, never married people increased by 92% (Statistics Canada 1977, 169). There was a major building boom in apartment construction (Miron 1985, 7.18, table 7.3.2), which was a response to such changes, and in turn also made such arrangements possible. As more and more women recognized that they might be on their own for more extended periods of their lives, they had greater incentives to establish themselves as income earners in their own right.

Women's Changing Paid Labour Force Participation

The percentage of women in the paid labour force increased steadily after 1945 and did so dramatically between 1960 and 1980 (Statistics Canada 2000).

In the 1960s and 1970s, most women tended to start employment after leaving school and to withdraw from the labour force after their marriage or first pregnancy. Increasingly by the end of the period, however, women tended to return to paid employment once the youngest child began school. Between 1965 and 1975, the number of employed women increased by 70% (increasing from 2,076,000 civilian workers to 3,515,000). In 1961, 28.7% of all women aged 15 and over were in the paid labour force. Between 1971 and 1981,women's participation in the paid workforce steadily increased from 36.5% to 52%, including almost 42% of married women by 1975 (Statistics Canada 1995). The formal labour force participation of Québec women during that period was slightly lower than that of the Canadian average, moving from 34.6% in 1971 to 47.8% in 1981 (Institut de la statistique du Québec 2007c). Undoubtedly, one must see in this discrepancy the effects of the sharp opposition to the participation of Québec women in formal labour by the traditional male-dominated local elites, trade unionists, intellectuals, and politicians, as well as religious authorities, who, until *la Révolution tranquille* (the Quiet Revolution), considered women's paid work more a threat to social cohesion than an achievement in itself.

However, in all provinces, in addition to changing demographic conditions and women's increasing desire to ensure their own financial autonomy, the expansion of women's formal labour force participation reflected the effects of structural changes generated by the bureaucratization of enterprises and states, both national and provincial, as well as the expansion of the service sectors (health, education, maintenance) where female labour was traditionally accepted, not to say confined. The increase in women's participation in the paid labour force was also at least partially attributable to the increasing availability of goods and services that in earlier times were produced and exchanged almost exclusively within private households.

The labour force was even more segregated by sex than it is now: the existence of a dual labour market based on the social division of the sexes considerably limited the range of paid jobs open to women. Most women had jobs in the clerical and retail sectors, where the labour market was expanding but where wages were low and benefits few or non-existent. In 1971, 64.2% of women in the labour force were confined to twenty professions in which they accounted for 70.2% of the entire workforce. All of these—except for the occupations of teacher and nurse—were located in devalued or undervalued professional categories in which employees had few or no responsibilities and few professional chances of mobility (Descarries 1980). In all these professions, the average wages were—and are still—

affected by the systematic undervaluation of women's work. Consequently in 1971, on average, Canadian women earned about 57.3% of what men earned, and the situation deteriorated even more by 1976 to merely 52.1%. Women of colour and immigrant women were almost always in the lowest paying, least attractive jobs, and most of them, despite their formal qualifications, had trouble advancing in their occupations.

In many workplaces, women faced explicit sexist discrimination and harassment, even though this reality was hardly recognized, let alone named and condemned. They also had to deal with dominant ideological values that maintained that "woman's place is in the home," and that as wives and mothers their obligation was to be at home full-time. Women had to juggle the competing demands of their paid employment and their domestic and family responsibilities, especially for child care, in a work and community environment that was usually hostile to such concerns and offered no support services. The concept of *articulation famille/travail*, balancing work and family, had not yet reached social consciousness, and women's demands for a more equitable sharing of domestic tasks was yet to be formulated (Luxton 1980). Women were captives of a patriarchal system, vigorously denounced by Simone de Beauvoir, that treated them like *le deuxième sexe* (the second sex), a situation also documented, significantly, by *Chatelaine* magazine under the editorial leadership of Doris Anderson (1957–77), as well as later on by Betty Friedan, who labelled and laid it bare in her landmark book, *The Feminine Mystique* (1963).[5] Such experiences meant that many women were receptive to feminist critiques of the double shift of paid and unpaid work and of sexist discrimination as these critiques became more widely available.

As the numbers of women in the paid labour force grew and as the labour movement began organizing new sectors such as the public service where there were more and more women, the proportion of women members in the labour movement increased. In 1962, women made up only 16.4% of all union members, but between 1965 and 1975, the number of union women increased by 144% (Ontario Women's Bureau 1977), resulting in the unionization of almost one woman worker out of four (23%) in 1976; rates of unionization did, however, remain uneven: relatively low numbers in Nova Scotia (16%) and Ontario (18%) compared to the strong advances in British Columbia (28%) and Québec (30%) (Akyeampong 1998).

While the labour movement in the early 1960s was male dominated and did not promote women's issues, it did offer women union members an organizational base in which and from which they could fight for women's concerns and urge their unions to begin to take up women's issues. The first claims dealt with the development of maternity leave programs and "equal pay for equal work"; this issue was not yet formulated in Canadian legislation in terms of "equal pay for work of equal value." Inside their unions, women held conferences, ran educational and training programs, organized themselves in women's caucuses, challenged the male dominance of union structures and issues, and progressively brought women's issues to the bargaining table. For example, in 1964 the United Auto Workers held its first conference for women workers and called for full equality (Sugiman 1993, 172–88). In 1965, the Ontario Federation of Labour set up its first women's committee, chaired by Grace Hartman, a vice-president of the Canadian Union of Public Employees. The next year, the Ontario Federation of Labour organized a conference on women and work (Crean 1995, 68). In 1968, the Canadian Labour Congress included the eradication of sex discrimination in its constitution (Canadian Labour Congress 1968, 9).[6]

The labour movement provided union women with education, and a forum in which to develop their demands. In Québec, documents put out by women's committees of the Confédération des syndications nationaux (1976) and the Centrale de l'enseignement du Québec (1974) were among the first to bring feminist issues into the open and to formulate an analysis in terms of the social relations between the sexes and power relations. As leading women in the union movement were also active in women's organizations, they provided mutually reinforcing links between the two arenas (Luxton 2001b). At the same time, women were making slow gains in professional occupations and in business. These women, too, faced sexism at work and in their professional associations, which prompted many of them to swell the ranks of the existing women's organizations, set up new professional and business organizations, and lend their support to equity struggles.

Gender Ideologies and Women's Realities

During the Second World War, the Canadian government launched major advertising campaigns urging women to enter the paid labour force and the military as part of their contribution to the war effort. A range of services, including limited child care, was implemented to enable women to do so. Immediately after the war, that effort was reversed. The government tried to ensure that returning servicemen were reintegrated into postwar society and given priority in the labour force. Women were encouraged to leave their paid work and return to the home, reorienting their lives around their domestic responsibilities as wives and mothers. The dominant image of women presented in the mass media, especially magazines, was the consumer of domestic goods whose main source of happiness was hearth and home. In this period, there was a factitious professionalization of the roles of housewives and mothers. Domestic chores became a creative art form according to the media. The "whiter than white" slogan of one soap company was complemented by the publication of numerous handbooks on child care. Dr. Benjamin Spock's *The Common Sense Book of Baby and Child Care* (1946) was published in pocketbook format. The book quickly became essential for a whole generation of mothers and sold more than 50 million copies throughout the world, an exploit exceeded at the time only by the Bible. The idea that women's main aims in life were marriage and motherhood was widely reinforced. Schools encouraged girls to learn home economics, while textbooks portrayed girls playing with dolls and mothers staying at home, in contrast with boys doing a range of activities and fathers going off to work away from home. Most middle-class girls were encouraged to get "just in case" educations that prepared them for jobs such as teaching or nursing. Such careers, deemed socially acceptable for women, were assumed to permit women to get jobs before marriage and allow them to return to those jobs either once their children were grown or in case the marriage failed.

Even the report of the Commission royale d'enquête sur l'enseignement dans la province de Québec (the Parent report) (1966), which was seen as a groundbreaking document in Québec and introduced real coeducation, was cautious about discussing women's access to higher education and promoted it only in a "just in case" tone. The notion of "women's education" persisted. In spite of real structural changes, the objective was still to develop women's predispositions and qualifications to prepare them for their roles as mother, wife, and housewife. Seen only as a complement or substitute, women's paid labour force participation was still described apologetically as a "counterweight to boredom," "auxiliary wages," or "pin money." Article 1019 of the Parent Report states, "to a certain extent, one must prepare them [girls] to be aware of married life's major problems and to become mothers capable of taking care of their children and raising them suitably. Lastly, one must provide all girls with training to hold jobs that will enable them to earn their living either before or during their married life, or after their children have been raised. Such preparation and holding a job can make a woman a sharper (more awake) and more interesting person, often more satisfied and more balanced, and possessing some security since it enables her, if need be, to help her husband financially, or to ensure the subsistence of the family if her husband were to disappear." Article 1020 recommends in part that "family and domestic education must be part of every girl's training and accustom girls to find both aesthetic and human enjoyment in domestic work." After advising boys "to be useful in society" (art. 1023), the report also suggests that boys acclimatize themselves to domestic realities: "Without wanting, of course, to transform men into *'bonnes à tout faire'* [all-purpose maids] or subjecting them to domestic tyranny, one can think of simplifying their participation in domestic life by giving them a certain preparation. In particular, they should be introduced to child psychology, trained to discuss the family budget, and prepared to see the problems which the woman must raise" (art. 1024).[7]

Dominant practices in women's health attributed various illnesses and depression, as well as lesbian sexual orientation, to the individual's failure to accept her appropriate feminine role. Religious organizations and leaders advocated marriage and motherhood as the best life for women and railed against anything that encouraged women to do otherwise. These gender ideologies were reinforced by a variety of laws, regulations, and policies that supported women's domesticity and thwarted their independence. Women could not get credit or make major purchases without their husband's permission. Many employers refused to hire married women and fired women workers if they got married. For a long time, it was illegal for married women to hold jobs in the federal civil service, and it was illegal for women to work in some jobs, such as mining, right up until the 1970s.

However, despite the almost hegemonic ideology of femininity in the 1950s, there were major discrepancies between the messages about the way women should live and the way most women were living. Racism meant that women who were not White and Euro–North American, like those who were not elite or middle class, were often actively prevented from achieving these "ideal" family lives. Many Aboriginal women's children were forcibly removed and sent to residential schools. Immigrant women, especially from the Caribbean, were not allowed to bring their children into Canada with them. Working-class women were in the paid labour force out of economic necessity, and White middle-class women were employed in ever increasing numbers—and not just in search of "pin money" either.[8] By the late 1950s, leading women journalists such as Doris Anderson and June Callwood noted these discrepancies and wrote controversial articles challenging that ideology and encouraging women to demand alternatives. In *Revue Populaire* (which became the French edition of *Châtelaine*), in 1962, Renée Pelletier-Rowan published an article that defied existing laws by discussing birth control and the joy of having a child by choice: "La régulation des naissances: la joie d'avoir un enfant quand nous l'avons voulu" (Birth control: The joy of having a child when we wanted to).

The Formal Political Context, 1966–76

By 1966, fifty years after some women won the right to participate in electoral politics,[9] a total of only forty-six women had been elected to provincial and territorial legislatures, eight women had been elected to the House of Commons, and nine women had been appointed to the Senate. Only one woman had led a political party: Thérèse Casgrain. Having belonged to the Co-operative Commonwealth Federation (CCF; predecessor of the New Democratic Party), Casgrain held office as president of the Québéc wing during the period 1951–57 (Trimble and Arscott 2003, 14). In 1972, Rosemary Brown became the first Black woman elected to a legislature (Brown 1989), and in 1974 Eleanor Millard was the first Aboriginal woman elected (Trimble and Arscott 2003, 30). Trimble and Arscott calculate that in 1970, women held only 2.1% of the key public positions in Canada (2003, 37). Formal politics was totally male dominated, largely hostile to women in politics, and, at best, indifferent to women's issues.

In the immediate postwar period, the federal state proposed to develop a comprehensive welfare system that would "institutionalize the government's, rather than the market's, ultimate responsibility for social welfare," in which an interventionist government "was seen as a principal instrument of economic development and social progress" (Ornstein and Stephenson 1999, 35). Subsequent governments never realized this promise, although, through the 1950s and 1960s, federal governments did expand welfare programs, based on regulation of the economy by fiscal and monetary means, not direct state intervention (Granatstein 1982). In the late 1940s, the federal government strove for labour peace in the face of major organizing initiatives by industrial workers through the recognition of trade unions and collective bargaining regulations designed to restrain the excesses of employers and limit workers' right to strike (especially the 1948 Industrial Relations and Disputes Investigations Act). Over the next two decades, the state took on the major costs of two components of social reproduction: expanded post-secondary education and health (for example, with the 1966 Medical Care Insurance Act). It also recognized limited collective responsibility for those who were unemployed or unable to hold employment by developing the social welfare safety net with the 1965 Canada/Québec Pension Plan, expanded unemployment insurance, and welfare payments. By the mid-1960s, Canada had developed a modest liberal welfare state (Campbell 1987, 94–116), whereas Québec established different programs that were seen by many as stepping stones into modernity. The Quiet Revolution—as the social, economic, political, and cultural changes that occurred during the 1960s and 1970s were designated—involved major transformations in the management of public and social affairs (especially health and education). Such transformations were founded on explicit economic nationalist objectives and called for the promotion of French-speaking Québécois and Québécoises who did not identify as "French-Canadians" anymore. The democratization of education, as well as modernization and the intervention of the Québec state, were seen as the means to reach this goal.

The Women's Movement of the 1960s and 1970s

In the 1960s, there was a resurgence of the women's movement in most countries (Rowbotham 1992, 2000). Under pressure from women's organizations internationally, the United Nations Status of Women Commission recommended that member countries conduct reviews of the status of women, and some began to do so. In Canada and Québec, the changing social, political, and economic climate strengthened existing women's organizations and led to a flourishing of new organizations and campaigns, and a widespread mobilization of thousands of women from all parts of the country. Together, a revitalized women's equality movement and a new, more radical women's liberation movement galvanized thousands of women who enthusiastically assumed women could and should challenge all areas of men's privilege.

In 1965, Québec's women's groups celebrated the twenty-fifth anniversary of winning their right to vote and decided to form a new coalition—the Fédération des femmes du Québec (FFQ)—which, to this day, plays an important role in the orientation and development of the Québec women's movement. In 1966, two church-based groups—Union catholique des femmes rurales and the Cercle d'économie domestique—combined to form the Association féminine d'éducation et d'action sociale (AFÉAS). Both FFQ and AFÉAS worked (and continue to work to this day) to reform Québec family law and to advocate a range of women's issues, becoming over the next decade increasingly radical, whereas the short-lived Front de Libération des femmes du Québec (1970–72) published the first feminist journal in Québec,

Québécoises deboutte, and gave impetus to the critical and socialist orientation of Québec feminism.

Aboriginal women came together, forming groups such as the Indian Homemakers Association of British Columbia (1960), the Mohawk Group of Women from a Canadian Indian Reserve, and Indian Rights for Indian Women, which was founded specifically to fight discrimination in the Indian Act (1971). When the Supreme Court ruled that Jeanette Lavell was not discriminated against under the Indian Act, despite the fact that First Nations women who married non-status men lost their Indian status, while First Nations men conferred their status on non-status wives, this controversial decision mobilized outraged protests and contributed to links of solidarity with non-Aboriginal women. A loose network of such groups led to the formal creation of the Native Women's Association of Canada in 1974 (Jamieson 1979, 157–77).

In the mid-1960s, many of the large national women's groups carried out joint lobbying efforts, such as the Canadian Committee on the Status of Women, formed to make a submission to the Special Joint Committee on Divorce in 1966 (Marsden and Busby 1989, 79). In the same year, realizing that most national women's groups were lobbying the government on the same issues, and assuming that they would be more effective if they coordinated their efforts, Laura Sabia, president of the Canadian Federation of University Women (CFUW) invited thirty-five national English-language organizations and the Fédération des femmes du Québec to send representatives to a meeting in Toronto in May 1966. Fifty women representing thirty-two groups attended. They formed a coalition called the Committee for the Equality of Women in Canada (CEWC) to pursue the rights of women in Canada, and amongst their actions they called and campaigned for a Royal Commission on the Status of Women (Luxton 2001b, 76–77). The following year, the Centennial year of 1967, CEWC's chair, Laura Sabia, threatened a march of 3,000,000 women to Ottawa if a royal commission was not established. In a much cited comment, Sabia later admitted, "I don't think I could have gotten *three* women then."[10]

At the same time, but quite independently, young women who were part of the generalized youth mobilization internationally and transnationally began to look at their own positions as women in the various student, anti-war, and anti-imperialist movements and New Left politics. They developed critiques of the sexism in the movements and organizations they were part of, formed independent women's organizations or groups, and began a range of services designed to meet women's needs and to challenge the sexism of existing institutions and services. Women's liberation activists were not particularly interested in parliamentary politics; rather they focussed on issues such as contraception and abortion, daycare, and sexism in law, employment, and popular culture. While women's liberation was an international movement (Rowbotham 1972b), its organizational forms were typically small and local. However, a shared political vision meant that important actions were taken up across the country.

Women and the Arts: A Feminist Cultural Revolution

As the social and political circumstances facing women began to change, women in the arts responded by creating new spaces for women, using their arts to explore women's lives in new ways, reclaiming traditional women's creative forms (quilting, embroidery), and rediscovering literary foremothers and oral narratives. Then, too, some women clearly laid the foundations of social and political change. Gabrielle Roy, for example, is widely credited with preparing the ground for Québec's Quiet Revolution with her extraordinary first novel, *Bonheur d'occasion* (*The Tin Flute*), which also provided a feminist critique of domesticity, years ahead of both *Le deuxième sexe* and *The Feminine Mystique*. Roy's novel, published in French in 1945 and translated into English in 1947, won the Prix Femina and the Governor General's Award, and it sold over three-quarters of a million copies in the United States. Originally from Saint Boniface, Manitoba, Roy set her novel in the poor, working-class, Saint-Henri neighbourhood of Montréal. *Bonheur d'occasion* is a pioneering work of urban realism and of feminist fiction, offering a powerful portrait of a family swept by the winds of change, the Depression, and war. Mother–daughter relations are central as teenage Florentine Lacasse struggles, with very mixed success, to not repeat the life of her mother Rose-Anna, whose happiness has been relentlessly leeched by too many children, too much poverty, and too little control.

A pioneer also of the new woman-centred fiction is Anne Hébert, who probes the raw psychology of women's guilt, passion, and search for freedom in such historical novels as *Kamouraska* (1970) and *Les enfants du sabbat* (1975). *Kamouraska* is a gothic romance based on an actual murder committed by one of Hébert's female ancestors in 1839 in the Québec village that still bears this name.[11] Important experimental feminist writers of the 1970s in Québec include Monique Bosco (*La femme de Loth* 1970; translated as *Lot's Wife* 1975), Louky Bersianik (*L'Euguélionne* 1976), Nicole Brossard (*French Kiss* 1974), and Madeleine Gagnon (*Lueur* 1979). They further dismantle patriarchal stereotypes of woman—virgin, madonna, whore—and challenge fundamental literary structures, including plot and even language itself. There is often a generational conflict, as children and adolescents rebel against and reject the unsatisfactory, even degraded, world of their parents; for example, in Marie-Claire Blais's *Une saison dans la vie d'Émmanuel* (1965) or *Manuscrits de Pauline Archange* (1968).

Not infrequently, these writers draw analogies between the oppression and struggle for liberation of women, and the colonization and fight for self-determination of the nation, including its distinctive languages (*joual* or *chiac*). This is strikingly evident in the gently revolutionary, and often comic, work of Antonine Maillet, born in Bouctouche, New Brunswick, a *porte-parole* for the aspirations of the Acadians. In a stunning example of the intertwining of art and politics, the actor who not just played, but seemed to embody, Maillet's beloved cleaning woman character, who knows her community in intimate and revealing detail (*La Sagouine* 1971), Viola Léger was appointed (in 2001) to the Senate of Canada. Léger performed the dramatic role more than 1,400 times in English and French, at home and abroad; Maillet has won many honours in Canada, Québec, and France, including the Prix Goncourt in 1979 for *Pélagie-la-Charrette*, her retelling of the story of the Acadian Expulsion and of a latter-day Évangeline.

A similar feminist cultural revolution was occurring in anglophone Canada. In 1963, Gwendolyn MacEwen's first book of poetry bore a portentous title: *The Rising Fire*. In 1968, Marian Engel's first novel *No Clouds of Glory* (republished as *Sarah Bastard's Notebook* in 1974) told the scandalous story of an iconoclastic female university lecturer, a "lady PhD," Sarah Porlock, who, equally proud of her breasts and her brain, is determined not to let her sexuality interfere with her career or vice versa. Sarah has had an abortion, a procedure still illegal in Canada at the time and a subject almost never mentioned in literature. Other novels of this period also frankly confront the issues of unwanted pregnancy (Margaret Laurence's *A Jest of God* [1966]) and abortion (Margaret Atwood's *Surfacing* [1972]). In real life, singer-songwriter Joni Mitchell found herself single and pregnant just as she was preparing to launch her career in Toronto. Seeing no viable alternative in 1965, Mitchell gave her daughter up for adoption, alluding to the painful loss later in songs such as "Little Green" (from *Blue*) and "Chinese Café" (from *Wild Things Run Fast*), which runs in part: "My child's a stranger / I bore her / But I could not raise her."[12] Some of women's deepest and long-suppressed experiences were at last being told, and in the first person.

In 1969, Margaret Atwood published her first novel, *The Edible Woman*, which deals with women's objectification and alienation in a patriarchal consumer society. Her poetry collection *Power Politics* (1971) is a cycle of poems criticizing the notion of romantic love that encourages women to find meaning in life by finding a husband, which Atwood believed kept women dependent upon men and vulnerable to exploitation. Like a battle cry in the so-called "war between the sexes," she penned the iconic four-line epigraph:

> you fit into me
> like a hook into an eye
>
> a fish hook
> an open eye (Atwood 1976, 1)

In a poem with the accusatory title "You Did It," she later sums up: "You attempt merely power / you accomplish merely suffering" (Atwood 1976, 158). Although it played into the ugly stereotype of the man-hating feminist, such a critique of patriarchal power masquerading as love was life-transforming for countless women who read it. By the mid-1970s, Atwood was earning a living as a professional writer, no easy feat in Canada.

Aboriginal women writers and singer-songwriters focussed on the often-harsh realities of their lives and enjoyed unprecedented popularity. Buffy Sainte-Marie, a Cree originally from Saskatchewan, became an important figure in international folk circles in the 1960s. Sainte-Marie's most popular works include the unsentimental love song "Until It's Time for You to Go," the protest song over broken treaties "Now That the Buffalo's Gone," and "The Universal Soldier," which became the anthem of the 1960s peace movement (Sainte-Marie 1964). Maria Campbell, a Métisse from northern Saskatchewan, in 1973 published *Halfbreed*, her autobiographical account of the brutal realities of poverty and racial discrimination, of drug abuse and prostitution, and also, ultimately, of rekindled pride and hope through lessons learned from Cheechum, her great-grandmother. The book has become a classic of Canadian and feminist literature, and Campbell an award-winning writer and university professor.

Thus, as feminism emerged on the public stage as a vibrant social and political movement, it also produced vital new themes and characters, new arts and culture, as part of its creative expression. Feminist literary, art, and music critics provided a critique of cultural activity and generated an interest in "women's culture." Visual artists, dancers, poets, novelists, playwrights, sculptors, and filmmakers expressed the excitement, concerns, and visions of the burgeoning women's movement, and offered a whole new take on "the lives of girls and women," as Alice Munro phrased it in the title of her book of interconnected short stories published in 1974. In short, the 1960s and 1970s constituted a period of intense creativity. Many important women writers and artists achieved public acclaim in this period.[13]

In 1971, Joyce Wieland became the first living Canadian woman artist to have a solo exhibition at the National Gallery of Canada. Entitled True Patriot Love, it was a collection primarily of Wieland's quilts and wall hangings, which made a powerful statement by bringing traditional female "crafts" into the domain of "art." In 1975, the exhibit Some Canadian Women Artists, held by the National Gallery of Canada to celebrate International Women's Year, presented the art of many more women to the public (Graham 1975). Feminist sculptor Maryon Kantaroff carved out a career in the almost exclusively male domain of monumental sculpture. In 1974, Kantaroff established the Toronto Art Foundry, casting bronze sculptures for herself and other artists in Canada and the US. Her works have been commissioned for public spaces such as galleries and hospitals. One six-foot bronze sculpture, The Garden, expresses Kantaroff's understanding of the interdependency of male and female, blending "hard" and "soft" elements, making them equal halves of a whole.

One of the most important efforts to promote women's arts and culture was the National Film Board's Studio D, which opened in 1974, the first government-funded film studio dedicated to women filmmakers in the world. A series of films on working women (in French by Anne-Claire Poirier and in English by Kathleen Shannon), had shown that there was a need to address women's issues in film and a female audience eager to view such films (including the newly emerging feminist and women's studies classes). Shannon recognized the systemic discrimination faced by women filmmakers and the appalling lack of films addressing women's issues, and she fought to redress both problems. In contrast, when Anne-Claire Poirier was asked to create the French counterpart to Studio D, she refused, arguing that it would be a women's ghetto, with limited funding and few chances to make good films. Instead, Poirier argued for funding for French films created by women to be on equal footing with the money provided for other French productions by men.[14] Studio D produced an impressive variety of films, many of them winning awards and breaking distribution records, and all of them articulating women's concerns. These included Would I Ever Like to Work (Shannon 1974), I'll Find a Way (Shaffer 1977), Not a Love Story: A Film about Pornography (Klein 1981), Forbidden Love (Fernie and Weissman 1982), If

You Love This Planet (Nash 1982), *Souris tu m'inquiètes* (Danis 1973), and *J'me marie, j'me marie pas* (Dansereau 1974).

With the development of low-cost, portable, easy-to-use cameras in the mid-1960s, video activists appeared; most thought of themselves as contributing to the counterculture, defined by left-wing political views and by adherence to the ideas of Marshall McLuhan. For McLuhan, electronic media shaped collective ideas and attitudes, and contributed to social and political consciousness-raising. Particularly because of the low costs involved, women were able to take up this art form relatively easily. Women artists and performers were able to overcome the sexist barriers of previous decades to make their mark on the art scene. Many of them used their talents to present feminist issues or to make feminist political arguments through their art.

As feminist criticism developed, two key issues emerged: first, the issue of representation as an investigation into images and as a theorization of relative institutional power; and second, the place of gender in the operation and writing of cultural policy. Feminists pointed out the ongoing underfunding of women cultural producers, the increasing wage disparity between male and female artists, the under-representation of women on boards of directors of cultural organizations and on policy committees, and the failure of most institutions to present women's works (much less feminist works) to the public. These issues related closely to the struggles of women in other fields, strengthening the links amongst feminist activists in many domains.

The Royal Commission on the Status of Women in Canada

In 1967, the Liberal federal government under Lester Pearson was forced, by growing public pressure, to launch a Royal Commission on the Status of Women in Canada to "inquire into ... the status of women in Canada ... to ensure for women equal opportunities with men in all aspects of Canadian society" (Royal Commission on the Status of Women in Canada 1970, vii). Chaired by journalist Florence Bird,[15] the commission embodied the popular commitment of the time to consultation; it held meetings in fourteen cities and received 468 briefs and about 1,000 letters of opinion. National and regional women's organizations, especially those involved in calling for the commission, actively mobilized their members to get involved. Women across the country were excited by the opportunity, and the commission received numerous submissions from small groups of women who came together in local communities in response to the opportunity provided. Even radical young women, for the most part sceptical about, or even opposed to, government commissions, were inspired to contribute. As women met to discuss possible submissions, they collectively identified problems and inspired one another to get actively involved in fighting for change. For many women and men, it would be no exaggeration to say that this commission was indeed, as Heather McIvor called it, a "national consciousness-raising exercise" (cited by O'Neill 2003).

The commission filed its report in 1970. After two years, the government had done little in response to its recommendations. The Committee for the Equality of Women in Canada and other supporters formed the Ad Hoc National Action Committee on the Status of Women and organized a conference in 1972. The agenda of this Strategy for Change conference, held in Toronto, was to evaluate the government's response to the 167 recommendations. Its steering committee included the older women's organizations and several of the new women's liberation groups such as the Ontario Women's Abortion Law Repeal Coalition and the New Feminists. Funded by the Liberal federal government, Liberal party women and government bureaucrats formed a significant part of those attending, but the 700 participants also included some of the key activists from women's liberation organizations, the labour movement, and other radical women's groups. There were workshops on most of the key issues, such as daycare, contraception and abortion, and employment and pay equity.

One of the major debates emerged when Liberal party supporters and government bureaucrats wanted the conference to endorse a government-appointed advisory council on the status of women rather than grassroots organizing. This council would be expected to evaluate all government legislation and policy to determine its impact of women. Many of the participants, and especially the more radical women, assumed that any government-appointed committee would have to conform to government wishes. They also argued that to rely on such a council would be to forfeit the opportunity to build autonomous women's organizations.

A radical caucus of about sixty women met to discuss the options. It brought together women from the established women's and labour groups, such as Kay McPherson, then-president of Voice of Women, and Madeline Parent, the secretary-treasurer of the Canadian Textile and Chemical Union, as well as younger women from Women's Liberation (McPherson 1994). They discovered that despite apparent differences in style and fashion, they shared similar politics, had much to learn from one another, and were more effective if they worked together. Susan Crean, at the time aged twenty-seven, described her experience: "We were definitely the jeans and bandana set.... I heard women of my mother's generation espouse politics closer to mine (despite the girdles and bouffant hairstyles) than the thirty year old right to lifers" (1995, 91). The caucus rejected the idea of a government-appointed council that they insisted would only be co-opted.

They called instead for the formation of a new umbrella organization of existing women's groups, whose main focus would be to monitor the federal government's response to the recommendations of the royal commission and lobby for laws and policies favourable to women's equality. It would also act to support and foster its member organizations, each focussed on particular issues or regions. As Madeline Parent argued, what was needed was not an advisory council responsible to Parliament but a Parliament responsible to the women of Canada. Their arguments were persuasive and, as the report on the conference noted, "The convention rejected the concept of a federally-appointed, federally constituted Status of Women Council" (Strategy for Change Convention 1972, 2). Instead, the convention declared the formation of the National Action Committee on the Status of Women (NAC), the organization that remained the leading voice of the women's movement for almost thirty years (Vickers, Rankin, and Appelle 1993).

Despite the rejection of the proposal by the Strategy for Change conference, the federal government created the Canadian Advisory Council on the Status of Women in 1973 as an arms-length agency (Eichler 1983). It worked with both government and community groups and produced important feminist policy research on a wide range of issues for over twenty years, until it was dismantled in 1995, ostensibly as a federal budget deficit-cutting measure. Some activist women were members both of NAC and its member organizations, as well as of the federal, provincial, or territorial advisory councils. Experiences such as these highlighted the value of coalition politics and consciousness-raising, and produced a women's movement in Canada that many claim is unique (Dobrowolsky 2000, 8–12; Timpson 2001, 4) and, at least up until recently, "one of the most successful women's movements in the world" (Rebick 2004, A21).

Feminist Issues and Struggles in the 1970s

One of the major mobilizations of the women's movement in the 1970s and 1980s was the struggle for access to safe contraception and free abortion, using such slogans as "we will have the children we want" and "we want complete control over our body."[16] Such claims carry a specific refusal of the social constraints that imposed maternity, and in that way they attacked the ideological context that sustains the social division of the sexes. On May 14, 1969, the law prohibiting the publicity and sale of contraceptive products or the diffusion of information on birth control was removed from the Criminal Code, and the House of Commons adopted amendments to authorize abortion for therapeutic reasons. However, the new legislation was judged too restrictive and unsatisfactory for women, who argued that the creation of the therapeutic committees still denied them control of their bodies and their reproductive rights. Thousands of women rallied around the issue of abortion, demonstrating in the streets, presenting a unified front, and giving public visibility of the strength and power of the women's movement. The Montréal Women's Liberation Movement supported the opening in 1969 of the first private abortion clinic by Dr. Henry Morgentaler. In Québec in 1970, le Centre des femmes, which identified itself as an "avant-garde" feminist core, formed to enhance the creation of an autonomous women's liberation movement. On Mother's Day, le Front de liberation des femmes organized a demonstration in support of free abortion on demand, and le Centre de planning familial du Québec published a pamphlet enti-tled, *100 femmes devant l'avortement*. In 1970, calling for free abortion on demand, an abortion caravan set out from Vancouver for Ottawa, picking up support (and supporters) along the way. Several women chained them-selves to their seats in the House of Commons Visitors' Gallery. In 1972, le Centre des femmes set up a private abortion clinic and published a "Mani-feste pour une politique de planification des naissances" (manifesto for a policy on birth control). In 1988 in the Morgantaler decision, the Supreme Court handed down a ruling stating that Canada's abortion law was in breach of Canada's Charter of Rights and Freedoms, tossing it out in its entirety. The following year, the Conservative government introduced a bill to make doc-tors responsible for decisions to proceed with abortions. If the woman's health was found to be not at risk, doctors faced a two-year jail sentence. Dur-ing the parliamentary debate, about a hundred doctors stopped performing abortions and a further 275 threatened to stop if the bill passed. The bill did pass the House of Commons but was defeated in the Senate by a tie vote. At that point, the government promised not to introduce a new law again.

Another key issue was violence against women. Gradually, although the problem continues to be downplayed or even denied, analyses of violence against women led the women's movement to identify all types of violence as a means of social control that sustains inequalities and power relations between men and the women. Feminists organized shelters to provide support and services to women and to do educational work and lobby for changes in the way such violence was understood and handled. In 1973, Interval House, one of the first shelters for abused women, opened its doors in Toronto, just seventy-five years after a woman in an "insane asylum" was given a gynaecological operation to "cure" her—a common practice around 1898—because she claimed her husband abused her (Prentice et al. 1996). Around 1975, there were five transition houses in British Columbia. Over the years, though at a pace inadequate to meet women's needs, regional and pan-Canadian networks were established to furnish assistance to women survivors and to work collectively to end violence.

Other radical organizing was small scale and local. In Toronto, for example, in the late 1960s and early 1970s, small groups sprang up: the New Feminists, the Radical Feminists, and Toronto Women's Liberation. Some published papers such as the *Other Woman* and *Broadside*, or opened centres like Women's Place or the Toronto Rape Crisis Centre. At the University of Toronto, activists took over a building and set up an infant daycare centre, occupying the president's office to ensure the funding necessary to bring it up to the required municipal standards. A few years later, in response to legal requirements that housed children over and under two years of age in different facilities, they organized a ten-month sit-in that resulted in the Campus Community Day Care Centre (Luxton and Maroney 1992). Similar organizational initiatives happened across the country, often independently of one another or relying only on informal, personal connections to make links.

As the women's movement grew and developed, it was forced to confront the extent to which women could unite around shared concerns, as well as the extent to which they were either divided—or, more appropriately, allied—with other political movements. Women began organizing around such divisions, exploring (often explosively) the extent to which alliances were possible and critiquing the exclusionary practices of many women's groups, which were considered to be dominated by White, straight, middle-class feminists. In 1970, more than 200 women from across Canada gathered in Saskatoon, Saskatchewan, for the first national conference on the women's movement. One of the main issues they debated was the relationship between sex, "race," and class. In her keynote speech, McGill University sociologist Marlene Dixon argued that "race" and class divided women too much to build an autonomous women's movement. In 1973, building on the momentum that had resulted in the 1969 decriminalization of "homosexual acts,"[17] the first National Lesbian Conference was held in Toronto. It brought lesbians together to discuss strategies for organizing autonomously and to consider the implications of working within the women's or gay men's movements. Other events occurred in many regions of the country, simultaneously demonstrating the widespread public interest in women's issues, bringing even more women and men to support feminism, and advancing political debates among feminists.

Even though the Canadian and Québec movements could rally together on particular initiatives, the question of national identities, the issues of linguistic and cultural differences, and the lack of networks among different women's groups imposed other constraints on the development of the Canadian women's movement; these internal divisions came to a head over the repatriation of the constitution in 1982. Over the years, different orientations and allegiances produced quite different strategies and politics, especially in women's relationship to the state. In addition, francophone feminists (in Québec and elsewhere) tended to make connections with feminists in France and other francophone regions, and in Latin America, whereas Canadian feminists working in English tended to orient to the US and Britain. Francophone and anglophone feminists had limited contacts with one another; Canadian anglophone feminists had very little knowledge of feminist literature written in French, and rarely used it in their own work. Both groups, however, struggled with class issues and often failed to recognize the specific discrimination that Aboriginal women, women of colour, lesbians, and immigrant women would mobilize around. As a result, links between activists from those various communities were (and still are) equally difficult to establish and maintain (Egan 1987).

In the 1960s and 1970s, the importance of fighting against the economic, social, political, and legal constraints that oppressed all women, regardless of their political affiliation, class, national origin, sexual orientation, "race" or ethnicity, religion, or other differences, produced an innovative cooperation among women (Hamilton and Barrett 1986). Despite the difficulties, politically, the women's movement has always understood, at least in principle, that it can survive only if it encompasses diversity, recognizing the existence of Québec as a nation within the Canadian federation, the reality of First Nations and Aboriginal societies, the regional diversity and organizational base of politics in Canada, and the centrality of immigrant communities, only partially integrated by a Canadian state unable to overcome racism (Adamson, Briskin, and McPhail 1988; Bannerji 1991; Maroney and

Luxton 1987; Rebick 2005). The political disagreements among feminists and the difficulties inherent in trying to grapple with systemic discriminations, inequalities, and the national question imposed major challenges as the women's movement confronted the growing political conservatism of the 1980s and the turn to neo-liberalism (Bashevkin 1998). Nevertheless, the political mobilizations and the massive social changes in the lives of girls and women in the 1960s and 1970s were the crucible of feminist scholarship and women's studies in the universities.

Women in Post-Secondary Education

In the 1960s and early 1970s, governments invested heavily in post-secondary education, establishing new colleges, CÉGEPs (Collèges d'enseignement général et professionnel), and universities. There was a major hiring boom for faculty, many of whom were educated in France, the US, and Britain, given both the lack of Canadian trained graduates and the stated preference on the part of university administrators for candidates with French, US, or British degrees. The numbers of students admitted, including women, increased significantly. However, the universities remained deeply sexist in their institutional culture, their curricula, and their faculty. In the mid-1960s, only about one in ten university professors was a woman, and most of them were clustered in education, nursing, household science, and arts. In 1969–70, women were 95% or more of students enrolled in household science, nursing, secretarial science, and physical and occupational therapy, but only 22% of graduate students. In 1969–70 women earned 20% of the master's degrees awarded and less than 10% of doctorates (Vickers and Adam 1977, 32, 59). By 1970, women made up 37% of full-time undergraduates, but they continued to be restricted to a few "female appropriate" fields. In 1975, Québec women obtained 40% of all university diplomas awarded at the first-cycle level. The proportion of masters and doctorates obtained that same year by women was respectively 33.4% and 23.2% (Descarries 1980).

In the early twenty-first century, when women constitute more than half of all university students and 35.5% of all faculty, full- and part-time (Robbins et al. 2005),[18] it is hard to realize how relatively recent women's access to university has been. When universities were first developing in Europe in the thirteenth century, for the most part they excluded women as students and teachers, and developed curricula based on Aristotelian philosophy that explicitly stated that women were inferior to men and incapable of rational thought (Allen 1985, 413). For about six hundred years, the recognized institutions of higher learning perpetuated the assumption that women could not be scholars, and they produced research that assumed and proved women's inferiority. During that time, some women and their male supporters challenged those assumptions, finally winning access to the universities in the latter part of the nineteenth century.

The first women allowed on campus in Canada were staff, hired to do things such as sew curtains, wash floors, and light the school fires. One of the first such women was Charlotte Turner who, in 1829, was paid 4s. 8d. "to Making 14 Curtens for the College"—that is, King's College in Fredericton, which later became the University of New Brunswick (UNB). Another was Joanna O'Leary, a cleaner, who, in 1853, became the first regularly employed support staff woman at UNB. The next women to be accepted on campus were students who, starting in the mid-1860s, demanded the right to attend university and to take degrees alongside the men. In 1865, Emily Stowe was denied admission to the Toronto School of Medicine and so took her degree at the New York Medical College for Women; she then made it her life's mission to gain access to medical training for women back home. In 1875, Mount Allison University in New Brunswick became the first university in the British empire to grant a degree to a woman when Grace Annie Lockhart received her Bachelor of Science (Robbins et al. 1991). In 1883, Stowe's daughter, Augusta Stowe-Gullen, became the first woman to graduate with a Canadian medical degree. In 1890, Bishop's Medical College in Montréal opened its doors to female students. Ten women completed their medical studies there before the merger of the medical school with that of McGill eliminated for a period women's access to medical studies in Québec.

Annie Marion MacLean, who was not only the first woman but also the first Canadian to receive a doctorate in sociology, had to leave the country in order to obtain her degree. She received her PhD from the University of Chicago in 1900 (Campbell 2000). In 1903, Emma Baker became the first women in Canada to receive a PhD in philosophy and Clara Benson was the first to receive PhD in chemistry, both at the University of Toronto (Prentice et al. 1996, 174–75). In 1904, after graduating from Saint-Paul University of Minnesota, Irma Levasseur was forced to get a bill through Parliament to enable her to gain admission to the Collège des médecins et chirugiens du Québec, thus becoming the first woman in Québec to practise a liberal profession.

In the early part of the twentieth century, the number of women teachers in post-secondary education slowly increased. The first women professors and administrators were hired, including Clara Benson and Annie Laird, both at the new faculty of household science at the University of Toronto (Sheinen 1998). A few women gradually moved into more senior ranks and positions. It was not smooth sailing. In 1912, Carrie Derick, a distinguished botanist at McGill University, became Canada's first female full professor (though the principal pointed out this was merely a "courtesy title," and it did not carry the usual increase in pay) (Forster 2004). By 1921, the percentage of full-time women faculty reached 15% (Dagg and Thompson 1988, 65), and by 1944, during the Second World War, a record high of 19.9% was reached (Backhouse 1988).

The real change came in the 1960s when, seizing the opportunities opened up by the expansion of universities, and in Québec the creation of CÉGEPS that made free post-secondary education available, women students moved into most fields of higher education in numbers and proportions unattainable by earlier generations. However, in 1976, the figure for women faculty of 14.0% was *lower* than it had been a half-century earlier (Robbins et al. 1991, 27). Since then, there has been a slow but steady increase, so that women full-time faculty in 2004–2005 constituted 32.6% of academic staff across Canada (Canadian Association of University Teachers 2006, 2, table 1).

Women also moved—glacially slowly—into senior administration. In 1925 in Halifax, as Mount St. Vincent evolved from a women's college to became a university, Sister Mary Evaristus Moran was appointed president (Mount St. Vincent University Archives 2007)—a first for Canadian women. In 1974, when Pauline Jewett moved to British Columbia as president of Simon Fraser University, she became the first woman president of a Canadian coeducational university. The data for women at the dawn of the twenty-first century show how few have managed to reach the top positions: women are 18.8% of full professors, 17.2% of vice-presidents, and 13% of presidents (Robbins and Ollivier 2007).

As women entered universities in larger numbers than ever before during the sixties and seventies, they confronted rampant sexism. University structures, personnel, and culture were all masculine and excluded women. The curriculum was profoundly androcentric, ignoring women most of the time, glossing the experiences of (often elite and White) men as representative of all human life in the profoundly ambiguous notion of "Man." It was often deeply sexist, reflecting entrenched beliefs that legitimated women's oppression with claims of biological and historical inevitability. The main prevailing theories of the human sciences in that period assumed that men and women were significantly different biologically and socially, and that any efforts to challenge or interfere with such sex differences were both

Table 1: Ratios of Students (Full-time Undergraduates) to
University Teachers, by Sex, in Canada

Year	Female Students to Female University Teachers	Male Students to Male University Teachers
1965	39.733:1	11.94:1
1967	35.06:1	10.43:1
1969	33.14:1	8.91:1
1971	30.88:1	7.62:1
1973	31.55:1	7.22:1
1974–75	30.58:1	7.06:1
1976–77	32.37:1	7:1
1978–79	30.35:1	6.48:1
1980–81	30.25:1	6.49:1
1982–83	32.15:1	6.98:1
1984–85	33.40:1	7.19:1
1986–87	33.37:1	7.19:1
1988–89	33.14:1	7.29:1
1990–91	32.58:1	7.43:1
1992–93	33.44:1	7.89:1

Source: 1965–73 data: Leacy 1983; 1975–93 data: Statistics Canada, 1975–93.

naively unrealizable and inappropriately socially disruptive. On many campuses, there were buildings and programs that explicitly excluded women.

Most undergraduate students even in the late 1960s had very few women
professors and those they had were typically part-timers or sessionals. Table 1
indicates the ratios of students (full-time undergraduate) to university teachers by sex in Canada from 1965 to 1993 and gives some sense of what women
faced. There was a serious lack of female mentors and role models, and male
professors were often indifferent if not antagonistic to women students. For
many young women trying to get an education, the women's movement
offered a way of making sense of their experiences and provided a vision of
how things might improve.

Feminist Scholarship and Women's Studies

In Canada as well as in Québec, the women's movement challenged existing norms of femininity and produced new cultural and social understandings of, and possibilities for, women. It was also the lever that made possible
their entry into sectors that traditionally had been closed to them. Through
its social criticism and its socio-political struggles, it encouraged the emergence of aspirations and the acquisition of skills, which prompted young

militants not only to assert their rights to a profession, but also to engage in the cause of women by investing in the development of research and study programs. In three capacities—as women, activists, and researchers—they consequently sought to denounce the androcentrism of the existing theoretical, scientific, and social models, and to promote feminism as an analytical tool and a perspective that would bring women to recognize and think of themselves as historical subjects. In universities, research institutes, government agencies, professional organizations, and trade unions, they came to conceive of their research practices, as well as the production and transfer of feminist knowledge, as a concrete act of militancy. At the same time, leaders of Canada's and Québec's women's movements called upon feminist scholarship to provide research on women. The women's movement used and "made public" knowledge and analyses developed by feminist researchers to sustain their actions and demands. The resulting recognition of feminist studies as a legitimate field of study helped to link the research concerns of feminist scholars with the practices and the needs of activists and grassroots workers, and fostered the exchange of knowledge amongst them. It also inspired young women entering universities to demand access to and legitimate space for feminist studies as part of the formal curriculum.

Feminism is both an intellectual project and a political movement. As a result, as feminist scholarship developed in the universities, it was significantly linked to the activist women's movement in ways that were (and continue to be) simultaneously exciting and productive, challenging and fraught. It was "an ongoing, difficult, frustrating, demanding, vital, and genuinely two-way connection" (Eichler 1992a, 135). Tensions emerged when efforts to strengthen academic feminism undermined activist commitments of time and energy to liberation politics outside the university. Ironically, while working in rape crisis centres or battered women's shelters, or fighting for employment and pay equity in the labour movement were seen as doing movement work and validated as activist political involvement, those teaching feminism to hundreds of students and fighting for employment and pay equity in universities risked accusations that they had abandoned feminist activism for individual career building.

Similar tensions existed (and continue to exist) among academics. Some faculty came from other academic fields to feminist studies with a primary orientation to the academy. In their efforts to establish legitimacy for feminist scholarship, they were sometimes cautious about appearing "too political," as many traditional academics still clung to the illusion that their teaching and research were somehow value-free, not marked by any ideological shading. Some were women's movement activists, either part of the liberal equality movement or from the radical women's liberation movement, committed to building feminist studies as an academic wing of the larger women's movement. Feminist scholars were drawn to one another by their shared critique of sexism, their mutual efforts to improve women's situations, and their excitement in building feminist scholarship. Their collaborative efforts created strong ties and were important in securing a place for feminism in the universities. At the same time, their different political orientations meant that feminist scholars were often divided by the differences in their theoretical and practical analyses and strategies. They often found allies among non-feminists who shared their discipline or liberal or left-wing political affiliations. Those feminists who oriented their time and research to popular activist issues risked accusations from the academy that their work was partisan and not academically sound. Such differences produced debates and sometimes tensions among scholars, and contributed to what later was identified by many as a problematic divide between academic and activist feminism, a simplistic formulation that obscures significant political differences among feminists and also obscures the real collaborations that took place (and still do) on women's issues.

The development of feminist scholarship and of women's studies as an area of intellectual investigation, as a site of innovative critical teaching and learning practices, and as a legitimate academic and administrative unit in universities around the world was one moment in the long struggle for women's access to education in general and to universities in particular, an expression of the dream for women to become formal knowledge creators. Women's studies was born in the 1960s, on the one hand, out of the frustration and anger women felt when their critiques of the academy were ignored or denied, and, on the other, out of their passion and excitement as they developed scholarship about women and gender relations and uncovered new ways of learning and knowing.

While some discipline-based scholars sought both to add women and to expose the androcentric assumptions of their own fields, others realized that no single dimension was adequate to explain the widespread persistence of gender hierarchies, and they began to look to multi- and interdisciplinary approaches for direction. Some departments were supportive of feminist engagements and created positive spaces for new scholarship; others remained hostile and refused to admit feminist approaches. Heated debates flared about whether it was better to work within disciplines to ensure that women's issues were fully integrated, to set up separate, interdisciplinary women's studies programs, or to strive for both on the assumption that they would support and strengthen each other. When separate programs were set up, there were debates about whether to call them women's studies or feminist studies (later equity or gender studies). The actual outcome depended on the resources and political climate of the specific university.

In francophone Québec, the establishment of feminist studies, rather than women's studies, occurred quite specifically on the basis of militant and academic arguments: Québec scholars chose to promote feminist studies within each discipline. In part, they were reluctant to initiate distinct women's studies programs. While they acknowledged that distinct disciplines could be isolating and restrictive, they feared confinement and ghettoization for themselves and their students in women's studies. More importantly, the majority of them opposed the women's studies strategy because they regarded the analysis of gender relations as a transversal object and a social and intellectual analytical perspective that must be applied to all disciplines, not as a discipline in itself (Descarries 2005a). They preferred to establish feminist studies as a perspective that promoted change in a theoretical and methodological training securely anchored within a given disciplinary framework. In the rest of Canada, most early initiatives involved changes to both existing disciplines and interdisciplinary programs, which ended up being formalized as women's studies when administrations rejected the name "feminist studies" as "too political."[19] Such debates continue even now.

The Emergence of Feminist Scholarship

Feminist scholarship both in Canada and Québec during the 1960s and the early 1970s was articulated around two main axes, distinguished by their theoretical, analytical, and strategic orientations. Initially, scholarship in that period was informed primarily by liberal egalitarian feminist thought and by struggles for the elimination of all laws and measures harmful to the exercise of equal rights and access. The analyses and research of this period tried with uneven success to make up for the androcentric blindness of knowledge systematically produced by humanities and social sciences. It answered a need to describe, to understand, and to clarify the contemporary situation of women in Canada and Québec and to reveal the history that had been ignored up to that moment. It concentrated on critiquing the hierarchy created by gender divisions and on questioning the differentiated and specialized places and roles assigned to women and men.

Within the framework of research conducted at the instigation of the Royal Commission on the Status of Women in Canada and under the direction of its executive secretary (1967–70), Monique Bégin, forty studies were commissioned. Both the main report (1970) and the supporting studies exposed for the first time various aspects of women's places and roles in the workplace, as well as in politics and the family. Although they were relatively descriptive, the mere production of these research projects raised questions about the barriers and policies that limited women's access to education, the workplace, and various other institutions. The report called for further studies on women's issues and opened the way for the deconstruction of the truncated representation of society and gender relations reproduced by the social sciences and humanities at that time.

As the political mobilization of the women's movement intensified, new questions emerged. For the first time, the assigned place of women in the private and public spheres was no longer interpreted as inevitable nature or destiny, but was treated as a social question, as an arbitrary situation that could be changed, even by liberal feminists who called for formal equality with men. For radical feminism, the political issue was explicitly identified as the reversal or abolition of patriarchy—a socio-political and economic system and a hierarchical principle that legitimize the superiority and the control of the class of men over the class of women. Socialist feminists problematized the division of labour that shaped women's place and role in society and the fundamental inequality inherent in class divisions as seen through a gendered lens. For the first time, too, reflecting the diversity of the currents of thought that framed its reflection and its actions, the women's movement adopted a theoretical and strategic vocabulary of its own to designate women's social and economic conditions. In the mid-1970s, sex/gender was introduced as an analytical category. Terms such as sexism, gender relations, sexual stereotyping, inequality, discrimination, exploitation, and sexual divisions of labour provided tools to name women's experiences of their place in society and the discrimination they faced, to open new perspectives, and to enable new analyses.

The Creation of Knowledge and Critical Feminist Theorizing

The second axis of development, which complemented and overlapped the first one, marked the real debut of a critical analysis of sex and class hierarchies and patriarchal society. It was marked by the radical political context of the 1970s and a feminist militancy that included a more virulent criticism of the state, of patriarchal institutions, and of heterosexist constraints, as well as an investigation of the relationship between sex and class hierarchies and oppressions. Epistemological ruptures sundered old-fashioned notions of neutrality, objectivity, and the universality of positivist sciences. Feminists attempted to demonstrate that it was no longer possible to think of the world and to conduct scholarship as before, that is, in a way that excludes women as subjects of history and knowledge, and ignores sex as a critical category of analysis. Discrediting the religious and naturalist notion of the complementary nature of the sexes, scholars were also concerned about developing a social history that recognized the domination of one social group, women, by another, men.

Within universities, research became more critical and more engaged. Feminist scholars transcended their first objective of denunciation and participated in the elaboration of feminist conceptual tools such as patriarchy, power relations, and social reproduction (Descarries 1998; Luxton 2006). In an exciting and vibrant explosion of theoretical and political elaborations, scholars and activists debated whether patriarchy is an autonomous system, whether women represent a class or not, and how to theorize the possibility of a "we" or "sisterhood" of women while recognizing some of the social processes behind the constructions of hierarchies between women and men and among women themselves (Armstrong and Armstrong 1987).

Consequently, empirical investigations, epistemological reflections, and theoretical debates converged, calling into question the double standard of the existing disciplines developed by male scholars and the interpretations and practices inspired by them. From various theoretical and disciplinary perspectives and various workplaces, they proposed feminist critiques of existing analyses and conceptual tools in order to develop an increasingly global reflection on gender relations or *rapports de sexe* as the result of a symbolic and social system that not only reproduces itself, but also contributes to the organization, structures, and reproduction of the interdependence of all social relations and hierarchies. They debated the relative value of the concept of "patriarchy" and whether male dominance could be argued to be universal or historically specific. By putting women at the centre of their conceptual and empirical reasoning and analysis, and by introducing sex/gender as a critical category, feminist scholars contributed to the development of various methodological approaches that make room for women's voices and experiences, and established a democratic and complementary environment in which to exchange knowledge. With this particular optics, the observations and criticisms that emerged concerned the mechanisms of power, the social construction of sexual identities, patriarchal constraints, and the social reproduction of the sexual division of labour, as well as the ideological and economic causes of the tacit reproduction of women's oppression. Social control, sexual assault, marital violence, prostitution, and pornography constituted, for the first time, legitimate issues and research themes.

Conceptually and theoretically, feminists contributed to the debates in the disciplines, but in doing so many came to argue that no single dimension, whether biological, sexual, economic, psychological, political, or historicist, is adequate to explain the origins and persistence of gender hierarchies or to offer guidelines for struggles for equality or liberation. Rather, they sought to understand women's situation as a multidimensional complex of material and ideological forces, fundamentally structured by power relations and importantly understood in international, comparative perspectives. As a result, they laid the basis for what became feminist theory, which simultaneously is linked to the theoretical frameworks of specific disciplines and is an autonomous body of ideas with a resolutely interdisciplinary and inevitably international orientation (Maroney and Luxton 1987, 1). To be genuinely effective, however, interdisciplinarity demands of its practitioners a thorough knowledge of multiple disciplines before it makes efforts to combine or integrate them. Few students had access to systematic programs of study that prepared them for one, let alone two or more, disciplines, and few academics had the time or resources to do the in-depth work required for sophisticated interdisciplinary research. One of the challenges facing the practitioners of the newly emerging feminist theory was how to avoid mobilizing theoretical concepts whose implications they only partially understood based on superficial understandings of various traditions, without demanding more of themselves than was expected of other scholars, most of whom happily ignored the newly burgeoning feminist scholarship in their fields.

In that political moment of the early 1970s, several types of initiatives sprang up simultaneously, often initially as individual, local actions, but each contributing to a growing intellectual and political project. Searching for the women "hidden from history" (Rowbotham 1977), research on women flourished and in turn generated pressure on publishing and distribution practices. Excited by the new questions raised by the politics of the women's movement and by newly emerging knowledge, students demanded courses and individual faculty fought to offer them. Their efforts and the resistance they encountered fuelled critiques of universities and led to a range of efforts to make universities more open to women and feminist scholarship. Drawn to one another by their excitement at their shared interest in feminist scholarship and women's studies, and by their need for support in the face of an indifferent or hostile world, feminist scholar-activists organized conferences and set up regional, national, bi-national and international organizations to foster feminist intellectual work.

In spite of their dynamism and the quality of their scientific work, however, the situation of feminist scholars and feminist studies through this period remained precarious. Under-financed and kept at the periphery of dominant social sciences and humanities, feminist studies had problems extracting itself from the margins to gain legitimacy. It was difficult to convince non-feminist scholars that their raison d'être and approaches were not valid if they failed to take account of women and gender relations. Few feminist works of this period succeeded in revising the thoughts of the "mainstream" or in challenging prevailing scholarship sufficiently to force it to integrate critical feminist perspectives, analysis, and criticisms into its corpus of knowledge. The real issues, then as today, were to participate in the building of new and generally recognized knowledge, and to create, from women's diverse points of view and their everyday lives (Smith 1987), an alternative, non-sexist humanities and social sciences.

Research, Publishing, and Distribution

There was so little material available that, as the first writings about women and sexism appeared, they were eagerly received and widely circulated. Before photocopying and the Web (and heightened concern for copyright laws), networks of people reproduced and circulated material by typing carbon copies or Gestetner stencils. Existing editors and publishers were often uninterested in, or hostile to, work on or by women, so activists set up new journals both popular and academic. When existing publishers rejected a collection of essays of Canadian material on women and their oppression, a collective formed the Canadian Women's Educational Press, later the Women's Press and published *Women Unite!* themselves (Discussion Collective No. 6 1972, 7–8). Frustrated by the lack of material on and for feminist and women's studies, Margrit Eichler and Marylee Stephenson established the *Resources for Feminist Research/Documentation sur la recherche féministe* as a bilingual scholarly journal in 1972. In 1974, in Vancouver, Press Gang became an all-women collective, offering printing services to local community and women's groups. In 1975, *Atlantis* published its first edition, and éditions du remue-ménage was founded in Montréal by a collective of women who wanted to present another side of the collective memory. The Canadian Research Institute for the Advancement of Women (CRIAW), founded in 1975, emerged and flourished to offer greater possibilities for exchange and dissemination of knowledge, although in 2007 even this strong, bilingual organization has had to make cutbacks and lay off staff. Through the 1980s, feminist productions and publications, as well as national, bi-national, and international infrastructures that support academic work, were thriving. The decline started to set in, however, in the 1990s.

Teaching, New Curricula, and Program Development

In the universities, individual courses were developed, sometimes in response to student demand, sometimes because individual faculty negotiated with their home departments to offer specific courses, usually "on women" in their discipline, occasionally because a visionary dean initiated innovative programs. Such courses increased the demand for more published materi-als and produced scholars eager to research and publish in the area, fuelling the growth of text-based scholarship. Most importantly, they took seriously the feminist slogan that "the personal is political" by challenging students and faculty to examine their own lives, exploring the contradictions of their desires and fears, and struggling for a self-understanding that appreciates the forces shaping one's life and anticipates possible future selves. As a result, while "on women" courses were often greeted enthusiastically by women students, their reception by the larger university was less certain. Often seen by the university establishment as faddish or dismissed as too political or irrelevant, the long-term success of such courses varied widely. Nevertheless, by 1975, at least 149 courses are documented as having been taught in Cana-dian universities. This probably represents about 80% of all courses that were actually taught (Eichler 1992b).

The timing and ways in which studies of women were taken up were significantly determined by discipline, institution, and region, and also var-ied from country to country. Despite their deep-seated sexism and periodic misogyny, sociology, languages and literature, and history recognized the importance of questioning female–male relations and were among the ear-liest in Canada to produce studies on women (Luxton 1984). Unlike the US, where sociology followed other disciplines (Stacey and Thorne 1985), and despite erroneous claims that the same thing happened here (McDaniel 1991, 307), sociology in Canada led, rather than followed, other disciplines.

By 1975, thirty-eight of the women's studies/feminist studies courses had been given in sociology, compared to twenty-two in languages and literature, nineteen in history, thirteen in psychology, six in education, and five in anthropology. Other disciplines had fewer than five courses at that time (Eichler 1992a). The emergence of social history with its commitment to "the recovery of the lives of those individuals and groups (including workers, women, farmers, and the poor) traditionally dismissed or ignored as marginal, inarticulate and powerless" (Iacovetta and Mitchison 1998, 7) encouraged research on women's role and place in history. A focus on writing by, for, and about women started to transform literature. Psychology was in the forefront in some institutions, but not in others. Political science and economics were more resistant and only began to generate a significant feminist scholarship in their fields at a much later date. As feminism was taken up by a particular discipline, the new scholarship drew on existing work from other disciplines, producing a combined and uneven development in feminist scholarship across the country.

Changing University Structures and Practices

Feminist scholarship and women's studies courses brought together faculty, students, and staff interested in feminist issues. They often provided a space for women to identify problems in institutional structures and practices, and a base from which women could organize for changes. On many campuses, women identified a chilly climate that was hostile to women. Women's groups called for a range of services from sexual harassment centres to campus child-care centres. They demanded university policies against discrimination, for the use of non-sexist language. In faculty unions, they called for women's caucuses and affirmative action hiring policies. In turn, efforts to undermine the chilly climate created support for women's studies courses and feminist scholarship.

The United Nations declared 1975 International Women's Year, calling on member countries to take stock of the situation of women in their countries and inviting them to celebrate women's achievements. In Canada and Québec, 1975 marked a change in the climate for feminist scholarship and women's studies, a kind of "coming of age." By that time, there was a small but thriving network of experienced teachers. Courses were offered in more universities, and the possibility of undergraduate degrees in women's studies was under consideration. The existence of feminist publications, journals, and emerging organizations gave the field a growing legitimacy. There was a new range of materials available for teaching, more faculty interested in teaching, and a supportive and interested student population. While it was still fledgling and vulnerable, women's studies and feminist scholarship had found a place in academic life and were poised to develop further.[20]

Notes

1 For an excellent history of women in Canada that offers details of the period discussed in this chapter and gives a wealth of further references, see Prentice et al. (1996). Another excellent source of information is *L'histoire des femmes au Québec depuis quatre siècles* (Collectif Clio 1992).

2 There is currently a widespread practice of using the plural when referring to "women's movements." While we appreciate the motivating political concerns, we think it reflects a problematic understanding of what a social or political "movement" is. A "movement" is by definition plural and diverse. The women's movement is transhistorical, inter- and transnational, large scale and amorphous, and comprised of individuals, groups, and organizations with the general goals of promoting social change to improve women's situation.

3 Women in Québec did not win the right to vote in provincial elections until 1940.

4 When we cite statistics for Canada, we are including the Québec data; statistics on Québec alone are also cited separately to show the distinct patterns.

5 Despite widespread claims that the 1960s revitalization of the women's movement began in the United States, a review of *Chatelaine* magazine under Anderson's editorial leadership shows that the issues of that phase of the women's movement were under debate in print in Canada a decade before they were in print in the US. The point is not to compete over who did what first, of course, but to recognize the political climate in which feminism can flourish, to note the politics of knowledge production, and to urge scholars to do more research on the history of feminism in Canada and Québec. Too often, US publications dominate and their claims are assumed, uncritically, to apply to Canada.

6 Academic women participated in their staff unions, and in 1972 the Canadian Association of University Teachers (CAUT), the umbrella organization of faculty associations, set up its Status of Women Committee.

7 Free translation of the articles by the authors.

8 *Pin money* originally referred to money given by husbands to their wives for the specific purpose of buying pins. It then came to mean money for private and personal expenditures, or for incidentals.

9 Most Aboriginal Women were prohibited from voting until 1960, when the federal franchise was extended to them. On January 28, 1916, some Manitoba women became the first in Canada to win the rights to vote and to hold provincial office. They were followed by Saskatchewan on March 14 and Alberta on April 19. The following year, 1917, British Columbian women were enfranchised on April 5 and Ontario women on April 12. Through the Wartime Elections Act of 1917, the federal vote was extended to women in the armed forces, and to female relatives of military men. At the same time, thousands of citizens naturalized after 1902 were disenfranchised. It was thus not a victory for Canadian women.

10   See Sabia (1985). Also, as O'Neill (2003, 2) notes, "pressure was also mounted by women journalists (women's pages in newspapers), in women's periodicals (French and English versions of *Chatelaine*) and on women's radio and television programs where the idea was promoted to audiences and support built for it. The pressure tactics were particularly impressive since women as a group were not a political constituency of any force prior to this."

11   The novel *Kamouraska* was turned into a internationally acclaimed film with the same title in 1973 by Claude Jutra, itself a milestone in Québec cinema, starring Geneviève Bujold.

12   The two were reunited in 1997, after Mitchell's daughter, Kilauren Gibb (born Kelly Dale Anderson), as an adult began a search for her mother (see Bliss 2007).

13   The growing space for, and recognition of, women writers is reflected in the list of winners of the Governor General's Literary Awards for the period 1966–76:

1966
English fiction: Margaret Laurence, *A Jest of God*
English poetry or drama: Margaret Atwood, *The Circle Game*
French fiction: Claire Martin, *La joue droite*
1967
English non-fiction: Norah Story, *The Oxford Companion to Canadian History and Literature*
French poetry or drama: Françoise Loranger, *Encore cinq minutes*
1968
English fiction: Alice Munro, *Dance of the Happy Shades*
French fiction: Marie-Claire Blais, *Manuscrits de Pauline Archange*
1969
English poetry or drama: Gwendolyn MacEwen, *The Shadow-Maker*
French fiction: Louise Maheux-Forcier, *Une forêt pour Zoé*
1970
French fiction: Monique Bosco, *La femme de Loth*
1971
French fiction: Antonine Maillet, *Don l'Orignal*
1972
no women
1973
English poetry or drama: Miriam Mandel, *Lions at Her Face*
1974
English fiction: Margaret Laurence, *The Diviners*
1975
English non-fiction: Marion MacRae and Anthony Adamson, *Hallowed Walls*
French fiction: Anne Hébert, *Les enfants du sabbat*
1976
English fiction: Marian Engel, *Bear*

14   A similar debate occurred over whether to set up autonomous women's studies departments or ensure that feminist scholarship was integrated into all existing disciplines. For the most part, while the rest of Canada ended up with distinct women's studies departments, Québec opted for integrating feminism into existing disciplines.

15 Chair Florence Bird was a CBC broadcaster who had reported extensively on women's employment. The other commissioners were Jacques Henripin, professor of demography, Montréal; John Humphrey, professor of law, Montréal; Lola Lange, farmer and community activist, Claresholm, Alberta; Jeanne Lapointe, professor of literature, Québec City, who had been involved with the Parent commission on education; Elsie Gregory MacGill, aeronautical engineer, Toronto; and Doris Ogilvie, judge, Fredericton.

16 Later, immigrant women and women of colour challenged those formulations, pointing out that class inequalities and racial discrimination prevented many poor and racialized women from having the children they wanted. In response, birth control and abortion rights demands were linked to demands that would make it possible for women to have the children they wanted: for free universal child care, decent-paying jobs, and adequate housing for all.

17 Pierre Trudeau, prime minister and author of the legislation, said famously in a 1967 media scrum outside the House of Commons, "There's no place for the state in the bedrooms of the nation." CBC television news, broadcast 21 December 1967. Available at: http://archives.cbc.ca/IDC-1-73-538-2671/politics_economy/omnibus/clip1. Accessed 26 January 2008.

18 This places Canada substantially below countries such as the United Kingdom (35.1%), Australia (36.0%), New Zealand (36.6%), and the US (39.4%) (Canadian Association of University Teachers 2006).

19 The Ontario Institute for Studies in Education was an exception to the general thrust in the rest of Canada by taking the same approach as Québec and declining to establish a department of women's studies or feminist studies when the opportunity for this arose.

20 A chronology of the ongoing development of women's studies, produced by Wendy Robbins and Laurie McLaughlan (now Laurie Fulton), can be found online at http://www.unb.ca/PAR-L/chronology.htm (Robbins and McLaughlin 2002).

Essays

Creating a Tradition of Canadian Women Writers and Feminist Literary Criticism

◉ *Clara Thomas*

AT YORK UNIVERSITY, I taught Canadian Literature in 1968–69 and Canadian Women Writers in 1975–76.[1] Both were the first such graduate courses at York, and many colleagues from across the country told me that the latter was the first such course taught at the graduate level in any university. Peggy Fulton[2] and I agreed that I was able to do it because York was still new and welcomed experiments. We began with fourteen students—thirteen women and one man. He didn't approve of us and left shortly. We had a wonderful time, exploring writers such as Mary Anne Sadlier and Lily Dougall, who had until then been completely forgotten, as well as the popular writers of our own day—Margaret Laurence, Marian Engel, and Margaret Atwood (just getting into her stride).

Cooking was one of my class's talents. I always held a dinner for my students, but this group suggested a second dinner, a potluck. They brought wonderful food. One student was True Davidson, who had been mayor of East York and was a force to be reckoned with in Ontario politics. Another who also had a strong presence was Susan O'Heir, who had taken a year off from being associate dean of nursing at the University of Toronto. I saved their research notes and final papers in a thick file, which now resides in the York University Archives. At least three of that class went on to become academics: Michèle Lacombe at Trent, Robin Andras at Alberta, and Lisa Bubbers at the University of New Brunswick.

I carried on with Canadian Women Writers for another year and then reverted to teaching other courses. In 1977, I taught a new course called

First-Person Narrative (autobiography and autobiographical fiction). My reading list began with three outstanding nineteenth-century women writers: Susanna Moodie, Catherine Parr Traill, and Anna Jameson.

Born a Feminist

I always say I was born a feminist. I was born in 1919, at the very crossover of an old world to a new, when having the vote was brand new, attendance at university was still a privilege for Canadian women, and the presence of women on university faculties was barely tolerated, if at all. University life was always my goal, implanted in me by my paternal grandfather, and, later, by my husband and male friends and professors. My grandfather McCandless had been a schoolteacher, and he loved to hold up to me the Baptist university, McMaster, as a goal.

I have always considered Eleanora of the University of Michigan, from the 1909 novel by Gene Stratton Porter, *A Girl of the Limberlost* (1993), as being an inspiration in my teenage years. Like many another female, however, I took great pains as a teenager to downplay my academic prowess, pretending to be much more stupid than I was, especially in things to do with the male world—sports and cars, for instance.

Two important role models were my mother and my husband's mother. My mother, an advanced woman in her day, worked in a dress shop throughout my childhood, finally becoming, to her intense pleasure, manager. My husband's mother, a widow, was a teacher. It seemed natural to me and to my husband for a woman to work outside the home. This was an important attitude and influence. At that time, the 1930s through the 1950s, much of society was hostile to the idea.

My Student Years in the 1930s and 1940s

My first days at the University of Western Ontario in the fall of 1937 were the unhappiest of my four years there. I had to find work to pay for my board, and I was utterly unprepared for the orientation rituals, which were boring, humiliating, and embarrassing.[3] I was equally unprepared the following spring, 1938, to be "rushed" (approached to secure a pledge of membership) by all three sororities. It never occurred to me not to join when asked, and likewise it never occurred to me to question their social elitism or out-and-out racism. Jewish and Chinese girls were not eligible, and Blacks were unthinkable (Thomas 1999, 69).

Throughout my years at Western, I had a close male friend who had a great influence on me—Brandy Conron. There was nothing romantic between us, but we studied together and we fantasized about having our own university with, of course, ourselves as prominent faculty members. Eventually Brandy earned a Harvard PhD and became a professor and principal of Middlesex College at Western. In having the backing of male friends and professors, and their advice and confidence, I was very lucky.

Truth to tell, I became a scholar only in my last two years at Western. Always obsessive, I wanted only two things: to marry Morley (which I did at age twenty-three, in May 1942, moving with him to his posting in Dauphin, Manitoba), and to go to graduate school. My graduate career began as an extramural student taking one senior course in world fiction at the University of Manitoba, and my teaching career began through Western's extension program on the station in Dauphin. Next, I moved to London, Ontario, working in the university library at Western while completing an MA, with a thesis on Canadian novelists from 1920 to the present. I graduated in the fall of 1944. Not only did I get the thesis through with no trouble, but, best of all, I became pregnant. I gave birth to my first son in July 1945, and Longman published my thesis in 1946.

Women were welcome for MA work but were looked upon as poor candidates for the PhD. Very few women were hired full time by Ontario universities—in fact, the only one I knew was Flora Roy of Waterloo Lutheran (now Wilfrid Laurier). In 1949, I first applied for admission to Toronto's PhD program. This was a major step for me, and I did it fearfully. My first application was speedily discouraged by a scathing letter from Brandy in which he accused me of competing with Morley and threatened to pull out his support for my teaching if I dared to go any further. It seemed that Carl Klinck was hoping to get his student, Harry Weaver, accepted for Toronto's PhD program that year, and the warning signals were up: "no one else with a Western affiliation need apply." When I went down to the campus to withdraw, Professor Woodhouse told me that my application had been one of the best. My entrance was thus delayed by seven years.

Our second son was born in March 1951. Instead of going to mothers' meetings in the hospital the week following the birth, I marked essays, which I had brought to the hospital with me from my extension class that had finished only the week before.

Discovering Anna Jameson

In 1939–40 at Western, the honours students in English took a course in Canadian literature. Women writers were prominent. I discovered Susanna Moodie, Catherine Parr Traill, and Anna Jameson, and from then on I had a ready-made dissertation project for the time that I would be able to undertake the PhD program. In the mid-1940s while working in Western's library, I shared in the excitement when our Canadian specialist, Elsie Murray, published an edited version of Jameson's *Winter Studies and Summer Rambles in Canada* (Jameson 1944). Later still, I became firmly fixated on Jameson. I can remember standing in the cafeteria line beside Murdo McKinnon, the English department chair, and telling him that I'd like to publish an article on Anna. I'd already had my MA thesis on Canadian novelists published by Longman, but no one, least of all myself, was impressed by that, and I was not surprised when he laughed unbelievingly.

I regarded *Winter Studies* to be the heart of Jameson's work. At the time, I was completely dim about the importance of her art criticism, to say nothing of her *Characteristics of Women* (1832), the study of Shakespeare's heroines that, in the 1830s, had established her as a well-known writer, both in England and on the continent. Anna Jameson and Lady Byron exchanged letters for years, as Anna also did with Ottilie von Goethe, the daughter-in-law of the poet.

From 1957 to 1961, I was at the University of Toronto doing my PhD. The Generals in those days consisted of six papers, starting with Anglo-Saxon literature, and, for me, a three-hour exam in Victorian, my major field. There was no Canadian field as such. In writing my doctoral thesis, "Anna Jameson: The Making of a Reputation," during 1960–61, I made as much as I dared of Jameson's early feminism and of her various crusades in her works to raise the standards and quality of women's education. I had always to keep in mind, however, that I was doing my research at the University of Toronto, until recently loath to have women in its PhD program at all, let alone a woman who argued too vociferously for the New Woman aspects of Jameson.

The second wave of the women's movement was in its infancy, and Ellen Moers' groundbreaking work, *Literary Women*, was not to appear until 1976. I was inhibited and cautious, for I was already doubly fortunate in my work, with Northrop Frye as my thesis supervisor and the easy acceptance by the department of my part-time schedule since I was juggling marriage, two children, and extension teaching. Eventually, I turned my dissertation into a biography, *Love and Work Enough*, which was published in Canada in 1967 and subsequently, on the recommendation of Malcolm Elwin, in England. The reviews in the Toronto papers were good, especially Carl Klinck's in the *Globe and Mail*, but there was one miserable review in the annual "Letters in Canada" section of the *University of Toronto Quarterly* by a very young historian, Michael Cross, who wondered why the press would publish a book about a "whining, self-pitying woman" (Thomas 1999, 147).

At graduation in 1961, I was again doubly fortunate in being at the very beginning of a real need for women academics—the expansion of the 1960s was just dimly on the horizon—and in having the good will and good advice of Professor A. S. P. Woodhouse, the renowned head of the English department. It was Woodhouse who told me that he had "sent my name to York," as in those days he placed his students in English faculties across Canada. I was interviewed by Hugh Maclean, who was looking for someone for the brand-new York University English department. He and I clicked at once. Before I could really realize my luck, I was interviewed by Murray Ross, the president of York, and hired. I did not mention to either Maclean or Ross that I had had a book published in 1946; I quite honestly did not think of that. "Publish or perish" had yet to become a term of universal academic awareness. It never occurred to me to have any requests, let alone demands, of my own, so when Ross told me my pay would be $5,000, I was delighted. I didn't exactly appreciate his reminding me that it was a generous sum to pay a woman, especially one in English, where many candidates were available, but I was in no mood to demur (Thomas 1999, 140–41).

The secretaries deserve a special chapter in any story of the young York University. Their secretarial skills were impressive, and so were their social skills, for they became the discreet confidantes of faculty and students alike. Florence Knight, my good friend, on one rare occasion when she was unavoidably away, called me to say, "Mrs. Thomas, please try to make Professor Maclean a good cup of tea." Every secretary dutifully made and served tea, coffee, or the ubiquitous sherry as part of her job (Thomas 1999, 153).

In 1978, the University of Toronto Press issued a paperback version of *Love and Work Enough*, and I was able to add an introduction that gave Anna Jameson at least her partial due as a nineteenth-century feminist. It was not until the mid-1980s that she was "discovered," celebrated by various young women scholars, and featured in such publications as *A Mazing Space* (Neuman and Kamboureli 1986) as the committed champion of women that she had always been.[4]

The Impact of Margaret Laurence

Reading Margaret Laurence's *The Stone Angel* for the first time in 1965 was a milestone in my life. Never before had I been so deeply moved by a book, so aware of its speaking directly to me, in an idiom completely familiar—my mother's, my grandmother's, my own. From the start, I thought it a turning point for Canadian literature, too, so much so that I had my students buy the hardcover edition that fall—a radical and expensive addition to their book list. After the publication of *A Jest of God* in 1966, I began to say that I had to write about all of Margaret's work. Soon Dave Godfrey, the editor for McClelland and Stewart's Canadian Writers Series, asked me to write something. The first little book, *Margaret Laurence*, I did in the Christmas holidays of 1968, my mother in the hospital in her last illness, myself at our kitchen table where I could easily watch various pots boil. From time to time, one or other of my family would find me in tears, for the juxtaposition of the heroine Hagar's situation and my mother's was unbearably moving.

I first visited Margaret in Elm Cottage in England in 1969, at the time of the publication of my *Margaret Laurence* book (a book that was wretchedly edited—I've always been somewhat embarrassed by it). That June day was the beginning of one of the most important and firmest friendships of my life—and our family's. We quickly came to call each other "dear sister." Margaret was coming over to take up her first post as writer-in-residence at the University of Toronto. The year 1969–70 was a hard one for Margaret. She and her husband had finally decided to divorce. She had long since found, to her grief, that she could not reconcile the demands of her work with her marriage.

During her stint as writer-in-residence, I made the first of many long gowns for her, all of them from the same pattern. One, in a bright coral print, she is wearing in the film *The First Lady of Manawaka*. For her installation as chancellor of Trent University, she picked out blue-green silky material and sent it to me to sew. Margaret used to love to say that she was the only woman in Canada whose dressmaker had a PhD. I loved that line, too!

Margaret was at our house when Beth Appeldoorn and Susan Sandler opened Longhouse Bookshop in Toronto in 1972, the first bookshop to stock Canadian books exclusively, and another landmark for Canadian writing. When cultural historians write of the yeasty 1970s, Appeldoorn and Sandler must be among our prime literary benefactors.

I had a sabbatical in 1973–74. Just before *The Diviners* was published in 1974, Margaret gave me the final typescript to read, because I was about to work on *The Manawaka World of Margaret Laurence* (1975) and she wanted me to be able to include her new book in my study. In June of 1986, she was with me when York honoured me with a DLitt.

Women's Studies

For all of those years, I was listed as a member of the women's studies faculty. I did not involve myself in the advocating of women's studies courses at York University, however, because, as I remember saying to Johanna Stuckey, I could not fight on two fronts at once. I had begun Canadian literature studies at York, and I was kept extremely busy seeing that it flourished and doing many thesis supervisions. Never, however, was there any doubt that I was all in favour of such developments as long as Canadian literature continued to flourish.

Speaking again of friendly male colleagues, I have Michael Collie to thank for seeing that I became president of the Association of Canadian University Teachers of English (ACUTE)[5] in 1971–72. I was the first woman president. Janet Lewis was secretary-treasurer, and we had a wonderful year. One of our projects was to canvass all English department women across Canada, finding out much about their situations and backgrounds. We sent out a questionnaire, which I had devised, to every female member of ACUTE. The numbers? I don't remember, but not that many—you'd be shocked at the meagre number. We got a 100% response rate from our cross-country colleagues.[6]

I continue to do a lot of reviewing for *Books in Canada* and *Canadian Woman Studies*. I am in my office in York's archives weekly. I very much enjoy talking to and advising the overseas students who come to do research on our writers, Laurence in particular, but others as well. Graduate studies remain very close to my heart.

Notes

1 A more detailed discussion of my life and career is in my published autobiography, *Chapters in a Lucky Life* (Thomas 1999).

2 E. Margaret Fulton went from Waterloo Lutheran University to become president of Mount St. Vincent University.

3 I was the girl in the notorious Western "Kiss Picture," which resulted in orientation horseplay being cut out entirely for some years. Two sophomores collared a girl and a boy and ordered them to chew on opposite ends of a piece of string. Some smart photographer took a picture of the two of us as we reached the middle, Canadian Press picked it up, and it was reproduced all over Canada. Ministers and the inevitable

guardians of public morals viewed it with alarm, and a tempest in a teapot ensued (Thomas 1999, 68).

4   See my *Chapters in a Lucky Life* (1999, 22), and *A Mazing Space: Writing Canadian Women Writing* (Neuman and Kamboureli 1986).

5   A second "C" was later added to the acronym when the association added the word "college" to its title.

6   The responses were sent, with the rest of the ACUTE material, to the next executive, which was centred at Western. As far as I know, there is no repository for the old files— they were scrapped long since, I believe.

Selected Publications by the Author

Thomas, Clara Eileen. 1962. Anna Jameson: The making of a reputation. PhD diss., University of Toronto.

———. 1969. *Margaret Laurence*. Toronto: McClelland and Stewart.

———. 1975. *The Manawaka world of Margaret Laurence*. Toronto: McClelland and Stewart.

———. 1978. *Love and work enough: The life of Anna Jameson*. Toronto: University of Toronto Press. Original edition, 1967.

———. 1999. *Chapters in a lucky life*. Ottawa: Borealis.

Mother Was Not a Person, So I Became a Feminist

Marguerite Andersen

WHEN I CREATED the interdisciplinary course Women in Modern Society, to be taught at Loyola of Montréal (later part of Concordia University) in 1971–72, I did not know that the course would turn into a book. It did, because I soon realized that what we were doing—our discussions, the essays that were being written, and the guest lectures that were being given—should be made available to more people than the forty-five women and five men enrolled in the course. The course was innovative and sometimes not all that middle class as, for instance, when I invited a Loyola professor of biology, a Jesuit, and Dr. Morgentaler to debate the question of abortion. The resulting book, *Mother Was Not a Person* (1972), had two editions, selling six thousand copies. It has for a long time been out of print and is difficult to find in second-hand bookstores. That must mean that people are hanging on to their copies or to the copies their mothers purchased.

I wrote in its preface, "The book risks being called reactionary and rightly so. It is a middle-class publication which will be read by middle-class women; it will serve middle-class purposes. The myth of sisterhood, of a sisterhood of all women, will, as Marlene Dixon explains in her analysis of the feminist movement, remain a myth and a myth which is doomed to collapse. I wish for better, but am forced to accept my own limitations. I am a middle-class woman living in a middle-class environment; I will not bring about *The Revolution*" (1972, 2). I still remember how, a few weeks after the book had come out, Father Malone, SJ, Loyola's president, assured me that his mother had certainly been a person; obviously, I had to explain the Persons case to him: Canadian women became persons in 1929 only, when His Majesty's Privy Council in London, having received a petition from five energetic Canadian women, overruled, after four days of debate, the Supreme Court of Canada. It had decided in 1928 that, under the British North America Act of 1867, women were not persons (see also the joint essay by Rosalind Sydie, Patricia Prestwich, and Dallas Cullen in this volume). He listened to me carefully and also accepted my recommendation that faculty and all other female employees be eligible for maternity leave with full pay ... something my female colleagues of that time still remember with glee. In the meantime, and with Loyola now being part of Concordia University, the benefits have changed again.

From Loyola, I went in 1972 to the University of Guelph, where I was appointed chair of the Department of Languages. Of course I very quickly met the feminists at the university, such as Norma Bowen and Joanna Boehnert, who unfortunately both died very prematurely, and Wendy Robbins (then Keitner) and Terry Crowley. We ran a successful brown-bag lunch seminar for faculty, staff, and students, to which the public was also invited; it brought such speakers as Jill Conway, June Callwood, Rosalie Abella, and Margaret Atwood to the campus. At that time also, I founded a group called the Guelph Freedom Ladies, together with non-academic Guelph feminists including Diane Goodwillie, Maureen Leyland, and Elizabeth Boyle. The group participated in the lunch series and, during International Women's Year, organized a weekend seminar, including a vaginal self-examination demonstration (mirrors provided), a bus trip to Nellie McClung's Ontario homestead, and a Women's Parade through the city; the latter had eight hundred participants!

I must mention the washroom struggle that took place within the Department of Languages. We were twenty-four full-time faculty members, a few part-time lecturers, and three secretaries, plus a great number of mainly female students, as languages are a favourite subject of women students in the arts and social sciences. There were two washrooms: one had two stalls, one urinal, and two sinks; the other had one stall and one sink—the bigger washroom was for the men. Male faculty represented at most half of the teachers, and male students certainly did not constitute half of the student body of the department, nor were there any male secretaries.

I thought it would be simple. As chair of the department, I would present figures concerning male and female users of the washrooms and simply put up signs declaring which washroom was for whom. A female visiting lecturer from Grenoble, France, Professor Simone Vierne, was most enthusiastic and even went to buy a green plant, which she deposited in the urinal promoted to become a plant holder.

I was wrong. All hell broke loose. A very tall member of the Classics Section wrote to inform me that one of the toilets in the men's room was taller than the other and that tall men need this elevation. I wrote back, wondering whether in his home such matters were considered. Men wrote to the dean, who wrote to me advising me to give up. I must confess, to my shame, that I did just that.

I have forgotten the university world since. Although I later on held the Nancy Ruth Chair for Women's Studies at Mount Saint Vincent University (which in 1999 conferred on me a doctorate of humane letters, h.c.), I slowly moved away from university life into a sphere that suits me better, that of creative writing, mostly in French. You can actually go to my website (http://margueriteandersen.franco.ca) and see what I have done since that glorious period of the second wave of feminism.

Today, I am asking myself how far we women have progressed. I knew right from the beginning that it would take several generations to change our position in society. It has. Have we reached our goals? Some of them. Canadian women have achieved equality before the law. But—and whatever one may see as progress, there is always a but—as recently as 2005, the equality of Muslim women in Ontario and in other provinces was threatened by the possible introduction of religious laws, such as *sharia,* into Canadian family law. Fortunately, the move was defeated. And what can one say about worldwide violence against women? We cannot yet rest. I am glad to know younger women are accepting the responsibility of carrying on the struggle and continuing "the drive and the thirst for a decent society and a good life" (Dixon 1969, 239).

Selected Publications by the Author

Note: Margret Andersen and Marguerite Andersen are variant spellings; since 1982 she has used the latter.

Andersen, Margret, ed. 1972. *Mother was not a person.* Montreal: Black Rose Books; Content Publishing.

Andersen, Marguerite. 1995. *La Soupe.* Sudbury, ON: Prise de parole.

———. 2002. *De mémoire de femme.* Montréal: Quinze. Original edition, 1982.

———. 2004. *Parallèles.* Sudbury, ON: Prise de parole.

Andersen, Marguerite, with Christine Klein-Lataud, ed. 1992. *Paroles Rebelles.* Montréal: Éditions du Remue-ménage.

Fanning Fires: Women's Studies in a School of Social Work

Helen Levine
with Faith Schneider

I WAS HIRED BY the Carleton University School of Social Work in 1974 to teach an elective course on women and social work. We named it Status of Women. The motivation for this addition to the curriculum was twofold. First, the school was shifting from a highly clinical approach to a political/structural emphasis on how human behaviour is rooted in, and shaped by, the institutions and structures of society. Second, the women's liberation movement was very prominent in the early 1970s. A group of women students had approached the director (and probably others), asking or demanding that a women's course be introduced. I was a trained and experienced social worker and a feminist heavily involved in the women's movement. There were few such social workers around at the time.

I had never felt at ease with traditional social work practice and didn't define myself as a professional, meaning someone a notch above those clients on the receiving end of professional service. I was a worker, a social worker. Nor did I subscribe to the traditional model of social work intervention that focussed heavily on pathology in working with women. At the time, I preferred small group and collective approaches as a respectful and dignified way of working with consumers of services. It seemed more useful and more democratic to enable people to share experiences and to work at problem solving together. All this fitted in with the developing philosophy of the Carleton School of Social Work.

I began as a Marxist feminist and gradually evolved into a radical feminist. This happened via a critical analysis of how male dominance is/was embedded in the major institutions of society, both personal and political, including the left-wing organizations I had been part of. Women's issues were invisible in most social change movements prior to the contemporary women's movement. As women, we had been blinded to our own membership in an oppressed group, and thus had collaborated with male-defined goals, priorities, and ways of working and, for the most part, performed secretarial and domestic services for the men. We were a majority (51% of the population) with minority status.

The writings of Betty Friedan, Nellie McClung, Simone de Beauvoir, Kate Millett, Dorothy Smith, Robin Morgan, and Adrienne Rich, among others, as well as the report of the Royal Commission on the Status of Women in Canada, made a huge impact on many women in the early 1970s. I recall buying ten paperback copies of Friedan's *The Feminine Mystique* (1963) to distribute and mail to friends near and far. This new literature and new consciousness became part of the Status of Women course, along with the very few social work articles from a feminist perspective that had been written by Sylva Gelber and Jim Gripton.[1]

It is important to note that social work literature had been replete with material about women, especially women in the family and women and madness. Long-established male norms in the helping professions promoted an acceptance of women's subservient and unequal place in the social structure and deemed to be sick those women who did not adjust. It required a distinctive feminist approach to question these norms and to address the changes required.

The dearth of relevant social work literature in the beginning forced me to be interdisciplinary in providing reading material for the course on Status of Women. Course readings were culled from English literature, political science, sociology, psychology, and psychiatry. This interdisciplinary practice remained of value but necessarily decreased as more directly relevant social work literature appeared.

In a field where the majority of workers and consumers of services were women, the school decided that training in social work required that all students develop a critical analysis of women's condition in society. The Carleton School was unusual at the time among most university social work programs in Canada, in addressing the importance of feminism in the curriculum.[2] I was given the opportunity and the task of developing course material and promoting consciousness of women's issues in the school at large. The Status of Women course evolved into Women and Welfare. Later,

Feminist Counselling also became a significant part of women's studies at the school.

I began to include quality student papers to enrich course outlines. This was a significant new source of material, and it paralleled a new approach to social work practice. It was a way of recognizing people without formal credentials as owning a valuable kind of knowledge. This was a departure from the notion of "the professional" or "the scholar" having ownership of all worthwhile knowledge.

The Status of Women course requirements included keeping a journal, which could deal with relevant personal issues and experiences or with reviews of class literature—or both; it was to be handed in at the end of term but not graded. The journals encouraged reflection, critical thinking, and writing in the women's movement at the time. Journal keeping was an invaluable tool in women's studies and another connection between the grassroots and academia.

Women's studies came to be characterized by radically alternative ways of thinking and acting, at both personal and political levels, in the service of social change. Our minds as well as our bodies had been colonized in a male-defined culture. Women's studies led to a redefining of patriarchal norms and assumptions that permeated women's lives, and that had been unconsciously internalized in women's psyches.

Feminist literature in the field of social work gradually emerged. Feminists analyzed social institutions such as the family and motherhood (Levine and Estable 1981). We critiqued the traditional family as a site of frequent male violence against women and children. We saw the home as a place where women's work was unrecognized and undervalued. I began to write articles and chapters on such topics as psychiatry, motherhood, and aging, and on women's paid and unpaid work.

Women and madness was another major issue being addressed by the early women's movement. It was partly by exploring my own experience as a psychiatric patient (1973) that I began to develop a major area of my work called feminist counselling. When the Addiction Research Foundation asked me to present a paper at their first conference on women and the use of legal drugs, I wrote a feminist critique of the conventional psychiatric system and its harmful effects on women. I revealed myself publicly for the first time as an ex-psychiatric patient. A cardinal principle of my speaking and writing from then on was to align my own personal struggles with those of other women. Thus the title of my first article, "On Women and on One Woman" (Levine 1976b).

I want to note the importance of consciousness-raising groups in the early women's movement. It was in these groups that many of us began to talk about what was really happening in our lives. In the process of breaking the silence, we found much common ground among us. We gained courage and strength from knowing we were not alone in our struggles. In my women's studies courses, I tried to replicate this approach to provide a milieu where students too could be open and thus learn and thrive. They often did. It reflected a commitment to process as well as product, an important feminist principle.

One of the joys of teaching women's studies was that it was a new field, and we were pioneering and learning as it evolved. It meant that I was largely unencumbered by standard academic requirements and free to explore and experiment. It was a rewarding personal and intellectual experience. There was, however, conflict in the school about the introduction and centrality of women's studies courses and content. The faculty was divided between clinical and political orientations. In the early years, many students came to the Carleton School because of its radical ideas, but some wanted more clinical skills and less critical analysis. It was a time of unparalleled ferment. I was the one feminist member of faculty in the early years and often a thorn in the side of others. My major focus was on students and on the women's movement—and we were in a militant mood in those early times.

Some important historical moments for women's studies at the Carleton School of Social Work:

- During the early 1970s, when women's studies was in its infancy at Carleton, Geraldine Finn organized a Women's Studies Association conference at the University of Ottawa. The theme of the conference was "Reason and Violence." As one of the speakers, I chose to use the opera *Lucia di Lammermoor* to illustrate the theme of women and madness—a huge departure for a social worker.
- In 1975, a small number of women faculty and students from the Carleton School of Social Work, along with two interested social workers from Toronto, organized what became a groundbreaking forum on Women and Social Work.[3] Rosemary Brown was suggested as keynote speaker. I was in awe at the thought of inviting a person of such stature, but we did and I was thrilled to introduce Rosemary at the conference. These new experiences were both exhilarating and terrifying. We women were accustomed to listening rather than speaking in the public sphere.
- In 1976, some feminist students joined me to form an editorial committee at the Carleton School of Social Work to publish an entire women's

issue of *The Social Worker*. The particular issue was called *'76 and Beyond*. It was here that I wrote about feminist counselling for the first time (1976a).

- My work with teaching assistants was collaborative and reciprocal. I learned; they learned. We met weekly after each Status of Women class to discuss strengths and weaknesses, and to plan the next class together. These were rich experiences.

- One year, teaching assistants in the Status of Women course and I formed a small collective to develop a handbook for women receiving welfare. The collective included a woman on welfare. The handbook provided practical information and support for women on public assistance (Research Collective 1975). It was a solid year's learning for us.

- An important adjunct to the early courses were afternoon showings of Studio D films (women's studio of National Film Board) with discussion following. Attendance was voluntary. Relevant topics included women's history, poverty, pornography, rape, and battered women. These remarkable films were a potent cultural force and added immeasurably to the Status of Women course.

- In the 1970s, some Carleton School of Social Work faculty organized a conference on Equality. Their list of speakers was all male. I raised hell, and they finally invited Dorothy Smith from the Ontario Institute for Studies in Education. I considered this belated tokenism and boycotted the conference.

- Also in the seventies, the School and the community organized a joint conference entitled Whither Social Work. All male speakers here, too (eight of them)—plus one female student. This time, I attended but rose at the beginning to point out the gender imbalance and to demand a reorganization of the conference before proceeding. Though I think my individual intervention was of value, I began to better understand the limitations of individual actions.

- I had attended a summer Institute of Women's Studies at Sir George Williams University in Montreal in 1974.[4] I was learning as I began to teach, a frequent practice in this new field of women's studies. Margaret Benston offered an invaluable course on the Political Economy of Women. She was a pioneer in women's studies at Simon Fraser University. As well as the course content, I learned a great deal from her about dealing with men in a women's studies class. On my return to Carleton, I began to implement some of her ideas. At the beginning of the academic term, during the first "shopping around" class, I outlined the course and its requirements. Usually there were many women and few men. To the men, I said something like this: "The university is full of what we might describe as men's studies courses reflected by the mostly male faculty and male-defined content. Male students have a tendency to take over discussion in class. Women tend to be silent. If you decide to remain in this course, though your active participation will be welcome, you will not be allowed to take over. Mainly, I see Status of Women as a rare opportunity for you to listen to and learn from women." Sometimes a few men and women decided not to continue the course because they felt I had been unfair to the men.

- There was ongoing cross-fertilization in the seventies between Carleton and the Maritime School of Social Work (Dalhousie University) around women's studies. My work and friendship with Joan Gilroy, a highly respected professor at the Maritime School of Social Work, developed into a fruitful collaboration. Like the Carleton School, the Maritime School had become less clinical and more political. Women faculty, staff, and students there worked together in many innovative ways. For example, Rosemary Brown, well-known Canadian social worker, feminist, and activist, was invited to the Maritime School as a visiting professor to teach and speak in both school and community on topics related to women. Inviting a Black feminist radical into a school of social work was a rarity at the time.

- Women from the Carleton School and the Maritime School helped spearhead an important women's caucus within the Canadian Association of Schools of Social Work. We helped found a newsletter/magazine called *Connections* for women faculty and students as a means of spreading new ways of thinking about and working with women as social workers.

Through all of this, feminist counselling in my life and work was one thread that went from community to university and back to community. Aside from becoming a women's studies course, feminist counselling was an example for me of forging a connection with women around personal and political issues. It involved the community and women's studies in a meaningful collaboration. I considered feminist counselling to be part of my political work.

Three central ideas from the women's movement and from women's studies have remained at the core of my philosophy of life: first, the personal is political—I agree with Margaret Benston who saw this as the major contribution of contemporary feminism to political thought (1969a, 1969b); second, the intrinsic value of self-disclosure among women, so that we can find common ground among us; third, the critical importance of women developing and utilizing a feminist framework/analysis with which to view our own and other women's life experiences, individually and collectively, as a basis for enduring social change.

Notes

This essay could not have been written without the support of my writing-group friend, Faith Schneider, at a time when my energy was depleted. Many thanks, Faith.

1 Sylva Gelber's influential work included her address to the Canadian Association of Social Workers, Vancouver, BC, June 8, 1973, published as "Social Work and the Status of Women" (1973b). Amongst her other works, published by the Women's Bureau in Ottawa, are *The Rights of Man and the Status of Women* (1969) and *The New Role of women* (1973). See also James Gripton, "Sexism in Social Work: Male Takeover of a Female Profession" (1974). During 1969–71, Gripton was part of a committee that developed the constitution of the newly formed Canadian Association of Schools of Social Work. With Mary Valentich, he co-edited such works as *Feminist Perspectives on Social Work and Human Sexuality* (1985).

2 The Maritime School of Social Work was doing likewise.

3 The Canadian Forum on Women in Social Work, in association with the Ontario Association of Professional Social Workers, at Carleton University, 1975.

4 Courses included Women's Studies, Psychology of Women, and Political Economy of Women. Sir George Williams University later became part of Concordia University.

Selected Publications by the Author

Berry, Oonagh, and Helen Levine. 2005. *Between friends: A year in letters.* Toronto: Second Story Press.

Levine, Helen. 1976a. Feminist counselling: A look at new possibilities. *'76 and Beyond.* Special issue of *Social Worker* 44: 12–15.

———. 1976b. On women and on one woman. In *Women: Their use of alcohol and other legal drugs,* edited by A. MacLennan. Toronto: Addiction Research Foundation of Ontario, 21–43.

———. 1989. Feminist counselling: A woman-centred approach. In *Women, work and wellness,* edited by Virginia Carver and Charles Ponee. Toronto: Addiction Research Foundation of Ontario, 227–52.

Levine, Helen, and Estable, Alma. 1981. The power politics of motherhood: A feminist critique of theory and practice. Occasional paper. Ottawa: Centre for Social Welfare Studies, Carleton University.

Feminism: A Critical Theory of Knowledge

Marie-Andrée Bertrand

I BECAME A FEMINIST without realizing it in 1965–67, during my doctoral studies in criminology at the University of California at Berkeley. At the time, I didn't have a name for my attitude toward the criminal justice system's unequal treatment of adult and young women. Entitled "The Myth of Sexual Equality Before the Law" (Bertrand 1967a), my first article discussed my analysis of Canadian and European criminal law, which at the time included offences specific to adult and young women (particularly sexual offences), and my observations on legal decisions in adult and youth courts in Canada (Bertrand 1967b). Day after day in these courts, supposedly neutral and universal standards were applied differently to women and men who had been charged with similar offences. In that period, the criminal justice system—like other state apparatus, health, education, and work— treated adult and young women unjustly on the basis of their sex. I was incapable then of explaining this phenomenon, and only in the title of my article did I attempt to condemn the hypocrisy of a justice system that draped itself in a cloak of fairness while administering inequality. Was this phenomenon specific to Canada, France, and Belgium—the three countries whose practices had been the subject of my study?

When I became an assistant professor at the Université de Montréal in 1968, I gathered up my very modest means and launched a vast comparative study of the treatment of adult and young women in Western and Eastern Europe and North and South America. In Eastern Europe (i.e., Hungary and Poland), adult women were not treated as minors and the provisions of criminal law were not as overtly sexist. Women represented one quarter of those who were charged and convicted, compared to 10% in Western Europe. Despite these differences, however, there was an emerging similarity: the sex of suspects gave rise to different treatments[1] regardless of the political (socialist or capitalist) and economic context (rich country, or poor, under-developed country). In that era, the word "gender" was not used; but the work of Margaret Mead in her books *Sex and Temperament in Three Prim-itive Societies* (1935) and *Male and Female* (1949) had convinced me that sex roles were socially and economically constructed. It was clearer to me— without my being able to explain why—that the law considered young and adult women criminals if they had sex outside of marriage, while the same behaviour in adult and young men was seen as normal and even applauded. In short, criminal law adopted to an extreme degree the most sexist aspects of the culture at the time, turning women into minors at the sexual disposal of their husbands.

Liberal feminism did not help me to explain this domination. The pos-sibility of developing a critique of capitalism and practices of racism opened up for me in 1972 when I enthusiastically accepted an invitation to teach for a year at the University of California at Berkeley. The questions of racializa-tion and class, barely present in the program of the Institut de Criminolo-gie at the Université de Montréal from 1960 to 1965, were central to the critical perspective being espoused in graduate studies in the same disci-pline at Berkeley. Through my contact with young professors and graduate students, I discovered Marx, developed a passionate interest in Engels and Hegel, and began to appreciate the ability of feminist theory to "explain" the process of domination and why and how women, the so-called "inferior races," disadvantaged classes, and even minors (in age) had become legal and economic outcasts. My assistants[2] were young people trained in Marx-ist theory by a few professors with big reputations who published exten-sively, little aware of the price they would pay for their theoretical positions.[3]

A similar movement appeared in Great Britain and Germany in 1973. In these countries, the leftist tradition was more entrenched than in the United States. In England, for example, three sociologists developed a brilliant cri-tique of social control theories and published two hugely successful collec-tive works (Taylor, Walton, and Young 1973, 1975) at the very moment their colleagues in Berkeley announced their radical critical criminology pro-gram. Together with sociologists and jurists in Norway, Holland, Sweden, Denmark, and West Germany, British academics created the European Group for the Study of Social Control, and I promptly joined them. The group held meetings parallel to the international criminology conferences that were like a breath of fresh air. At the beginning, this European group didn't pay much attention to feminist and post-colonialist concerns, but by 1968 there appeared British feminists like Frances Heidensohn (1968) and especially, Carol Smart (1976). They had become, by 1970, a very influential force within the group and in the field of law and society in Great Britain as a whole.

My "coming out" as a feminist dates back to this period. The year I returned to Berkeley to teach (1972–73), the editors of the review on criminology and the sociology of deviance were the graduate students who were assisting me with my courses. In addition to in-depth articles on criminology and criminal policies, this periodical, *Issues in Criminology*, published a series of "Dialogues" with sociologists and jurists who were well known for their critiques of law, criminology, and criminal policies. While I was there, I was asked to participate in one of these dialogues (Bertrand 1973a).[4] The interview was prepared with great care: the interviewers read all the publications and the CV of their interviewee. The "dialogue" was held over several sessions, and the transcripts were immediately given to me. I quickly realized that my thinking about the issues confronting criminology, and my theoretical hypotheses about the status of women and the relationships between women and criminal law, did not go far enough, and that, if I wanted to give my questioners proper answers, I would have to seriously study critical theories. During the winter semester of 1973, I devoured the major works of the Frankfurt School—Adorno, Horkheimer, Benjamin—and the sociologists and political theorists examining law as it related to poor and non-White people. My interviewers had decided to focus the interview on the gaps in criminology literature as it was being taught in Montréal and Berkeley, at the time the two leading centres in the field. The first part of the interview was about class and "race" bias in the program structure and individual courses; in the second part, I talked about criminology's silence when it came to women, and I spoke—too hastily and not clearly enough—about the theoretical shortcomings stemming from these three weaknesses.

This interview and my teaching appear to have left a strong and positive impression on several colleagues, because in a recent collection on critical criminology, two of them, Julia and Herman Schwendinger, recall this period in the history of criminology at Berkeley, portraying me as an accomplished feminist who shared their goal of renewing the epistemology of criminology (2002). This is very flattering to me, because in 1973, I was still in the process of finding myself.

My thinking and lectures during the winter of 1973 did, however, enable me to propose to the organizers of the first conference of the European Group for the Study of Deviance and Social Control, set to take place in Florence, a paper entitled "The Hegemonic Conception of Criminal Law and Criminal Policies" (Bertrand 1973b), a hypothesis that I later developed and which became a chapter in the first anthology on critical criminology in Canada (Bertrand 1978).

During all these years, I knew my knowledge of feminist authors and writings was seriously flawed. I hadn't read much of the "classics," and de Beauvoir did not appeal to me. To make up for my ignorance, I could think of nothing better than to propose the creation, in 1989, of a graduate seminar on women's issues, a collaborative teaching activity that would bring together colleagues from different disciplines who had already published works on women. The Faculty of Graduate Studies at last gave the project the go-ahead in 1990 after refusing it the year before. It was, in short, a graduate-level digest of feminist studies that were being taught already in several neighbouring universities, but not at the Université de Montréal. The women who participated in this adventure, which lasted ten years, were sociologists (Nicole Laurin and Danielle Juteau), a social psychologist (Marisa Zavalloni), historians from the Université de Montréal and McGill (Bettina Bradbury and Andrée Lévesque), a specialist on the Old and New Testaments (Olivette Genest), a philosopher (Louise Marcil-Lacoste), and me. The seminar, entitled Le féminisme au carrefour des disciplines (Feminism at the crossroads of the disciplines), dealt with the state of teaching and research on women in our respective disciplines (see Juteau's essay in this volume). Starting in 1992 or 1993, the seminar became a forum for the analysis of feminist theories. In addition to presentations by each of the institution's female professors, the seminar featured talks by leading feminists from several countries, among them Christine Delphy and Colette Guillaumin from France; Drucilla Cornell, Sandra Harding, and Jane Flax from the US; and Isabelle Stengers from Belgium.

In preparation for this course, my research assistants and I spent the summer of 1989 meeting feminists who taught in different universities in Montréal; they readily offered to spend half a day with us, for free, to present their empirical work and theoretical hypotheses. In this preparatory work in the summer of 1989, Francine Descarries was most useful, presenting us with an overview of feminist movements, a chronology of basic works, a chart of different currents of feminism, and an axiologic proposal. Our group then commenced a period of feverish reading and discussion. By the time of the first formal sessions of the PLU 6013 feminist theory seminar, we had a foundation of shared knowledge. The seminar was attended by master's and PhD students (women and men) from widely varying disciplines, including engineering, mathematics, business economics, education, theology, and social sciences. They took the course for credit or simply audited it; many came back for a second year. Five of the six or seven instructors taught free of charge[5] and the faculty granted two teaching credits to the seminar director. This experience profoundly influenced my publications over the last fifteen years.

In 1991, at the request of two US colleagues, Dorie Klein from Berkeley and Kathleen Daly from Yale, I co-organized an international event, the International Feminist Conference on Women, Law, and Social Control, held in Mont Gabriel. It was funded by the National Science Foundation in Washington, DC, the justice departments of Québec and Canada, and the Centre international de criminologie comparée at the Université de Montréal.

Taking part were sixty-one feminists invited from twenty-eight countries in the global North, South, East, and West, all authors of recognized papers on women and penal law. Among other things, this meeting revealed the cultural limitations of theories formulated in Northern and Western countries that sought to comprehend and explain the condition of women. In addition to topical presentations illustrating the diversity of contexts and social and penal practices, Western women were challenged by African and Asian women and by feminists from poor countries; we were forced to recognized the limits of Western "reason" and theories produced in "rich, White countries" when it came to the "gender" and "colour" of law.

To pursue my studies in feminism, I decided to devote my sabbatical year in 1993 to the subject. I arranged to meet with feminist theorists in the US, and they hosted me for a few weeks in their university. They included Sandra Harding, to whom I owe my conviction about the epistemological nature of feminism; Drucilla Cornell, who discussed post-structuralist and postmodern theories and their position in feminist currents; and, especially Seyla Benhabib, whose affinities with the Frankfurt School (Adorno in particular), which she has incorporated so well into her feminist analysis, continue to enlighten me. I spent a semester at the McGill Centre for Research and Teaching on Women before going to Germany for a six-month stay in the Aufbau und Kontakstudium Kriminologie at the University of Hamburg. From there, it was easy for me to work on the last stage of my research on women's prisons in Northern Europe[6] while at the same time carrying on a rich dialogue with a legal sociologist, Johannes Feest, of Bremen, and a sociologist of social institutions and deviance living in Hamburg named Fritz Sack. I also benefitted from my stays in Northern Europe in 1993 and 1994 to meet with feminist theorists in the law and sociology faculties of Norway, Denmark, Germany, and Finland, interview them, and write a profile on feminist studies in law and legal sociology in these four countries (Bertrand 1995b).

After the study on women's prisons (1993–98), in 2003, I began to completely rewrite a monograph on women and criminality (Bertrand 2003). The updated statistics were an eye opener: I saw that the official figures showed a clear increase in women's crime rate, and an alarming multiplication (three times higher) of women's incarceration rate. This was while male criminality in Canada was declining.

My most recent article, which has just come out, is entitled "Féminisme, perspective épistémologique" (Bertrand 2005). In it, I review the major stages in the history of the women's movement and feminist theorization, and show that, in recent works, feminism is used as a theory of knowledge. A number of authors are doing this. Others view feminism and gender theory rather as a heuristic proposition. Feminist epistemology takes different forms, depending on the authors, but in general, it is an epistemology of the subject based on the individual and collective experience of women's standpoint. Often, it is deterministic and structuralist, and attentive to the constraints that, if unrecognized, exert control, even over the mind. It is an emancipatory theory, and, in most authors, modern in its faith in reason, science, and progress.

A feminist in retirement, I don't have much time for rest, nor do I desire it. I'm still teaching the epistemology seminar for the PhD program in applied humanities and social sciences; I supervise graduate students and am part of a research team (SSHRC Major Collaborative Research Initiative). I was a consultant with the Law Commission of Canada for the What Is Crime? project (2004–2006), and, taking over from Francine Descarries, I played an active role on the Policy Research Fund at Status of Women Canada during 2001–2004.

Notes

1   The study was called *Étude de la criminalité féminine comparée* (1970), and it took place under my leadership at the Centre international de criminologie comparée, Université de Montréal; researchers included André Payette, Henrik Tham, Paul Doucet, Marianne Harvey, and Rodica Stanoiu. The study was funded by the Canada Council for the Arts (grants 680083 and 680976).

2 I had one undergraduate course, for which over 450 students registered; I was given ten assistants, all of them master's and doctoral students.

3 This group and their publications resulted in the three youngest members—Anthony M. Platt, and Julia and Herman Schwendinger—being refused tenure; they had to leave Berkeley. At the time, Ronald Reagan was the governor of California, giving him the title of president of all the state universities; university regents were well-known figures like, for example, the San Francisco press magnates, the Hearsts. Tenured professors and the university senate tried in vain to resist this denial of freedom of expression. The regents imposed their decision and later, in 1978, ordered the school to cease its activities. Created in 1949, the Criminology School closed its doors for good in 1978.

4 Virginia Enquist Grabiner (BA, MCrim) was the interviewer; she was a doctoral student engaged in research on suffrage movement and theoretical aspects of sexism.

5 Of the six or seven professors participating in all the sessions, only one was given credit for it each year.

6 This study gave rise to a collective work entitled *Prisons pour femmes* (Bertrand et al. 1998). We did field research in twenty-three penal institutions for women, closed and open, in eight different countries.

Selected Publications by the Author

Bertrand, Marie-Andrée. 1967. The myth of sexual equality before the law. In *Actes de la Société de criminologie du Québec*, edited by Société de criminologie du Québec. Montréal: Centre de psychologie et de pédagogie.

———. 1967. Self image and social representations of female offenders. PhD diss., School of Criminology, University of California, Berkeley.

———. 1978. Penal interventions against women: An illustration of male hegemony in the making and application of penal law. In *The New Criminologies in Canada*, edited by T. O. R. Fleming. Toronto: Oxford University Press.

———. 1995. Le pouvoir des théories féministes dans la reconsidération radicale des théories du contrôle social. In *Theoretical discourse/Discours théoriques*, edited by T. Goldie, C. Lambert and R. Lorimer. Montréal: Association des études canadiennes.

Bertrand, Marie-Andrée, and André Payette. 1970. *Étude de la criminalité féminine comparée, 1968–1970: Canada, Europe de l'Ouest et de l'Est et Amérique du Sud*. Montréal: Centre international de criminologie comparée.

Women's Studies: A Personal Story

Dorothy E. Smith

THERE ARE MANY WAYS of telling the story of one's life. I begin, then, with the simplest fact, that I was born in 1926, so, as I write this in 2005, I am seventy-nine years old. The life that I connect with this one that I'm still living started when I went to the London School of Economics at the age of twenty-six (having tried a variety of training and jobs, including a few years of secretarial work). I had no idea of an academic life, but I knew that the key to better jobs was a bachelor's degree. I read in sociology and anthropology, and was fascinated. I graduated, got married, emigrated to the United States to do graduate studies at the University of California at Berkeley, had two children, finished my doctorate, got divorced, and left the US (ultimately) to work in Canada at the University of British Columbia (UBC).

In Canada, I was exposed to the period of Canadianization, which was very influential in my work as a sociologist. I came to understand that the sociology centred in the US, but claiming universality, essentially placed me, as an academic, in much the same position as a docent in an art gallery or museum. I should reproduce; I should not originate. I had been trained to impose the orthodoxies of the US sociological establishment on Canadian students and not to think for myself. I was the intellectual colonist. The Canadianization movement taught me to reject this role; I discovered the possibility of calling on sociology to think about the actualities of the society in which it was being discussed. This was something that sociology did not do well.

A second and greater challenge to who I was as a sociologist and who I would become emerged with the women's movement. This was of a different

order altogether. If the inadequacies of the sociology I knew how to practise had emerged, at least for me, in the politics of Canadianization, the
women's movement went much, much deeper, both in me and in my
grandiose proposal for a total transformation of sociology (Smith 1987,
2005). Like many other women in sociology at the time, I was astonished to
discover the degree of women's exclusion from the discipline in multiple
ways: we weren't wanted in sociology faculties; we weren't mentioned in
sociological writing and research; and we were excluded conceptually in the
order of sociological discourse. For me, however, there was another problem: we were never the subjects, never the knowers of sociological discourse.
Examining sociology from this perspective suggested a more fundamental
problem than that unmasked by the Canadianization movement: the conceptual ordering of sociology could not perform other than by constituting
people as objects. Constituting them as objects denied them/us presence as
subjects. Writing a sociology for women would thus entail a reconstruction
of sociology's conceptual order such that it would be capable of beginning
from where people are in the actualities of our lives and exploring from
there the relations and organizations that shape us without our knowledge.
This would be the business of sociology; this would be its professional commitment.

All this was happening at a major juncture in the women's movement that
is hard to recover once it has passed. It's hard to recall just how radical the
experience of the women's movement was at its inception for those of us who
had lived and thought within the masculinist regime against which the
movement struggled. For us, the struggle was as much within ourselves,
with what we knew how to do and think and feel, as with that regime as an
enemy outside us. Indeed, we ourselves had participated, however passively,
in that regime. There was no developed discourse in which the experiences
that were spoken originally as everyday experience could be translated into
a public language and become political in the ways distinctive to the women's
movement. We learned, in talking with other women, about experiences
that we had in common and others that we had not shared. We began to
name "oppression," "rape," "harassment," "sexism," "violence," and others.
These were terms that did more than name. They gave shared experiences
a political presence.

Starting with our experiences as we talked and thought about them, we
discovered depths of alienation and anger that were astonishing. Where had
all these feelings been? How extraordinary were the transformations we
experienced as we discovered with other women how to speak with one

another about such experiences and then how to bring them forward publicly, which meant exposing them to men. Finally, how extraordinary were the transformations of our selves in this process. Talking our experience was a means of discovery. What we did not know, and did not know how to think about, we could examine as we found what we had in common. The approach that I have taken in developing an alternative sociology takes up women's standpoint in a way that is modelled on these early adventures of the women's movement. It takes up women's standpoint, not as a given and finalized form of knowledge, but as a ground in experience from which discoveries are to be made (Smith 2005, 7–8).

The women's studies courses that I started teaching with Helga Jacobson (anthropology), Meredith Kimball (psychology), and Annette Kolodny (English) at UBC in 1973 were an integral part of the speaking of our/women's experiences that was at that time central to the political dynamic of the women's movement. We did not originate women's studies at UBC though we were involved in its origination. There had been a series of feminist lectures that women in the Alma Mater Society had created, and these were our inspiration. If I now forget their names, it is partly an effect of distance in time and partly of my age, which blurs the boundaries and differentiations of the years. A number of women faculty then developed an initiative within the university to establish a women's studies course. I was not directly involved in these struggles though I certainly supported them. I don't know why I was not involved; perhaps because I was at that time very active in various women's organizational initiatives in the community. Helga kept me informed. She told me of the difficulties of convincing the almost exclusively male members of the fifteen committees, before whom the case for a women's studies course had to be argued, of the academic legitimacy of the enterprise.

Feminist academic material, women's studies academic material, simply did not exist. When we four, Annette, Helga, Meredith, and I, who designed and finally taught the courses, looked for appropriate course readings, we were hard put to find anything. I have collected copies of the course outlines we devised, but I am writing now from memory, and I remember looking for books or other materials that might be relevant and finding only two or three works in sociology that were remotely related to the topic (one of them being Jessie Bernard's 1964 book, *Academic Women*). I know that others drew on materials that could be interpreted from a feminist standpoint, as I did. There was, however, no theory, very little substantive material from the point of view that we were necessarily developing, and certainly nothing remotely approaching a textbook.

The course we designed had a dual structure. We appropriated in each of our departments two courses, or released time for two courses. One course was a three-session-a-week general course in which we all participated. In addition, each of us, representing anthropology (Helga), English (Annette), psychology (Meredith), and sociology (myself) taught a once-a-week seminar in our own fields. Students had to register for both courses. This was, I remark, an excellent design because it enabled issues arising in the general course to be developed in more specialized disciplinary settings evoking critiques that could not have been foreseen or, at that time, enunciated in the general course.

Our ignorance, the absence of material to be taught, and the women's movement's distinctive commitment to working from women's experience turned into extraordinary advantages. In a course with sometimes eighty students, we engaged in dialogue. The differentiation between students and professors in knowledge was not great. True, we had skills that they might not yet have, but when it came to knowledge of women's lives, they could contribute from their own experiential knowledge as much as could any of the four of us, let alone the literature we drew on. I came to think of each hour of the three hours a week as the *real* university. It was in those three hours that, like the children who followed the Pied Piper into the world of light through the door in the mountain, we entered the real university of dialogue, argument, varied views, learning, learning, learning. Jürgen Habermas's (1970) ideal speech situation was nothing to this. Nothing I've experienced before or since was like this. Everyone had knowledge to draw on; everyone had ignorance to be remedied; everyone was passionately concerned to learn as well as to teach.

Of course, this could not last. The administration cunningly (and not for the last time in my experience) had allowed us the released time to set the course/s up just as we wished and, once we had things running, withdrew part of the time available so that we could run only the general course. In part, and over time, the magic of dialogue faded. The real university disappeared, to be replaced by traditional academic method. A feminist literature came into being; there were theories to be taught and substantive studies to be introduced. We ourselves wrote papers that became part of the course reading list. We became the experts, and our students became those it was our responsibility to teach.

This was not all of my life in the women's movement, nor all of the lives of those with whom I worked. There was so much, it is difficult to patch together the different pieces and their timing, much less to write a coherent account. Foundational to all this were my children and household (I was a single parent), and a job that was essential to our domestic economy yet competed in multiple ways with the work of being parent, house carer, neighbour, and whatever else might enter into the scope of home. In and during this and, in part, because of this course or these courses, as well as the activism in the community that I could not resist, I was changing.

I was changing in ways that are now so deeply integrated into who I have become that I cannot remember a former state of being Dorothy Smith. I have written elsewhere of the changes as taking place over a period of time, of having a kind of pace and inevitability that I have compared to the labour of giving birth to a child. In giving birth, a massive muscular process, independent of will or intention, takes over the body. It has its own determinate destination and will go there. I was seized by such a process—not a muscularity of the body but of the psyche, of mind. I had begun to find myself differently in the world than I had done formerly. I had been responsible, responsive, relatively conformist (though perhaps, in retrospect, a little odder than I imagined). I did not become wild or strange, but I had practised, probably since I had started to read, a form of consciousness that located me, as subject, outside myself as a girl and as a woman. I had learned how to situate my consciousness in the world of art and intellect written by men. I could read Wordsworth's *Prelude* (1850) without awareness that it was written by a man from his standpoint and experience, and that I was not that.

It was this that was changing. What was difficult, of course, was to discover an alternative base for subjectivity. I did not then think of it in that way. I did not know quite what was happening, though I adopted for myself a phrase that I had picked up from earlier work by Noam Chomsky, that the responsibility of intellectuals was to tell the truth. I used this phrase rather differently than he intended it because I came to see that telling the truth meant refusing the boundaries of whatever institutionalized discourse was operative in any given context and drawing upon whatever was in me that I knew was (a) relevant and (b) not necessarily acceptable within institutional conventions. I had to learn to have the nerve to do this. I was going through a process of discovering, in who I was, who I might be as a woman, and specifically, in this context, as a woman academic.

Over the two year or so period that I was caught up in this, as well as learning new skills in thinking, writing, speaking, and working politically, I also for a time felt that I had lost contact with the world in which others participated. I did not feel mad because, for the first time, I could recognize that coherence was always in the making and that it required a recognition of who I was, what I was drawing on, and what I found in me through the various situations that I encountered. A friend of mine, going through a rather similar process, described to me how, for a period of time, she could not see herself in the mirror. In its time, this period of labour, of being caught up in a process that had a destination that I could neither foresee nor choose, came to an end. It was not that the processes of change ceased, but that the foundational changes had been put in place, and from then on it was up to me to make choices, to take chances, to develop skills, and to envisage possibilities.

I cannot say that the work experience of the women's studies course, as I described it earlier, was all that was implicated in this process; but it was, I think, a major precipitating component. In that classroom, in the room of light that we entered through the door in the mountain three times every week, we were engaged in the discovery of ourselves as women and as subjects. As women, we had never been subjects in the world of intellect and art. We were discovering it practically, each time we met, in talk and reading, and in building a knowledge based in the dialogic of women's experience. How could we not be changed who had never known this before? It was on the basis of being thus changed that I could see how to go forward in developing an alternative sociology that would begin in the actualities of women's/people's/our lives as we experience them.

Selected Publications by the Author

Smith, Dorothy E. 1977. *Feminism and Marxism: A place to begin, a way to go*. Vancouver: New Star Books.

———. 1978. A peculiar eclipsing: Women's exclusion from men's culture. *Women's Studies International Quarterly* 1 (4): 281–96.

———. 1987. *The everyday world as problematic: A feminist sociology*. Toronto: University of Toronto Press.

———. 1990. *The conceptual practices of power: A feminist sociology of knowledge*. Toronto: University of Toronto Press.

———. 2005. *Institutional ethnography: A sociology for people*. Lanham, MD: Altamira Press.

Contributing to the Establishment of Women's Studies and Gender Relations

◉ Anita Caron

AS A STAFF WORKER in Catholic Action groups in Montréal from 1950 to 1962, I became aware of the alienation and exclusion experienced by many women in Québec and elsewhere. In 1962, when I began working on a master's degree, and later when working on a doctorate in religious sciences, I became more interested in women's place in the Judeo-Christian tradition. This was the period of preparation for the Vatican II Council: an ideal opportunity to present formal recommendations.

Recommendations on the Place of Women

I, and some women who, like me, had worked with l'Action catholique therefore began to study works and articles featuring theoretical arguments for the effective recognition of women as full-fledged persons. Simone de Beauvoir's *The Second Sex* was a key influence as we drafted a paper for the bishops who would be participating in the council sessions. This paper was a synthesis of observations, aspirations, and recommendations on women's status and role in the family, society, and church. The text we submitted to the bishops was also published in *Le Devoir* (a Montréal daily newspaper) in the autumn of 1965. It generated other media coverage as well, notably on the issue of women's access to the priesthood. In me, it aroused the desire to contribute to the recognition of women as subjects. My duties as professor at l'Université du Québec à Montréal (UQAM) later gave me this opportunity.

Creation of Courses on Women and Gender

Hired as a professor when UQAM opened in 1969, I was eager to introduce a course on women and religion in the curriculum that was being developed. Of course, feminist studies had not yet appeared. Then, in 1972, a history course attended by more than 200 students sensitized the university to the need for a program on "the status of women" (see Nadia Fahmy-Eid's essay in this volume). The human sciences sector examined the possibility of offering a certificate addressed specifically to women working in women's groups.

Perspectives on a Program

I and some other colleagues were invited to a meeting to discuss the goals and content of this certificate program. The women who participated in the consultation decided against the certificate format due to the inherent risks of professionalization and ghettoization. We agreed, though, that it was important to propose to the university the creation of courses, research projects, and community services specifically addressing women and gender relations. A working group was created to identify the academic activities that already existed in this field of study and to explore the possibility of creating others. In meetings attended by women professors, lecturers, students, and professionals, we regularly updated each other on the work being accomplished to organize courses, identify research projects underway, and follow up on training requests from women's groups.

We realized right away that the process would be interdisciplinary and closely linked to the women's movement. Issuing from the aspirations of a couple of dozen women professors in diverse disciplines, the group taking shape sought organizational forms that would foster links among researchers in different disciplines, as well as partnerships with women's groups. The proposal we submitted to the UQAM administration described a group whose mandate would be to offer educational activities, coordinate research projects, and respond to requests for expertise.

Creating the Groupe interdisciplinaire d'enseignement et de recherche sur les femmes—The Women's Education and Research Group

In 1976, in response to our proposal, the curriculum committee created the Groupe interdisciplinaire d'enseignement et de recherche sur les femmes (GIERF), conferring on it the following mandate:

- ensure the coordination and creation by the different disciplines of credit courses on women and gender relations
- promote and coordinate research conducted in this field of study and foster the sharing of this knowledge
- establish links with women's groups in order to respond to their needs in terms of research, lectures, consulting, and conferences

Before becoming an official body, the group existed for three years in an experimental form. I was responsible for coordinating the first four courses given in the autumn of 1976. Three years later, GIERF was officially recognized as a teaching and research body and formally entitled to a coordinator. The group was already proposing to create a broad field of research and teaching about the condition of women and gender relations. It also provided diverse services to women's groups and proved to be a vibrant force for women in the university, ensuring the publication and distribution of their work and action both internally and externally. In 1990, the creation of a research institute confirmed and strengthened this role. At the beginning of this third millennium, the Institut de recherche et d'études féministes continues to pursue GIERF's mandate, highlighting the contribution of feminist studies to a critical and renewed vision of the different dimensions of knowledge.

It was a privilege for me to have been associated with the creation and development of the group initially responsible for its direction and dynamism. I am also very fortunate to have benefited from its support myself in recent years, with my own research work on gender relations within the church,[1] and on the network of women researchers and practitioners involved in implementing policy and practice to reduce women's poverty.[2]

Notes

1 Les femmes et leur participation au pouvoir dans l'Église (Fonds pour la formation des chercheurs et l'aide à la recherche [FCAR] 1986–88); Groupes de femmes et participation au pouvoir dans l'Église (FCAR 1988–90); Femmes, formation théologique et emplois (Conseil de recherches en sciences humaines du Canada [CRSH] 1990–92); Des alternatives aux représentations traditionnelles des rapports hommes–femmes dans l'Église (CRSH 1993–96).

2 L'économie sociale et la lutte contre l'appauvrissement des femmes (CRSH 1997–2000); Réseau féministe pour un renouvellement des théories et des pratiques économiques et politiques (CRSH 2000–2003).

Selected Publications by the Author

Caron, Anita. 1984. *Les parents et le statut confessionnel de l'école au Québec*. Sillery: Presses de l'Université du Québec.

————. 1985. *La Famille québécoise, institution en mutation? Analyse de discours et de pratiques de groupes intervenant auprès des couples*. Montréal: Fides.

————. 1987. *L'éducation morale en milieu scolaire: Analyse de situation et perspectives*. Montréal: Fides.

————. 1991. *Femmes et pouvoir dans l'Église*. Montréal: Agenda de distribution populaire.

Caron, Anita , and Lorraine Archambault. 1993. *Thérèse Casgrain: Une femme tenace et engagée*. Sainte-Foy: Presses de l'Université du Québec.

Feminism and a Scholarly Friendship

◉ *Jill Ker Conway*
  Natalie Zemon Davis

WE BEGIN THIS ACCOUNT of our 1970–71 course Society and the Sexes in Early Modern Europe and the United States by tracing the intellectual and personal paths that led up to our conceptualization of what a course on the history of women should be like. We blended two very different disciplinary trainings and fields of research with our personal and political histories.

Natalie My interest in feminism began early. By the time I was a student at Smith College in the late 1940s, I knew I wanted to combine a scholarly career with marriage—already something of a challenge to gender mores of the day. I was active in the "progressive" and Marxist groups on campus. When I met and eloped with my left-wing husband at the end of my third year, an egalitarian marriage was part of our commitment (he typed my senior thesis for me).

My interest in the history of women and gender began seriously only much later. Though Smith was a women's college with women professors and a history of feminist action, I don't recall that we ever studied women specifically in any of my history and literature courses. In graduate school (at Harvard, and then at the University of Michigan), I decided to do social history—not because of my teachers, but because my initial interest in Marxism turned me in that direction. Surprisingly, one of my Michigan professors (a man—after my Smith years I had no women teachers) urged me to do a seminar paper for a Renaissance course on Christine de Pizan. I turned it into a social study—"Christine de Pizan as a Prototype of the Professional Literary Woman"—and explored her pioneering writings on women in terms of her own position in early fifteenth-century society. For background I read Mary Beard's *Woman as a Force in History* (1946)and Eileen Power's writings on medieval women (1922, 1924, 1975), and found these works fascinating—but I did not want to make Christine the subject of my doctoral dissertation as he urged me to do. By 1952, I was focussing on issues of religion and social class during the Protestant Reformation, especially the urban artisans and workers, virtually never studied in this connection. Christine de Pizan would have taken me into the rarified circles of the court and the nobility (de Pizan 1998), and also at that time I could not see the connection between her life choices and ideas, and the larger questions of social and cultural organization and change that I wanted to probe.

Until the late 1960s, my historical research and publication on sixteenth-century France, carried on in the United States and after 1962 in Toronto, concerned the lower classes, their resistance movements, trade union activity, and beliefs. Women entered into the story as, for example, recipients of poor relief. When I began to teach economic history at the University of Toronto, I introduced a section on women in the labour force; but women and gender were not at the centre. That early social history work was helpful, however, for later work on women: it gave me experience in finding sources that were claimed by traditional historians not to exist; it got me thinking about dichotomies of resistance and oppression; and it gave me the habit of comparison—across class and across religion.

Similarly, my political activities up to the mid-1960s did not have feminist questions at the centre. Until 1960, my husband and I were much concerned with civil liberties issues; he was a target of the House Committee on Un-American Activities and had a case going in the US courts. I had had my passport revoked. Once this was over, we moved to Toronto in 1962 so he could teach mathematics at the University of Toronto, since he had been blacklisted in the US. The civil rights movements in the southern US and the early movement against the Vietnam War then absorbed our attention.

Including women at the centre of things came from several sources. By now I had three children and had started collecting materials, just out of curiosity, on childbirth and early child-rearing in early modern Europe. I had begun to teach, first at Brown University, and then at the University of Toronto (political economy, history). Either I was the only woman in a department or part of a little group of female lecturers and assistant professors. I recall that around 1964, one of my male colleagues at the University of Toronto referred to all the men in the department as professor and me as "Mrs." I could see the struggle of women in the graduate programs at the University of Toronto, especially those trying to juggle marriage and children as well. Together with several of them, I organized a questionnaire for those graduate women at the University of Toronto who were also mothers. We submitted our mimeographed report ("A Study of 42 Women Who Have Children and Who Are in Graduate Programs at the University of Toronto") with recommendations on things like flexible schedules, daycare, and library hours to the University of Toronto administration in 1966. We didn't get an answer.

In the next years, the women's movement exploded at the University of Toronto, along with the debates about restructuring the university. I also had the delight of getting to know Jill Conway. Over many a lunch, I learned of her research on the first generation of American women to undertake graduate study, and understood how such a topic was a new road to central issues in the cultural and social history of the United States. By then, my own research was going in a more cultural direction, as I began to work on festivities and the connection between the carnivalesque and resistance movements, topics in which gender symbolism had a role to play. Out of this wonderful interchange came our plan for a comparative course: Society and the Sexes in Early Modern Europe and the United States.

Jill I had the standard British training in history as an undergraduate at the University of Sydney in the 1950s. This meant a neo-Marxist orientation toward the primacy of economics as a causal factor, combined with a British imperial focus on administrative and institutional history. I knew the dates of every imperial war, and the actual identifying numbers of the major Colonial Office memoranda applying to the settlement and governance of Australia, but little social history, and the history of ideas only as it related to English high culture. It was exasperation with this curriculum that sent me off to Harvard for doctoral study in American history.

Women figured in this British imperial narrative only as the occasional reformer of prostitutes or as spectacular sexual adventurers, or in the persons of monarchs like Elizabeth I or Queen Victoria, always treated as under the guidance of their male major political advisors. It is an indication of the lack of attention to women as historical figures that, shortly before I left for Harvard in 1960, I, just a beginning graduate student, was asked to write the biographical pieces on some key women figures, such as Elizabeth MacArthur, in the settlement of Australia for the first systematic effort to produce a *Dictionary of Australian Biography* (Pike 1967, 379–81).

My graduate work at Harvard was unusual for the 1960s because, to my astonishment and delight, my thesis director, an intellectual historian, treated women intellectuals Jane Addams (1860–1935), Gertrude Stein (1874–1946), and Mabel Dodge Luhan (1879–1962) as important social thinkers and influencers of the development of uniquely American styles of thought, taking them as seriously as William James, John Dewey, or Thorstein Veblen.

With this encouragement I chose a dissertation topic in the history of women. I wanted to understand why, one hundred and thirty plus years after women had gained access to education in North America, Europe, and Australia and New Zealand, they had so little to show for it in terms of roles in the professions, politics, and the academy. To answer that question, I studied the first generation of American women to undertake graduate study, and their subsequent careers. This topic required reading the American pioneers of sociology, the history of the professionalization of learning, the founding of the "female professions," and a prosopographical study of thirty or so pioneering women who undertook graduate education in the sciences, social sciences, and humanities, along with their counterparts who became important public intellectuals.

The lives of these women were case studies in the way discrimination worked to close off opportunity despite access to education. But what interested me more as I worked my way through their papers and publications was why women so basically self-aware, rebellious, and critical of the accepted romantic life plot for women still described themselves and their lives to others in stereotypically romantic terms. This set me thinking about the ways cultures censor what can be thought and felt, many decades before postmodernism and the study of narrative made these questions routine (Conway 1982).

At the University of Toronto, where I joined the history department in 1964, I was encouraged to teach an upper-level undergraduate seminar in US history, where it was expected that I would draw on my doctoral work to develop research projects for students. This experience set me thinking about periodization and whether the major turning points in the history of women fit with the definition of time shifts used to characterize trends and eras in standard history.

So far as my political interests were concerned, my departure from Australia represented a political act, a refusal to accept the definition of the past treated as authoritative within the profession in Australia. Moreover, by choosing to study in the US, I was also rejecting the Oxbridge tradition dominant in Australian culture. My departure was prompted, too, by experiences of outright discrimination, though I still thought of this in personal terms until a second encounter with discrimination in my own promotion and pay as a young instructor and assistant professor at the University of Toronto. This time my studies had shown me that mine was not a personal predicament, and so I acted to mobilize other women faculty to study rates of promotion and differentials in pay unrelated to performance. My zest for the fight was enhanced by a husband who was a strong feminist and supporter of my career.

As these events were unfolding, I had the great good fortune to meet Natalie, and we began to schedule regular lunches together to discuss our work. She taught me how one studies the non-literate and finds the voices of the people left out in standard historical sources. I learned an entirely new approach to texts and documents from her, and began to broaden my thinking about how to study more than an educated elite. We discussed my puzzle about my non-romantic romantic women, and my speculation that cultures might expropriate feelings just as Marx and Engels said capitalism expropriated the creativity and the product of labour. We discussed theology and witchcraft and the polluting female in early modern times, to which I juxtaposed the modern social sciences and their model of women as "failed males," or people in a lower stage of development than men, the fear of women undermining "standards" in professional groups, and the worry that women would be emotional if able to become political leaders. These conversations eventually evolved into plans for teaching a new kind of history.[1]

Both We had no model to follow, no pre-existing syllabus. We had to decide on our topics, our ordering of themes, our explanations, and our ways of seeing connections between gender relations—relations between "the sexes" as we called them—and other forms of social life and historical changes. We ended up with a course that went in several new directions, departing from current social and intellectual history courses in its ordering and interdisciplinarity. Rather than starting off with the usual population, geography, and economics, we started off each semester—the European semester and the American semester—with "Images of the Sexes" found in different writings over time. That is, we began with a version of the "construction" of gender. We then moved to demography (a relatively new topic for history courses), family relations, and sexuality (including same-sex relations), and then on to women in economic and professional life, women in religious life, and finally women in politics. In the European section, we opened by comparing Christine de Pizan (waiting in Natalie's notes for twenty years), with the images from the *Malleus Maleficarum* (Institoris 1485), a handbook on witch prosecution; we ended comparing Mary Wollstonecraft's *A Vindication of the Rights of Woman* (1792) with Rousseau's chapter on "Sophie" from his *Émile* (1762).

We also privileged primary sources—that is, books written by women and men at the time—over theory and recent interpretive efforts, such as they were; but then we had to find the sources, in the face of skeptics who said they did not exist. For Jill, this meant seeking well beyond the century she knew best in US history; for Natalie, this meant starting from scratch, looking in rare book collections and in little-known printed transcriptions of manuscripts. We ended up with an impressive Works Cited, which we circulated widely in mimeographed form and the American section of which Jill subsequently published.

Jill For me, this meant adding complexity to the assumed progressive dynamic nearly universal in treating nineteenth- and twentieth-century US history by deconstructing the history of supposed progress in women's education in the US, frequently described in works with titles such as "A Century of Progress," by linking it to the history of discrimination that resulted in the establishment of the underpaid and non-research-based women's professions. Much care was taken to balance the assessment of what these segregated female professions achieved, by examining the record showing how stereotypes of the female temperament fostered such adjustments to prejudice, and by recognizing the extent to which marginalization in those professions gave women professionals a perspective on society that produced the great Progressive women reformers.

To the extent possible, I used the same structure and categories as Natalie used in the first half of the course, replacing theology with social science, social protest with reform (linking temperance women's smashing of liquor barrels with the bread riots of early modern Europe), and drawing on medical texts for the images of female sexuality presented in the earlier texts on witchcraft. Where the structure differed in the second half of the course was in the examination of the ways in which apparent gains in one area in women's status and rights were compensated for conservatively in another social arena. Thus we studied how the success of the suffrage agitation was quickly followed by the new discipline of psychology, which defined an interest in power or the non-domestic world as a sign of female sexual maladjustment. By contrast with early modern Europe, a non-traditional society had great flexibility in maintaining the status quo alongside the appearance of change in sex roles. In the section on demography and fertility, we analyzed the tactics of feminist reform, and how the birth-control movement's use of the courts to secure women's access to information made a potentially revolutionary redefinition of female sexuality relatively conservative.

A totally new departure was the section on anti-feminist thought and organizations, in which students were introduced to texts that showed how and why opposition to expanding women's rights made sense to the participants at a personal level, while at the same time such opposition was symptomatic of larger social and political problems in an aggressively competitive and profoundly acquisitive era.

Natalie Conceptually, we made several leaps. How were gender systems connected with other forms of social organization? For me, this meant seeing the ways, both symbolic and experiential, that the male/female hierarchy reinforced (or allowed inversion of) the social/political hierarchy that marked Old Regime Europe. As for change over time in gender relations, I explained them with several variables rather than focussing on a single one (economic or religious): I used neither a simple model of progress to modernity nor a narrative of decline from an aristocratic, pre-industrial, golden age. Though especially interested to locate women's strategies for resistance or for carving out space for themselves, I—like Jill—saw women neither as absolute heroes or victims. Women were a group often diverse in interest and in viewpoint; they had varied relations among themselves (from intimate to hostile) and with men.

Both Teaching Society and the Sexes in that first year, 1971–72, was enormously exciting. We had lots of students, mostly women. That year, and in subsequent years when Jill taught alone, we had marvellous teaching assistants, several of whom—Veronica Strong-Boag, Elizabeth Cohen, and Linda Kealey—went on to become leaders in women's studies in different parts of Canada. Within the University of Toronto, perceptions of the course's scholarly Works Cited, conceptual rigour, and balanced treatment of causation helped create a willingness to teach on subjects relating to women, both within established departments and in new programs. Society and the Sexes did not, however, prompt a strong interest in recruiting women scholars to the history department, where some years elapsed before another line appointment was filled by a woman. The course syllabus and Works Cited became nationally and internationally known and frequently drawn upon in teaching in the field. Jill's decision to publish her section accompanied by commentary on key issues in the field came in response to the enduring interest in the course and its Works Cited.

The year 1971–72 turned out to be the only time we taught the course together, for Natalie left for a professorship at the University of California (UC) at Berkeley, and, after teaching the American section herself for several years, Jill left in 1975 to become president of Smith College.

Natalie But the course changed us. I went on to teach Society and the Sexes in Early Modern Europe first at UC Berkeley and then at Princeton, and helped found a Women's Studies Program both places. My work in cultural history and my interdisciplinary reach were much expanded, and my historical publications (as in *The Return of Martin Guerre* and *Women on the Margins*) integrated women and gender fully into the central narrative.

Jill I continued my exploration of gender and social systems as president of a college for women where curriculum, finances, student recruitment, and faculty training were all influenced by the nature of the student body, and the institution's one-hundred-year history of advancing the education of women. I wrote about this in an autobiographical volume entitled *A Woman's Education* (Conway 2002). The experience of the course enlarged my focus on the subject and led to several decades of work on women's access to education in non-Western countries and more recently on the educational needs of women workers in contract factories in the global economy.

Society and the Sexes taught me the importance of text, and my own research illuminated the impact of gender stereotypes on female self-reporting. This prompted me to write a series of memoirs (*The Road from Coorain* [1989], *True North* [1994], and *A Woman's Education* [2002] and to publish three anthologies of women's memoirs, drawing on little known, unpublished, or out-of-print materials (*Written By Herself: Autobiographies of American Women* [1992]; *Written By Herself*, vol. 2, *Women's Memoirs from Britain, Africa, Asia and the United States* [1996]; and *In Her Own Words: Women's Memoirs from Australia, New Zealand, Canada and the United States* [2003]). In my own writing I have been particularly concerned with establishing narrative patterns that are impossible to interpret as romantic, though many readers and some movie script writers still manage to do so.

Both How would we teach this course today?

Natalie I would not necessarily have "the sexes," that is, gender, as the organizing topic or central narrative theme of a course. If you always start with the category of "gender" and the group called "women," you inevitably focus on the theme of likenesses and differences, and simply find repeated evidence for them. Likeness and difference are essential categories in all comparative history, and a major contribution of women's studies has been deepening the understanding of the forms of analysis for other fields, such as peasant studies and ethnic studies; but limiting yourself to this process yields familiar results and the political and conceptual paradoxes to which Joan Scott (1996)and Wendy Brown (2003) have called attention. Thus, I might take a theme—such as political action and violence, or health and healing, or economic production and exchange, or immigration and diasporas, or friendship and sexuality—and let it carry the narrative over time, while gender questions would be raised each week under that rubric. I would expect gender meanings to emerge in new ways. This is certainly what I found in my recent book, *The Gift in Sixteenth-Century France*, where focussing on gift exchange led subsequently to surprising discoveries about women's attitudes.

Jill Today I would build my section of the course around the impact of migration on settlers and indigenous people, environmental change, and responses to environmental degradation, especially in Asia, Africa, and Latin America, where such damage has been a driving force in female-led environmental movements. I would treat women's working life in a global perspective, making sure to link it to the migration patterns of males in modern times. The sections concerning education and cultural roles would focus as much on the politics of women's education globally as on curriculum and outcomes.

Like Natalie, I would choose to study major changes and movements of the modern world to enable students to see that, though differently embodied, and consequently lodged in gender systems, women and men inhabit the same social world. Therefore, they are affected by the same political and economic transformations that are characteristic of modernity. Like her, I would also aim to link the study of gender to our understanding of a post-colonial world that can no longer be viewed from a Western perspective.

Both By now, as our own research has taken us well beyond Europe and North America, and as a global and post-colonial consciousness is essential for thinking about our troubled world, we would expand the perspective in our course. We would bring in women historians from non-Western regions to lecture to our students. Indeed, were we to teach the course at the University of Toronto, in this regard we would simply be catching up. Our students would be part of families from all over the world—a composition more richly varied than our class of 1971–72. We would have colleagues who are exemplars of this global consciousness, such as Shahrzad Mojab, current director of the Institute for Women's Studies at the University of Toronto.

Our aim for a jointly revised course would be to enable our students to understand contemporary feminism, not simply in the context of the West, but through awareness of feminist positions found in Africa, the Middle East, and Asia. Only through understanding the political, religious, and social links of these different feminisms to the past and their links to the current conflicts and movements for change can we assess gender relations today and their possibilities for the future.

Notes

1 I did not in 1970 see myself as a pioneer in the history of American women. There were many predecessors in the field, such as Julia W. Spruill, *Women's Life and Work in the Southern Colonies* (1938), Mary Sumner Benson, *Women in Eighteenth Century America: A Study of Opinion and Social Usage* (1935), and Mary Beard (only begetter of the Berkshire Conference on the history of women), *Woman as Force in History* (1946). These and many other works based on extensive research were all unread and out of print in 1970, but I was much indebted to this earlier generation.

Selected Publications by the Authors

Jill Ker Conway
Conway, Jill Ker. 1989. *The road from Coorain*. New York: Alfred A. Knopf.
————. 1992. *Written by herself: Autobiographies of American women; An anthology.* New York: Vintage.
————. 1994. *True north: A memoir.* 1st Canadian ed. Toronto: A. A. Knopf Canada.
————. 1996. *Written by herself.* Vol. 2, *Women's memoirs from Britain, Africa, Asia and the United States.* New York: Vintage.
————. 2002. *A woman's education.* New York: Alfred A. Knopf.
————. 2003. *In her own words: Women's memoirs from Australia, New Zealand, Canada and the United States.* New York: Vintage.

Natalie Zemon Davis

Davis, Natalie Zemon. 1975. *Society and culture in early modern France*. Stanford: Stanford University Press.

————. 1976. 'Women's history' in transition: The European case. *Feminist Studies* 3: 83–93.

————. 1983. *The return of Martin Guerre* Cambridge, MA: Harvard University Press.

————. 1995. *Women on the margins: Three seventeenth century lives*. Cambridge, MA: Harvard University Press.

————. 2000. *The gift in sixteenth-century France*. Madison: University of Wisconsin Press.

Midwife to the Birth of Women's Studies at McGill

Margaret Gillett

WHAT A PLEASURE and honour it is to be asked to participate in this project. Even while it forces me to face the astonishing fact that I am now more than three-quarters of a century old, it also gives me licence to indulge in nostalgia for a rapidly receding decade. How far away 1966–76 now seems! Fortunately, I have always been a pack rat for paper, so, if memory fails me, I can still put my hands on old CVs, bibliographies, clippings, letters, and notes. These are important because, as a perceptive feminist reminds us, "We censor ourselves by not writing down our thoughts, by not keeping what we have written, by throwing away leaflets publicizing our demonstrations, or by overlooking even the importance of keeping minutes at group meetings" (Leslie 1992, 72). So enough of self-censorship! It's fun to overcome reticence and also to remember that "the personal is political."

I really don't need documentation to remind me that, all my life, I have been alert to gender differences and have wanted equality. I was the youngest of a happy family of five children. I had two brothers and two sisters, all loved, but I envied my brothers the household tasks they were given (chopping wood rather than washing dishes) and the more convenient clothes they wore (pants rather than skirts). In elementary school in the 1930s, spelling bees and other contests regularly pitted the girls against the boys: girls shone in English and, to the chagrin of the boys, quite often in science and math. My most important secondary schooling was at an all-girls school, so scholastic gender differences retreated. At the University of Sydney in the

1940s, all the professors were male, and I can recall only one female course assistant. However, I clearly remember that in my undergraduate English courses I read Virginia Woolf and deliberately chose to write papers dealing with Shakespeare's heroines, seeing that the best of them were bold; in history, I became acquainted with Mary Wollstonecraft and Emmeline Pankhurst and was incensed by the often-violent struggle for women's suffrage; in anthropology, I learned more from Margaret Mead and Ruth Benedict about gender roles and the existence of matriarchal societies. During the 1950s, I marched through Sydney with other student-teachers demanding (unsuccessfully) equal pay, and I continued to fight for that cause after I began teaching high school. I had a constant reminder of the financial injustice women suffered because it came with every pay cheque—I was receiving just over half the salary of my male colleagues.

After I had been out in the world for a while and returned to Sydney from two years of travel and teaching in Europe, I worked with the administration of the Colombo Plan (an organization established in 1950 that provides economic aid to parts of South and Southeast Asia). There, I met someone who was the single most significant influence on my intellectual development and my social values: Dr. Monika Kehoe, an American almost twenty years my senior, put a new perspective on everything for me.

Monika was brilliant, self-possessed, and unafraid of convention. She freely criticized the male superiority entrenched in Australian mores, she smoked cigarillos, and, in an era when practically no single women drove their own cars, she buzzed about in a japonica-coloured TR3 with the top down. She fascinated some people, infuriated others. Previously, I had had an inkling of gender inequality, but she saw through the whole scam. I was extremely fortunate to have known her. She was a significant mentor, and her ideas about feminism, as well as her out-spoken conviction that women can do anything, continue to inspire. It was with great appreciation, but some trepidation, that I considered her suggestion that I apply for funding for graduate school and come to North America.

This was in the mid-twentieth century when everything seemed to be in a whirl of changing, conflicting values—hippies, "race" riots, the Beatles, the push for the Equal Rights Amendment. Like so many other awakening women, I avidly read the bestseller *The Feminine Mystique* (Friedan 1963) and, on Monika's recommendation, *The Second Sex* (de Beauvoir 1949). At that time, I had to get special permission from a librarian to borrow Simone de Beauvoir's classic, presumably because it was too bold and shocking for open shelving.

While I was earning my doctorate in comparative education at Columbia University in New York, I stayed with Monika. She taught me not only the ways of American higher education, but also how to play aggressive tennis and to take command of the net. It is amazing what that did for my self-assurance. When I had my degree, I came to Canada as assistant professor of education at Dalhousie University in Halifax. Monika became dean of women at the University College of Addis Ababa, Ethiopia. Quite soon she wrote to tell me that, after a failed coup attempt, the emperor of Ethiopia had donated one of his palaces for the establishment of the Haile Selassie I University and, obviously, there would be need for qualified faculty. I sent off my CV and waited. Finally, I had an encouraging response but no definite offer. Dal wanted to renew my appointment, but the possibility of Africa was alluring. What to do? Should I choose the security of Halifax or the adventure of Addis? When faced with this dilemma, I took one of those giant leaps that make life exciting and worthwhile. At the end of the academic year, I resigned from Dal and flew off to Ethiopia—with my cat but without a contract.

In due course, I became the first registrar of the Haile Selassie I University. What a wonderful, professionally demanding, personally enriching experience that proved to be. But a couple of years at high altitude and high pressure were enough, and I accepted appointment as associate professor of education at McGill.

When I first arrived in Montréal, I was not aware of feminist ferment here, and my CVs show that my first publications mostly had to do with education. However, in my first published book, *A History of Education: Thought and Practice* (1963), I made a point of including material on women's education, and in my classes I usually discussed gender issues, deploring the conventions that directed girls and women into limited "female" courses and occupations.

From the beginning of the next decade, I was far less reserved. We all were. "The times they were a-changing" and, without doubt, the spirit of the 1970s must have had a very stimulating effect on me as it did on so many people. The Royal Commission on the Status of Women in Canada published its significant report in 1970, and more and more feminist books, journals, and organizations began to appear. Early in the decade, I met and worked with Montréal women who had previously been unknown to me: Margret Andersen, who hosted a colloquium on Sisterhood at Loyola College; Christine Garside Allen and Greta Nemiroff, who offered a Summer Institute on Women at Sir George Williams (1973) and laid the groundwork for the Simone de Beauvoir Institute; Marie-Andrée Bertrand, who inspired her colleagues and students at the Université de Montréal; and Mona Forest and Jackie Manthorne, who set up the Montréal Women's Centre, where I joined the board (see the essays by Andersen, Nemiroff, and Bertrand in this volume).

Meanwhile at McGill University, the senate began an inquiry into "Discrimination as to Sex in the University" (1969–70), which was chaired by Dr. Rose Johnstone of biology. A series of open meetings on women stimulated interest in feminist issues. The Women's Union, which had been defunct for several years, was revived with "a room of one's own," and undergraduates established the Women's Collective Press. Importantly, religious studies professor Erin Molloy encouraged students to circulate a petition demanding courses in women's studies. Some classes focussing on women were actually given then, but they were few in number and were disguised under "innocent" titles such as Meg Bruce's Special Topics in English. A former student reminded me recently that everyone in class knew that my Social Foundations of Education was essentially women's studies and that we had to fight general complacency, as well as specific hostility to us as perceived radicals. Meanwhile, some dedicated women faculty members began meeting at my apartment to make plans for systematic program development.

I admit that I was not what has been called "one of those proverbial loud, nasty, bra-burning, shit-kicking, radical 'Women's Libbers' that everyone was warned against" (Zaremba 1992, 110). Yet I was not afraid to speak out and became known for my "unorthodox" views. In 1971, I gave unabashedly feminist talks to local consciousness-raising and networking groups, as well as to women's professional organizations and even to men's groups like the Rotary Club. I excited the students, if not the administrators, of Russell Sage College, Troy, New York, with a convocation address about indoctrination into gendered roles, and, in 1973, my paper on "Women in the Montréal Area" was one of several welcomed at the National Conference on Women in the University held at Queen's. For International Women's Year in 1975, I took advantage of being editor of the *McGill Journal of Education* and produced a special issue on *Women and Education* (volume 10, no. 1), which became a useful text. That year, when I talked about "Sexism in Higher Education" to the Canadian Association of Foundations of Education and about "Sexism in Schools" to the PEI Teachers' Federation, I ruffled quite a few feathers and generated protest from incredulous male colleagues who were still in denial. By 1976, my papers, such as "Women in Canadian Universities," given at conferences in England and the United States, were well received by both male and female colleagues—perhaps because these dealt safely with Canada rather than England or the US, or perhaps because they had benefitted from the impact of International Women's Year!

At that time, we were aware that we had a great opportunity to uncover the discrimination and bigotry that traditionally had been overlooked, and to make women-oriented changes to age-old attitudes, social practices, and even language. Women professors were most often referred to as "Miss" though men were, accurately or not, "Professor" or "Doctor." Remember that the general use of "Ms." was still a long way off, that the woman who chaired our Royal Commission was "Mrs. John ..." not "Florence Bird," and that the term "feminist" was still not widely used.[1] We were not all enamoured of emerging designations—"women's libbers" or just "libbers" seemed always to be said with derogatory overtones, and "womanist" never caught on.

Be that as it may, I canvassed support from male administrators and received a small grant from Principal Bob Bell to prepare an oral history of women at McGill, and, with colleagues Janet Donald, Erin Malloy, and Andrea Vabalis, a grant to undertake a study of the nature of the teaching and research on women throughout McGill. Our study, completed in December 1975, revealed a considerable amount of legitimate academic interest in women's issues in diverse disciplines and faculties. We found that by then there were nine three-credit courses with "women" in their titles—including my two, Women and Education, and Women in Higher Education, plus my six-credit Seminar on Women's Studies.[2] Among our recommendations was the establishment of a formal Women's Studies Program and a McGill Centre for Research and Teaching on Women.

The following year, these proposals were accepted, an advisory board representing half a dozen faculties was appointed, and I was named acting director. We had a grand party to celebrate. I found that very gratifying and was encouraged to undertake further research, which ultimately resulted in the publication of We Walked Very Warily: A History of Women at McGill, the first full-scale history of women at any Canadian university (Gillett 1981).

All was going well. The diversity of the advisory board and the fact that it was chaired by McGill's first woman dean, Donna Runnalls of religious studies, appeared to be a great strength. Alas, this proved to be an illusion. I learned the painful lesson that all women academics do not share feminist values, in spite of the fact that they are all, without doubt, the beneficiaries of feminist-generated social progress. Misunderstandings and disagreements developed, and I resigned from the advisory board on a matter of principle. I felt unhappy and betrayed, even though Vice-Principal Sam Freedman formally wrote to tell me that I would henceforth officially be known as the founding director of the McGill Centre for Research and Teaching on Women. This was cold comfort, but probably our little drama at McGill was not unlike the growing pains and power struggles in many another women's studies program. Life goes on. After a brief period in limbo when Dr. Prue Rains of sociology filled the breach, the centre recovered with the happy appointment of Dr. Peta Tancred from McMaster University as director, and, though chronically underfunded, it is currently holding its own under the able leadership of Dr. Shree Mulay of the Faculty of Medicine.

Notes

1 According to the *OED*, the word "feminist" first appeared in 1850 meaning "the qualities of women"; Virginia Woolf used it as we understand it in *Three Guineas* (1938). There are many other early examples in the literature.

2 These were McGill's first officially approved courses with "women" in their titles. See Gillett, Donald, Malloy, and Vabalis (1976). *The Women's Studies Undergraduate Handbook 2004–05* lists sixty-six courses.

Selected Publications by the Author

Gillett, Margaret. 1963. *A history of education: Thought and practice.* Toronto: McGraw-Hill of Canada.

———, ed. 1975. *Women and education.* Special issue of *McGill Journal of Education* 10 (1).

———. 1981. *We walked very warily: A history of women at McGill.* Montréal: Eden Press.

Gillett, Margaret, and Ann Beer, eds. 1995. *Our own agendas: Autobiographical essays by women associated with McGill University.* Montréal: McGill-Queen's University Press.

Gillett, Margaret, and Kay Sibbald, eds. 1984. *A fair shake: Autobiographical essays by McGill women.* Montréal: Eden Press.

Gillett, Margaret, Kay Sibbald, and Elizabeth Rowlinson, eds. 1996. *A fair shake revisited.* Montréal: McGill Printing Services.

How the Simone de Beauvoir Institute of Concordia University Grew from Unlikely Beginnings

◉ *Maïr Verthuy*

IF THE STORY NARRATED in this book stops in 1976, then the Simone de Beauvoir Institute doesn't belong here as it saw the light in March 1978. I hope, however, the readers will indulge me if I discuss how the institute came about.

My own relationship to women's studies is a little strange, as it didn't occur to me until I started teaching at Sir George Williams University that such courses might be necessary. This is not to suggest that Sir George was less open or progressive than other institutions; indeed, the opposite proved to be true. In 1965, however, I'm not sure the expression even existed.

I simply took it for granted that women enjoyed the same space as men in the university curriculum. We all have our moments of naïveté! But I had been brought up like that, both at home and at school. In the grammar school, in Great Britain where I did my pre-university training,[1] we read as many women authors as men, in English, French, and German. In history, because we were in Britain, we necessarily studied powerful women and queens regnant. The same story played out in science, art, and so forth and so on. When I arrived at university, the first author we studied in French was a woman, Marie de France. *Time and Tide* (1920–79), a proto-feminist journal of social, political, and economic issues, founded by Lady Rhondda and employing mainly women journalists, was "voluntarily" compulsory reading for most of us. Before coming to Montréal, I taught a few years in collegiates in Ontario and was always allowed to choose my own literary texts, and I obviously included women.

Then, on arrival at Sir George, I was asked to teach a six-credit course on the history of French literature and was provided with a copy of the extracts used by the chair of the department, who had previously taught the course, plus his outline. I almost went into anaphylactic shock. Not one woman was on the list. I immediately asked the chair if I could change the selection to include women, and he immediately agreed. It had just never occurred to him to put women writers on the list! His ready acquiescence was not typical. So Marie de France, Louise Labé, Madame de Lafayette, Ninon de Lenclos, Madame de Staël, George Sand, Rachilde, and others quickly appeared among the extracts while those written by less interesting men disappeared. Our readings of the male writers would also and again obviously depend at least in part on the women's point of view. What could have been more normal? But I imagine that must have been my first involvement with women's studies as a nascent discipline.

This attitude necessarily spilled over into my other courses, and supportive rumblings were being heard from our female students. I imagine this was also true at Loyola College. In the sixties and early seventies, Concordia University did not yet exist. Sir George Williams University existed downtown; Loyola College in the West End was the anglophone undergraduate campus of the Université de Montréal. Women in various departments in both institutions were busy raising their own consciousness and that of many students. One need only think of Allannah Furlong, Sheila McDonough, Susan Hoecker-Drysdale, and Gail Valaskakis, to name but a few.

The resistance from our male—and some female—colleagues was amazing and lasted down the years (and decades, in some cases). For my first four years in the French department, where I was the first, and for a while, the only female full-time professor, most of my colleagues spent far more time and energy on trying to get rid of me than on their more academic and professional pursuits. Fascinating though it was to receive so much non-stop attention from so many men, life wasn't entirely easy; but I hung in there and won, in effect. Some of my male colleagues even apologized to me in later years for their unacceptable behaviour. I should say, in defence of reluctant women professors, that their position within the university was always at that point precarious. Although very few women were hired, many more women were refused tenure than men—until we organized.

While all this was going on in my department, women colleagues from other disciplines in both institutions were also growing more and more aware, although most were spared my siege. A friend in anthropology explained she could no longer stand listening to colleagues making remarks such as, "The Inuit tradition involved offering their wives to tourists," as if wives were objects, not members of the Inuit community. More and more of us were now actually engaging in feminist research.

In 1970, thanks to the combined efforts of Greta Hofmann Nemiroff and Christine Garside Allen, as they were then known (see Nemiroff's essay in this volume), and some others, a joint project involving Loyola, Sir George Williams, and McGill burst upon the scene: the first official interdisciplinary women's studies course. It was a great moment. Immediately, other courses started to spring up, in anthropology, English and French, history, religious studies, theology, classics, and psychology, as well as courses on Native women; there are too many to list. By 1976, when Loyola and Sir George finally merged, we had enough courses to introduce a minor in women's studies and could already envisage a major (1978). I think all those of us who lived and breathed women's studies, students as well as faculty, lived also in a permanent state of revelation, particularly those who were just discovering the existence of women. One could almost envy their joy in discovery.

The Simone de Beauvoir Institute grew out of this euphoria, and was voted into existence on March 9, 1978—one day late for International Women's Day! We were given part of one of the old houses on Bishop Street, the very one that had earlier and for so long housed the famous lesbian bar Madame Arthur, which Marie-Claire Blais mentions in her novel *Les nuits de l'underground* (1990). One brief anecdote: Simone de Beauvoir was asked if she would agree that we give her name to the institute. She scrawled back a very brief answer ("Oui, probably!") on a sheet of her usual square-lined paper torn out of her exercise book, with no date, no address, nothing. The university lawyer was shattered, as were many of us, so we wrote again, and this time, while using the same kind of torn sheet of paper, she gave her full name, address, and the date, before writing a complete sentence to indicate her agreement.

The institute was to house women's studies and engage in a well-developed program of parallel activities, such as workshops on very eclectic but helpful topics. There were quarrels and in-fighting, but the institute went on. Our very first student members included heroines of the long struggle for women's rights in Québec, such as Simonne Monet-Chartrand and Jacqueline Béïque. Thérèse Casgrain visited regularly and gave us much support. Younger names of future advocates and militants also spring to mind: Howard Scott, Gail Scott, Jeanne Maranda ...

I was the first, the "founding" I suppose, principal of the institute (1978–83). During my mandate, in 1981, we organized the first pan-Canadian conference on women's studies (Parlons-En), bringing together members of the Aboriginal and Black communities, as well as a variety of minorities. That encouraged us to be more ambitious. In 1982, we succeeded in organizing a ten-day conference on teaching and research related to women, which brought together participants from over eighty countries, ensuring, at the same time, that visitors from so-called "developing countries" made up over half of the number. That was their first experience of not just being "alibis."

The institute functioned because of all the help we received from members of the university community. Not all of them, of course. But the rector, the provost, and many women in the administration, from budget officers to receptionists, supported our activities. Students and part-time and full-time faculty worked beyond requirements to ensure its success. The Montréal community became heavily involved in our worldwide conference. That all still arouses a certain amount of exhilaration.

Before ending, I must add that I'm not convinced that all our research and teaching have had the effect they should have had on the approach of many male—and some female—scholars. Keep up the good fight!

The institute has changed over the years and that is as it should be. That is another story for another day.

Note

1   Our teachers were on the whole not particularly young (or so it seemed to us then!). Several of them had been among the first women actually to obtain degrees from Oxford or Cambridge universities. Until quite late, women were allowed to pay for their studies, take courses, and pass the exams, but not to receive the parchment. Oxford granted them their degrees starting in 1920 and Cambridge in 1947. They were probably all closet feminists, but the subject was never discussed.

Selected Publications by the Author

Verthuy, Maïr, ed. 1987. *Colloque international sur la recherche et l'enseignement relatifs aux femmes, 26 juillet–4 août, 1982.* 2 vols. Montréal: Institut Simone de Beauvoir, Université Concordia.

———. 1988. *L'expression "Maîtres chez nous" n'existe pas au féminin: Pleure pas Germaine et La nuit; Femmes et patrie dans l'oeuvre romanesque de Laure Conan.* Montréal: Institut Simone de Beauvoir, Université Concordia.

———. 1992. *Fenêtre sur cour: Voyage dans l'oeuvre romanesque d'Hélène Parmelin; Essai.* Laval, QC: Trois.

Verthuy, Maïr, and Lucie Leguin, eds. 1996. *Multi-culture, multi-écritur: La voix. migrante au féminin en France et au Canada.* Montréal: L'Harmattan.

Verthuy, Maïr, and Jennifer Waelti-Walters. 1988. *Jeanne Hyvrard.* Amsterdam: Editions Rodopi.

Moments in the Making of a Feminist Historian

◉ *Alison Prentice*

WAS IT IN 1965 or 1966 that someone from the University of Toronto phoned in late June to ask if I would take on five history tutorials in September? And when exactly did I meet Natalie Davis? I remember both occasions vividly. On the first, I was in the middle of scrubbing the kitchen floor. A former history teacher with an MA, I was now at home with two boys—except when interesting university teaching work materialized. On the second, I was at a university wives' gathering that would change my life. The first event convinced me that I wanted more control over what I taught and when. The second led to a volunteer job looking at how some U of T students juggled doctorates and parental work (Davis et al. 1966), as Natalie had done before them (see Jill Ker Conway and Natalie Zemon Davis's joint essay in this volume). If they could do it, why couldn't I?

From my 1967 interview with the graduate secretary of Toronto's history department, I remember only two questions. "What, Mrs. Prentice, do you plan to do with the PhD when you get it?" he asked. I finally answered that I hoped to teach. I must have looked stunned at his next question, however, because he answered it himself: "Who will look after your children?" Well, his wife would undoubtedly suggest that I find "a good Scotch body." I was admitted to the program forthwith, and, from then until my comprehensive exams, there were no more personal questions from the history department. Maurice Careless and Michael Katz, who jointly supervised my thesis, were outstanding mentors.

A strange moment did occur one day, when I chanced to encounter a physicist colleague of my husband's on campus. He wanted to know what I was doing at the university. "A PhD in history," I replied. "Oh," he exclaimed, "if *my* wife did that, I'd *kill* her." A favourite former professor was less outraged, but sceptical. "Why in the world would you do a doctorate?" he wondered. "If you have something to say, write a book!"

The comprehensive exams were the next trial. I wrote my thesis during my husband Jim's sabbatical in 1971–72, and, that spring, the brother of a friend from my MA year tracked me down in the wilds of Illinois to tell me about a job at York University's Atkinson College. Happily, I was hired as a lecturer and found myself in a supportive department, shared with two women colleagues, and loving the opportunity to teach mainly mature students, many of whom were women. But I still hadn't taken the "comps." I'd done the thesis first, since writing it up fitted better with Jim's leave. During my first term teaching at Atkinson, I wrote six short essays, choosing an option created during the late 1960s for those who preferred writing papers to exams. When, at the comprehensive oral, I faced four male professors, three of them younger than me, I lost it. The queries of my advisors seemed to display either how boring my field was, or how ignorant I was of others. The third examiner then announced that one of my six papers had interested him (implying, I felt, that the five others had not). "In the introduction to that paper," he went on, "you declared your intention to show that women are a social class. *But your paper did not prove that women are a social class!*"

Could anyone articulate the concept of gender in 1973? Certainly not I—but I knew when I was angry. Sweeping an accusing hand around the room, I said what was obvious at least to me: "*You* are all men." And, pointing in the direction of the main office: "Down the hall the secretaries are all women. Are you trying to tell me that women aren't a social class?" The examiner had no further questions. I answered the fourth examiner's somewhat trivial query incorrectly and then stood in the hall for a very long time, finally learning that I'd received a "compassionate" pass. I did know something about the history of education, and my advisors liked my thesis; I'd clearly had a bad day.

Within a year, I'd put the finishing touches on "The School Promoters: Education and Social Class in Mid-Nineteenth-Century Upper Canada" (eventually published in 1977), and the 1974 thesis oral defence was a happy event. Slowly (it took seven years), I'd managed to get a PhD and a university job, but I'd upset a few apple carts along the way. No longer the exclusively family oriented wife and mother doing some studying on the side, I'd also learned, with the help of Kate Millett, that I was a feminist.

At Atkinson, I twice experienced challenges arising from the mere fact of being with other women faculty. Our informal women faculty group was vitally important to all of us, I think; we were generally a support to one another, and we exchanged information, for example about the "assertiveness training" that was being offered to women at York who felt they needed it. But we hadn't realized how visible and apparently threatening to male faculty we were. The most disturbing challenge happened when five women, who met once a month for lunch, were sitting together in the far corner of the otherwise empty faculty lounge. "Aha," crowed the dean as he looked in the door. "If I shot all of you, that would finish the women's movement at Atkinson, wouldn't it?"

More positive moments occurred in connection with my first conference paper on gender. Invited by Harvey Graff to join a session at the Canadian Association for American Studies conference on women in the spring of 1974, I prepared a paper on the feminization of teaching. At the conference, I met Barbara Roberts, a vibrant sister historian, then completing her doctorate; later, I was thrilled when my paper was accepted by *Histoire sociale/Social History*, a journal that has done much for women's history.

In my second year at Atkinson, I proposed a course called The History of Women, the Family, and Education in Canada. Although one male colleague questioned its intellectual coherence, another quickly corrected him; the course was adopted and I learned much from teaching it. A graduate assistant was available for bibliographical research, and a call to the graduate secretary of York's "day school" history department easily arranged Beth Light's employment. At the end of our conversation, this colleague congratulated me on the course title. The "history of women," in his words, was infinitely preferable to that dreadful phrase, "women's history." Click! From then on, it was women's history to me.

Around this time, I heard Natalie Zemon Davis, Gerda Lerner, and Carroll Smith-Rosenberg deliver brilliant keynotes at a women's history conference in Berkshire, Massachusetts. Even more important was meeting Susan Mann (Trofimenkoff) there; tellingly, we had never met in Canada. Meeting Canadian feminist historians like Barbara Roberts and Susan Mann was crucial; at some point in the mid-seventies, it became apparent that we were a community. Impressed by the women's history books published by the Canadian Women's Educational Press, such as *Women at Work: Ontario, 1850–1930* (Acton, Goldsmith, and Shepard 1974), I joined those who wanted more. Even if we had to plan an essay collection leaning over the seats of an airplane, as Susan and I did on the way home from a Canadian Historical Association (CHA) meeting one year, feminist historians were now in contact. The Women's History Committee of the CHA was born in 1975 and became an important institutional locus of our activity and activism. In Toronto, I was similarly inspired by the York/U of T Women's Studies Colloquium, which began meeting monthly sometime in the mid-1970s.

In the fall of 1975, I joined the history and philosophy department of the Ontario Institute for Studies in Education (OISE). Once at OISE, I happily participated in the interdepartmental Group for Research on Women created by Margrit Eichler. I also became involved in my department's Women's History Project (WHP). Established before I came to OISE, the WHP employed Marion Royce, who had worked in education and in international organizations, and had been the first director of the Women's Bureau in the federal Department of Labour. Soon, Beth Light joined the project, bringing expertise in Canadian women's history generally, as well as her skills in computer data entry. The project was a joy. But there was ongoing murkiness about the allocation of secretarial time and, eventually, the great computer heist, when a male colleague for several frustrating months occupied the computer terminals we relied on. In part for these reasons, we moved the WHP to the OISE Centre for Women's Studies in Education, founded in 1983 (see Frieda Johles Forman's essay in this volume). Drafting the centre's constitution and acting as its first chair were challenging. How could one fit a feminist centre into an institution whose practices were so gendered?

Increasingly, my primary focus became women's history. A major goal was establishing the field at all levels of schooling, and eventually Paula Bourne and Pat Staton joined the WHP team, to promote this aim through conferences and workshops, as well as research and publication. Another goal was to challenge and develop our field. We no longer wanted to fit women into previously constructed stories about historical movements and events; we were ready to show that they were also movers and shakers. Moreover, their history as mothers and daughters, sisters and workers, was important. We wanted to explore the structures that created gender and, in my case, especially to understand gender constructions in the world of teaching. Finally, we began to explore our own subjectivities, both as women historians and as second-wave feminists. Attempting to trace developing interests among contemporary Canadian historians of women, Susan Mann and I pointed first to the history of women's organizations and suffrage; then to the history of women's work, culture, and the family; and eventually to the growth of areas like the history of women and medicine, education, religion, and sexuality (Trofimenkoff and Prentice 1985). Not that we had lost interest in the earlier topics; our field had endless room for expansion, it seemed, as well as for revisionist interpretation. Certainly, later analysts would call attention to "race" in a way that earlier historians of women had not.

Over the years, the WHP team, in collaboration with other scholars, published articles on the history of women and education;[1] an annotated bibliography (Strong-Boag and Light 1980) and a three-volume documentary series dealing with Canadian women's history more generally;[2] a volume documenting the history of women teachers in Ontario (Staton and Light 1987); and an essay collection focussing on the history of women's work (Bourne 1985). By the early 1980s, we were also ready to tackle a more difficult task. I was part of a WHP-supported collective planning a textbook in Canadian women's history. In our lighter moments, we thought of titles like "Cooking and Mending our History," or "Women, Eh? Why Not?" It finally appeared, more soberly, as Canadian Women: A History (Prentice et al. 1988).

I once gave a brief talk on the writing of this book at a University of Toronto colloquium dedicated to documenting the progress of feminist history. Afterwards, a member of the audience commented that she hadn't known I could be so funny. The humour in fact masked several tragedies, which woven together marked my life and the progress of Canadian Women. In the course of six years, I lost not only my son Matthew in a car accident, but two of my closest friends, who were also members of the textbook collective. Pat Schulz, who was to have been our expert on the history of contemporary feminism, died of cancer in 1983; Marta Danylewycz, who specialized in the history of Québec, died when her deranged brother killed his entire family in 1985. Two other members of the original textbook collective dropped out for practical reasons.

These events were crushing. But we gradually reconstituted the collective, and eventually six women were involved in an extraordinary process. Gail Brandt, Paula Bourne, Beth Light, Wendy Mitchinson, and I critiqued the first drafts of our chapters with—and at the home of—Naomi Black, who happened to live near a great Toronto deli. We would spend an entire day, sometimes more, going over each chapter sentence by sentence, nourished by the delicious lunches that Naomi prepared. We'd gained weight by the time the book was finished, but had also become fast friends. The meals and comradery were key, but there were many other highlights to this adventure. Near its end, Gail Brandt and I got together in the Glendon College library to finalize the tables and graphs for the text. We had still not finished when Gail had to retrieve her son Gregory from the Glendon daycare. Nothing daunted, she arranged for us to keep the key to the daycare so that after supper we could carry on our work there while Gregory played. So we sat, two mums on tiny chairs at tiny tables, with our papers spread all over the daycare, until the job was done.

Then and later, I also had the fun of working on a monograph with Susan Houston and on essay collections with Australian and Swedish scholars Marjorie Theobald, Alison Mackinnon, and Inga Egqvist-Saltzman, all of whom influenced me enormously. Collaborations with Sandra Acker, Paula Bourne, Beverly Boutilier, Ruby Heap, and Elizabeth Smyth—Canadian colleagues who shared my interest in the history of women's professional work—proved similarly fruitful. For me, it seemed then and still seems a feminist thing to do, writing or editing with another woman or two—or, for that matter, five. I'm quite sure that this idea sprang from our experiences of the late 1960s and early 1970s, when the seeds of working collectively for common feminist goals were sown.

Writing autobiographically also seems feminist—and perhaps all historical work is, at some level, autobiographical. Mine reflected my experience as a woman teacher, as the mother of two schoolchildren, and as a woman married to a scientist, who supported my work and also influenced my explorations in the history of women in physics.[3] In the end, my passion for women's history gave me the joy of working with many other passionate, feminist women and men whose stories, companionship, and good food have enriched my life.

"What is the major theme of your textbook in Canadian women's history?" someone once asked. "Survival," was my instant reply. One might say the same thing about feminist scholars and scholarship in the second half of the twentieth century.

Notes

1   WHP articles by Marta Danylewycz, Ruby Heap, Susan Laskin, Beth Light, Alison Prentice, and Marion V. Royce are listed in the bibliography by Diana Pederson, *Changing women, changing history* (Ottawa: Carleton University Press, 1996), 22–23, 26, and 28–30; many are also described and cited in "Workers, professionals, pilgrims: Tracing Canadian women teachers' histories," in Weiler and Middleton (1999).

2   Beth Light and Alison Prentice, eds., *Pioneer and gentlewomen of British North America, 1713–1867*; Beth Light and Joy Parr, eds., *Canadian women on the move, 1867–1920*; and Beth Light and Ruth Roach Pierson, eds., *No easy road: Women in Canada, 1920s to 1960s* (Toronto: New Hogtown Press, 1980, 1983, and 1990).

3 The connections between my life and work are elaborated in Prentice (1999) and Gorham (1997).

Selected Publications by the Author

Prentice, Alison. 1975. The feminization of teaching in British North America and Canada, 1845–1875. *Social history/Histoire sociale* 8:5–20.

———. 1999. Workers, professionals, pilgrims: Tracing Canadian women teachers' histories. In *Telling women's lives: Narrative inquiries in the history of women's education*, edited by K. Weiler and S. Middleton. Buckingham: Open University Press.

Prentice, Alison, Naomi Black, Gail Brandt, Paula Bourne, Beth Light, and Wendy Mitchinson. 1988. *Canadian women: A history.* Toronto: Harcourt Brace.

Prentice, Alison, and Marjorie R. Theobald, eds. 1991. *Women who taught: Perspectives on the history of women and teaching.* Toronto: University of Toronto Press.

Trofimenkoff, Susan Mann, and Alison Prentice, eds. 1985. *The neglected majority: Essays in Canadian women's history.* Vol. 2. Toronto: McClelland and Stewart.

Doing Feminist Studies Without Knowing It

Micheline Dumont

for ANTOINETTE BABOYANT

FIRST, I WANT TO BE very clear about one thing: for me, in 1965, there was simply no such thing as feminist studies. In my three years in the history program at university, the possibility of studying women's history never once came up. I took courses with Guy Frégault; he was the only professor who truly impressed me. His courses convinced me that for history to be authentic, it must be social, and that, as a discipline, history can inform only if it interrogates the past with worthwhile and original questions. I never put these convictions into practice though, because, after university, my research activities came to an end.

In 1965, I was thirty years old and living in Paris, where I had followed my husband, who was studying for his PhD in sociology. I had a five-month-old daughter, and my life had just taken a new direction. I had taught history and history pedagogy in a teachers' training college from 1959 to 1965. During these years, whenever I thought about my future, I was faced with a dilemma: love or work? Love meant getting married and raising my children. Work meant continuing my teaching career. Getting married *and* working still seemed problematic to me. I think that today it's hard for people to imagine the powerful hold of social and religious dictums on the young women of that era. For me, the idea of becoming a university professor was unimaginable. To combine marriage with an intellectual life, I dreamed of marrying a university professor, and my dream came true.

Back in Montréal in September 1967, people persuaded me to continue teaching at the teachers' training college in a period when these institutions were closing one after the other. I accepted a part-time post. It was to be the last step of my professional career before plunging into family life, as I was pregnant. I didn't know then about maternity leave. This social measure was non-existent, both in actual fact and in my consciousness. I got myself a replacement for two months and returned to school with a six-week-old baby. Luckily, I had a babysitter and had to work only two days a week. After the last afternoon class, I sprinted home for the four o'clock feeding.

In the spring of 1968, Monique Bégin, then–executive secretary of the Bird Commission (the Royal Commission on the Status of Women in Canada), proposed that I write a thirty-page essay on the history of the status of women in the province of Québec. The school year was over: why not do this little contract in my leisure (!) time? I accepted because I was still hungry for the intellectual life. I was given an essay that had already been written, called "The Cultural Tradition of Canadian Women: The Historical Background" by Margaret Wade-Labarge (1971a). I was the one of the first people to read it, and it gave me an excellent overview of Western traditions. I was struck by the influence of three powerful institutions: Greek philosophy, Roman law, and Christian theology. I realize now that the word *patriarchy* was absent from this text. My aim was different: I was to discuss women from the "*province* of Québec," as we were still calling it back in 1968, rather than "Québec."

Where to begin? I still don't know how I did it: there was *nothing* to work with. Where were the archives of information about women? Failing archives, at least there were the official histories, those which had already been written. I was sure about one thing: if such a history existed somewhere, it certainly hadn't been available to me when I was in university.

I went to the Gagnon Room at the Montréal Library where a librarian, Mademoiselle Baboyant, suggested several works to me: anthologies of biographies on women; *Cinq femmes et nous*, by Bernard Dufebvre (1950); anthologies about the religious congregations in Québec; *Les femmes du Canada: leurs vies et leurs oeuvres* (National Council of Women of Canada 1900); *La femme canadienne française* of 1936, devoted to French-Canadian women; and, especially, *Canadiennes*, by Albert Tessier (1946). This last volume was a history of Canada—as we said in those days—that incorporated into the traditional historical framework anecdotes and other facts about women that had been ignored by official histories. I found it interesting, although a little too pious, and above all, presented in the traditional political history format. I felt that a history of the situation of women should extend beyond individual lives and the confines of political history and reveal the circumstances of most women. But how was I to learn what this was? Where were the writings about ordinary women?

The librarian also directed me to recent history and introduced me to texts of which I had been unaware until then: *La Bonne Parole*,[1] the convention proceedings of the Fédération nationale Saint-Jean-Baptiste, *La Sphère feminine*,[2] and *Le Journal de Françoise*.[3] Last, she told me about Catherine Cleverdon's work, *The Woman Suffrage Movement in Canada* (1950). There was a chapter on Québec. It wasn't much, but it was a beginning. Studious, I also discovered old letters of Elisabeth Bégon and Julie Bruneau-Papineau, the first two volumes of the *Dictionnaire biographique du Canada* (G. W. Brown 1945), and Jacques Henripin's writings on demography. I plowed through the *Revue d'histoire de l'Amérique française* (Institut d'histoire de l'Amérique française 1947) and came up with a meagre harvest of two articles.

A woman friend with whom I had spoken about my project told me of a recent publication: *La condition de la Française d'aujourd'hui* by Andrée Michel and Geneviève Texier (1964). The first volume included an extensive historical section and an overview of the condition of French women during the ancien régime. Here was an excellent starting point for me, because I would have to discuss the French régime. The book was indeed so enthralling that I rushed out and bought it. I excitedly annotated the historical sections and went to the library of the Université de Montréal to read all the cited works. I began to feel well versed with the legal position of women as I came to understand that, fundamentally, "the status of women" was determined by the rules of civil law. I consulted a notary, Bérengère Gaudet, who was also at the time preparing a study of family law in Canada (Gaudet 1971). She helped me through the labyrinth of civil legislation and proposed headings to guide my analysis of the articles of the Civil Code. She gave me the manuscript version of an article by Jacques Boucher: "Histoire de la condition juridique et sociale de la femme au Canada français" (1970).

Mademoiselle Baboyant, with whom I had been discussing the progress of my research, gave me a list of women to interview. We could meditate at length on the role of librarians in the dawning of feminist consciousness! I then met with the president of the Fédération nationale Saint-Jean-Baptiste, Marie-Ange Madore. Thérèse Casgrain received me in her living room and told me about women's campaign for the vote. Yvette Charpentier, the "midinettes" trade unionist, talked to me about the women of the garment trade and their strikes during the 1930s. I wrote to Laure Gaudreault, founder of the first teachers' union in 1936, and she sent me copies of *La petite feuille*.[4] Florence Fernet-Martel, the second woman to earn her bachelor's degree, described women's awakening after the Second World War. I also met with Gabrielle Farmer-Denis, who told me about the Cercles de fermières (farm women's groups), and Flore Jutras, who talked about women in business. Because I wanted to present an overview of women's presence in the principal professions, I wrote to all the professional orders and asked them for the number of women members of the profession in 1968. Unfortunately, the Centrale des enseignants du Québec refused to provide me with statistics by level of education.

Going through my own library, I came upon a book by Jean Lemoyne called *Convergences* (1961), a section of which contained essays about women, including "La femme dans la civilisation canadienne-française," "La littérature canadienne-française et la femme," "Comprise par elle-même," and "La femme et son avenir ecclésial." These essays opened up vast new horizons for me while at the same time raising my ire. I was getting a double message: women had been dominated by men—of this I had been convinced since reading Simone de Beauvoir's *The Second Sex* (1953) in 1958. At the same time, since women's role was so central in our history, it was being described as a form of matriarchy. I was not at all persuaded by this matriarchy idea, but how could I argue against it? The first article was a sweeping description of four centuries of history that pointed me to certain events or facts that could serve as the basis for discussing women as a group. They were reported from a male perspective, but it would be possible to examine them from another point of view. I was even able to identify an overall plan of sorts, which I developed in three sections:

1. *The French régime*, in which I intended to discuss the *Coutume de Paris* (Paris Custom), the legal foundation that determined women's status; the *fondatrices* (women founders) of religious communities, who were much discussed in "official" histories, but about whose contribution I wanted to offer a new interpretation; and the *Filles du Roy* ("King's Daughters"), these ordinary women whose lives I wanted to revisit, particularly in terms of that famous issue of women's fertility, a favourite theme of male historians.

2. *The nineteenth century*, in which I planned to discuss the Civil Code of 1866 (women's legal status), political life, the new women founders of religious congregations, the first women writers, and mothers.

3. *The twentieth century*, where I intended to discuss women's associations (I didn't use the adjective "feminist" then), access to university education, participation in the work world, the right to vote, the reform of the Civil Code, women artists and writers, and the new situation of women since 1950.

I decided I would meet with Margaret L. MacLellan, who was preparing the "Canadian" version of the study (1971; Wade-Labarge 1971b). I wanted to ask about her outline and present my own outline to her. I thought that, given our parallel research topics, it would be a good idea to coordinate. Her outline was very different from my own. She made rapid mention of the historical context and then concentrated on women's struggles to transform their condition: civil rights, right to education, right to exercise a profession, political rights, participation in active political life, and the role of women's organizations. I was disconcerted by our discussion, because I found in it no echo of my desire to describe the lives of ordinary women. Moreover, she believed we should not discuss women writers and artists because they didn't have to fight for the right to artistic expression. Her research was clearly political in tone, which was not where I wanted to go with my own work. This meeting left me quite troubled. I decided I would stick to my plan; to my regret, however, I did drop the sections I had planned to devote to women writers and artists. I would have loved to write about the women who signed the Refus Global!

All that remained to do was write. My paper was taking form, yet I didn't see the picture that was emerging. During the ancien régime, women lived in a context that enabled them to get around the restrictions imposed by law. In the nineteenth century, women's situation deteriorated, but the religious life "represented the only avenue for women's social advancement" (Johnson 19). In the twentieth century, Québec women woke up, and quickly caught up to their Canadian sisters.[5] "This optimistic vision of history, including the negative impact of Victorian/Napoleonic/capitalist institutions, was not specific to Québec. It was the vision of Andrée Michel and Geneviève Texier in *La condition de la française d'aujourd'hui* (1964). It was also the perspective adopted in the first histories of women in the United States and in European studies of modern history" (Dumont 2001, 84). At that time, except for the French book, I was unaware of any of the other works; I discovered them only much later. I submitted my paper to the people in Ottawa in August 1968.

I finished the final corrections of the English translation of my text in June 1969, eighteen hours before giving birth to my third daughter. I was then caught up with my move to Sherbrooke in 1969 and the life of a full-time mother with three daughters of preschool age. During this happy period, someone phoned me in 1970 with an offer to teach in the history department of the Université de Sherbrooke "if I sent in my CV." So I returned to teaching history, realizing that I too could teach at university, and also, that I had to work outside the home if I didn't want to go crazy. The research on "women's condition" drifted out of my mind.

When the research sponsored by the Bird Commission was published in 1971, I discovered that this "contract," published under the title *Histoire de la condition de la femme dans la province de Québec* (History of the Status of Women in the Province of Québec), was actually a pioneering work. I was immediately inundated with requests for interviews and speaking engagements, including, with my husband, Rodrigue Johnson, the keynote address for the convention of the Fédération des femmes du Québec in June 1972. My work, which I had thought unremarkable, was apparently nothing of the kind. Jennifer Stoddart, a history student at the Université de Québec à Montréal (UQAM), arrived in my office and asked me to take part in a collective multidisciplinary seminar being planned for the autumn 1972 session at UQAM (see Nadia Fahmy-Eid's essay in this volume). She also asked me to supervise the master's thesis she was writing with Marie Lavigne on women workers in Montréal between the two world wars. In June 1973, organizers of the convention of the Canadian Historical Association approached me for my comments on two papers: one by Susanne Cross, "The Neglected Majority," and the other, by Jennifer Stoddart and Véronica Strong-Boag, on domestic workers.[6] There was a huge crowd at this meeting. I read my comments in French, but the lively discussion that followed was in English. The notion of "women's history" had just emerged and I realized that this was a new research field. Without knowing it, I had formulated my first epistemological reflections on women's history. This was a springboard for the intellectual discoveries that I presented in *Découvrir la mémoire des femmes* (2001). It was not until 1976 that I gave my first course in women's history, but after that, my commitment to women's history and feminist studies was definitive and absolute.

I realize now that I had always had a feminist consciousness, probably ever since my teens. I discovered among my papers a "feminist" text dating back to 1953: "Ta ta ta, ma fille!" is an article in which I criticized the editors of *Vie étudiante* for never writing about job orientation for girls. My volunteer work in Jeunesse étudiante catholique (Catholic student youth) had taught me that girls' ideas were just as interesting as boys' ideas. The works of

Simone de Beauvoir, Margaret Mead, and Evelyne Sullerot helped shaped my thinking between 1957 and 1965. Discussions with friends, women and men, enriched this consciousness as did discussions about the Bird Commission, for which two of my women friends were working. At some point—I don't recall the exact date—I decided that the fact that I was a woman should not prevent me from achieving my dreams. It was women's responses to my writings that revealed their subversive impact to me. I should also add that the broader context of the years between 1974 and 1980, during which the feminist movement was in full effervescence, could not help but influence my thinking. Lectures, actions, and demonstrations generated a need for knowledge about women's history. Women's history opened the door to a new perspective on the world and knowledge. I enriched this perspective when, starting in 1982, I launched myself into a busy period of feminist activism in Sherbrooke. I believe that the combination of activism and reflection/theory constitutes a powerful catalyst.

For a long time, then, I was—like Monsieur Jourdain in Molière's *Bourgeois Gentleman* (2001), who for years spoke prose without knowing it—a Madame Jourdain who did feminist studies without knowing it.

Notes

1 Magazine of the first feminist association in Québec, the Fédération nationale Saint-Jean-Baptiste, founded by Marie Gérin-Lajoie (mother) in 1907.

2 Magazine of the Alliance canadienne pour le vote des femmes du Québec, founded by Idola Saint-Jean in 1928.

3 Magazine published by Robertine Barry from 1902 to 1913.

4 Newsletter of the Fédération des institutrices rurales from 1937 to 1946.

5 Today, I am dismayed by the long list of errors contained in this paper that I signed using my married name, Micheline D. Johnson.

6 I never read the second paper, because, as I learned just five years ago, they were told by their professor that such a paper would be damaging to their careers.

Selected Publications by the Author

Dumont, Micheline. 1989. The influence of feminist perspectives on historical research methodology. In *The effects of feminist approaches on research methodologies*, edited by W. Tomm. Waterloo: Wilfrid Laurier University Press.

———. 2001. *Découvrir la mémoire des femmes: Une historienne face à l'histoire des femmes*. Montréal: Éditions du Remue-ménage.

Dumont, Micheline, Michèle Jean, Marie Lavigne, and Jennifer Stoddard, eds. 1982. *Histoire des femmes au Québec depuis quatre siècles*. Edited by C. Clio, *Collection Idéelles*. Montréal: Quinze Collection.

Dumont, Micheline, and Louise Toupin, eds. 2003. *La pensée féministe au Québec: Anthologie 1900–1985*. Montréal: Éditions du Remue-ménage.

Johnson (Dumont), Micheline. 1971. Histoire de la situation de la femme dans la province de Québec. In *Tradition culturelle et histoire politique de la femme au Canada: Étude preparée pour la Commission royale d'enquête sur la situation de la femme au Canada*, edited by the Commission. Ottawa: Imprimeur de la Reine.

A Matrix of Creativity

◉ *Frieda Johles Forman*

I BECAME A POLITICAL activist during the Vietnam War. Although my anti-war group in New York was entirely made up of women, many of whom were mothers of young children, I did not at first consider gender as a component of our work, nor sexism as an issue worthy of serious political engagement. In the mid-sixties, I regarded feminism as a diversionary tactic, taking us away from the "real" problems—the war, capitalism, racism, imperialism—and their manifestations. As the women's movement in New York became more prominent, its political actions more visible, the scales fell from my eyes and I began to see the centrality of women in revolutionary struggle. It helped to have Lenna Jones, my good friend and a long-time activist, elucidate the links between sexism and other forms of oppression.

In 1970, by then a committed feminist, I immigrated to Canada with my husband and two children, in search of a more humane and progressive environment. Shortly after arriving, I joined the Toronto Women's Caucus, heavily dominated by Trotskyites, but the only women's group I found that welcomed new members. Despite my misgivings about its hidden agenda, I felt I had found an authentic home in Canada, where friendship and political activism were integrated. In our weekly consciousness-raising sessions, I felt deeply connected in sisterhood, as though reborn into a world where we were free to express our thoughts, reveal our experiences, and envision another way of living in the world.

My association with the Toronto Women's Caucus brought me into the public sphere, where I identified myself loudly and assertively as a "shrill feminist." I spoke out at meetings, gave media interviews, and was an occasional "women's lib" guest in university classes. These expressions of my feminism were still outside formal educational institutions. In 1971, thanks to a fundamental educational revolution at the Ontario College of Art (OCA), I was hired essentially to develop and teach any course I wanted. I declared myself a feminist and proposed, along with courses in philosophy and literature, a course called Women and Art. Although I had a good background in art, I was not an art historian; but, buoyed by the spirit of feminism, I did not hesitate to offer this innovative course.

Since my students had chosen to attend art school rather than university, the curriculum had to reflect that inclination. At that time, few resources on women artists or feminist aesthetics were available; nevertheless, it was a paradisical period in my life and, I believe, in the lives of the women students at the OCA. For the first time, they felt free to reveal the sexual harassment they experienced at art school, where women artists as teachers were a rarity. We also spoke of the invisibility of women's contribution to art. We read everything that was available because, in those days, we could still read everything that emerged from feminist presses.

Slowly, however, anthologies emerged that included articles on women in the arts. Linda Nochlin's "Why Are There No Great Women Artists?" (1971) was for many of us the first rigorous, theoretical piece on the subject. The students were totally smitten. When we invited practising artists to our classes, our students were visibly moved to see themselves reflected, often for the first time, in another woman artist. Another faculty member, Margot Smith, also taught a women's studies class, and by the second semester we joined efforts and team-taught a large, lively class.

Our success in the classroom inspired us to organize a weekend conference on women in the arts—the first, I believe, in Canada. Held in 1972, it included a panel that brought together visual artists, filmmakers, and theorists: Kay Armatage, Vera Frankel, Katja Jacobs, Bonnie Kreps, and Joyce Wieland. They were all feminists, and they delighted and mesmerized the students. During my tenure at OCA, we also mounted the first women's art show in Canada: an exuberant multimedia exhibition contained in a matrix of creativity designed to redress centuries of isolation and *encavement*.

By the time I left OCA (due to major changes in administration), we had also founded Kids Can Press, dedicated to publishing non-sexist, multicultural Canadian children's books (still thriving today, but with a different mandate), which sprang from a class I taught on children's literature. I speak not self-servingly of these triumphs, but to highlight what was a reality during the early seventies: infused with a new sensibility and a collective sisterhood that informed our actions and thoughts, we were convinced we could accomplish world-changing deeds, unfettered by hesitation or practicality. To be "realistic" was considered pedestrian, lacking in imagination. We saw ourselves as part of a revolution, which unlike all previous progressive movements, put women at centre stage, central to the struggle. Exhilarated by all the feminist expression around us—be it political, spiritual, psychological, or intellectual—we felt blessed and privileged to be part of this worldwide social transformation.

Because the times were generous, I was able in 1974, with the help of feminist friends, to move to the Ontario Institute for Studies in Education (OISE), which stood then at the forefront of educational change: oriented towards inclusivity, equity, and, in general, presenting a progressive, emancipatory stance. When I joined the Women's Kit Project as a researcher, the kit was already completed and on its way to being tested in secondaryschool classrooms. Since I was not in any significant way involved in its development, I can be lavish in my praise of this remarkable multimedia box covering a wide range of subjects about women: family, work, education, health, women's history in Canada and other parts of the world, artistic representation, and media representation. Every item included contributed to consciousness-raising, in those days a familiar term. The Women's Kit, created by Pam Harris, still ranks decades later as the most brilliant kit for women's studies ever produced. Issues of class and racialization were integrated, but not in the divisive way in which they would emerge later in the women's movement.

By 1974–75, women's studies was gaining ground, and thanks to the urging and pressure of students, feminist courses were offered in the departments of sociology, history, and philosophy. Some were team-taught with graduate students. Dr. Gloria Geller stands out as a major contributor to this effort. As the demand for feminist studies grew, the Women's Kit Project became something of a magnet for students and researchers. Not only was our office a welcoming and stimulating place, but it also contained a growing collection of feminist resources: books, periodicals, archival documents, and a range of ephemera, such as posters and flyers from across the world. Word spread about our project and, informally, we became known as a feminist centre.

The founding and development of the Women's Educational Resources Centre is a glorious event in the history of Canadian women's studies. Only after its naming did I learn that the root, the radical meaning, of the word "resource" is from "resurgere," to rise again—thus a centre where women would rise again. In the OISE scheme of elevation, we rose from the fourth floor to the sixth, the sociology in education department, and then to the eleventh, where we joined our two sister projects, the journal *Resources for Feminist Research*, brought to OISE as a feminist research newsletter by Margrit Eichler, and the Canadian Women's History Project. Together, we formed the Centre for Women's Studies in Education (see Alison Prentice's essay in this volume).

The Women's Educational Resources Centre (WERC) was not a gift from the administration, though a certain largesse prevailed in those days, the mid-seventies. It was, rather, the result of feminist struggle, passion, and vision to achieve a centre of our own—more than a room of our own. We envisioned this enterprise, this project, as an assembly, a resurgence of women's scholarship, and research, and expression of women's experience. It was a place for sisterhood to emerge—where every document, every modest newsletter, every manifesto, mattered to us as part of our work towards a transformed world.

The maintenance and growth of the centre was a labour of love, and sometimes just plain labour, of many devoted and dedicated (in its traditional meaning) feminists. In those days, every research project at OISE (on pain of death) had to include a faculty member as "principal investigator." That collaboration, in our case, became itself an expression of sisterhood. In 1975, Margrit Eichler, one of the early feminist scholars at OISE, introduced Mary O'Brien to our project. She urged Mary, who had just signed her first contract, to accept the responsibility of serving as co-principal investigator with me. This was understandably a difficult decision for Margrit and Mary: in the male-dominated department where the project was housed, I had a reputation of being scrappy and uncooperative. The match, however, was made in heaven: Mary O'Brien and I shared perception and vision, and the recognition that we were participating in an intellectual, political, social, and spiritual revolution. That thought was with us always.

In 1998, as I was organizing and preparing the centre's holdings for the move to the Jackson Library, amidst the sorting and sifting and much sighing, I recalled Mary O'Brien and her presence in the centre and in the women's studies program at OISE. Mary loved teaching above all else, and this love of teaching extended to others. I recall so vividly a class of students from SEED (from Shared Experience Exploration Discovery), an alternative high school,[1] who wanted to know just what this thing we called "theory" was. I was their facilitator, but I wanted them to learn from the feminist theorist, the feminist philosopher, in our midst. I asked Mary, who rarely said "no" to any worthy request. And so, every Tuesday morning, stretching over months, she spoke about theory, drawing upon the early philosophers and moving into modernity and contemporary feminism. I doubt that any group of teenagers has ever sat so still, so enraptured by intellectual history. Her writings, teaching, and great spirit remained with us after she retired. *Reproducing the World: Essays in Feminist Theory* (O'Brien 1989), her book of collected essays, was her praxis.

Since I was responsible for the day-to-day running of the centre, my praxis followed an anarcho-feminist model: no means/ends division, no hierarchical structures. All who came were treated with the same respect, be they eminent scholars, community activists, or high school students. It was a haven, which all who entered felt immediately; visual expressions of this philosophy were everywhere—for example, posters claiming "Women are history" greeted our constituency, our public. I realized this sense of belonging as woman after woman said, "Do we have such and such a book?" Rarely did I hear, "Do you have?" Friends of the centre who travelled across the globe brought us manifestations of the worldwide women's movement in all manner of publications, local women's newsletters, and flyers. WERC became a treasure trove of the international women's movement as well as an archive of the past. The centre was always meant to be a home for scholars, researchers, university and college students, secondary school students (women's studies was part of the curriculum then), women's services, and community groups: in a phrase, the swirling world of women's enterprises. From conception and inception, our holdings included a substantial French component (about 10% of the collection) that in time contributed to the development of French women's studies guides for the secondary school level in Ontario.

The vertical files comprised a unique collection of materials assembled over twenty-three years, a period of tremendous development in women's studies. They included rare, original documents, conference proceedings, unpublished papers, special issues of periodicals, out-of-print publications and archival resources; they came to the centre from every region of the world. These historical treasures could not be found anywhere else in Canada, and their value to researchers and scholars who came from across the globe was immeasurable.

Lest I leave the impression that once we had our centre all our trials were over, let me add a note of reality. Though we may have created a feminist utopia, the OISE administration continued, more or less, in its own bureaucratic ways. Since the WERC was classified as a research project, we had to apply for funding annually (occasionally, we were granted multi-year funding). This annual rite not only robbed us of much-needed time, but also gave us a permanent sense of impermanence. In 1998, after twenty-two years of women-centered service to the widest community, the WERC was dissolved, its collection sent to the main OISE library. The University of Toronto no longer wanted to support this unique, so very useful centre for women's studies. I took early retirement; I could not bear to preside over our lost paradise.

There was no happy ending for the centre; but the friendships that were forged in that brilliant period are alive. Angela Miles was a loving ally during all the years of the centre's existence, and happily, her theoretical work on integrative feminism continues to influence the current generation of women's studies students. Paula Bourne and Philinda Masters, models of sisterhood through the decades in which life brought us together, continued their work with dedication.

Note

1   SEED was the first alternative public school in Ontario, founded in 1968. It is located at 885 Dundas Street East in Toronto. SEED is the name by which it is known, an acronym coming from Shared Experience Exploration Discovery.

Selected Publications by the Author

Forman, Frieda, ed. 1989. *Taking our time: Feminist perspectives on temporality.* Oxford: Pergamon Press.

———. 1996. Sister voyager: The feminist ticket to Yiddish culture. Paper read at Di Froyen: Women and Yiddish, New York, NY.

———. Forthcoming 2008. *We escaped: Jewish refugees in Switzerland during World War II.* London: Valentine Mitchell.

Forman, Frieda, and Mary O'Brien, eds. 1990. *Feminism and education: A Canadian perspective.* Toronto: Centre for Women's Studies in Education, Ontario Institute for Studies in Education.

Forman, Frieda, Ethel Raicus, Sarah Silberstein-Swartz, and Margie Wolfe, eds. 1994. *Found treasures: Stories by Yiddish women writers.* Toronto: Second Story Press.

Transforming the Academy and the World

Deborah Gorham

IN SEPTEMBER 1971, during my third year as an assistant professor at Carleton University, I offered a course in women's history for the first time. I recognized from the outset that teaching the course was the most exciting, enriching, and challenging work I'd done in my brief career. It was a genuinely transformative experience for me and for many of the students who took this and other feminist courses I taught in the 1970s.

However, in the early 1970s, I did not think seriously about my work as a contribution to a collective academic enterprise. For me it was, rather, an extension of my commitment to the women's movement. It was only in the 1990s that I carefully examined the contribution that historians, women and men based in Canada in the early 1970s (myself included), had made to the creation of women's history at Canadian universities. It was only then that I discovered that Carleton's History 04.345, Women and Society, the course I offered in 1971, was one of the two earliest courses in women's history offered at any Canadian university (Gorham 1997, 1996).[1] It was only then that I fully recognized the contribution that a group of scholars and teachers at Carleton made to the creation of Canadian women's studies. These important people include the late Elinor Burwell, professor of psychology, and Joan Jonkel, with whom I taught a third-year seminar on women, history, and literature in 1973–74. We were indeed "inventing feminist scholarship and women's studies in Canada," not only with the mounting of discipline-based courses, but also with the introduction of the first women's studies course at Carleton in 1974–75 and with the preparation of the brief that created the Interfaculty Committee on Women's Studies, the forerunner of the Pauline Jewett Institute of Women's Studies at Carleton.

Most of my working life has been informed by feminist scholarship. In my contribution to this volume, I look back on this fortunate circumstance, focussing on two points. I comment on the feminist theorists and mentors who have mattered most in my life, then and now, and I offer my assessment of the impact that feminism has had on scholarship in Canada.

Feminist Theory

When I began working as a feminist teacher and scholar, the authors who turned my thinking in new directions were the passionate activists of the 1960s and 1970s, among them Germaine Greer (1970), Kate Millett (1970), Charnie Guettel (1974), Robin Morgan (1970), and Margaret Benston (1969a). Greer's analysis of "the Stereotype," the forever young, hairless, odourless, sexless "Eternal Feminine," the object of desire, resonated deeply with me. No actual woman could be "the Stereotype," Greer pointed out. Any real woman was forced to be a "female impersonator." "I refuse," said Greer (1970, 61–62). The central concept of women's liberation was articulated most fully by Kate Millett, in *Sexual Politics*: "The term 'politics' shall refer to power-structured relationships, arrangements whereby one group of persons is controlled by another … The following sketch, which might be described as 'notes toward a theory of patriarchy,' will attempt to prove that sex is a status category with political implications" (1970, 23–24).

Millett's concept of sexual politics was a genuine "invention," a concept that brought about a paradigm shift, to borrow Thomas Kuhn's famous term (1962). The older paradigm—one that feminists themselves adhered to—was that political, social, educational, and legal redress would remove discrimination against women. The concept of sexual politics makes evident the fact that male dominance—patriarchy—is embedded in private, as well as public, behaviour, and that the "private" or personal is, in fact, political.[2]

Sexual Politics mattered deeply to me personally. I did not become a feminist because of the second-wave literature. I was lucky: raised as a feminist by my politically engaged, unconventional, left-wing parents, I grew up believing that women had a right to equality with men, and that as a girl I had as much obligation as a boy to do well in school and prepare myself for useful work. As a young girl, I read about feminism. My father gave me Virginia Woolf's *Three Guineas* (1938) and Vera Brittain's *Testament of Youth*

(1978) to read when I was in my early teens, and he made sure that I read de Beauvoir's *The Second Sex* in 1952, when it first appeared in English. My energetic mother provided an example of a successful working woman. She ran her own advertising agency and contributed more to the household financially than my novelist father.

Still, my family of origin was not without its traumas and contradictions. Inequalities were a significant if unacknowledged part of my parents' marriage. In spite of their commitment to feminism, my father was the privileged person in our family. He was the writer, after all. My mother merely made the money. Neither of them questioned that the writer came first. Later, when I was in my twenties, these patterns reproduced themselves in my own life, as I struggled to balance marriage, motherhood, and career. In the early 1970s, reading Millett and others was transformative for me. *Sexual Politics* as a theoretical tool deepened my understanding of my own situation and reinvigorated my commitment to feminism.

I became a feminist first, a teacher second, and a scholar third. As a teacher and scholar, I was fortunate indeed. Trained initially as a British social historian, I knew about the fine work on women's history that had been done by an earlier generation of scholars (Pinchbeck 1969; Clark 1992; Power 1922; M. Campbell 1968), and many historians of women active from the 1960s to the 1980s influenced my own teaching and scholarship. It is difficult to select among them, but I was profoundly influenced by Joan Kelly's questioning of traditional male-centred periodization and by her bold discussion of the "feminist theory" embedded in the fifteenth-century "Querelle des Femmes" (1984). I was inspired by Linda Gordon's historical work, and also by her analysis of the relationship of feminism to scholarship (1986). Natalie Zemon Davis's brilliant insights into early modern French history remain, decades later, an indispensable contribution to understanding the historical relationship between women and power (1975). Finally, Gerda Lerner, who as early as the late 1960s was offering cogent theoretical frameworks for women's history, provided both inspiration and tools for teaching women and gender (see Zinsser 1993).

Even in the 1970s, feminist scholars, like feminist activists, did not always agree with one another. Among feminist historians there would be, by the 1980s, sharp divisions between historians embracing post-structuralism and those who were critical of this approach. The most crucial fault lines, however, concerned racialization, ethnicity, and nationality. Did women's liberation have a universal message, or was it merely the voice of a privileged, White, largely American elite?

Many answers to this question have been proposed. For me, Gerda Lerner's recent work stands out. In the "Rethinking the Paradigm" chapters in *Why History Matters* (1997), Lerner grapples with the question of "difference" and points out that the analytic and theoretical work that has come out of theorizing "difference" has been fruitful: "Women's Studies ... has made an enormous intellectual contribution to transforming thought and reconfiguring curricula by making the question of power and 'differences' among women the focus of serious debate ... In fact, the debate on 'differences' represents the most serious challenge to traditional thought and traditional ways of organizing knowledge so far" (146). Lerner's own theorizing represents a convincing synthesis and a creative expansion of our understanding of the relationship between gender, class, and "race."

Transforming the Academy and the World

Feminism and feminist scholarship have enriched my life enormously, as they have enriched the lives of many of my colleagues and students, but what else has women's studies accomplished? Have we changed the academy? Has the academy changed the world? Feminism has had an impact, but not the impact many of us hoped for in the early 1970s.

In 1973, at a conference in San Diego, California, Robin Morgan spoke in support of women's studies. Answering those who opposed any attempt to use the male-dominated academy to forward feminist objectives, she said, "Yes, it's odious to have to go to the Man for [educational tools] but we must take them and use them in a new way. Not to move up the ladder; to destroy the ladder." "I want to have everything," she added, "feminist colleges, feminist universities, a feminist world" (2004, 73–75).

Morgan's vision was to transform the academy, but she spoke as a writer, not as an academic. Annette Kolodny, who, in contrast to Morgan, has been a university professor for most of her working life, has written about her experiences at the University of British Columbia (UBC) in the early 1970s when "the energy and enthusiasm of feminism was international and infectious. Nothing, it seemed, was impossible" (2000a, 276–90). Kolodny was involved in one of the shrewdest, best-planned examples of women's studies institution building in the history of Canadian university life. In 1973, four faculty members, including Kolodny herself, Helga Jacobson, Meredith Kimball, and Dorothy Smith developed an "extraordinary collaboration" (see the essays by Kimball, Kolodny, and Smith in this volume). After considerable struggle, the four achieved the acceptance of a women's studies core course, along with four discipline-based seminars. However, while feminist scholarship grew at UBC, the original interdisciplinary vision was soon eroded: "By 1978, the original year-long, twelve-credit program which integrated a truly interdisciplinary lecture course with discipline-based seminars, had virtually disappeared. The truth is, there was simply no institutional support" (Kolodny 2000a, 289).

Feminist scholarship and women's studies have achieved much in Canada since the 1970s, but some of our victories may be pyrrhic. Marginal groups who seek recognition from indifferent and sometimes hostile institutions often find that they are faced with the seeming inevitability of co-optation. As I have said elsewhere, this has happened to women's studies scholars in Canadian universities (Gorham 1996). The establishment of women's studies degree programs may look like solid recognition, but often they serve to disguise our continued marginalization and dampen the power of our initial demands.

Often, the "victim" gets blamed, but that is not my intention here. Sad to say, as feminist scholars our choices have been limited by the entrenched sexism of universities.[3] Feminist scholarship and women's studies emerged in Canada, as they did in the United States, at the height of the success of the women's liberation movement; but that success was not sustained. As Alix Kates Shulman puts it with wry humour, the women's movement became "tainted." By what? "By its close association with women": "gradually, perhaps inevitably, with the passing years the vitality of the women's movement was sapped as our victories were taken for granted, our ideas co-opted or subverted, our quarrels magnified, our truths accepted as truisms and overlooked ... that oppressive female taint ... soon appeared once again on whatever women do" (1995, 89–90).

Difficult enough, though, that "female taint" is for fortunate women like myself; it is minor when compared with the terrible experiences that women endure in unsettled, war-torn parts of the world. The *Globe and Mail* is the newspaper I read at breakfast. As journalist Stephanie Nolan documents for the *Globe*, in some parts of the world, women suffer mercilessly from rape, which continues to be used as a weapon of warfare. As I write this, such brutality is occurring, for example, in Congo and in the Sudan (Nolan 2005).[4] Earlier it was Bosnia.

We can take some comfort from the fact that, in 2005, journalists like Nolan are fully aware that rape is a political act. It was the work of feminist writers in the 1970s, most notably Susan Brownmiller, who redefined the meaning of rape as the exercise of male power over women (1975). Feminist thinking, then, can change the world, but sadly only to a limited extent. For me, feminist scholarship was always meant to be part of feminist activism. Naming and understanding women's oppression is only a beginning. Actually eradicating misogyny—Shulman's "taint" of womanhood—in Canadian universities and throughout the world is proving to be no easy task.

Notes

1 The University of Toronto course, taught by Natalie Zemon Davis and Jill Ker Conway, was of course much more famous.
2 The origin of the term "the personal is political," now embedded in our language, is not known. See the discussion on the Women's Studies list WMST-L on the matter, at <http://research.umbc.edu/~korenman/wmst/pisp.html>.
3 Some, of course, claim, quite falsely, that feminists have "taken over." See, for example, Christina Hoff Sommers (1994). For continued sex discrimination in Canadian universities see Elena Hannah et al. (2002).
4 On women and rape in warfare, see Robinson (2002).

Selected Publications by the Author

Gorham, Deborah. 1996. In defense of discipline-based feminist scholarship. In *Graduate women's studies: Visions and realities*, edited by A. B. Shteir. Toronto: Inanna Publications.

———. 1997. Women's history: Founding a new field. In *Creating historical memory: English-Canadian women and the work of history*, edited by B. Boutilier and A. Prentice. Vancouver: UBC Press.

Reminiscences of a Male Supporter of the Movement Towards Women's Liberation and Social Equality

Leslie Marshall

HERE'S A BRIEF DESCRIPTION of my involvement in creating the first Women in Literature course at the University of Guelph. I hope it will give a sense of how things developed, at least as far as my participation went. I proposed the course to the English Department curriculum committee in 1974 and taught the first section in the winter term of 1975 to a class of thirty-five women and one man. At that time, the department was looking for suggestions to fill the recently introduced Themes and Forms slot at the 200 level. Themes and Forms courses were expected to be introductory courses with a wide appeal, and a course on women's writing seemed to me to be an obvious choice. I knew that a group led by Norma Bowen and Joanna Boehnert in psychology, Nora Cebotarev in sociology, and Donna Lero in family studies was working towards the establishment of a women's studies program at Guelph, and, of course, there was a lot of talk of "women's liberation" and "consciousness-raising." Since my daughter Tina was born in 1972, I had a special interest in what was happening, and to support the movement in a general way I was planning to direct Doris Lessing's 1962 drama, *Play with a Tiger* (1996), to celebrate International Women's Year.

The course proposal, as I recall, was not contentious, and it was readily approved. I suppose some people may have thought it odd that a man would teach such a course, but, if so, I was not made aware of such reservations. The convention in the department was that, if you suggested a course, you would be expected to teach it, and I simply saw myself starting an interesting course that I thought we should be offering. One must remember, too, that, in those days, there were relatively few women in the department on the permanent faculty. In the 1974–75 academic calendar, there were five out of a list of thirty: Nancy Bailey, Linda Marshall, Mary Rubio, Elizabeth Waterston, and Lesley Willis. Amongst the contractually limited faculty were Lois Gottlieb and Wendy Robbins (Keitner). The women who were interested were soon involved. As early as the spring term of 1975, my wife Linda Marshall and I were teaching a section each, and, shortly thereafter, Nancy Bailey became the principal instructor. In 1978, Women in Literature was given a permanent number, 37–288. I enjoyed teaching the course and did so as often as I could. Altogether, I taught it five times between the winter of 1975 and the winter of 1984.

I didn't think of it as a women's studies course as the term is now understood, and it would be misleading to think of me as a pioneer in this respect. I did consider myself a supporter of the movement towards women's liberation and social equality, but I offered no cogent political analysis. I thought of the course, rather, as an introductory 200-level English course with the usual aims of the improvement of thinking, reading, and writing, but with the significant introduction of gender into the equation. For me, it was an exploratory exercise, though I did think that, if I were successful, it could lay the groundwork for future courses in women's writing.

Virginia Woolf's *A Room of One's Own* (1929) gave me the framework for the course, and my approach was largely influenced by Alice Munro's story "The Office" (1968b) and an interview with Graeme Gibson (Munro 1972) in which she talks about the difficulties she thought women of her generation had in telling the truth about their situation. Both Woolf and Munro talked about the problem of being a woman and a writer, so I thought the course could be useful, not only in sketching a brief history of women's writing, but also in encouraging the women in the class to try to overcome some of the inhibitions Woolf and Munro described. The aim was a kind of "liberative" writing—an idea that owed much to the concept of "confronting" texts that was current in the drama of the time. Simply, rather than submit to the text, students were invited to measure what they read against their own experience.

I recognized that my gender was a problem. Woolf and others had led me to believe that women were unlikely to talk frankly and without inhibition in the presence of a man. I was also aware of the danger that, however unwittingly, I might join Woolf's legion of men pontificating about women. To try to get round these problems, I made a reading journal the main course requirement. The journal served two main purposes. The first was to give me access, in an ongoing way, to what the class was thinking and feeling, which helped me to plan classes and to decide what issues to raise. The students were encouraged to hand in journal entries whenever they felt they had something interesting to say or any question they wanted to discuss. I asked them to date the entries to encourage them to make their journal writing a regular part of their schedule. Students were free to include in the journal anything from any source that they felt was pertinent to our subject, and I found that this stimulated discussions outside class that fed back into the stream.

The second and related aim of the journal was to encourage the kind of independent thought I've mentioned above. The thesis essay, useful though it is in helping students organize ideas, always seemed to me to constrain their thinking. In the journal entry, in contrast, there was no obligation to arrive at a conclusion. I encouraged students to carry their ideas from one entry to another so that they began to get a sense of thought as an evolving process. I tried to get them to think about their thinking and what conditioned it, to think concretely and historically, and to look for contradictions. It took time to get some students to stop writing their entries as if they were miniature essays, but, once they overcame their fear of contradictions and came to see them as opportunities to think something through, they produced some remarkable results. Whenever I could, I read interesting or provocative entries in class to give them a sense of how others were approaching the exercise. Behind it all, of course, was my hope that the process would open their minds to the possibilities of social change.

I've spent some time describing the journal because, though I devised it as a stratagem to overcome an obstacle, it soon became central to the structure of the course. The fact that I was able to begin each class with material or questions that the students themselves had provided and that they were able to respond to my response, both immediately in class and later in their journals, opened up a special kind of dialogue. What I remember most vividly about 37–288 is the delight of teaching classes where, because of their genuine interest in the subject, the students themselves developed the momentum that carried the argument forward. A distinctive tone developed in class discussion as the term progressed and the women discovered the strength of their connection with one another.

This is not to imply, of course, that everyone felt equally involved or that they agreed with one another or necessarily liked one another. Most of the discussion, in fact, involved women's relationship with men, and there was lots of vigorous debate. For example, though there was general agreement about the effects of patriarchy as Woolf describes them—discrimination, inhibition, discouragement, distraction, and self-destruction—not everyone agreed with her looking to androgyny as a solution. I encouraged them to read *A Room of One's Own* as a historical text, and someone usually insisted on the importance of anger for the contemporary woman. I realize that it would be easy to present the concept of "sisterhood" in the seventies in rather a sentimental and idealized way. The bond between women, as I saw it evolve, was a dynamic idea, forged through argument.

Now, I say that I felt I had a genuine interaction with the classes. Of course, I'll never know how it appeared from the other side of the lectern. You might well get a different picture from some of the students in the class. By the same token, I'll never really know how successful a teacher of Women in Literature I was. The only time I recall being seriously challenged in my role was during a discussion of Sylvia Plath's *The Bell Jar* (1963) when a visitor to the class claimed that, as a man, I was either incapable of seeing or refused to see Esther as the victim of an oppressive patriarchal medical establishment. Of course, she was right, and this illustrates what I said earlier: that the course lacked political edge. I don't remember much coming of the intervention, but I do remember feeling that the class was too inclined to protect me. I imagine that the young women of today would be less accommodating.

How do things appear to me today? It seems to me that the co-opting of feminist ideas by the forces of global consumerism and neo-liberal political philosophy constitute a major threat to the women's movement. Earlier this summer, a young woman crossed my path, bare-midriffed, tattooed, navel-pierced, with "It's All About Me" emblazoned across the seat of her track pants. The slogan, in some fashion, derives from the consciousness-raising I've described above, but clearly, too, such rhetoric of female empowerment and related imagery of woman's liberation is used in today's advertising to sell everything from chewing gum to spa treatments and botox injections. It might also be seen to be the epitome of the Thatcherite philosophy of duty to oneself first, which was making its presence felt just about the time I stopped teaching 37–288. Caryl Churchill's *Top Girls* (1982) shows how destructive Thatcherite careerism can be of the social aims of feminism and the bond of sisterhood.

In a review of a BBC series entitled *Big Ideas That Changed the World* (Cholmondeley 2005), Germaine Greer is quoted as accusing globalization of "peddling an extreme version of the female stereotype, the updated version of the female eunuch … with all her accoutrements, her lipstick, her nail varnish, her hair dye, her enhanced breasts, her high heel shoes, the works, alive and well and thriving in every society on the planet." She is further quoted: "The cultural expression of globalised consumerism is pornography, and pornography expands daily, exponentially, multiplying itself across cyberspace. Where is feminism, now that we need it more than ever?" (Joseph 2005, 27). It seems to me that Greer has a good point. Although significant gains have been made over the last thirty years for middle-class women, the basic problems of poverty, discrimination, and violence persist in Canada and throughout the world.

The message doesn't seem to be getting across to the young women of today. Linda Georges, coordinator of women's studies at Guelph, tells me of her concern that the average female student of today, though she takes for granted all that has been accomplished by the women's movement, will decline to call herself a feminist. Whereas, in the seventies, feminism offered a promise for the future, today it seems to be a label from the past.

How, then, can the importance of the women's movement be communicated to the present generation? Not, according to Catharine Lumby, director of media and communications at Sidney University, by replaying the feminism of the seventies. Or, at least, in her view, Germaine Greer is not the woman to do it. "The world needs feminists of all persuasions on display," Lumby concludes, "whether as prime ministers or reality TV contestants. If younger women are expected to find feminism relevant, then all feminists need to show they are open to understanding the lives young women live and the culture they embrace" (2005). Not without some regret, Lumby dismisses Greer as out of date and out of touch (Joseph 2005).

Andrea Dworkin, another icon of 1970s feminism, was discarded in similar fashion by Berkeley Kaite, professor of cultural studies at McGill University. Kaite (2005) was responding to a sympathetic obituary for Dworkin written by Margaret Viner, which concluded, "in an academic environment which has allowed postmodernism to remove all politics from feminism, we will miss Andrea Dworkin." Kaite, in response, insisted that Dworkin had been "surely and rightly" ridiculed, in part, for "pushing an outmoded agenda—that of the singular voice of feminism." "The legacy of postmodernism," Kaite's letter to the editor continues, "is its insistence on the politics of the local, the multiple, the plurality of voices and differences, indeed the waning of the authority of the 'master narratives.'"

What is there, then, to replace the old analysis that will give direction to the next phase of the struggle? Is the waning of master narratives an indication that feminist energies are dissipating? It is clearly an important time of transition in the women's movement. As I scan the Internet trying to get a sense of what is happening, I am conscious of a lot of discord and name-calling. I am not sure if I am listening to sisters arguing or to different sisterhoods in internecine strife. Is it disarray or creative ferment?

It strikes me that it would be very interesting to teach 37–288 today. There are lots of contradictions to think through. If, by some miracle, I were offered the opportunity, I might begin by having the class invent a reality TV show that a feminist could play in good conscience. It's difficult to think back thirty years without a degree of nostalgia, and I hope I haven't presented too distorted a picture of those days. May I say, in conclusion, that I consider myself lucky to have had the opportunity to teach 37–288.

Selected Publications by the Author

Marshall, Leslie. 1980. *Review of The novelistic vision of Doris Lessing: Breaking the forms of consciousness*, by Roberta Rubenstein. *WLWE* 19(2) (Autumn 1979): 178–81.

You Just Had to Be There

◉ Greta Hofmann Nemiroff

A Women's Studies program should offer the student knowledge, an opportunity for personal growth, and a challenge to affect the direction of society in the future … it should address itself to the following three questions: "What is and has been women's situation?" "Who am I … this woman, here?" "What can I do as a woman to make things better in the world?"
— Christine Garside Allen (1975, 51)

Beginnings

IN THE FALL OF 1970, the first women's studies course to be taught at a Canadian University was taught at Sir George Williams University in Montréal.[1] Team-taught like many early women's studies courses, it was offered by me and Christine Garside,[2] as she was known at the time. Team-teaching was a good strategy for early women's studies courses. Considering that women's lives and works do not fit neatly within disciplinary boundaries, an interdisciplinary approach involving faculty grounded in different disciplines provided a wide knowledge base from which to address the subject of women. As well, team-teaching provided the pioneers in women's studies with support within the chilly confines of universities that were not very receptive to the field.

Christine was a member of the philosophy department and I was a member of the English department at Sir George Williams, but our professional partnership grew seamlessly from our "private" lives. We met at a stiffly social departmental event through our then-husbands who were members of the philosophy department at McGill University. We would meet for lunch and talk enthusiastically about our research and teaching. Late in the summer of 1968, within a few weeks of each other, we both gave birth to boys.

When the babies were a few months old, Christine brought her children to my house for a visit with me and my children. Through the afternoon, as we earnestly attempted to talk about our current research interests—Kierkegaard for her and Kafka for me—we were continuously interrupted by the children's needs. As Christine prepared to leave, she wryly commented on the difficulty of academic discourse under these circumstances. I responded, with due respect to those literary gentlemen under discussion, by saying that perhaps our attempt at intellectual exchange in this situation was even more interesting than they were. Should we not be researching and teaching about ourselves?

Christine sank back into a chair; before long we were discussing de Beauvoir, Friedan, and the Royal Commission on the Status of Women, which was in session at the time. We were aware of feminist demonstrations in the United States and were sympathetic to the free speech, anti-war, and Black civil rights movements, all of which were touched upon in that conversation. Our focus, though, was on our own experience as women, on ourselves as subjects, and on the exciting possibility of exploring how we as women could theorize our lives. As a philosopher, Christine was most interested in "women's identity" while, as someone grounded in the arts, I was interested in ways in which women were represented, our "images."

Over the next months we designed our course, Woman's Identity and Image, and proposed it to both our departments. As we formulated our thoughts, we became increasingly conscious of the virtual invisibility of women in the academic discourse of our disciplines. The intellectual generalities men formed about themselves under the guise of "human nature" automatically were applied to women, a subset of "humanity" … except when they weren't, when we were either ignored, condescended to, or subjected to misogynistic commentary. We knew that unless the course were offered for credit, it would have no real status in the university. Notwithstanding the fact that it took some convincing for our departments to agree to list the course for credit, we naively believed that all it would take to convince people of the subject's academic merit was information and sweet reason. In our enthusiasm, we not only underestimated the depth and power of systemic misogyny, but we didn't have the concepts or words to describe it.

Woman's Identity and Image: 1970–76

Our original objectives for the course were to counter ways in which women had been defined and represented by men, to research and define women from women's point of view, to exhume long-buried works by and about women, and to promote women's rights to equality in every sphere. At the outset, we didn't consciously address issues of racialization, class, ethnicity, ability, or sexual orientation in themselves. Women as a subject was so vast and confusing that our first time round focussed on developing frameworks for interrogating the often-elusive subject of women, testing and refuting generalities about women, and finding resources of information.

In 1975, in a published interview with Jean-Paul Sartre, Simone de Beauvoir posed the following question: "est-ce que les femmes doivent entièrement rejeter cet univers masculin ou s'y faire une place? Est-ce qu'elles doivent voler l'outil, ou changer l'outil? Je veux dire aussi bien la science, que le langage, que les arts. Toutes les valeurs sont marquées du sceau de la masculinité. Faut-il, pour cela, complètement les rejeter de réinventir, à partir de zéro, radicalement autre chose? Ou faut-il s'assimiler ces valeurs, s'en emparer, s'en servir, à des fins féministes?" (Should women entirely reject that masculine universe or make a place for themselves there? Should they steal or change the tool? I am referring to science, as well as language and the arts. All values bear the mark of masculinity. For that reason, should one totally reject them and try to reinvent from zero something radically different? Or should one assimilate those values, take possession of them, and use them to feminist ends?) (de Beauvoir and Sartre 1975; translated by G. H. Nemiroff).

Feminist intellectuals at different times have followed both of de Beauvoir's alternatives: for women to appropriate men's tools of analysis and to invent our own. An important initial step for us in "pioneering" women's studies was to counter misconceptions within the intellectual history we best understood, that of White European-based culture. This process, widely practised in early women's studies courses, motivated extensive feminist production in intellectual, artistic, scientific, and social fields. These critiques fed into the development of feminist theory and research. In the first few years, Woman's Identity and Image included works by men, which were both critiqued and used to formulate new theories.

Initially, and at least until 1975, our course was based on what we called "conceptual history," a historical approach to how women had been defined in our culture. Although we realized that there were serious problems with Jung's insistence on the universality of archetypes, we developed a fairly loose structure using archetypes as a conceptual framework for our course. We identified and consecutively explored six archetypes, the first three of which—woman as evil temptress, woman as virgin goddess, woman as earth mother—have strong historical roots in Western culture. The final three archetypes, covered in the second term of the course, were more contemporary in their focus: woman as passive object, woman as genius, and woman as political activist.

Assigned readings drew upon anthropology, art history, biology, classics, history, literature, philosophy, political science, psychology, religious studies, and sociology. Clearly, we were not well-versed in all of these subjects, so, when greater expertise was needed, we invited colleagues to lecture to our classes. We assiduously followed and were influenced by the work of new feminist scholars and the preoccupations and publications of women's groups and organizations emerging in the late 1960s and early 1970s. As the course progressed for the next nine years, we focussed less on critiquing male writers and more on the research and writings of other feminists in order to construct new theories regarding women in our culture. Later on, research on women in other cultures and situations illuminated our work and steered us away from illusions of universality to a more realistic understanding of how material and cultural differences mediate and shape women's experiences.

Texts and Other Resources

While we had to assign specific texts to our students, we also drew on numerous other resources to give depth to our understanding and treatment of the subject of women. In 1970, the central feminist texts available to us were de Beauvoir's *The Second Sex* (1953), Friedan's *The Feminine Mystique* (1963), and Virginia Woolf's *A Room of One's Own* (1929). We introduced the concept of archetypes with reference to the writing of Jung, Plato, and de Beauvoir. For example, for woman as evil temptress, we initially assigned parts of Genesis and Hesiod's *Theogony* (1966), excerpts from Milton's *Paradise Lost* (1968), Pope's *Rape of the Lock* (1944), and poetry and short stories by women, including blues by Bessie Smith. Some male writers presented and critiqued from a feminist point of view were Aristotle, Engels, Bebel, and Freud. As we addressed contemporary issues, we referred to the report of the Royal Commission on the Status of Women (1970) for information on women's situation in Canada.

Women's publications burgeoned in North America between 1970 and 1975. Newsletters and pamphlets published by women's groups in Canada brought us into touch with contemporary issues identified by women. Those were heady times for developing a language for reflecting on ourselves and others qua women. Naming our experiences with new words like "sexual harassment" and "marital rape" made it possible to develop new subjects for research and new epistemologies, and to undertake action for change.

The intellectual fervour of the time was driven by talk. Some women participated in consciousness-raising groups; others just sat up late at night discussing our experiences and thoughts. While the "breaking the silence" experience was an important and empowering aspect of the time, so was the discussion of new ideas, new research, and new discoveries. Christine and I met every Tuesday before class for dinner at the Coffee Mill on rue de la Montagne. Our discussions would move freely back and forth between our "private" and "public" lives, often generating subjects for further investigation and inclusion in our research and lectures.

Early women's studies conferences were important sites for sharing ideas and pooling our meagre resources of information. In 1973, I keynoted the first official women's studies meeting at the Learned Societies at Queen's University. A very enlightening conference was held at the University of Toronto in the autumn of 1974, with feminist academics from across the country, many of whom would become well-known scholars in the field. While women's studies research and content were discussed at early conferences, we also discussed the social and economic contexts in which we worked. When Christine and I co-presented a paper on our approach to women's studies at the founding convention of the American Women's Studies Association in San Francisco in 1976, I was surprised to discover that half our audience of about 125 women had been so grateful for the opportunity to teach women's studies courses that they did so for no extra pay above their regular course loads. Another important feature of conferences were the book tables, which exhibited and often sold new publications such as books, journals, and even unpublished articles. I still possess a faded mimeographed copy of Naomi Weisstein's much anthologized "Psychology Constructs the Female" (1971), purchased for ten cents at a conference in New York.

After 1973–74, we were able to supplement de Beauvoir, Friedan, and Woolf with excellent anthologies.[3] Because we used readings from diverse sources and wanted to keep costs down for the students, we developed our own "course pack." This comprised a large transparent plastic envelope containing a folio of readings for each "archetype" to supplement books we had assigned with salient passages from the Bible, scholarly articles, short stories, and poetry. We were able to draw on some anthologies of women's poetry (Segnitz and Rainey 1973; Berkinow 1974; Iverson and Ruby 1975), as well as new feminist criticism (Showalter 1971), for the literary part of the course.

Innumerable works of the time influenced our thinking. I was and still am most stimulated by theoretical writing that turns my thoughts upside down. We drew upon numerous Canadian publications, such as Marylee Stephenson's early anthology, *Women in Canada* (1973), which had important articles by Dorothy E. Smith, Margrit Eichler, Patricia Marchak, and others. Other Canadian sources we drew upon for our work were Margaret Benston's "The Political Economy of Women's Liberation" (1969b) and *Women Unite! An Anthology of the Canadian Women's Movement* (Discussion Collective No. 6 1972). Articles by American feminist scholars that affected me and are still relevant included Cynthia Ozick's "Women and Creativity: The Demise of the Dancing Dog" (1971), Linda Nochlin's "Why Are There No Great Women Artists?" (1971), Naomi Weisstein's "Psychology Constructs the Female" (1971), Phyllis Chesler's "Patient and Patriarch" (1971), and Anne Koedt's "The Myth of the Vaginal Orgasm" (1973). As I prepared this article, I reviewed various political manifestos we included in assigned readings, such as "The Witch Manifesto" (Anonymous 1969), "The SCUM Manifesto" (Solanas 1969), the San Francisco Redstockings' "Our Politics Begin with Our Feelings" (1969), and the "Bitch Manifesto" (Joreen 1969). They brought back the excitement of those times and the readiness to be "outrageous," qualities missing in the current safety of many women's studies publications. As I participated in a number of feminist groups that operated in constant search of egalitarian forms of self-government, I especially appreciated an article by Joreen (Jo Freeman) entitled "The Tyranny of Structurelessness" (1973).

We addressed issues of social class through the work of Engels, Bebel, Goldman, and Mitchell. Aside from poetry and blues, the first work we assigned on women of colour was Catherine Stimpson's article, "Women's Liberation and Black Civil Rights," from *Women in Sexist Society* (1971). Joyce Ladner's *Tomorrow's Tomorrow: The Black Woman* (1971), with its critique of "White" social sciences, had a great influence on me. Other important works were Mary Daly's *Beyond God the Father* (1973) and Kate Millet's *Sexual Politics* (1970). I developed feminist interpretations of novels such as

Jane Austen's *Pride and Prejudice* and Charlotte Brontë's *Jane Eyre*; it was also refreshing to work with fiction arising from an overt feminist imagination, such as Doris Lessing's *The Golden Notebook* (1967) and *Martha Quest* (1964), Margaret Laurence's *The Stone Angel* (1965) and *The Diviners* (1974), and Fay Weldon's *Down among the Women* (1971), a witty and stylistically innovative feminist account of the times.

In the early 1970s, many more women's studies courses were introduced at Sir George Williams University and other universities in Québec and Canada. I remember hoping that women's studies would change the disciplines and "feminize" the universities. I sometimes had a queasy feeling when I realized that it was also entirely possible that its presence in the university would instead institutionalize women's studies.

Pedagogy

Woman's Identity and Image classes were scheduled in the evenings to accommodate the needs of women at home with children, women in the paid work force, and day students. Our first class had about seventy-five students in it. However, there were an additional fifty or so students who were very committed to auditing the course. Subsequent classes met in a larger room and averaged between 100 and 150 students plus auditors. From the beginning, about ten percent of our students were males. Although there were a few men who had come to scoff (but not for long) or ostensibly to "meet chicks" and discover "what turned them on,"[4] most of them were seriously interested in the subject. What remains with me from the first years is the hunger our students had, not only for information, but for the tools to understand their own lives. As Marcia Westcott explains in "Women's Studies as a Strategy for Change," "Women students are no longer studying material that is totally outside themselves, but are learning about the ways in which their social contexts have shaped them as women. In this process, social knowledge and self-knowledge become mutually informing ... For them the personal becomes intellectual and the intellectual personal" (1983, 211). There was a passion and intensity to learning that, in my view, has somewhat faded as women's studies has become more institutionalized over the past twenty years.

While we encouraged as much class discussion as possible, it was clear that many students were shy to speak up in so large a group, especially on a subject so intimately connected to their lives. By 1973, I was teaching in Québec's community college system where I became a founding member of the New School of Dawson College, an alternative program based on theories of humanistic education.[5] I continued at the university as a part-time lecturer in women's studies until 1979. My experience with the self-disclosing pedagogy of humanistic education convinced me that our university women's studies students needed a safe venue to discuss issues related to feelings evoked by the course material.

Since one of our objectives was to empower women, we had to acknowledge that "the empowerment of students means encouraging them to explore and analyze the forces acting upon their lives. It means respecting and legitimizing students' own voices in the classroom" (Weiler 1988, 149). Because of the size of our classes and the fact that the students did not know one another, we decided to pilot a voluntary conference group that would meet for two hours a week after class. I volunteered to facilitate the first conference group in 1973–74. The conference agenda was open and much time was spent discussing the relationship of our personal lives to the subjects covered in class. There were intense discussions and arguments, moments of extreme sadness, and times of great laughter. This opportunity for discussion helped students to critically process the readings and to elaborate upon their own opinions. At the end of the year, members of the group unanimously expressed the opinion that conferences should be continued, with the stipulation that they be optional since not all students had the time or the desire for such participation. From that time until 1979, students in Woman's Identity and Image had the option of joining conference groups led by students who had done well in the course.

In order to assess the climate of our class and the needs of the students, at our first class we asked each student to do the following written exercise: "If the Goddess were to award you a perfect answer to one and only one question regarding women, what would your question be and why?" The students' written responses gave us a very good idea of their concerns and the climate of our class, and they informed how we contextualized our ideas for them. Almost without exception, women belonging to groups struggling for equality (women of colour, Québécoises, women from ethnic minority groups, lesbians) would pose some version of the question: "What am I first? What is my first oppression? A woman or a …?" Students chose their own subjects for their research papers; we learned from their research proposals, papers, and bibliographies. Some students proposed and carried out extraordinary projects in fine arts, film, and other media.

Although our class time was mainly devoted to lectures, our teaching style was quite informal; students addressed us by our first names and often took issue with our ideas. We were both present at each class and would comment on or add to each other's lectures. Where possible, we divided the subject matter according to our training in the disciplines, as well as to our particular interests. Neither of us was trained in the social sciences, and so the learning curve was steep and exciting. For example in addressing "women as passive object," Christine lectured on Aristotle, Schopenhaur, Rousseau, Nietzsche, and de Beauvoir, as well as social scientists such as Bardwick and Chodorow. I covered the "psychological and sexual dynamics of passivity" with reference to Ibsen's *Hedda Gabler*, a story by Joyce Carol Oates, and several poems, but also with reference to Freud, Horney, de Beauvoir, and Friedan, and other readings in philosophy, psychology, and sociology.

You Just Had to Be There

The years 1968 to 1976 were among the most intellectually exciting years of my life. While I had enjoyed my years of traditional studies in English literature and fine arts in the 1950s, they had not filled me with the passion that I experienced once I "dropped" everything else for women's studies. For me, women's studies and the women's movement were simply different branches of the same enterprise: understanding and improving women's situation in the world. This involved becoming an autodidact, addressing and never fully resolving the "nature/nurture" debate, listening to other women recount their experiences and feelings, reading deeply, and learning concepts and methodologies about which I was totally uninformed, critically examining my own life, risking many relationships, and undertaking political struggles, especially when I was just too enraged not to participate.

When I attend academic conferences these days and listen to the presentations of younger colleagues, I am often impressed by their intellectual acumen but worry about their being co-opted by the academy and socialized by the raw ambition and competitiveness it takes to succeed in that environment. I find myself wondering if they have ever been active in women's groups and if they have developed the kind of friendships that were so material to our progress at the time. I am ambitious for these bright young women; my hope for them is that in thirty-five years they will be able to say to their bright young women about the current period in women's studies: "you just had to be there."

I have always told women's studies students that you "can't go home again"; you cannot unlearn feminism or enjoy a life unexamined through a feminist lens. When I recall the intense feeling of those early years, what I remember most is a continual sense of exploration and newness. As you headed for the next corner, you did not know what you would find as you turned it. There were painful discoveries and deeply uncomfortable moments, but it was also a period of unprecedented intellectual collaboration among women. Participating in the "invention" of women's studies changed my life forever.

Notes

1 In the late 1970s, Sir George Williams University joined with Loyola College to become Concordia University.
2 Christine Garside changed her name to Christine Allen after her divorce. In 1979–80 she joined the Roman Catholic Order of the Sisters of Mercy. Thereafter, her name became Sister Prudence Allen. In this article, I will refer to her as "Christine," as she was known to me at the time.
3 The most significant collections were edited by Vivian Gornick and Barbara K. Moran (1972), Julia O'Faolain and Laura Martines (1972), Alice Rossi (1973), and Betty and Theodore Roszak (1969).
4 At our first class in one of the early years, a young man told the entire class that these were his reasons for taking the course.
5 For information on the educational philosophy of the New School, see Nemiroff (1993).

Selected Publications by the Author

Afkhami, Mahnaz, Greta Hofmann Nemiroff, and Haleh Vaziri. 1998. *Safe and secure: Eliminating violence against women and girls in Muslim societies.* Bethesda, MD: Sisterhood Is Global Institute.

Nemiroff, Greta Hofmann. 1987. *Women and men: Interdisciplinary readings on gender.* Markham, ON: Fitzhenry and Whiteside.

———. 1989. *Celebrating Canadian women: Prose and poetry by and about Canadian women.* Marham, ON: Fitzhenry and Whiteside.

———. 1993. *Reconstructing education: Towards a pedagogy of critical humanism.* New York: Praeger; Toronto: OISE Press.

———. 1999. *Women's changing landscapes: Life stories from three generations.* Toronto: Second Story Press.

The Second Wave: A Personal Voyage

Sandra Pyke

IT WAS 1966. Armed with a newly minted PhD, I was about to begin my first full-time academic job at York University. Having just moved to the city, my spouse and I went shopping for bedroom furniture in one of Toronto's huge department stores. At the customer service desk, I filled out an application form for a store credit card. "What is your husband's name?" I was asked. Puzzled, I replied, "Why is that relevant?" I learned that the card must be registered in my husband's name, not mine. Increasingly loudly voiced protestations that I was gainfully employed while he was not, that I was a Canadian citizen, that I paid taxes, that my parents and my grandparents had been born in Canada, that I had a good credit rating, fell on deaf ears. Apparently it was the policy of the store that married women could not have their own credit cards. Confronted with such egregious discrimination, I was (almost) struck speechless. Threatened, among other dire outcomes, with the loss of a substantial sale, the manager of the credit office ultimately agreed that a breach of the policy seemed a reasonable solution. It was an incredible, demeaning experience, which still has the power to evoke anger, bewilderment, and shame, and it marked a turning point in my life. The pursuit of equality and equity for women became a central focus, a raison d'être.

Toronto in the sixties was a hotbed of grassroots feminist organizations.[1] I was introduced to one of them, the Toronto Women's Caucus, by a graduate student at York, and in turn I encouraged some of my colleagues (e.g., Mary Stewart) and graduate students (e.g., Frances Ricks) to attend the weekly meetings on Adelaide Street. The focus of the group was mass action, and the decriminalization of abortion was a key issue. Coalitions were readily formed around the abortion issue, and hundreds of activists bussed to Ottawa, bearing our banners and signs, to bring our concerns to the attention of the Canadian government. The academic study of abortion was the early research focus for another feminist colleague at York, Esther Greenglass, who published several articles (1972, 1975) and a book on this topic (1976). My own first sortie into writing on feminist issues was an article entitled "Sugar 'n' Spice" that appeared in *The Velvet Fist* (1971), the in-house publication of the Toronto Women's Caucus. As is obvious from the title, the piece focussed on the differential socialization messages for girls and boys, one of the themes frequently addressed in consciousness-raising sessions.

One of the most conservative of the social sciences, psychology, my discipline, provided relatively little sustenance to feed a hunger for feminist content and analysis. Three main themes were prominent in the literature. A number of feminist psychologists of the day were focussed on documenting discriminatory practices in hiring, rates of promotion, the nature of assignments, and remuneration for services, along with rebutting the argument that women were less productive than men and that children would suffer if their mothers worked outside the home (Kimball 1973). Bear in mind that this was the era when Lionel Tiger's socio-biological perspective was, if not normative, at least widely endorsed (Tiger 1969; Tiger and Fox 1972). Other feminists critiqued the prevailing models of therapy, noting the androcentric bias and its inappropriate application to women clients, as well as drawing attention to the incompatibility between traditional sex and gender role prescriptions and good mental health (Kimball 1986). Still others tackled the topic of sex differences, arguing that such differences were a result of sex-based differential socialization practices in the home, in the school, and in the media. For example, a number of researchers documented the negative consequences for female children resulting from teachers' differential expectations for boys and girls derived from traditional socialization patterns (Caplan 1973, 1975; Serbin et al. 1973).

One intriguing theoretical perspective on the etiology and consequences of sex differences was authored by a colleague at York, David Bakan. His popular book *The Duality of Human Existence* (1966) attracted the attention and enthusiasm of the small feminist community in psychology, as well as feminist scholars from other disciplines, and it continues to be referenced in the contemporary literature. Bakan's erudite and scholarly treatise rests on three key assumptions. First, all living beings are characterized by two basic modalities—agency and communion. Agency is identified by such individualistic qualities as self-protection, self-assertion, self-aggrandizement, separation, differentiation, and alienation. Communion, in contrast, is characterized by qualities of union, contact, cooperation, openness, and being at one with other organisms. The second assumption is that agency is more typical of the male, while communal tendencies are more characteristic of the female. The third assumption is that pure agency (i.e., agency unmitigated by communion) is detrimental to the organism.

Bakan argues that agentic tendencies have been reinforced by the Industrial Revolution, capitalism, science, Protestantism, and the general decline in the effectiveness of religion. Child-bearing and child-rearing experiences may act as buffers, protecting females from the full effect of these agentic forces in the environment. Males, for their own survival, are exhorted to develop or give expression to communal qualities, but the developmental task for females is, in the words of the song, to "Stay as sweet as you are." Indeed, Bakan cautions that "the clamor for equality comes from the agentic feature of the female personality" (1966, 140). By and large, psychologists have tended to misinterpret Bakan, assuming that he was postulating a form of androgyny, a balance of agency and communion for both sexes. Although a number of researchers have reported findings consistent with Bakan's approach, Frances Ricks and I found only limited support for the applicability of his model in a study of ten pairs of male and female voluntary social organizations (Ricks and Pyke 1973).

Interest in androgyny was, of course, not limited to psychology, as scholars in other disciplines latched on to the idea (Pyke 1980). Carolyn Heilbrun (1973), for example, has generated a compendium of illustrations of androgyny from the fields of art and literature. However, within psychology, operationalization of the construct by social psychologist Sandra Bem (1974; 1975a; 1975b) triggered a virtual barrage of empirical studies. Bem argued that masculinity and femininity, rather than constituting opposing poles of a single dimension (more femininity automatically means less masculinity), were, in fact, orthogonal. She proffered two principal hypotheses: (1) androgynous individuals (regardless of sex) are more adaptable and flexible than those with a feminine, or masculine, or undifferentiated sex-role orientation, and (2) androgynous folks are psychologically healthier than individuals of other sex-role persuasions. In general, though, the majority of comparisons reveal no statistically significant differences between androgynous subjects and those of other sex-role groups. Even where significant differences are found using the Bem Sex-Role Inventory, they fail to provide unequivocal support for Bem's hypotheses. The most parsimonious explanation for the aggregated findings is that a masculine sex-role orientation is associated with greater psychological well-being, as well as with greater adaptability/flexibility. Eventually, the construct, which had been hailed with such enthusiasm as a way out of the masculine/feminine dichotomy, pretty much disappeared from the literature.

Nevertheless, in spite of these contributions at home and abroad, it is probably fair to say that, by and large, Canadian mainstream academic psychology was oblivious to the second wave of the women's movement. The positive side to this void in psychology was that virtually any feminist work was essentially breaking new ground. As a consequence, many of the early feminist psychologists were generalists, writing on a variety of topics—there was so much grist for the mill. For example, my first feminist research study involved an investigation of the depiction of gender roles in children's literature (Pyke 1975). Similarly, I explored the presentation of women on television and the number of women authors of published articles. A critique of traditional counselling interventions with women and a description of feminist counselling formed the content of three other of my early articles, while teacher attitudes and perceptions vis-à-vis sex roles were discussed in two studies.[2]

Of course, finding a forum for disseminating feminist contributions was a significant challenge. In the early 1970s, submissions with feminist content were not welcomed by the Conference Program Committee of the Canadian Psychological Association (CPA). Fed up with what appeared to us to be sex-based discrimination, several untenured faculty and graduate students associated with York University decided, in 1972, to mount our own symposium, held in conjunction with, but independent of, the CPA convention. The official symposium title was On Women, By Women, but, since it was located in a hotel adjacent to the convention venue and reached via an underground pedestrian avenue, the event came to be known as the "underground symposium" (Bowen 1973). At least two hundred convention delegates attended this unsanctioned event, which received unprecedented press coverage. Notwithstanding this inauspicious beginning, CPA moved fairly quickly to "get on board." For example, the very next year, one of the symposium participants, Esther Greenglass, was one of the convention's invited speakers. A year later, I was asked to join the CPA Task Force on the Status of Women in Canadian Psychology that was struck in recognition of International Women's Year (1975). Frances Ricks and I subsequently served terms on the CPA Board of Directors and, a decade after the event, I was elected president of the association.

An important development stemming from the Task Force was the establishment of the CPA Section on Women and Psychology in 1976. This organization created a community of feminist psychologists in Canada, providing opportunities for mentoring and support and the forging of friendships and collaborations with colleagues from across the country. One of its initiatives, the brainchild of Cannie Stark, was the creation of an institute, a one-day event held the day before the convention proper. For the first time, feminist psychologists had a forum especially designed for the presentation of theory, research, and practice relevant to women—a significant advance from the days of the underground symposium. The proceedings of the 1978 inaugural institute were published in a book edited by Cannie Stark-Adamec (1980).

Another notable outcome of the Task Force was the establishment of the CPA Status of Women Committee, initially chaired by Elinor Ames from Simon Fraser University and subsequently by Cannie Stark from the University of Regina. This committee was charged with the responsibility of overseeing the implementation of the more than one hundred recommendations generated by the task force.

Dissemination of feminist material remained a challenge, however; local newsletters, journals with limited distribution, or book chapters were often the only available publication venues. Many of the items referred to above appear in non-refereed vehicles such as *Ontario Psychologist* while others can be found in *Interchange,* another Ontario publication, or *Special Education in Canada.* Indeed, many of my early articles were contributions to a regular column about women in the *Ontario Psychologist,* a feature that did not survive my resignation as journal editor.

These were the halcyon days of the feminist movement. Progress was evident everywhere. Sexual harassment was out of the closet, named, and deplored. Date and marital rape were identified as crimes. The prevalence of the sexual abuse of young female children and the attendant trauma were recognized. Abortion was legalized. Courses on women appeared in university curricula. Women were moving into the labour force, into the professions, and into universities in ever-increasing numbers. Journals devoted to the publication of material relevant to women were established. Granting agencies began to fund research on women. Task forces on sex bias in research and in counselling and therapy produced reports, and guidelines were developed for the non-sexist delivery of therapy and for the conduct of research. It was an exciting, energizing period for feminists, and I feel privileged to have played a small part in these efforts to achieve equality for women.

An unrelenting commitment to feminism has sustained and nurtured me throughout my academic and personal life. It has influenced the courses I taught (Women, Sex Roles, and Society; Psychology of Women); the organizations I joined (Canadian Psychological Association Section on Women and Psychology; the American Psychological Association Society for the Psychology of Women); the journals I subscribed to (*Canadian Woman Studies*; *Psychology of Women Quarterly*); the administrative positions I accepted (director, graduate program in women's studies; advisor to the president on the status of women); the topics I researched (androgyny, the chilly climate); the theses and dissertations I supervised (on PMS; on the coming-out process); the charities I supported; my parenting style; and the relationships I treasured. While the voyage was sometimes rough, with occasional bouts of seasickness, I can honestly say that it has been a truly amazing trip.

Notes

1 See Ricks, Matheson, and Pyke (1972) for a description of four such groups.
2 See Pyke (1974c; 1974d; 1975b), Pyke and Ricks (1973), and Pyke and Stewart (1974).

Selected Publications by the Author

Pyke, Sandra W. 1975. Children's literature: Conceptions of sex roles. In *Socialization and values in Canadian society*, Vol. 2, edited by R. M. Pike and E. Zureik. Ottawa: Carleton Library Series, 51–73.

———. 1977. Sex-role socialization in the school system. In *Education, change and society*, edited by R. Calton, L. A. Colley, and N. J. MacKinnon. Toronto: Gage, 426–38.

———. 1980. Androgyny: A dead end or a promise. In *Sex roles: Origins, influences and implications for women*, edited by C. Stark-Adamec, 20–32. Montréal: Eden Press.

———. 1997. Education and the "woman question." *Canadian Psychology* 38 (3): 154–63.

Pyke, Sandra W., and Cannie Stark-Adamec. 1981. Canadian feminism and psychology: The first decade. *Canadian Psychology* 22 (1): 35–54.

A Lifetime of Struggles to Belong

◐ Vanaja Dhruvarajan

IN 1972, I OFFERED the first course on gender, called Sociology of Sex Roles, in the department of sociology at the University of Winnipeg. The course caused a big uproar in the department because I included Robin Morgan's book *Sisterhood Is Powerful: An Anthology of Writings from the Women's Liberation Movement* (1970) on the reading list. My success in mounting the course and the uproar it caused both reflect my struggles to belong in the academy in North America.

My husband and I moved from India to Chicago in the early 1960s in search of better economic opportunities. It was a tremendous shock culturally and in many other ways. Not too many people of my kind were found in Chicago. Being away from kith and kin was isolating. This was made worse by the attitudes and social practices of racism prevalent at the time. African-American feminist theorist bell hooks has written about the difficulties involved in feeling at home among strangers, particularly when one is devalued as a person because of aspersions cast on one's "race" and culture (hooks 1994), and my struggles against these challenges were feeble at best. Our efforts to move back to India did not work out because of a lack of jobs as India was struggling after centuries of colonial domination. But Canadian universities were expanding and provided job opportunities for us.

In 1967, the year that United College became the University of Winnipeg, I arrived in Canada and joined the faculty in the Department of Sociology as a sessional lecturer. I had a master's degree in sociology from the University of Chicago and a bachelor's degree in economics, philosophy, and sociology from the University of Mysore, India. I was told in no uncertain terms that I was getting a chance to teach because of the degree from Chicago. Degrees obtained in a so-called "third-world" country were, and often still are, not recognized in North American academia. Fortunately at Chicago, with the support of a couple of sympathetic teachers, I was allowed to pursue my studies for an MA, although only after I proved my ability by taking several courses at my own expense.

It took several years to get an assistant professor's position at the University of Winnipeg, which was given to me in 1973 on condition that I would complete a PhD in sociology as soon as possible. Because of family commitments, it took me until 1974 to start on my PhD program; eventually I got my degree in 1981. The pressure was intense for me to complete the degree soon, as my tenure and promotion were all contingent on that achievement, yet I had difficulties in choosing a research topic for my dissertation. When I expressed my interest in studying the lives of Hindu women, I was told that I could study families but not women because the latter were not considered a legitimate research topic. With the dominance of structural-functionalism as the theoretical framework and positivism as the research methodology in the department, I was compelled to toe the line drawn by the gatekeepers of knowledge in the university and conduct my research within the specified guidelines.

What Philomena Essed (1991) terms "everyday racism" kept me on alert and anxious throughout most of my student days. At Chicago, it was routinely assumed that as a student of colour I was less capable, and the onus was always on me to prove otherwise. The experience was remarkably similar in Winnipeg as well. One administrator once remarked to me in a matter-of-fact manner that he had a gut feeling that I was not a good teacher. It is difficult to count the number of times my authority was undermined, my expertise questioned, and my judgements ridiculed. A chilly climate in universities prevails for women of colour, not only because of their gender, but also because of their "race," religion, and culture (Bannerji 1993; Dhruvarajan 1997). Racism was and still is part of academic common practice in North America; the inferiority of non-White people, our culture, and our ways of life are taken for granted in the curriculum and pedagogy. Resisting it is often interpreted as our lacking in scientific spirit and our inability to view things objectively. For example, it was argued in one of the courses at Chicago that children who grow up in non-nuclear family settings, such as extended families, lack strong superego development and therefore suffer from personality deficiencies. The professor argued that this explained why non-White people were colonized and how it was for their own good. Critiques of Western knowledge monopolies, such as those by Audre Lorde (1984) and Essed (1991), point out how differences are not viewed in non-hierarchical terms within Western cultural common sense since Western culture is assumed to be superior.

As a student, I belonged to a study group, which helped me survive the suffocating racist and sexist environment at the University of Chicago. I still remember the members of that study group—all White—who proved in ample measure that not all White people are racists, and not all Americans imperialists. The Government of India's report of the Committee on the Status of Women in India (1975) showed the growing influence of feminism in India, something that was very important for my own personal development. I learned a great deal about the growing influence of second-wave feminism during this time. The first United Nations World Conference on Women in Mexico and the declaration in 1975 of the Decade of Women added to the significance of the women's movement, which I celebrated. Remembering both my mother's trust in my abilities, and the pride in my "race" and culture instilled by my teachers in India helped me to maintain confidence in myself and nurture my inner strength, which in turn helped me to withstand the racist and sexist onslaughts.

I became involved with the Canadian Association of University Teachers (CAUT) in the 1970s and served as a member of the Status of Women Committee of the University of Winnipeg Faculty Association. In that capacity, I participated in conducting a study to assess pay equity across genders in the university. The study revealed that female professors consistently did worse than their male counterparts, but our efforts to redeem that inequity were not successful. I conducted on my own a research project to find out if there was prejudice and discrimination against racial minorities on campus. When the word spread regarding this study, I was summoned to the dean's office and asked a number of questions regarding the reliability and validity of my findings. The study did show evidence of prejudice and discrimination, but the sample size was small and therefore I decided not to publish the study.

The Sociology of Sex Roles course I developed was successful and was eventually changed to Dynamics of Sex and Gender, reflecting our growing understanding of the area. I had difficulty in the early years including anti-racism perspectives in the course since research and publications on women of colour were sparse and the gender paradigm popular at the time was not inclusive. I did try to bring to the class my own experiences but with great difficulty and mixed success. The classes had mostly White students who reflected the "common sense" position prevalent in the larger society that "there is no racism in Canada" because it is a democratic society with equal rights. Over the years, I proposed several other courses in the area. I also participated in our struggles first to establish a women's studies program and then to win a federally funded chair in women's studies. Both of these efforts were successful.

At the University of Winnipeg, my membership in the Professors'/Professionals' Action Committee on Education (PACE) provided a great deal of support, facilitating my involvement in different kinds of feminist activism. PACE, a voluntary association, was established in the 1970s and included mostly women. A few men who agreed with the association's mandate to raise consciousness regarding gender inequality in society were part of the group. We held workshops, conferences, colloquia, and lecture series on issues pertaining to women. We had many potluck dinners where we discussed strategies to establish a women's studies program.

I did not always feel at home in this group, since the colour of my skin, my culture, and my history separated me from the rest. For example, when the group was celebrating the accomplishments of Nellie McClung, I could not participate. Nellie McClung played an important role in getting "women" the vote. Being a strong believer in the racial superiority of White people, she argued that White women deserved the vote before people of colour. Her sense of sisterhood extended only towards White women, and thus I could not find any reason to celebrate. And to my dismay, when I took the initiative to organize a colloquium on Visible Minorities in Canada, all of my White colleagues treated the conference as irrelevant to them. I often wondered whether I could truly belong anywhere.

To belong means to be accepted and deemed as having entitlements. One's needs and wants are judged important because one is considered an insider, a part of the community, imagined or otherwise. Marlene Nourbese Philip (1992) argues that identity should include a sense of belonging—not just in the legal and civic senses, but also in the sense of feeling at home and at ease. It is only in belonging that we will eventually become citizens in a meaningful way. If there are questions or doubts regarding this matter, then one is marginalized (Dhruvarajan 2000). These borderlands are occupied due to differences in gender, racialization, class, or nation, among others. When you are left in these borderlands, as Anzaldua (1997, 241) argues, possibilities exist for resistance to bring about social transformation. This is done by exploring and integrating different cultural traditions to bring about new consciousness—a *mestiza* consciousness; but this may not always lead to effecting social transformation. For example, I have tried to show in many discussions with my White cohorts how, within the Hindu religious tradition, women's ability to achieve is not questioned because of the existence of the goddess along with the god, but because of social conventions, a woman's wisdom is questioned when she veers away from the roles assigned to her on the basis of her sex. In contrast, in the Western context, the Enlightenment tradition has been used to legitimize gender equality, but, because of the absence of feminine representation in the godhead of Western religious traditions, women in the West face different kinds of challenges. Such awareness has helped me in my own struggles, empowering me in a significant sense. Communicating these ideas to my White colleagues has been a challenge since they often did not want to move beyond the politics of recognition and make an effort to know, respect, and value my cultural tradition. Instead, I was often made to feel that I should be grateful for their generosity in allowing me to keep my tradition and to speak about it. This experience is one of isolation and alienation, which can lead to despair and a feeling of helplessness.

I have struggled, over time, to resist such an outcome. My struggles against gender discrimination began quite early and have continued to this day. My immigration to North America meant that I had to struggle against racism, imperialism, and colonialism, in addition to sexism. Therefore, the kind of feminism I have practised necessarily endeavoured to address all these concerns.

Choices of my research topics have been primarily coloured by my preoccupation with resisting discrimination on the basis of gender and racialization. In my book *Hindu Women and the Power of Ideology* (1989), I explore the limiting and often debilitating impact of the androcentric ideology of Pativratya—husband worship promoted by Hinduism—on the lives of Hindu women. My preoccupation with the empowerment of women has resulted in several research projects on Hindu families and lifestyle within Canada.

The successful efforts of feminists during this period resulted in the eventual establishment of women's studies programs and departments, thereby providing contexts for the generation and dissemination of knowledge from feminist perspectives. But feminists who criticized men for using men's experiences to generalize to all human experiences, thereby ignoring differences of gender, went ahead to commit a similar error by ignoring differences among women. There is a growing awareness of this tendency because of the challenges of scholars from marginalized groups. In spite of these efforts, the experiences of marginalized groups are not yet fully integrated into the mainstream of women's studies.

Within sociology, the impact of feminism has been remarkable particularly in the subfield of family with which I am familiar. For example, in the *Journal of Marriage and the Family*, it was at one time almost impossible to find an article on violence in families. As more and more feminists entered the academy, the field of sociology was transformed to reflect their concerns and interests. Considerable efforts were also made to identify variant patterns of family lifestyles by sociologists of colour, but we still have some ways to go to transcend the White middle-class bias in family studies. Mainstreaming feminist research findings in order to influence policies to empower women has been an uphill task in India. Similar challenges are faced in Canada also to mainstream gender-sensitive research in order to influence policy decisions. The main reason for this state of affairs is that research pertaining to women is still marginalized.

My recent co-authored book *Gender, Race and Nation: A Global Perspective* (Dhruvarajan and Vickers 2002) is an attempt to address many of these issues. We have endeavoured to develop a "one-world" perspective to study women by recognizing both the commonalities and differences among them. We show how gender interacts, intersects, and interlocks with other dimensions of social status such as "race," class, and sexual orientation, to name a few. We also extend our discussion to devise strategies to forge alliances across differences, and to confront and resist forces of domination and oppression. The book argues for a paradigm shift to address issues of concern for all women, all people for that matter. The book questions the Western knowledge monopolies and practices that treat differences in hierarchical terms. I am influenced in these efforts by the writings of scholars such as Himani Bannerji (1993), Chandra Mohanty (1991), Patricia Hill Collins (1990), bell hooks (1994), and Audre Lorde (1984), among others. More recently, I have been extending this discussion to study the impact of globalization on marginalized people, and the process of marginalizing non-Western knowledge systems around the world and privileging and naturalizing Western knowledge systems. In this context, I share the concerns expressed by scholars such as Vandana Shiva (1997), Noam Chomsky (1997), and Walden Bello (2001).

My particular interest in recent years is to explore possibilities of identifying viable alternatives to the neo-liberal paradigm and corporate globalization. I took early retirement from the University of Winnipeg in 2001
and am currently an adjunct professor in the Pauline Jewett Institute of
Women's Studies and the sociology department at Carleton University. I
continue to be involved in promoting anti-racist feminist causes: through
my research and writing; by teaching recently developed courses on gender
and anti-racism in higher education at the Ontario Institute for Studies in
Education of the University of Toronto, at Carleton University, and at the University of Ottawa; as an invited speaker at several universities in India and
Canada; and as a member of the Steering Committee of the Association of
Researchers and Academics of Colour for Equality.

I have been fortunate in obtaining support and encouragement from
some of those in positions of influence whose consciousness was raised
regarding these issues and who were motivated to bring about changes. In
spite of the mixed success of my efforts, my involvement with feminist
research, scholarship, and activism continued in the path charted during
the earlier period. My growing awareness of struggles among those in similar predicaments strengthened my convictions, giving me the courage to
continue over time with my own struggles.

Selected Publications by the Author

Dhruvarajan, Vanaja. 1989. *Hindu women and the power of ideology*. Granby, MA:
    Bergin and Garvey.
———. 1997. Chilly climate in B. C. universities. In *Equity and justice*, edited by
    D. Hearne and M. L. Lefebvre: CWSA Conference Proceedings.
———. 2002. Feminism and resistance to globalization of capitalism. In *Global
    shaping and its alternatives*, edited by Y. Atasoy and W. Carroll. Aurora, ON:
    Garamond Press.
———. 2005. Colonialism and capitalism: Continuities and variations in strategies
    of domination and oppression. In *Teaching as activism: Equity meets environmen-
    talism*, edited by P. Tripp and L. Muzzin. Montréal: McGill-Queen's University
    Press.
Dhruvarajan, Vanaja, and Jill Vickers. 2002. *Gender, race, and nation: A global per-
    spective*. Toronto: University of Toronto Press.

Once Upon a Time There Was the Feminist Movement ... and Then There Was Feminist Studies

Nadia Fahmy-Eid

TO RETHINK KNOWLEDGE in every field! An intellectual revolution of this order—because this is indeed what it was—cannot be explained outside of the social context from which it emerged. We must go back, then, to the feminist movement of the 1960s as it existed in a number of Western societies, particularly the United States, because this was the first source of inspiration for feminists in Canada and Québec. Feminists in Québec, in addition to being influenced by what was happening in the US, were also looking to France, because of the linguistic and cultural ties already linking us to this country. Meanwhile, feminist organizing and the creation of feminist studies courses and programs developed in different ways and at a different pace from one society to another. The shock wave that hit the US in the mid-sixties quickly spread through Canada and Québec, evolving at a pace and in ways specific to our societies.

When we speak about the beginnings of the feminist movement in the US, it is hard to say which event was the trigger: the report of the President's Commission on the Status of Women in 1963, or the publication in the same year of Betty Friedan's *The Feminine Mystique*. Whatever the case, it's clear that from then on theory and action were inseparable in the US feminist movement. Starting in 1966, we kept a close eye on the campaigns of the National Organization for Women (NOW); in 1968, the Women's Liberation Movement put out *Voice of the Women's Liberation Movement* magazine and organized the first national congress. The feminist movement in the US quickly radicalized in an effervescent social climate marked by anti-racist struggles (led by Black Americans) and the movement protesting the Vietnam War. Articulated in several breakthrough writings, the thinking of US and other feminists, as much as their actions, made a considerable impact on feminists intellectuals here in Canada. We all read *Sexual Politics* (1970) by American-born Kate Millet, *The Dialectic of Sex* (1972) by Canadian-born Shulamith Firestone, and *The Female Eunuch* (1970) by Australian-born Germaine Greer.

As for France, in the wake of the revolt of May '68 we rediscovered, at the same time as French women, Simone de Beauvoir's *The Second Sex* (1953). We also closely followed the actions of French feminists, who, in 1970, created the Mouvement de libération des femmes composed of women of many ideological backgrounds, which was quick to partner with other feminist groupings, including the Mouvement pour la liberté de l'avortement et pour la contraception, Gisèle Halimi's group CHOISIR, and the Ligue du droit des femmes, to get abortion decriminalized. The Ligue gave birth to another organization, SOS Femmes-Alternatives, which set up the first shelters for battered women, a model that existed already in the US and that inspired feminist activists throughout Canada.

Because we were francophones, we in Québec were aware of the actions and writings of French feminists and discussed their ideological differences before our counterparts in the rest of Canada. I'm thinking in particular of reviews that were central to our thinking and discussions like *Partisans*, *Questions féministes*, and the *Cahiers du Grif*, from which we learned of Christine Delphy's and Colette Guillaumin's theories about the roots of the oppression and exploitation of women. There was also the publication in 1975 of Benoîte Groult's seminal book *Ainsi soit-elle* (1975), which had a long-lasting impact with its revelation of the existence, across different societies and eras, of discourses and practices that created and perpetuated violence against and even hatred of women. While the issues raised in these writings were theoretical and practical in nature, they were, for the most part, rooted in the experience of all women. Whether it concerned contraception, abortion, work, or education, we all felt directly concerned. It isn't surprising, then, if these subjects were prominent in our later courses on the status of women.

The social climate of the late 1960s in Canada and Québec, like that of the US and France, although on a smaller scale, was marked by intense political and social activity. In Québec, particularly, the 1970 October Crisis and the repression of the Front de libération du Québec (FLQ) inflamed nationalist sentiments and distrust of government. Then, the political conflicts that continued through the mid-seventies led to intense labour struggles and repeated confrontations between workers and the government. It wasn't long before the capitalist economic system as a whole was being challenged by Marxist and extreme leftist groups. Feminist organizing was thus going on in Québec against a backdrop of multiple radical challenges to the status quo. When workers protested exploitation, women began to realize that they were doubly exploited, both as workers and as women. The consciousness of oppression specifically linked to their sex extended beyond the issue of wages and jobs, and encompassed all aspects of their lives as women. Not only that, they followed the struggles of women in other places, and these movements lent even more legitimacy to their own demands.

In Canada, this legitimacy began to be established back in 1970, with the report of the Royal Commission on the Status of Women (Bird Report). The commission had published a disturbing report on discrimination experienced by Canadian women in many areas of life. Its recommendations, notably those concerning family law and employment, reinforced the feminist campaigns in these areas. Already, in Montréal, where the feminist movement developed rapidly, the Montréal Women's Liberation Movement, founded in 1969 by anglophone women connected with McGill and Sir George Williams (later Concordia) universities, was actively working on the issue of contraception and abortion, publishing the *Birth Control Handbook* (over two million copies sold) and creating, with the help of Dr. Henry Morgentaler, a "free-standing" abortion clinic (free of the restrictions imposed by the hospital system).

A year after their anglophone sisters, francophone women founded the Front de libération des femmes (FLF). Led by a group of radical feminists—many of whom had already been active in nationalist and socialist groups—the FLF wanted to place the struggle for women's emancipation at the centre of its revolutionary program. Although political differences meant that the group did not formally survive for more than two years, it left a lasting impact, both in terms of consciousness-raising and actions. Two years was all it took to draft a manifesto and create a newspaper, both of which generated much discussion. First, there was the *Manifeste des femmes québécoises* (Groupe de femmes de Montréal 1971). Published by two FLF members, it was an extended cry of revolt, denouncing the exploitation of women, not only in patriarchal society, but also within the new revolutionary groups where sexism was rampant and feminist concerns unwelcome. Next, there was *Québécoises deboutte*, one of the first newspapers to express a radical feminist perspective; like the *Manifeste*, it was devoted to articulating a vision of women's struggle that was linked to global social change, affirming that "the personal is political." FLF members also worked with the Centre des femmes, which took over the publication of the newspaper and actively supported the Comité de lutte pour l'avortement et la contraception libres et gratuits. The Centre des femmes also set up a documentation centre to distribute women's health information. The centre was an important discussion space in which I was fortunate enough to occasionally participate.

Finally, among the initiatives that contributed to my commitment, was the work of women's committees created by feminists in the central labour bodies. The first, in 1973, was the Comité de la Fédération des travailleurs et des travailleuses du Québec (FTQ), whose report, *Travailleuses et syndiquées*, highlighted the double day and the plight of women workers with children (Fédération des travailleurs et des travailleuses du Québec 1973). The next year, the Confédération des syndicates nationaux (CSN) and the Centrale de l'enseignement du Québec (CEQ) followed suit (1974). The CEQ's Comité Laure Gaudreault drew members' attention to the multiple stereotypes conveyed by school textbooks. This is a study to which I would later often refer in my women's history courses.

The Beginning of Teaching and Research on Women at UQAM

The context from which feminist studies emerged at the Université du Québec à Montréal (UQAM) in the early 1970s constituted what we would now call a *cadre social porteur* (propitious social framework). In 1971, there had been a teach-in at Sir George Williams, which brought together several hundred women, including teachers, students, and activists. It was the first time a university had opened its doors to such a diverse public. The popularity of this event and the richness of the discussions it engendered was a trigger of sorts. This was where the idea of organizing more formal discussions within a university framework originated.

Already, since the beginning of the decade, Canadian feminists, following in the footsteps of US feminists, began setting up the first incarnation of women's studies programs in a few English-speaking universities. At the Université de Montréal, a women's history course was offered in 1972 in the continuing education program. As for UQAM, the first course on women, also organized in 1972, took the original form of a group-run multidisciplinary course (see Anita Caron's essay in this volume). Over two hundred students registered, including a dozen men! On board for this adventure—for adventure it was—were twelve professors, including two male colleagues and three sessional lecturers from ten different disciplines. Faced with the university administration's reluctance to manage this unheard-of format, the professors, by common agreement, decided to teach the course for free, so that the lecturers and teaching assistants working with them could be paid. Taking place in an atmosphere of intense excitement, this course was truly the kick-off of what would later become UQAM's feminist studies program.

The next year, many of us negotiated with our respective departments to create a course focussing specifically on women. Between 1973 and 1976, at least one such course was included on the official course list of the history, sociology, religious science, and biology programs. An important step had been taken. Running this enterprise and seeing to its survival were a group of only five or six of us who, semester after semester, dealt with the bureaucratic red tape in the departments concerned. This ranged from discussions on the conditions of course registration to negotiations about the photocopying budget. We had to photocopy texts ourselves, as well as ensure their distribution to the departments concerned.

At first, we called ourselves the Groupe interdisciplinaire pour l'enseignement et la recherche sur les femmes (GIERF), a name that did not become official until 1978. Our group didn't benefit from institutional recognition, however, because it didn't fit into UQAM's organizational structure. It must be acknowledged that our informal status gave us a wide margin to manoeuvre, but at the same time it deprived us of the practical means to operate. We weren't anxious to alter our status, however, because we found the "women's studies" model of the anglophone academic world risky. At GIERF we realized that this model could facilitate the development of feminist studies and research programs, but at the same there was a risk of ghettoizing the new knowledge about women by isolating it from the different disciplines. We believed that the knowledge we were constructing should be integrated as quickly as possible into all the fields if we wanted to succeed in complementing, correcting, and thereby revolutionizing all the fields of human knowledge from within.

We would realize several years later that the autonomy we were so anxious to maintain, fearing state interference that would ultimately lead to outside control, held a high price tag because it deprived us of valuable institutional technical and administrative support. It prevented us from gaining access to the information networks linking the existing academic units, thereby diminishing our visibility within the institution. I must say, though, that during this period the UQAM administration was very open to the feminist agenda. It was then a young university with a progressive philosophy, claiming openness to change. Several senior managers actually proposed to us on a number of occasions that we integrate into the existing academic structures, but we continued to be mistrustful. The only "concession" we made, in 1978, was to agree to make our group's name official and informally become part of UQAM's organizational structure; but it was a complex matter to formalize a grouping like GIERF, which was resolutely multidisciplinary while running a range of courses, none of them part of any particular program. For the academic world, the model was original, to say the least.

My First Course on the History of the Status of Women (1973)

In the history department, the idea of a new course on the status of women did not meet with any real opposition. Naturally, some colleagues thought the idea was absurd. They didn't understand its usefulness but didn't really oppose the project either. A passing whim on the part of overexcited feminist activists? This vision of things was certainly present, but it was never expressed out loud. My conversations in the hallway revealed to me that, actually, more of our colleagues believed that women's history did not really constitute a new field of knowledge because women had always been present in historiography. How could we claim that women were invisible, with all those saints, heroines, and famous queens dotting the pages of any good historical overview? Fortunately, those holding this position decided there was no point in formally opposing us. Other colleagues, a minority who could be described as leftist intellectuals, turned out to be valuable allies. Their cooperation was even more productive given that in 1973 the process of creating a new course was free of the bureaucratic red tape we know today.

In 1973, when I developed my first course on women's history, I was very fortunate to have the enthusiastic participation of a young colleague named Denise Julien. When I gave the course, I also benefitted from the collaboration of Marie Lavigne and Jennifer Stoddart, two young teaching assistants who were at once competent and very committed and who had both taken part in the big teach-in of 1972. This first course was called Histoire de la condition des femmes au Canada et au Québec, de la Nouvelle-France à nos jours. An overly ambitious goal, one that I had to bring down to more modest dimensions! As it turned out, this first course was an intellectual and educational adventure that was at once extraordinary and perilous; perilous, due to the absence of any constituted archival sources on women or historical summaries focussing on women. This "neglected majority," as it was called in 1973 by the historian Suzanne Cross, was the subject of a short study written in 1971 by the historian Micheline Dumont as a submission to the Bird Commission. Entitled "History of the Status of Women in the Province of Québec," this fifty-page portrait served as an important starting point, but it was clearly insufficient (see Dumont's essay in this volume). As for the archive hunt, the results were disappointing, so I had to find alternative solutions fast.

In hindsight, as far as methodology is concerned, the scarcity of historical sources had a positive impact because it forced me to resort to what turned out to be a salutary multidisciplinary approach. It was an opportunity to turn, not only to sociology and historical anthropology, but also to literature. I suddenly realized that in literary works, unlike official history, women were a strong presence. In many of these sources, I discovered a gold mine of information on women's living conditions, their education, and especially, their status and role in the family. These sources turned out to be very rich, in that they spoke not only of household work, but also of women's paid work outside the home, whether as school teachers or, later, as workers. With the appropriate analytical framework, certain novels—like *Trente arpents* (Ringuet 1938), *Le survenant* (Guèvremont 1945), and *Bonheur d'occasion* (Roy 1945)—turned out to be fantastic historical sources. I also learned to examine the writings of women themselves: personal diaries, memoirs and letters, and, especially in the early twentieth century, women's magazines, which gave women a forum of expression and represented a new voice in the public sphere.

In addition to a diversified approach to archival sources, my courses benefitted from the methodological and theoretical questions that marked this period of feminist reflection on women's history. Berenice Carroll's book *Liberating Women's History* (1976), in particular, was a key work in this regard. Appearing in 1976, it presented theories and raised issues that feminist historians were just beginning to discuss: the need to rethink the traditional periodization of history in order to adapt it to women's history; the necessity to examine not just the history of famous and intellectual women, who were capable of speaking for themselves, but to also focus on poor women, whose limited schooling had relegated them to silence; and last, the necessity to highlight the significance of women's history by constantly locating it within the broader context of history as a whole. Our first women's history courses greatly benefitted from all these questions that still constitute the richness and originality of a feminist teaching of history.

In this essay on my first experiences of feminist studies, I wanted to show how much this experience and the commitment it inspired are connected to the development of the feminist movement itself. The feminist revolution that took shape in the mid-sixties left its mark on all the women students, young people and adults, who took my courses. The enthusiasm of women students, their intense curiosity about anything connected with women's history—now their own history—and their new consciousness about the close link between knowledge and power, all this was happening within a social framework in which feminist scholarship went hand in hand with feminist action. It was indeed this particular juncture that made my first women's history courses one of the richest intellectual and personal experiences I had during those years.

Selected Publications by the Author

Fahmy-Eid, Nadia. 1991. Histoire, objectivité et scientificité: Jalons pour une reprise du débat épistémologique. *Histoire sociale/Social history* 24 (47): 9–34.

———, ed. 1997a. *Femmes, santé et professions: Histoire des diététistes et des physiothérapeutes au Québec et en Ontario (1930–1980)*. Montréal: Fides.

———. 1997b. L'histoire des femmes. Construction et déconstruction d'une mémoire sociale. *Sociologie et sociétés* 29 (2): 21–30.

Fahmy-Eid, Nadia, and Micheline Dumont. 1983. *Maîtresses de maison, maîtresses d'école. Le rapport femmes/famille/éducation au Québec*. Montréal: Boréal Express.

———. 1986. *Les couventines: L'éducation des filles au Québec dans les communautés religieuses enseignantes (1840–1960)*. Montréal: Boréal Express.

Women's Studies at the University of Alberta

Rosalind Sydie
Patricia Prestwich
Dallas Cullen

ALBERTA WOMEN HAVE often been in the forefront of feminist activity, despite, or perhaps because of, their province's politically conservative nature.[1] The most obvious example is the Famous Five of the Persons case. In 1928, five Alberta women—Henrietta Edwards, Nellie McClung, Louise McKinney, Emily Murphy, and Irene Parlby—appealed to the Supreme Court of Canada for clarification of the wording in the British North America Act. The act used the word "persons" when it referred to more than one person, and the word "he" when it referred to one person. As a result, many people argued that only a man could be a person, and women could not participate in government or politics. The five asked that the court rule that women would also be considered "persons." Their appeal was denied, so they took their case to the Privy Council of England, which was at that time Canada's highest court of appeal. On October 18, 1929, the Privy Council ruled that women were indeed "persons." The Famous Five of the Persons case are Canadian icons and, whilst they are the most well known, Alberta has many other examples of early feminist activity and activism.

The Legislative act that established the University of Alberta in 1906 stated "the Senate shall make provision for the education of women in the university ... [and] no woman shall by reason of her sex be deprived of any advantages or privileges accorded to male students of the university." In the first graduating class of medical students in 1925, there was one woman, Leone McGregor (Hallstedt), in a class of eleven. When the University of Alberta opened in September 1908, there were seven women graduates in the first class of forty-five students. These women graduates formed Club SIS (Seven Independent Spinsters). Since married women, even ones with degrees, were not supposed to work outside the home, only spinsters could be independent. The next year, the Wauneita Society was founded as a successor to Club SIS. All women students at the university automatically belonged to Wauneita (which is Cree for "kind-hearted"), and, in the 1950s and early 1960s, there was a women-only Wauneita Lounge in the Students' Union Building. The president of Wauneita was a member of the Students' Union Council, but, as women became more involved in campus affairs, interest in Wauneita declined, and it ceased to be an active organization in 1973.

By that time, however, second-wave feminists, both collectively and individually, had emerged at the University of Alberta in the form of an organization for academic women, a task force on the status of women at the university, and new courses on women. In the fall of 1973, Jean Lauber, a professor of zoology, and Naomi Hersom, a professor of education, went through the campus telephone directory for the names of women faculty members, and invited them to an informal dinner to discuss issues of interest to women academics. Approximately seventy-five women attended the dinner. These casual dinners continued until March of 1975, when the group decided to become a formal association, the Academic Women's Association. The impetus for this was the tabling of the report of the Senate Task Force on the Status of Academic Women.

In 1973 as well, the Edmonton Club of the Canadian Federation of University Women (at the request of Jean Lauber) had petitioned the senate of the University of Alberta to establish a task force to investigate the status of female staff members at the university. Members of the senate at the University of Alberta come from both the university and the public at large; the senate thus serves as a link between the university and the wider community. The senate's purpose is both investigative and advisory, in that it examines and advises on specific issues of long-term importance to the university. The goal of the task force was to determine whether there was discrimination against both academic and non-academic women on the campus. However, the complexity of the job classification system for non-academic staff led the task force to recommend that there be a separate study of the status of women in that group. The "Senate Task Force on the Status of Women: Report on Academic Women" (1975) comprised three parts: an attitude survey of male and female faculty members, a statistical analysis of the salary structure and career patterns of women academic employees, and a narrative account of the results of interviews with a number of staff members. The report also contained very specific recommendations directed to different university administrators (e.g., the president, the deans, and others). The informal women's dining group became the Academic Women's Association in order to lobby for the implementation of the task force's recommendations.

At the same time, a number of individual faculty members were developing women's studies courses. Rosalind Sydie was the first; as she explains, it was not easy.

Rosalind Sydie I developed a new course, Sex Roles (later renamed the Sociology of Gender), in 1970. I was pregnant with my first child and coping with the problems of organizing daycare. It was talking about this problem with others in the same situation that fired up my "sociological imagination," and the rest was history in the sense of my subsequent teaching and research. The course had a small enrolment of thirteen students in the first term and around twenty-five in the second term. In the following year, the enrolment exploded, with over two hundred students registered in each term. It was an exciting, but demanding, course to teach. Demanding, largely because of the lack of material and information to use in class; exciting because of the discoveries I made in my archival searches of past feminist writings and activities. Initially, I used a variety of materials ranging from novels to statistical information, such as information from Statistics Canada. Subsequently, of course, the text lacuna was remedied; indeed, feminist research bloomed rapidly and in ways that crossed disciplinary boundaries.

Developing the course was made somewhat more difficult in the first few years by the attitude of my colleagues (all male at that time), who regarded it as superficial, not really solid sociology. Countering the assumption that it was peripheral to the central preoccupations of "legitimate" sociology was complicated by the fact that I was a sessional instructor at the time and thus not a full-time faculty member able to defend the focus of the course (and incidentally my own research) in department forums. It was the popularity of the course, indicated by the constantly escalating enrolments, that provided some legitimacy in the department. I became an assistant professor in 1974, and the next appointment of a woman, Dr. Sharon Abu-Laban, was made in 1975. The rather "chilly climate" in the department was made less onerous by the interest of several graduate students in gender and feminist issues and by the expanding circle of feminist researchers in the university, as well as in various professional associations, who provided critical inspiration and support. For example, one of my PhD students, Maureen Baker, finished her thesis on "Women as a Minority Group in the Academic Profession" in 1975 (see Baker's essay in this volume). That year, I also acted as chair for a Social Sciences and Humanities Research Council conference on the economics of sex roles held at the University of Alberta. The other organizers were Ann Hall of the Faculty of Physical Education and Dallas Cullen.

Patricia Prestwich came to the University of Alberta after studying in the US during the 1960s anti–Vietnam War movement and pursuing her research in France after May 1968. Unlike Ros Sydie, she had a supportive department head.

Patricia Prestwich I established the first course on women's history at the University of Alberta in the academic year 1973–74, three years after being appointed to teach French and European history in the Department of History. I was unaware of any women's history courses taught in North America that I could use as a model, and I did not even know that Ros Sydie, who worked in the same building, had recently established a course on women in sociology. My course was a senior undergraduate seminar on women in European history, and the following year I established a lecture course in the same area. These courses have been taught on a regular basis since, and form part of a program in women's history offered by the department.

I began these courses because I was intellectually challenged by the claims of radical feminists who argued that women had always been oppressed victims of the patriarchy. As a trained historian, I suspected such sweeping and categorical assertions, but I did not know of any recent scholarship on the topic. (In my formal study of history, from my undergraduate courses to the PhD, I can recall only one mention of women's activism, a sniggering reference by a lecturer in an undergraduate course to what he considered to be the hysterical antics of British suffragettes.) In good academic fashion, I decided to teach a course in order to discover what had happened to women in the past.

I was fortunate to be in a department with a liberal attitude toward history and women. When I arrived in 1970, the Department of History had recently made an effort to hire women: I was the sixth woman appointed in a department of nearly thirty full-time staff; two women, Annelise Thimme and Helen Liebel-Weckowicz, were full professors. I thought I had died and gone to heaven! The department had for the past ten years been expanding its offerings in non-traditional areas, such as Asian, African, and African-American history. When, as an untenured assistant professor, I informed the chair that I wanted to start a course on women but that there was almost no recent scholarship available, he offered me a half-course teaching release to prepare this new area.

I approached these courses, not within a theoretical framework of oppression and victimization, but rather by looking at specific historical situations and trying to determine what barriers and what opportunities existed for specific groups of women. The courses met with enthusiastic student response, and I found increasing intellectual stimulation in the perspectives and theoretical tools that women's history offered me. Equally important, I soon found both firm support and a wider perspective through contact with women in other disciplines, particularly through the Academic Women's Association.

Dallas Cullen was the first woman appointed to a tenure-track position in the Faculty of Business. She had a supportive dean, Edward Chambers, who was aware of her previous feminist activism. While she was on a post-doctoral fellowship at Educational Testing Services, she and another post-doctoral fellow, Mimi Keiffer, had surveyed women in American university psychology departments in an attempt to document the discrimination they faced and develop recommendations for ways to improve their situation.

Dallas Cullen When the Wauneita Society disbanded in 1973, the then–dean of women, Isabel Munroe, was concerned that women would have fewer opportunities to develop leadership skills. She asked the deans of the faculties of Arts, Business, and Education if they would be willing to offer a course on women and leadership. Dean Chambers knew that I would want to teach such a course. He had earlier recommended me for membership on the senate task force, where I was responsible for the design and analysis of the attitude survey. I had spoken about the task force at Jean Lauber and Naomi Hersom's first dinner.

The course, Women in Administration (now Gender Issues in Organizations), was first taught in 1974–75, and has been offered continually since then. Finding relevant readings was difficult (as it was with all early feminist courses): the limited material that did exist had to be found without the benefit of electronic databases and search engines. Much of that original course focussed on male-female differences and similarities in various behaviours associated with management and leadership. There were eleven women and one man in the course; he took it because, he said, he knew that, once he was working, he would be supervising women, so he wanted to learn about them. He actually brought an interesting perspective to the class, since he often articulated or expressed (other?) men's responses to women's aspirations. We had some very intriguing discussions.

All The academic research and policy initiatives undertaken in those early years made for exhilarating times. At the University of Alberta by 1975–76, we had several women's studies courses and an active network of women faculty doing gender/feminist research. In 1975–76 the Academic Women's Association put on a non-credit "sampler" of women's studies courses that was exceptionally successful. Since that time, the vitality of both women's studies/feminist research and practical policy initiatives has increased in exciting and innovative ways at the University of Alberta. For example, the women's studies program cross-lists some sixty courses; the Academic Women's Association remains active; and a later development, Women in Scholarship, Engineering, Science and Technology, founded in 1982, under its vice-chair Margaret-Ann Armour, was (and still is), a leader in encouraging young women's participation in science and engineering.

Note

1 Our contributions to this essay are equal; our names are listed in the order in which our courses were created.

Selected Publications by the Authors

Dallas Cullen

Cullen, Dallas. 1994. Feminism, management and self-actualization. *Gender, Work and Organization* 1: 127–37.

———. 1997. Maslow, monkeys, and motivation theory. *Organization* 4:355–73.

Cullen, Dallas, and Lise Gotell. 2002. From orgasms to organizations: Maslow, women's sexuality and the gendered foundations of the needs hierarchy. *Gender, Work and Organization* 9: 537–55.

Hall, M. Ann, Dallas Cullen, and Trevor Slack. 1989. Organizational elites recreating themselves: The gender structure of National Sport Organizations. *Quest* 41: 28–45.

Nakamura, Masao, Alice Nakamura, and Dallas Cullen. 1979. Job opportunities, the offered wage and the labour supply of married women. *American Economic Review* 69 (5): 787–805.

Patricia Prestwich

Prestwich, Patricia E. 1993. Women and madness in a nineteenth-century Parisian asylum. In *ReImagining Women*, edited by S. Neuman and G. Stephenson. Toronto: University of Toronto Press.

———. 1994. Family strategies and medical power: "Voluntary" committal in a Parisian asylum, 1876–1914. *Journal of Social History* 27 (4): 797–816.

———. 1998. Germaine Poinso-Chapuis et les femmes du MRP. In *Germain Poinso-Chapuis, Femme d'Etat (1901–1981)*. Aix-en-Provence, France: Edisud.

———. 2002. Modernizing politics in the Fourth Republic: Women in the Movement Républican Populaire, 1944–58. In *Crisis and renewal in modern France, 1918–1962*, edited by K. Mouré and M. Alexander. New York: Berghahn Books.

———. 2003. Female alcoholism in Paris, 1870–1920: The response of psychiatrists and of families. *History of Psychiatry* 14 (3): 321–36.

Rosalind Sydie

Adams, Bert N., and Rosalind A. Sydie. 2001. *Sociological theory*. Thousand Oaks, CA: Pine Forge Press.

Sydie, Rosalind. 1987. *Natural women, cultured men*. Toronto: Methuen.

———. 1989. Humanism, patronage and the question of women's artistic genius. *Journal of Historical Sociology* 2 (3): 175–205.

———. 2003. Feminist challenges to sociological theory. In *Advances in sociological theory*, edited by N. Genov. Opladen: Leske and Budrich.

———. 2004. Sex and the sociological fathers. In *Engendering the social*, edited by B. Marshall and A. Witz. Maindenhead, UK: Open University Press.

Women's Studies and the Trajectory of Women in Academe

Annette Kolodny

GRADUATING FROM A United States college in 1962, I don't think I even realized how invisible women were in the education I had just received. Although Lorraine Hansberry's *A Raisin in the Sun* was the Broadway hit of 1959, the year I was a sophomore English major at Brooklyn College in New York, no women of colour were on any reading list. Only because one of my sisters tapped into a closeted lesbian grapevine and brought home a much-worn copy of Radclyffe Hall's 1928 novel *The Well of Loneliness* did I divine there might be anything like a tradition of lesbian literature. With precious few exceptions, for my generation, women were either altogether absent from the arts and public life, or they were the invisible helpmates of significant males.

Then, as the 1960s progressed, personal and political discontents exploded—and came together: the civil rights movement, the anti–Vietnam War movement, the United Farm Workers' movement, the American Indian Movement, the early gay and lesbian rights movement, the beginnings of the environmental movement, and the general questioning of unjust authority and inequitable treatment between and among different groups in the United States. What we then called the women's liberation movement was a part of it all; and many of us came to it through our prior involvement in one or more of the other great catalysts of the decade.

I earned my PhD in English and American literature at the University of California at Berkeley in the period that began with the Free Speech Movement of 1964 and terminated with the Vietnam Day Commencement of

May 1969.[1] With the idealism and boundless energy of the young, I participated in all of it, including my first feminist consciousness-raising group.
But for me and for many other women I knew, literature was also a vital
part of our political awakening and a vital marker on our path to self-aware-
ness. Whether we studied literary texts in graduate school or in small independent reading groups, we sought anything we could find written by women
in order to recover a sense of our past, our prior accomplishments, and our
shared sisterhood of struggle across lines of "race," religion, ethnicity, class,
region, and sexual preference. Those of us who studied literature in graduate programs were determined to rediscover our literary foremothers, even
when our male professors told us there weren't any. We were determined to
examine all the ways in which literature—by men and by women both—had
constructed and deconstructed femininity and gender roles. And we were
determined to find some space in academia to share our discoveries with our
students.

I did not immediately or easily find such a space. After I left Berkeley, my
first "real" job was as a member of the English department at Yale. I introduced women writers into my courses wherever possible, but Yale (newly
coeducational that year) had no courses into which one might fit the kind
of cross-disciplinary and thoroughgoing analyses of women's materials that
I had experienced in the consciousness-raising group in Berkeley.

Then, that fall, I fell passionately in love with one of my undergraduate
students, and we were married right after he graduated in June 1970. In the
spirit of the times, our wedding cake was topped by a peace symbol rather
than the conventional bride-and-groom figurines. The war in Vietnam, a
war we both opposed, was forcing us to flee the country. In the draft lottery
that began in the fall of 1969, my husband-to-be had drawn number twenty-
three, placing him near the top of the list for induction. He applied for Con-
scientious Objector status but, stubbornly honest, he refused to lie about
religious convictions he did not hold. We applied for positions in Canada (a
country from which United States draft resisters could not be extradited
because Canada had no draft law).[2] Happily, we received several offers. I
accepted an assistant professor position in the English department at the
University of British Columbia (UBC), and my husband accepted a graduate fellowship in the same department.

Vancouver was alive with feminist projects—projects organized around
poverty issues, domestic violence, and rape prevention. I was about to be
embraced by the best professional experience of my life: together with three

other dedicated and wonderful women faculty—Dorothy Smith, Meredith Kimball, and Helga Jacobson—I would help establish the first academically credited women's studies program in Canada.[3] Because I have elsewhere written at length about the difficult process of gaining academic approval for our innovatively interdisciplinary and cross-disciplinary program, I will here only note that when we did finally succeed in getting our courses into the schedule, the students who enrolled were nothing short of ecstatic (Kolodny 2000a).[4] One of the former students from my literature seminar, Leslee Silverman, remembers that "suddenly women's literature was no longer a thing apart but discussed in an inter-disciplinary context." For the first time in her educational experience, she had been "given the lenses of psychology and sociology to illuminate poetry and novels and, conversely, to begin to see how literature informed the other systems of describing reality." To her, "this was academic Nirvana."[5]

However exhilarating the program and however enthusiastic our students, it couldn't last (see the essays by Dorothy E. Smith and Meredith Kimball in this volume). By 1978, the original year-long, twelve-credit program that integrated a truly interdisciplinary lecture course with discipline-based seminars had virtually disappeared. There was simply no institutional support. No dean or vice-president at UBC was interested in taking either financial or administrative responsibility for women's studies, thus leaving the program vulnerable to the vagaries of departmental patronage. Those of us who had worked so hard to get women's studies established were paying too high a price in our home departments. Three of the four women's studies faculty members had to teach course overloads, in part because most of our departments refused to give either major or minor credit for women's studies, and we were thereby required to teach a full complement of courses for our home departments in addition to our women's studies responsibilities. Salary increases were minimal, relations with colleagues or department heads were strained, and promotions and tenure were too often denied.[6] By 1980, three of the four original faculty members were gone.

I left in the summer of 1974. The Vietnam War was winding down, and my husband had been reclassified into a status where he would not be drafted and was eager to return home. I was more ambivalent, having fully invested myself in the women's community in Vancouver, but I understood my husband's psychological need to be done with what he experienced as exile, so I accepted an advanced assistant professorship in the English department at the University of New Hampshire (UNH), assured by the chairperson who hired me that tenure would accompany the publication of my first book.

The Lay of the Land: Metaphor as Experience and History in American Life and Letters, which appeared in January 1975, was unapologetically feminist in its methodology, a fact that seemed to shock some of the senior men in the department (there were no senior women). By the time I came up for tenure review in late fall 1974, I was already involved in working with students and a few women faculty members to develop a women's studies program at UNH. Because I had published several important articles as well as the book, and because my teaching and service records at UNH had been evaluated as outstanding, I was wholly unprepared for a negative decision. But like my women's studies colleague at UBC, I, too, was denied promotion and tenure. The reason given was "collegiality," a term that did not even appear in the faculty handbook and that I came slowly to realize was code for any woman, especially a feminist, who makes the men uncomfortable. Five years of legal battles followed, as I sued UNH for sex discrimination and anti-Semitism, finally prevailing in a precedent-making out-of-court settlement in 1980.[7]

The experiences at UBC and UNH taught me precious lessons, however. I was now much more savvy about how to forge coalitions and galvanize constituencies—including students, faculty members, community leaders, and even sympathetic administrators—in order to initiate curricular change. I understood the need to reorganize institutional structures so that they could support, rather than thwart, inter- and cross-disciplinary teaching and scholarship. I had learned how to turn a feminist academic agenda into the institution's professed agenda of equality and excellence. In other words, I had learned how to align my language with the institution's language about itself. I also understood, as I had never fully understood before, just how vulnerable were the untenured women of my generation who risked their careers to make substantive institutional change.

All of these lessons played out in later years when I became dean of the College of Humanities at the University of Arizona. Again, because I devoted an entire book to detailing what a committed feminist can accomplish in higher education administration (Kolodny 1998), I won't repeat any of it here. Instead, I want to highlight a lingering bit of feminist naïveté and underscore its shortcomings. In a nutshell, those of us who worked to establish women's studies programs in the 1970s believed we were on a clear trajectory. We thought the introduction of women and women's materials in *our* programs would surely filter out across the campus and alter the shape of the curriculum in *all* the departments and disciplines. In this project, we have certainly enjoyed at least some success. Even if many of our non-feminist colleagues did not want to retool and embrace the new scholarship on women, their graduate students—and hence succeeding generations of faculty members—certainly did. As a result, most campuses are now home to a variety of new cross-disciplinary inquiries—from gender studies to cultural studies—that trace their roots to the explosion of new subject matters and experimental methodologies originally nurtured by women's studies programs. Women's studies itself has continued to develop and evolve as an exciting field of study.

But, as we started out in the 1970s, women's studies advocates knew that this was only part of what we aimed at. We believed that, along with our curricular innovations, we would also attract increasing numbers of women into graduate programs in all fields and disciplines, and in short order more and more women would attain PhD degrees and move into the professoriate. From there a new cohort of women scholars would transition into higher education administration and gradually change institutional structures so that the academic workplace, over time, could become a level playing field for women and men alike. The campus would also become a more hospitable workplace for women and for those with families.

Sadly, too little of this has yet happened. I know it can all be done; and I offer practical strategies for achieving these ends in *Failing the Future: A Dean Looks at Higher Education in the Twenty-first Century* (1998). But right now, that just isn't happening. The trajectory is stalled. In both the United States and Canada, women faculty *have* reached numerical parity with men in a few selected fields like English and education.[8] Still, the question remains: why haven't women reached parity with men in *all* fields and disciplines; and why is progress for women still so slow in academe?

The answer is multifaceted and complex, but we can easily identify at least a few problem areas that are significant in their impact:

1. Inadequate family-friendly policies and family-care support systems in academe have a more severe impact on women than on men.

2. Tenure timetables and promotion and tenure procedures at too many institutions remain predicated on an outdated model of a male faculty member without significant family responsibilities (and certainly no pregnancies).

3. The makeup and behaviour of hiring committees can prove an obstacle to the hiring of women. In some fields, all-male hiring committees still sometimes ask improper questions of female candidates during the interview process, usually personal questions never asked of male candidates. Female and male job candidates are also asked different *kinds* of questions. For example, a male candidate may be asked about his future

research or teaching plans while a female candidate is grilled on her basic knowledge of the field—somewhat like a second PhD oral—in order to "see if she knows her stuff."

4. In too many fields, the lack of senior *networked* female PhD advisors and dissertation directors puts women PhD candidates at a grave disadvantage when they apply for post-doctoral fellowships or for tenure-track positions. Male advisors are generally more aggressive in supporting their male students than they are in advancing the career opportunities of their female students.

5. Finally, because there are too few senior policy-making women administrators in academe, there is a real lack of political will to make the necessary structural changes required to ensure the success of women and minority faculty. Most especially, there are too few *feminist* administrators. Women are routinely assistant deans, but not deans; or they are associate provosts, but not provosts. We need feminist administrators who make policy (not just implement a supervisor's policies); and we need women controlling the budget, which is, after all, the true conscience of the university.

In closing, let me return to the themes that opened this essay. Much has changed for women students since I was an undergraduate. Women no longer find themselves invisible in the curricula of most fields and disciplines. Women's studies programs and feminist scholarship have transformed—and continue to transform—the shape and subject matter of intellectual inquiry across campus. Yet women faculty have not achieved the level of progress we might have expected by now. The few women who *do* become senior administrators are often too timid about seeing themselves as agents for change. Now that I have retired from the University of Arizona and contemplate different paths for engaging as an activist, it strikes me that there is one abiding lesson that I took from women's studies and from feminism in general. It is a lesson that keeps one alive and energized. The lesson is this: so much has been accomplished, yet so much still remains to be done.

Notes

I wish to express deep gratitude to my graduate student research assistants, Tom Hillard and Randi Lynn Tanglen, who helped with the research for this essay and prepared the final draft for publication. I could not have met the deadlines without them.

1 The Free Speech Movement began when, bowing to conservative political pressures, the university administration attempted to curb student rights to disseminate

information about political issues and political candidates along the sidewalk area in front of the campus at Bancroft Way and Telegraph Avenue. The Vietnam Day Commencement honoured the soldiers killed in Vietnam who would never experience their own commencement exercises; it was an occasion for many political, entertainment, and educational leaders to speak out against the war in a large, solemn open forum.

2   My husband, the novelist Daniel Peters, offered a fictionalized version of this episode in our lives in his first novel, *Border Crossings* (1978).

3   In the early 1970s, many Canadian universities had credited courses on women's studies topics located within traditional departments. To the best of my knowledge, UBC's was the first attempt at an integrated program of courses credited *as* women's studies. We designed linkages between courses, and we required students to enrol for twelve credits.

4   A shorter version appears in *The Politics of Women's Studies: Testimony from Thirty Founding Mothers*, ed. Florence Howe (Kolodny 2000b).

5   I am deeply grateful to former colleagues and students who, with enormous generosity, shared reminiscences.

6   One faculty member was denied promotion and tenure in the Department of Psychology at UBC. Another tenured faculty member was repeatedly denied promotion from associate to full professor in a different department.

7   I have written about the entire experience of being denied promotion and tenure, taking on a five-year legal battle, and the financial and emotional cost of it all in Kolodny (1989).

8   The 2006 Canadian Association of University Teachers *CAUT Almanac* reports that women dominated the field of education, representing 68.6% of doctorates awarded in 2004. In the humanities/social sciences, women were near parity with men, receiving 48.8% of doctorates in 2004. In business administration and public administration, women remained slightly below parity, representing 44% of doctorates awarded. In the sciences, women represented 38.4% of all doctorates granted and just 28.3% of doctorates awarded in the physical sciences. However, at 60%, women's presence exceeded men's presence in the scientific subfield of multi/interdisciplinary studies. Compared to other fields in the sciences, women were also a significant presence in the biological and biomedical sciences, representing 43.1% of doctorates granted. In mathematics, and computer and information sciences, women were awarded just 25.3% of doctorates in 2004. Women's participation was also low in the field of engineering, where women were awarded 16% of doctorates in 2004.

Selected Publications by the Author

Kolodny, Annette. 1975. *The lay of the land: Metaphor as experience and history in American life and letters*. Chapel Hill: University of North Carolina Press.

———. 1989. I dreamt again that I was drowning. In *Women's writing in exile*, edited by M. L. Broe and A. Ingram. Chapel Hill: University of North Carolina Press.

———. 1998. *Failing the future: A dean looks at higher education in the twenty-first century*. Durham, NC: Duke University Press.

———. 2000a. "A sense of discovery, mixed with a sense of justice": Creating the first women's studies program in Canada. *NWSA Journal* 12 (1): 143–64.

———. 2000b. "A sense of discovery, mixed with a sense of justice": Creating the first women's studies program in Canada. In *The politics of women's studies: Testimony from thirty founding mothers*, edited by F. Howe. New York: Feminist Press.

Women's Studies at Simon Fraser University, 1966–76: A Dialogue

Andrea Lebowitz
Honoree Newcombe
Meredith M. Kimball

THIS DIALOGUE CAME out of an evening of reminiscence about the founding of women's studies at Simon Fraser University (SFU). Andrea Lebowitz and Honoree Newcombe were members of the committee that worked to establish women's studies at SFU. Meredith Kimball was the first tenure-track appointment in women's studies. In the following dialogue, speakers are indicated by their first names.

Meredith How did women's studies come about at SFU?

Andrea Our commitment to creating women's studies came from our backgrounds in various anti-war and civil liberties actions. Some, like me, had worked for various anti-racist and women's organizations. Some came from political groups on the left. In the late sixties, the Women's Caucus emerged as an independent group out of the left-wing political movements at SFU. The caucus organized into four workshops: Working Women, Education, Reproductive Rights, and Media. The caucus also published *The Pedestal*, a local women's paper. Maggie (Margaret) Benston and I were active in the Education Workshop, or as we called it, the "ed wing." Fired by our sense of injustice, the need for women to have control over their own bodies and history, the idea that simple justice demanded that women be equally present and studied in the university, and that this was an important arena for furthering the goals of feminism, we began the process that, by 1972, led to the formation of a committee to design a women's studies program.

Honoree When I came to SFU as a student in 1970, the caucus had already begun to split into many different political projects. I was aware of the caucus, but didn't see myself as particularly a feminist. Then in the spring of 1971 I went to Maggie Benston's non-credit workshop on women's issues, held at a Burnaby community centre and library. That was the "click!" moment for me. I quite suddenly became passionately interested in women's issues, especially women's work. I immediately began doing some work on *The Pedestal*, which then had become quite separate from the caucus, and a short time later, along with several of the women who attended that workshop, became involved with the drive that ended with the founding of the Association of University Clerical Employees at SFU and the University of British Columbia (UBC), another outcome of the Women's Caucus.[1]

Andrea We were also able to try out various credit versions of women's studies courses in existing SFU courses that gave us room. We were fortunate to have several male colleagues who shared our ideas and who were willing to offer courses jointly with us. One of these, the Geography of Gender, certainly raised a few hackles and a few guffaws, but it was a very successful seminar and generated more student interest and pressure. Bob Horsfall invited Maggie and me into the course, and the three of us jointly directed it. Students from many departments were admitted.

Honoree Remember the Canadian studies course, the one that in a later incarnation became the women's studies course, Women in Canada, 1920 to the Present? Andrea taught the course, and Cindy Kilgore, a student member of the organizing committee, was the teaching assistant. There were ninety students in the course, more than any other Canadian studies course had enrolled, and we used this as more evidence of student interest in a full credit program in women's studies.

Andrea The Canadian studies course was amazing. The enthusiasm among the students was great. There was also a demand for courses on women in other areas. In English (my department), we tried to respond to the interest by using existing courses for the introduction of women writers who had never been taught before. For example, Evan Alderson and I used a Nineteenth-century American Literature course where we read Alcott, Chopin, and other women writers. Needless to say, there were a few howls from our colleagues, but students voted with their feet and the course filled.

It was the first time that I taught Chopin's 1899 story *The Awakening* (Chopin 1976).

Meredith Certainly you demonstrated lots of student interest. Were students also part of developing the credit women's studies program?

Honoree Very much so. It really was the students who started the bureaucratic ball rolling. As I remember a group of students, including Kate Braid, went to Bob Brown, dean of the Faculty of Interdisciplinary Studies (FIDS), asking for a real women's studies program. He sent them to talk with Andrea and Maggie about setting up a committee to develop a program. There were many students, both undergraduate and graduate, on the committee that developed the Women's Studies Program.

Meredith So how was this committee formed?

Andrea Basically it was anyone who was interested and wanted to join. Usually twenty or more people came to the meetings. There were faculty, staff, and students who contributed to the discussion. When the final proposal was written, political considerations led to a choice of people representative of the groups involved.[2] An interesting part of this committee was that there were only three faculty members, and Maggie and I were the active faculty contributors. Not surprisingly, we two got to carry the case to the larger community.

Meredith What were the models you considered for the program?

Andrea Three models were considered—a series of non-credit courses like the ones that had already been given at places like the local library, credit courses added to existing departments and programs, or a stand-alone program. We were convinced right from the get-go that if we didn't have a room of our own, a program with an organized set of courses, the power to appoint faculty into the program, and control over it, we would not be intellectually coherent. We would also be political sitting ducks when a department decided to drop a course, or a faculty member teaching a course left the university, or when times got tough. We also thought that as a program we should confer a degree, since credentials are coin of the realm in universities. I have to say that our analysis was right on. When the economic downturn of the late 1970s began, many women's studies non-credit programs fell by the wayside and single courses were cut. But we had put together a minor program that conformed to the general university norms for minor degrees and it weathered the financial storms. It was also our great good fortune to have the FIDS in existence at SFU. Since our program was interdisciplinary, there was a faculty to house the program. Many interdisciplinary women's studies programs had no institutional place to call home. But the interdisciplinary battle had already been won at SFU.

Meredith The difference FIDS made is clear, comparing your experiences to mine at UBC during the same time period. Although we fantasized about a whole program, we knew that it was politically impossible through the Faculty of Arts at that time. So the only thing we really considered was one interdisciplinary course plus four seminars, which were housed within existing departments.

Andrea It's amazing to remember that interdisciplinary study was looked on with such suspicion in the 1970s—especially today when interdisciplinary teams are sought after.

Honoree I remember that Maggie was determined that we build in safeguards so that women's studies did not become just another academic program, but remained true to and reflected the feminist politics that were its foundations. Having our own program with our own faculty was one of those safeguards.

Andrea Yes, and our separate existence, as well as the use of joint appointments between women's studies and another department in the early years of the program, encouraged and supported the development of courses about women and gender in other departments. So we did have an influence on changing departmental course offerings, although for many years we did not designate courses in other departments towards a women's studies minor, and to this day women's studies limits the number of designated credits that may be counted towards women's studies degrees. We have always felt that it is necessary to maintain a clear and shared core of courses in women's studies. Our first move towards a major in the early 1990s was to develop several joint majors with other departments, but the essence of a joint major at SFU is that each department maintains its own basic core. Hence, once again, SFU's institutional structures fostered cooperation, but women's studies had also demonstrated its strength both in women's studies courses and in courses developed in other departments.

Meredith Moving on, once you had the proposal, what was the process of implementing it?

Andrea It took two years and meetings with eleven committees before we were launched. As the two faculty members involved in the proposal, Maggie Benston and I went to all the meetings as representatives of the committee. We met with departments, faculties, subcommittees of senate, and finally the full senate on July 7, 1975. It was dark and stormy. Outside, one of Vancouver's rare thunderstorms was in full swing. Inside the Senate, sound and fury prevailed. Arguing for the program were Maggie Benston and myself—both very junior faculty members. We were fielding the usual questions about discrimination toward men (poor helpless things) when we were stopped by an interesting Catch-22. One senator opined that we had no research to back us up. This was largely true. We had done surveys of student interest and reviewed other programs across the continent, but in the early 1970s there wasn't much research. This was exactly one of our points. We needed to create a program that would be committed to fostering just such inquiry. The other marvellous comment came from a rumbling voice that suggested that giving us a program was tantamount to allowing the prisoners to create a prison education program. We maintained our decorum for that one.

Honoree But in spite of all the ruckus, it did, of course, pass.

Andrea Yes, and in terms of the vote it passed easily. Pauline Jewett, herself a feminist, had just been appointed president, and she made it very clear that she supported the creation of a program. Her position and the existence of FIDS were probably the two most significant institutional supports we had. That plus our own brilliance and hard work won the day! The next January (1976), Anita Fellman gave our first course, Introduction to Women's Studies.

Meredith In addition to the importance of FIDS and Pauline Jewett, were there other allies who were important to establishing women's studies?

Honoree Bob Brown, who was dean of FIDS, was a strong supporter from the beginning, as were several other faculty, such as Bob Horsfall in geography and Evan Alderson in English, who opened their classes to teaching early versions of women's studies courses. And it's very important to remember the support that students provided through their interest, their work on the planning committee, and their political support for a program.

Meredith And staff like you and Sara David. It is interesting to me how many people from all areas of the university were involved in the development of the program, which contrasts with my experience at UBC. Although there was much student support, which was important to getting the program implemented, the proposal was developed and written by myself and the other three faculty members who first taught in the program. Turning to a related issue, what theoretical frameworks did you use, both to envision the program and to teach courses like the Geography of Gender and the Canadian studies course Women in Canada in the Twentieth Century?

Andrea Maggie and I definitely looked to left-wing theoreticians for frameworks, but we both felt that while we agreed about their class analysis, we thought that their analysis of "the women's question" was out to lunch. Maggie published her very famous essay, "The Political Economy of Women's Liberation" (Benston 1969). When you asked about which theorists we relied upon, my answer would have to be—ourselves. Maggie was one of the clearest in her analysis. Even now, many years after her death, I miss her cogency and breadth of knowledge. We certainly challenged the monolithic scholarship that denied any diversity or difference and claimed to speak for "Humanity," but primarily we looked to ourselves and other young women for inspiration and ideas.

Honoree We also published and reprinted some of our work and used those as readings in the early courses.

Andrea Yes, we would reprint articles from The Pedestal and other sources and use these in workshops and classes. We also did some of our own publishing through the Corrective Collective.[3] *She Named It Canada: Because That's What It Was Called* (Corrective Collective 1971) was published when the Women's Caucus organized the Vancouver stop on the Vietnamese women's tour of Canada. Since that was during the Vietnam War, the Vietnamese women could not enter the US, so women's and peace groups in the US and Canada invited them to Canada, and women from the US travelled here for the meetings. The Corrective Collective wrote *She Named It Canada* in order to correct and inform many of the American women who had very little knowledge of Canada, including how it was different from the US. *Never Done: Three Centuries of Women's Work in Canada*, a follow-up work by the Corrective Collective (1974), was used in early women's studies courses at SFU.

Honoree Another form of theory was the caucus's use of humour in the agitprop theatre project.

Andrea Yes, I remember "Miss Cherry's Charm School," which was a hoot. In 1969–70, Miss Cherry appeared in several SFU classes where instructors were welcoming. Dressed in a slinky outfit with many feather boas, Miss Cherry led in her troops to the chant: "We must, we must develop our minds." A good deal of fun was had by all.

Meredith Were there any works in early feminist literary criticism that you found important to your thinking?

Andrea Of course there were *A Room of One's Own* (Woolf 1929) and *The Second Sex* (de Beauvoir 1953), but the works of literary criticism that first stopped me in my tracks were *Of Woman Born* (Rich 1976), *Literary Women* (Moers 1976), and *The Madwoman in the Attic* (Gilbert and Gubar 1979). I was very impressed that these authors did not analyze literature and authors as objects, but rather engaged in a conversation with the text and the author. This was so opposite to the New Criticism, which still held pride of place in English studies.

Meredith What would you say has been the main contribution of feminism to scholarship?

Andrea Feminism opened up the university to diversity. Women were the first "other" in the door.

Meredith How was diversity among women understood in the early development of women's studies at SFU?

Andrea We certainly did know that middle-class women were not the standard for all women. While we all undoubtedly became more attuned to questions of diversity, we knew it from the start. Wendy Eliot-Hurst, who had an anthropological background, convinced us that including the course

Women in Cross-Cultural Perspectives was necessary, and this was one of the first courses we offered. When the Corrective Collective began work on *She Named It Canada* (1971), we talked with several local Native women activists in Vancouver and invited them to contribute to this project. They couldn't do this as they were already too committed and busy with their own projects. When we asked them what we as non-Native women should do, they told us not to presume to talk about them, but to write what we knew. Therefore, on the title page of *She Named It Canada*, we included a statement acknowledging this situation.[4] Likewise, in *Never Done* we included a statement, along with our acknowledgements stating our awareness that both Asian and Native women's stories were important, but that we could not presume to speak for them.[5]

Meredith Can you briefly describe the development of women's studies at SFU since 1976?

Andrea We began with a minor program. In the mid-1980s, we introduced an MA program in women's studies. At the time, we decided to move to a graduate program rather than an undergraduate major because of limited resources—we simply could not offer enough courses with the existing faculty to create an undergraduate major. The other main development of the 1980s was the establishment of the Ruth Wynn Woodward Professorship.[6] In the 1990s, in preparation for the introduction of a major, we established a number of joint majors, the first two being with English and psychology. In 1994, the major was established. In recognition of the strength of the program, in 1991 senate approved a change in status from program to department for women's studies. Although this change did not result in immediate practical changes in the functioning of the department, it was symbolically significant. Since 2000, both a PhD program and a minor in gender studies have been implemented. Over the years, both students and faculty have produced an impressive body of scholarship.

Honoree The strength of women's studies has been evident in the university from the start. Not long after the program got up and running, in the early 1980s, there was a series of cutbacks; in fact, that was when we lost FIDS. I was on the board of governors at the time and remember very clearly that, during the long and acrimonious debates around which programs should be cut, women's studies was never really mentioned.

Andrea I should also add that women's studies faculty and students have been very good university citizens. Faculty members have filled many administrative posts in addition to their achievements in teaching and research, while students have excelled in professional and academic careers. In other words, we earned it.

Meredith What effect did all this have on both of you?

Honoree My interest in feminism, and subsequently women's studies, altered the whole course of my life. Women's studies gave me a methodology for analyzing what happens in the world around me. Many of my friends are people that I connected with through women's studies—faculty in the program, students, and people in related organizations. Women's studies has given me a very personal stake in SFU where I work—I have really cared about the program, its courses, and students. In the workplace, I hope and believe it has helped me to be more responsive to the problems women staff have in balancing homes, families, and professional obligations.

Andrea Well, I am now retired from the university, but I had a wonderful career. I was the first chair of women's studies and went on to do a great deal of administrative work, as well as work within women's studies. My first department was English, but when I retired thirty-six years later, I had switched to the women's studies department. Originally the appointments in women's studies were joint with an existing department. The idea was that in case our department went belly up, there would be a place for the orphaned faculty. Of course this never happened and, eventually, in addition to the jointly appointed faculty, there were full-time appointments in women's studies. The mix of joint and full-time appointments works very well. Also several faculty who were in other departments, like Maggie and myself, or faculty jointly appointed, moved full time into women's studies.[7] And the consequences for me? Quite simply, women's studies changed my life—professionally and personally.

Notes

1   Jill Stainsby, Honoree Newcombe, Jacqui Parker-Snedler, and Paul Reniers (1993).

2   The names on the proposal included faculty (Maggie Benston, Jamilla Ismail, Andrea Lebowitz); staff (Sara David, Honorée Newcombe); and students (Wendy Eliot-Hurst, Dana Janssen, Cindy Kilgore, Bertie Rush, and Marilyn Webb).

3 Members of the Corrective Collective included Karen Cameron, Pat (Hoffer) Davitt, Colette French, Marge Holligaugh, Andrea Lebowitz, Barbara Todd, Cathy Walker, and Dodie Weppler. Different subgroups worked on specific publications.

4 This statement reads: "The history of the native people was omitted at their request. This omission in no way suggests that we are unaware of the crucial importance of their history on this continent" (Corrective Collective 1971).

5 This statement reads: "This history confines itself to a study of European women in Canada. The absence of Oriental and Native women from these pages does not imply their lack of importance but rather our lack of knowledge" (Corrective Collective 1974).

6 In 1985, SFU received one of the five $500,000 grants from the Women's Program, Secretary of State, to establish an endowed chair in women's studies. By 1987, through the generosity of Ruth Wynn Woodward's daughters (Mary Twigg White and S. Elizabeth Russ) and other donors, the Ruth Wynn Woodward Professorship became the first fully funded endowed chair at SFU.

7 Sue Wendell, who was originally jointly appointed with philosophy, and Mary Lynn Stewart, who was originally jointly appointed with history, also moved over full time into women's studies.

Selected Publications by the Authors

Meredith M. Kimball

Kimball, Meredith M. 1986. Developing a feminist psychology of women: Past and future accomplishments. *Canadian Psychology* 27 (3): 248–59.

———. 1995. *Feminist visions of gender similarities and differences*. Binghamton, NY: Haworth Press.

———. 2001. Gender similarities and differences as feminist contradictions. In *Handbook on the psychology of women and gender*, edited by R. Unger. New York: Wiley.

———. 2003. Feminists rethink gender. In *About psychology: Essays at the crossroads of history, theory, and philosophy*, edited by D. B. Hill and M. J. Krall. Albany, NY: SUNY Press.

Andrea Lebowitz

Lebowitz, Andrea. 1991. *Star gazing: Charting feminist literary criticism*. Ottawa: Canadian Research Institute for the Advancement of Women.

———. 1996. *Living in harmony: Nature writing by women in Canada*. Victoria: Orca Book Publishers.

Lebowitz, Andrea, Gillian Milton, and Gilean Douglas. 1999. *Gilean Douglas: Writing nature, finding home*. Victoria: Sono Nis Press.

Honoree Newcombe

Stainsby, Jill, Honoree Newcombe, Jacqui Parker-Snedler, and Paul Reniers. 1993. *AUCE and TSSU: Memoirs of a feminist union, 1972–1993*. Burnaby, BC: Teaching Support Staff Union Publisher.

Nascent, Incipient, Embryonic, and Ceremonial Women's Studies

Linda Christiansen-Ruffman

Introduction

IN 1964, WHEN I started graduate school, becoming a feminist professor was not yet imaginable. Not even one woman taught in the graduate faculty of sociology at Columbia University when I was in residence (1964–67), and I then knew of no women's studies books, articles, courses, or women's movement. I was dumbfounded when a student recently told me that I had taught her women's studies in 1968. It challenged my reflective, contextualized understandings of women's studies development (Christiansen-Ruffman 1998).[1] I now theorize my early women's studies experiences within four overlapping stages of developing individual and collective action and consciousness: nascent (before 1966), incipient (1965–73), embryonic (1972–76), and ceremonial (International Women's Year, 1975).[2]

Nascent Women's Studies

As a student, I was generally not conscious of the fact that both inside and outside the academy, women were absent, invisible, undervalued, and/or oppressed. The full force of society's discrimination against women personally hit me in 1964 when I tried to find a job with my new Honours BA. My qualifications were treated as irrelevant. Potential employers asked if I could type (to become a secretary). I was furious at a woman personnel officer whom I overheard saying that I could be hired at a bargain (two-thirds the advertised pay and with better qualifications than any man). I remembered her actions as discriminatory in contrast to fond memories of the man who hired me. My misogyny, then, did not let me see her as negotiating a break for me, although my experiences during the hiring process did lead me to opt instead for graduate school.

At Columbia University, courses rarely mentioned women. I remember four exceptions: the presence of women's committees of political parties during African independence; a field methods project initiated by two of us on dance-hall girls; the methodological importance of including "sex differences" along with other structural variables in all research; and examples of what is now called "gender" in discussions of different role theories. I gradually understood problems with the role examples, but it took much longer to understand deeper "patricentric" biases in sociological theories (Christiansen-Ruffman 1989), including the depictions of men as actors and women as servants to men.

From Nascent to Incipient Women's Studies

Usually, I participated as a graduate student as if my gender did not matter. Occasionally, however, my guise as honorary man was interrupted when deep structures of patriarchy treated me in sexist ways. In 1965–66, for example, I was initially rejected as a Columbia Fellow because females were not considered to be serious scholars. I successfully appealed using the incipiently feminist argument that, as a woman, I would have more intellectual freedom and could do more innovative academic work because I would be less constrained by careerist norms than men. The insight was later connected to another "aha" moment (1966–67) when as students we could not name one woman sociologist who was not "sponsored" by a famous male sociologist as his wife or mistress.

At Columbia University, I was distressed by social relationships among faculty: the climate of disrespect, games of arrogance, and dysfunctional, individualistic, publish-or-perish academic norms that undermined ideals of good scholarship and collaborative community. I consciously tried to create a better intellectual climate around me when I moved to Halifax in the fall of 1967. I arrived in Nova Scotia, newly married (with equalitarian wedding vows we wrote). I expected to be treated equally, an increasingly challenging expectation.

Initially, at Columbia University, I had adopted what I now see as patriarchal standards: I enjoyed abstract theory (the more abstract, the better) and belittled practical work. Over time, I began to develop alternative ideas and analyses that, by the 1980s, I would call feminist. I had to rethink my academic approach when I taught outside sociology at the Maritime School of Social Work (see Helen Levine's essay in this volume), which became Dalhousie's in 1969.[3] I challenged myself and my students to develop "appropriate methodologies" for research to counter racism and the silences of the poor, and to promote real social change. In my first courses, a focus on equality issues associated with racialization, class, and nationality had equal billing with sex or gender; movements for peace, civil rights, students, anti-poverty, and international independence all had "currency" then.

Through both research and teaching, I also learned that I could not apply the sociology created in the United States to the world around me. I began research for, about, and with the community, using "bottom up" approaches to "politics." During research on local planning and political change processes and groups, such as MOVEment for Citizens Voice and Action, my research approach shifted from "research on" to "research for and with" participants. I helped create ecology and reproductive rights groups, and established a street-front family planning office in the "north end," the poorest part of the city with a large Black population. Two of us hired and trained outreach workers from that community, as well as an executive director and staff, and used what might now be considered action research in a variety of ways.

I had not considered my Columbia University dissertation, "Newcomer Careers: An Exploratory Study of Migrants in Halifax" (1976), to be related to women's studies. I was not consciously writing it as a woman. Literally, it was not written mainly *about* women, *for* women, or *with* women. Nevertheless, I now see signs of incipient women's studies in its approach. Its critiques of "patricentrism," its grounded theorizing, its implicit women's standpoint, its holistic analysis, and its qualitative, multifaceted methodologies would be categorized as feminist in the decades after its submission.

Students in my first full courses—taught under the titles Introductory Sociology (as a part-time lecturer at Mount Saint Vincent, 1968) and Sociology of Kinship and Family (as a full-time assistant professor at Saint Mary's, 1970)—now tell me that I taught them women's studies. Until recently, I thought my first women's studies course content was Marylee Stephenson's *Women in Canada*, which I introduced upon its 1973 publication into Modern Sociology. Now I imagine that the sociology of the family students were reacting to the course design, which was based on socially constructed age and "sex" (now called gender) roles within various family forms around the world. It is harder to explain why my introductory sociology students thought that their course was women's studies. It might have been that I was speaking as a woman, "first" naming women's realities as different, using examples from my life, and analysing gendered structures.

From Incipient to Embryonic Women's Studies

The transition between incipient and embryonic women's studies began when the growing women's movement focussed its change strategies on the academy. When I arrived at Saint Mary's University in 1970, I was hired in a tenure-track position as a sociologist but at a lower rank and at $2,000 less or only 80% of the salary of my male counterpart. When I discovered these differences, I sought equality. University administrators could not name any criterion on which he excelled. They changed the rank but not the salary, which was corrected, presumably, upon unionization. At the time, it was easier to see employment discrimination than to see patriarchy in scholarship.

In sociology in Atlantic Canada, the urban American bias was more apparent than the patriarchal bias. Theories did not fit, and I could not even translate my local research on citizen participation into interesting sociological questions. With Pat (Loiselle) Connelly, I eventually wrote a paper on "who participates" as a citizen in public meetings. It was boring. We could not come up with questions to create the sociology I longed to do. The several competing paradigms from graduate school did not help directly but held out hope for alternatives. I embraced local, Canadian, and international sociology. I was the first elected vice-president of the Atlantic Association of Sociologists and Anthropologists in 1975 and president in 1976.

Embryonic Women's Studies

As I began to see the world through women's eyes, I sought out other women with whom to press for collective change. The patriarchal games of "being good" did not work, and we needed the power of working together to change discriminatory structures. We began to talk and to act. I organized women's caucuses at Atlantic sociology/anthropology meetings and at Saint Mary's, as we were doing in the community. The faculty association appointed me as corresponding member to the Canadian Association of University Teachers' Committee on the Status of Women.

Meanwhile, in 1970, the International Sociological Association agreed to establish Research Committee 32 on Sex Roles (later Women in Society), which held its first meeting in 1974. Pat Connelly and I presented a paper, adapting C. W. Mills's (1959) dichotomy of private troubles and public issues to focus on women (Connelly and Christiansen-Ruffman 1977).[4] We did not use the comparative framework of sex roles because it reproduced and legitimized sexism. *Women,* especially "autonomous women," had more ana-lytic and political power, as the women's movement taught us at the same time that it helped to create "woman" and "women" as powerful. I could begin to glimpse the exciting possibilities of research by, for, about, and with women as a challenge to what we later called patriarchal knowledge.[5]

I was one of three Halifax sociologists (with Susan Clark from Mount Saint Vincent University and Lynn McDonald from Dalhousie University) who planned a major Canadian research/book project designed to make visible the many invisible women in history and in contemporary times. After lengthy planning, Canada Council (the Canadian research funding agency then responsible for social sciences and humanities research) turned down our major funding proposal. The officer claimed that no research on women existed on which to base the books. We disagreed, and to harness our momentum and the limited funding possibility suggested in our meeting with the council, Susan and I planned a Canada-wide conference.

The 1976 conference, Research on Women: Current Projects and Future Directions, grew exponentially. We first expected only thirty Canadian women, whom we had located for the book project. We were overwhelmed by the enthusiastic response to a call for papers, sent in the summer of 1976. We expanded the conference and secured funding from Canada Council, the Department of Employment and Immigration, and the Secretary of State. The conference included academic and community-based researchers from across Canada, and one day of the conference was designed to be acces-sible to community women. Excitement and energy abounded. The confer-ence clearly demonstrated the power and potential of even the existing research by, for, about, and with women. I edited a selection of the confer-ence's articles for *Atlantis* (Christiansen-Ruffman 1977). This conference "coupled" with the Ottawa initiative to become the Canadian Research Insti-tute for the Advancement of Women (CRIAW/ICREF). CRIAW's many produc-tive years of annual conferences helped to establish women's studies/recherche féministe in Canada.[6]

Ceremonial Women's Studies

Canada celebrated International Women's Year in 1975 with a public "Why Not?" campaign and new social space and resources for women. In 1975,

Saint Mary's University introduced its first titled women's studies courses. They were in anthropology and psychology, not in sociology or English, the two departments with the most active feminist faculty.[7] As women, we came together to conduct participatory action research, to present briefs to organizations such as the Nova Scotia Task Force on the Status of Women, and to found groups and coalitions along the way. The ceremonial International Women's Year helped us to attract new members, added legitimacy to our advocacy work, and spurred us to speak out. For example, when we heard that Canada Council would be meeting in Halifax (the chair's home city), we demanded a hearing. I represented the Saint Mary's Women's Caucus, and we spoke out on issues of discrimination against women in Canadian research.

To celebrate International Women's Year, Canada's Ministry of State for Urban Affairs sponsored research on women, and my Saint Mary's University research team won the contract.[8] Our "multifaceted methodology" was designed by, for, about, and with women, and we took the innovative approach of holding a public meeting to discuss draft findings in order to ensure community feedback. Urban Affairs liked our research, but it was not only the ceremonial 1975 that was short-lived: the ministry itself was dissolved in 1976.

Conclusion

With the end of International Women's Year, committees and caucuses, which had been established to advance the status of women, were dismantled by Canadian professional organizations. I remember being appalled to hear women members saying that a focus on women was divisive or that women's issues should be mainstreamed. I knew that women needed those committees and "more" rather than "less" to make real change in society. As I reflected on this dismantling of women's spaces, I decided to focus energy on developing women's studies and women's organizations. I understood that this would not be "popular" or easy but saw no alternative. I had learned that I could not escape being seen as a woman, even as a professional. My only hope was to work with other women for change. Only after I identified fully as a woman and worked specifically with women did I become conscious of the many layers of patriarchy in research, theory, knowledge, and society. Only then could I even imagine a world and a scholarship free from outmoded patriarchal assumptions, an alternative, caring world of life possibilities.

This essay began by describing my students' and my own different perceptions about when I began to teach women's studies. I now agree with my students that I was teaching with foundational assumptions of women's studies in my first courses. At the time, however, I was not conscious of doing so, and I doubt that students, then, would have said "women's studies." The new field needed some years to become part of societal consciousness, with institutional supports, a body of knowledge, and a recognized name. Recently, after another round of neo-patriarchal incursions in Canada, women's studies lost the clarity of its foundational assumptions. Fortunately, women's movements are again leading the way, both analytically and politically (see, for example, Antrobus 2004; Ricciutelli, Miles, and McFadden 2004; Vaughan 2007).

Notes

1   In my 1998 book, which introduces a feminist perspective into a series of regional books designed by the International Sociological Association, my essay, entitled "Developing Feminist Sociological Knowledge: Processes of Discovery," locates the development of women's studies in Canada at a later date than this present book.
2   My analysis and examination of early stages of individual and public "consciousness" is not psychological but social, implying different levels and meanings of awareness, analysis, action, and relationship.
3   In 1968–70, I held two of my four irregular teaching positions there.
4   After the International Sociological Association conference in Toronto, I received a letter asking me to submit my paper for review to the new *Canadian Journal of Sociology*. Since the letter was only addressed to me, I was pretty sure that they wanted the paper I had presented on part of my thesis. I remember making a decision to consult with Pat and proposed we submit the paper on women instead. In shortening it for publication, the editors removed the long quotations from women, which were not (yet) considered to be appropriate. It was published in volume 2, no. 2 with the title, "Women's Problems: Private Troubles or Public Issues?"
5   In fact, use of the word "woman" in my research in 1975–78 in small, isolated Labrador communities challenged me, my notions of expertise, my middle-class (anti-woman) feminism, and sociology's assumptions about traditional women, unilinear progress, and modernity. My paper on this research was presented at the Canada Research Institute for the Advancement of Women (CRIAW) in 1979, and published in 1980 as "Women as Persons in Atlantic Canadian communities" in *Resources for Feminist Research* as a Special Publication of volume 8, 55–57.
6   For a history of CRIAW, see Clippingdale (1996); the bilingual name was invented in 1991 at a meeting in Ottawa as part of our peer review (with Francine Descarries and Mary Lynn Stewart) of SSHRC's Women and Work Strategic Grants Program.
7   The new courses in 1975–76 were the following: Women: Anthropology's Other Half (Anthropology 201.0), which was taught by part-time faculty Rose Marie Jaquith as a continuing education course, and the Psychology of Sex Roles (Psychology 348.1/.2), which was initially taught by Irmingard Lenzer, a full-time faculty member, but then,

for many years, by part-time faculty. In 1979–80 Sociology's course Women in Canadian Society was formally introduced.

8 The team consisted of Faith Chao (mathematics), Ruth Hafter (chief librarian), Wendy Katz (English), and Helen Ralson and me (sociology). In May 1975, we produced a 204-page report, *Women's Concerns about the Quality of Life in the Halifax Metropolitan Area.*

Selected Publications by the Author

Christiansen-Ruffman, Linda. 1977. *Research on women: Current projects and future directions.* Special issue of *Atlantis* 2 (2): part 2.

————. 1980. Women as persons in Atlantic Canadian communities. *Resources for Feminist Research* 8 (Special Publication): 55–57.

————. 1989. Inherited biases within feminism: The "patricentric syndrome" and the "either/or syndrome" in sociology. In *Feminism: From pressure to politics*, edited by A. R. Miles and G. Finn. Montréal: Black Rose Books.

————. 1998. Developing feminist sociological knowledge: Processes of diversity. In *Feminist perspectives: The global feminist enlightenment; Women and social knowledge*, edited by L. Christiansen-Ruffman. Madrid: International Sociological Association.

Christiansen-Ruffman, Linda, Ruth Hafter, Faith Chao, Wendy Katz, and Helen Ralston. 1975. *Women's concerns about the quality of life in the Halifax metropolitan area.* Halifax, NS: Saint Mary's University.

Connelly, Patricia M., and Linda Christiansen-Ruffman. 1977. Women's problems: Private troubles or public issues? *Canadian Journal of Sociology* 2 (2): 167–78.

To Challenge the World

Ⓐ Margrit Eichler

IN 1966, I FOUND myself as a scholarship student from Germany at Duke University. I was twenty-four years of age, in love, and engaged to a German student. I had accepted a scholarship to study abroad against my fiancé's wishes—and our families, both of them very patriarchal, were pretty horrified that I would do such a thing. However, I felt that any true love would withstand a one-year separation and went, intending to stay for the year that my scholarship lasted. A year later, my fiancé's grade in his *Diplom* (about equivalent to an MA) was too low to qualify him for a PhD, and he decided to join me in the United States. I was offered scholarships to continue my studies, we married, and in 1968 I was pregnant. While not planned, the pregnancy was not unwelcome, but I was very unsure how my future would evolve. I had been raised with the firm understanding that having children as well as a job was not a viable option for a woman.

Along came women's liberation. I joined a consciousness-raising group consisting of students, faculty, and "faculty wives" from the University of North Carolina and Duke University. Twenty-two years later, in 1990, when we started meeting again once a year in one another's houses (which now are spread across two countries and two coasts), we found that this group had had a life-changing effect on all of us.

In 1968, we asked the question of how being female had shaped our lives. Today, we might formulate it as "what was the effect of gender on our lives?" The consciousness-raising meetings opened up new vistas for me, but I was often dissatisfied with the answers that we—and those whose mimeographed articles we read hungrily—came up with. My experiences as a student were no less frustrating. In my sociology classes, we had not learned anything that I considered helpful in this endeavour, nor does my PhD thesis, written during 1969–71 on leadership in secular and religious millenarian movements, reflect any feminist concerns. Nevertheless, it was at that time that I made a conscious decision that I would dedicate my academic life to pursuing these types of questions.

Since I had a brain-drain visa that required me to leave the US after four years and I was not quite finished my thesis, I decided to apply for a job in Canada in 1970, stating that I wished to teach about women. That kept me closer to my one-and-a-half-year-old son and then-husband. Two universities replied. St. Francis Xavier inquired whether my husband would accompany me (I had foolishly indicated on my CV that I was married, and it was not yet illegal to discriminate on that basis). I explained that he would come later, and they told me that they were a Catholic university that required that spouses live together. The University of Waterloo did not care about my family status and offered me a job.

I had no significant problems introducing the first course, Sex Roles, and subsequent courses, since I had been hired to do just that. Two of the (male) professors at Waterloo had been involved as consultants in the Royal Commission on the Status of Women and were thus already sensitized to the importance of research on women.

The president of the university regularly invited new faculty members to a reception in their first year. I received an invitation as "Mrs. My-then-husband's-first-and-last-name." I called the president's office to object and to request an invitation in my own name. It did not occur to me that this might not be a smart thing to do as a young sessional instructor on her first hire. It did get the president's attention; he checked and changed the policy, sent me a new invitation, and appointed me to head a committee on the status of women at the University of Waterloo, which reported its results two years later (*Gazette* November 1973).

As a foreign student in the US, I had never had the opportunity to teach. The first Sex Roles course enrolment surpassed two hundred students. There were no teaching assistants, so I divided the class into twenty groups, identified leaders, and gave them all a project to work on. The best of the resulting papers I mimeographed, bound, and used as a resource in subsequent years.

Being a foreigner in Canada, I was determined to educate myself about this country and to use only Canadian sources to the degree possible. This orientation was reinforced by my first attendance at a meeting of the Canadian Sociology and Anthropology Association, which was in the forefront of pushing the Canadianization of social science. As a result, I read everything Canadian dealing with women that I could put my hands on, but did not read some of the other important sources from outside the country. This determination to catch up with Canadiana is a factor, I believe, in my being woefully late in my career in integrating racialization and disability as intersecting factors into my work.

As noted, I was married (although my husband stayed at the University of North Carolina to finish his PhD), and universities had anti-nepotism rules—meaning that spouses could not be employed at the same university. It was a far cry from the reverse today—spousal appointments. I was also the mother of a toddler and, to all intents and purposes, a single mom plus the sole breadwinner. Social conventions took no account of this at all. Laws were openly sexist. For instance, only the head of household—in married couples, by definition, the male—could precede the rest of the family into Canada. This meant that my husband had to escort me over the border, and my immigration application was assessed on *his* likelihood of eventually landing a job, although I had a firm contract in my pocket.

Intellectually, I operated within a huge vacuum. In the beginning, I did not know a single other person who was struggling with the same issues. It was a very different situation from that in larger universities located in metropolitan centres where people worked in teams. I found exactly two English-language Canadian resources: the report of the Royal Commission on the Status of Women (1970), which I used as a textbook, and a report on the status of women in the federal government (Archibald 1970). Marylee Stephenson, then at the University of Windsor, sent a letter around in 1971 to organize the first session ever on women at the Canadian Sociology and Anthropology Association (now the Canadian Sociology Association). My chair passed the letter on to me, Marylee and I talked on the phone, then met, and I promptly fell sick and Marylee took over looking after my two-year-old son (see Stephenson's essay in this volume). It was a firm basis on which to build a friendship and cooperation. We decided to found the *Canadian Newsletter of Research on Women/Recherches sur la femme—Bulletin d'information canadien* (now *Resources for Feminist Research/Documentation sur la recherche féministe*). In the first issue we described its purpose as follows:

1. establish and/or improve communication among people in Canada who are doing research on women

2. list ongoing research on Canadian women in particular
3. list selected relevant information on the international scene
4. provide for an exchange of ideas on courses about sex roles or women

I received a grant of $50 from my department to help with the postage. We did everything ourselves: creating the text, typing it, running it off, stuffing the envelopes. In 1974, the Minister Responsible for the Status of Women, Marc Lalonde, contributed $10,000. We were awed by this huge amount of money!

The newsletter solved the problem of isolation instantly. I was now part of a network of feminist academics. In addition, the library at Waterloo had already a collection on women and they set aside $50,000—a princely sum at the time!—to upgrade their holdings. I basically could order anything I pleased. One thing seemed clear: all of sociology—and *all* other scholarship—needed to be revised. We considered ourselves to be starting completely from scratch, with a boldness that was, in retrospect, a mixture of hubris, ignorance, and actual daring, leading to some very innovative results. Yet there was still enough commonality between what we were doing and mainstream academic culture to allow us to operate—to some degree successfully—within the academic setting.

We challenged all conclusions by looking at whether they applied to women. This disposed neatly of theories about "rational man," "homo sociologicus," "economic man," "political man," and class theory in which women's class position was defined through their husbands or fathers. We argued that the prevailing presumption of universal applicability located this radical critique still within the context of scholarship, although it stretched its boundaries. Most subfields expanded highly unwillingly. The critiques were not limited to theories derived from male data, but also to the methods employed. Some feminist scholars argued that only qualitative data allowed us to find new truths, while others, including me, argued that we needed to critically assess and revise *all* methodological tools, and not restrict ourselves to only a few.

One of the major challenges we faced was that we discussed issues for which as yet no terminology had evolved. Concepts such as "sexist" and "sexism" had not yet gained currency; "patriarchy," "matriarchy," and "gender" had quite different meanings. I remember vividly the first American Sociological Association conference I attended (as a student) in 1969, at which we founded Sociologists for Women in Society and debated what to call what we were planning to do. We eventually settled on "sex roles"; "gender" was still a strictly grammatical term. It meant we were thinking about things for which no appropriate language had yet been developed. It was hard work!

What helped us mount the challenge was the women's movement and the desperate desire of the 30% of students who were female and who yearned to learn something, anything, that spoke directly to them and their experiences. Students flocked to the courses, and audited—if necessary, illegally—when they could not enrol. My classrooms were always overflowing, with people sitting on the floor because there were not enough seats. Because of strong student interest, the administration was willing to let such courses be mounted. Since the women's movement was news in the press, there was also a considerable amount of public attention paid to anyone who lectured or did research on these issues. Being located in the relative backwater of Waterloo, I became instantly publicly visible, was invited to give lectures elsewhere, and was thus able to connect with like-minded people.

I held myself accountable to the feminist movement. Creating a bridge between a popular movement and an academic structure presented a considerable challenge—particularly because universities then were even less oriented towards popular involvement than they are today. Topics that we researched often emerged from the movement, and we were all activists trying to improve the situation of women, not just through research, but also through other forms of social engagement.

The biggest hurdles were an almost complete lack of knowledge and of resources, and the fact that there were so few of us, without any institutionalized means to find out even who those few were. We had to create such means—newsletters, journals, organizations, networks—from scratch. Mainstream journals would not accept our articles; most mainstream book publishers were wary of unknown territories as well. The many rejection letters I received usually argued that my critique was either false or irrelevant, because the scholarship I was critiquing had conclusively shown itself to be right.

The issues debated included "Is it permissible to make money on the women's movement?" In other words, is it morally acceptable to teach about women if this is part of your paid job? We debated hotly whether women's studies should become its own discipline or whether it should stay within the existing disciplines and strive to change them. Some of us, including myself, felt that double-tracking (doing both) was the thing to do, and at the collective level that is what actually happened.

In 1975, the Ontario Institute for Studies in Education (OISE) invited me to apply for a job. The students in the Department of Sociology in Education had successfully lobbied for a person who would teach about women, and I ended up with the job, the only woman in a department that, at that time, consisted—except for myself—exclusively of White men.

The first year was simply terrible. I had been hired as a feminist, and felt that no one heard or saw *me*; instead they reacted to the caricature of a feminist that they carried in their head. In desperation, I started a group to which I invited all female faculty and research officers (GROW, the Group for Research on Women), which became the nucleus of the later Centre for Women's Studies in Education. Two years later, Dorothy Smith and Mary O'Brien joined the department. That almost magically ended this particular problem. We were all three outspoken feminists, but very different, so people had to see us as individuals.

We worked across departments to hire more feminist faculty, and fairly soon had a critical mass. Alison Prentice had been hired at the same time as myself; Jeri Wine audited one of my courses and then started to teach feminist courses; Helen Lenskyj, Kathleen Rockhill, Ruth Pierson, Paula Caplan, and later Roxana Ng, Kari Dehli, and Sherene Razack, among others, started teaching at OISE. Feminist research officers, including Frieda Forman, Marion Royce, and Paula Bourne, added immeasurably to the vibrant intellectual fabric. For a number of years, we had potlucks for the feminist faculty, while city-wide dinner meetings for women from York University, the University of Toronto, and OISE (at that time still an independent institution) created intellectual and personal contacts.

In the 1980s, we could have had a women's studies department at OISE if we wished. It was a difficult decision not to pursue this road. Those of us within Sociology in Education, who felt well supported by the department, did not wish to withdraw from our unit, while faculty in other departments, who had to struggle against pervasive sexism, would have preferred to form an independent department. Around that time, I conducted, together with Rhonda Lenton and with Rosonna Tite as the research assistant, the first large-scale study on women's studies professors in Canada, surveying almost nine hundred professors who had taught at least one feminist or women's studies course (*Atlantis* 1990).

OISE has been my home for over thirty years now, and I consider myself highly privileged to have been able to work at an institution that was centrally located, numerically small, open to experiments, democratically oriented, and—although never quiet or without problems—always a centre for social activism and new thought. In 1996, OISE was integrated into the University of Toronto, which brought a new set of challenges and opportunities.

I served as the first director of the Institute for Women's Studies and Gender Studies at the U of T (1999–2003), and have since returned to my home department.

Looking back, what has been our collective effect? Certainly less than we had wanted and expected—it would be a gross exaggeration to state that mainstream scholarship today is no longer sexist—but we did spawn a new scholarship, which has made some substantial inroads. While Canadian society certainly continues to be sexist, we have made some significant progress. The Charter of Rights and Freedoms has resulted in much improvement in law. Some young women and their partners today take for granted maternity/paternity parental leaves, women's artistic contributions have flourished, and women students now outnumber male students at the university, although the professoriate is still male dominated.

Much of the current discussion is now among feminists of different generations, and of different racial and ethic backgrounds, types of abilities, and theoretical and methodological orientations. This is a sign of success: there are enough of us to make such a dialogue (and sometimes struggle) meaningful. However, it worries me that too little attention seems to be oriented towards what is still a mainstream scholarship that has been only peripherally touched by a feminist vision, and that too much of our efforts seem inward directed rather than oriented towards changing, not just scholarship, but the social world around us.

Selected Publications by the Author

Eichler, Margrit. 1980. *The double standard: A feminist critique of feminist social science*. London: Croom Helm; New York: St. Martin's Press.

———. 1988. *Canadian families today: Recent changes and their policy consequences*. 2nd ed. Toronto: Gage.

———. 1991. *Nonsexist research methods: A practical guide*. New York: Routledge.

———. 1997. *Family shifts: Families, policies and gender equality*. Toronto: Oxford University Press.

Eichler, Margrit, and Mary Anne Burke. 2006. *The BIAS FREE framework: A practical tool for identifying and eliminating social biases in health research*. Geneva: Social Forum for Health Research.

From Male and Female Roles to Sex and Gender Relations:* A Scientific and Political Trajectory

🌀 *Danielle Juteau*

IT IS HARD TO PINPOINT exactly when I became a feminist because the process was gradual and non-linear. One does not wake up one morning and say, "I'm going to be a feminist!" Individual consciousness evolves as part and parcel of a broader social movement with which it intersects. "Western" feminism emerged in the wake of decolonization and the internal struggles traversing industrial societies, including the civil rights movement, nationalism, student revolts, and May '68. Also important, in my case, were the education I received at the Collège Marguerite-Bourgeois, a French-Canadian classical college for girls in Montréal where nuns encouraged us to become doctors, not marry them; the disappointment of my mother, who had fought for the vote only to be relegated to the traditional role of women; and finally, the gap between our dreams and social expectations. All of this provided fertile ground for feminism.

I went to the University of Toronto in 1968 as a doctoral student in sociology. Feminism was on the move, but feminist studies had yet to be invented or even imagined. My PhD thesis focussed on the transition from French-Canadian to Québécois nationalism and the transformation of the power relations underpinning ethnic and national boundaries. The fact that I was working on majority and minority relationships was not, as Colette Guillaumin made

---

*I explain in this text how the object became « les rapports sociaux de sexe », an expression hard to translate into English. Its importance is a central focus on the social relations that construct sexualized categories.

me realize later, an accident. Actually, many feminists, Andrée Michel, for instance, initially studied other minority-related issues like racism and immigration before gender became an object of research and a perspective on "reality."

I clearly recall the early days of the feminist movement in Toronto, notably a conference at U of T in which Joan Johnson, a member of a radical feminist group, explained to us what feminism was all about. The reporter from the student paper *Varsity* wrote that he was pleasantly surprised when he saw that the woman on stage spoke in modulated tones and was even pregnant—not at all the Amazon he'd been expecting with a gun in the place of a left breast! During meetings of the Learned Societies held at McGill in 1972, a session was organized to discuss feminism in sociology, and I was eager to attend. Why? I'm not too clear, but I identified with this cause that I felt was connected to my being. I'm not sure if my memory is accurate, but I recall women talking while seated in a circle on the floor. Among us were Margrit Eichler and Dorothy Smith, who "was not amused" by a man who accused feminists of having no sense of humour! (the essays by Eichler and Smith in this volume). "Would you level a criticism like that to the Black liberation movement?" she retorted sharply. I continued to participate in the women's caucus of the Canadian Sociology and Anthropology Association, where I met Peta Sheriff Tancred, who later founded McGill's Centre for Teaching and Research on Women. I subscribed to *Resources for Feminist Research*, published at the Ontario Institute for Studies in Education (OISE); at the time it was a newsletter, and it is still an essential reference.

When I got a position at the University of Ottawa in 1972, I was asked to teach a course on the sociology of the family because I had two children, which of course made me an expert on the subject. I used this opportunity to discuss male and female "roles," as we called it then, and I discovered a world I had never dreamed existed: Mary Wollstonecraft (1792), a pioneer who has remained contemporary; John Stuart Mill (1869), whose analysis and behaviour were edifying; Harriet Martineau (1838), a neglected methodologist and sociologist; Virginia Woolf and her amazing *A Room of One's Own* (1929); de Beauvoir (1953) on the social construction of femininity; Shulamith Firestone and her scathing analysis of romantic love as an ideology masking sexual inequality (1972); Juliet Mitchell, on the articulation of patriarchy and capitalism (1970); and Millett on sexual politics (1970). This intellectual endeavour was also political. We were transforming knowledge and power, and changing our disciplines and departments. I have always believed that sexism affects all women, including those in universities. Consequently, fighting in that environment was not to be discarded as bourgeois. As feminists, we rejected the notion of a revolution where the oppressed would face the oppressors on a battlefield at a specific time. It was necessary to act on all fronts at all times, using every means possible. If the "personal is political," it was because power relations exist in all spheres of society, including the family—previously thought to be sheltered from such forces.

With Ann Denis, who joined the department in 1973, and who was always a great feminist and an excellent strategist, I proposed the creation of a new course, timidly entitled Rôles masculins et rôles féminins. We presented it to the department meeting and then to the faculty council, where it was approved without much trouble. We argued that it was a developing field, so there would be no lack of students, and it would put the University of Ottawa on the leading edge! I gave this course for the first time in the winter of 1975, changing the title several times in keeping with theoretical advances. The students and I learned about earlier feminist struggles, how they had been hidden from history, and our disciplines' shortcomings when it came to an understanding of women's oppression. In addition to the classics, we read Margrit Eichler and Dorothy Smith, from whom I dissociated myself because at the time she identified capitalism as the main enemy, considering the oppression of non-proletarian women (and, therefore, sexual oppression) of secondary importance. We also discovered Têtes de pioche[1] and the Manifeste des femmes québécoises (Groupe de femmes de Montréal 1971), which examined the relationships between feminism, nationalism, and capitalism, and the specific situation of Québécoise women. We were driven by an extraordinary intensity, and much in-depth work was produced as a result. Activism? Academia? They were inseparable, as is true of all theory that is developed by the oppressed and enriched by their experience. During this period, Susan Mann, Marie Laure Swiderski, Naomi Goldenberg, and Elisabeth Lacelle, among others, formed an interdisciplinary group to start a Women's Studies Program at the University of Ottawa. The project was a success, and today the university has a Joint Chair in Women's Studies with Carleton, an institute, and several specialized programs.

We were also active off campus. For Franco-Ontarian women, feminism raised the issue of a double, even triple, oppression. This was seen (Juteau-Lee and Roberts 1981) not simply as a sum of oppressions, but as a situation characterized by interlocking social relations. The founding meeting of Canadian Research Institute for the Advancement of Women (CRIAW), in which I participated in 1976, united practitioners, scholars, and politicians in an association seeking to pursue feminist action beyond International Women's Year (see Jill Vickers's essay in this volume).

So much remained to be done. However, our mission was clear, we were passionately committed, female students were excited, dissertations were written, research was conducted, and the androcentrism of the social sciences was challenged—a new field of study was emerging. A few male colleagues, most of them Marxists, it must be said, were irritated, but the administration supported us. There was much writing about the process that had begun with the inclusion of an object of research and progressed from viewing sex as an independent variable to a specific social relation that had to be explained. We understood that writing "sex explains wage differentials" didn't, in fact, explain anything. What was "sex" as a social category? What was the origin of this mode of categorization? This is what we called the Copernican revolution, a shift away from biological sex to gender.

Later on, we started discussing sexual categories themselves as a social construct, and studying what we call in French *les rapports sociaux de sexe*, namely the relations constituting sexualized social categories. It is impossible in this essay to retrace all the debates of the period (Juteau and Laurin 1988); I will therefore focus on my own itinerary. In France and Great Britain, theoretical and political debates pitted Marxist or socialist feminists against radical feminists, while in the United States, radical feminism was confronted by criticisms from women belonging to minority groups, including "Black" African-American women. In Québec, the opposition between Marxist and radical feminists also intersected with nationalism; indeed, the *Manifeste des femmes québécoises* linked women's liberation to national liberation. This caused a split between francophone and anglophone Québécoises, and also between Québécoises and Franco-Ontarian women. At the founding conference of the Regroupement des femmes québécoises in June 1978, I was refused the right to join the association.[2]

I disagreed with Marxist feminists. For me, capitalism did not cause patriarchy; rather, capitalism intersected with and oriented patriarchy. While I identified with the North American radical feminists, I was disappointed by their lack of theorization concerning the construction of sex classes. Biological differences do not ipso facto generate sexual categories, no more than skin colour creates "races."

It was during a sabbatical year spent in Paris in 1979 that I discovered a convincing theoretical approach that has served me ever since. Neither essentialist nor Marxist, feminist materialism—notably the decisive works of Christine Delphy (1970), Nicole-Claude Mathieu (1971), and Colette Guillaumin

(1978)—theorizes the specific social relations that construct sex classes. Borrowing from the Marxist notion of class, Delphy (1970) showed how the main enemy—the class of men, not capital—is constructed within the domestic mode of production. She countered not only the theories of Marxist feminists, but also the essentialism of differentialists who praised the superior virtues of femininity. She engaged in a heated debate with socialist feminists who challenged her approach, the latter arguing that women cannot form a class because they already belong to antagonistic classes. If they did not seem concerned about the fact that the proletariat belonged to different sexual categories, it was because they didn't conceive of the latter as social; at least, they didn't view them as the main contradiction.[3]

Mathieu (1971) was, to my knowledge, the first—long before Juliet Butler made a big splash—to interrogate the social construction of sexual categories and theorize social sex as distinct from biological sex and gender. For her, it is not sufficient to say that sex and gender are distinct, because we must understand how sexual categories themselves are constructed. They are erroneously conceived as being biologically based, even by those who separate gender construction from biological sex. This is where Guillaumin's analysis (1978) becomes crucial. Her theory of *sexage*, the collective and individual relations of appropriation that constitute sex classes, focusses on the basis upon which social categories are founded. If one is not born woman, one becomes one, not so much by learning sex roles as by being assigned the unpaid labour of caring for others. In viewing the social relations between the sexes as preceding capitalism, she did not insist on domestic labour and household production as the principal site of oppression. All women belong to the sex class and their labour, even that of single women, is appropriated within diverse sites, including the family.

I then understood that nuns, about whom I had been thinking and whose major contribution to French-Canadian society had been unheralded, belonged to the class of women, as they were furnishing labour that was being appropriated within the framework of the church—*et voilà*, I was set to commence, with Nicole Laurin, our major study of the work of nuns in Québec. Since 1981, I had been at the Université de Montréal, where it was harder to get feminist studies into the curriculum. Others are better placed to talk about that than I am: Francine Descarries, who as a student pushed for and then taught the first feminist sociology course (in 1978); Nicole Laurin, who was hired in this period; and Marie-Andrée Bertrand, who fought tirelessly to ensure the recognition of feminist studies (see Bertrand's essay in this volume). As soon as I arrived in the department, I worked with Nicole

Laurin to develop this field of study. We taught undergraduate and graduate courses, and workshops; we used the existing course names and inserted our content. Guillaumin was invited to give a seminar. I supervised theses and dissertations. Nicole Laurin and I successfully carried out this prodigious project thanks to some large grants, and six women who assisted us as students over a three-year period.[4] We published articles (1988) and books—in short, the sector was galvanized. But we didn't create new structures, centres, programs, or courses with official course names, which I now believe was a mistake. The lack of visibility and institutional structure hampered the field's sustainable development. I did take part in the interdisciplinary seminar Marie-Andrée Bertrand organized in 1988—after much effort because our superiors worried that the content would be unscientific. Her conviction and determination made possible what turned out to be an intense, productive, and unforgettable intellectual experience of sisterhood: an interdisciplinary critique of androcentrism, a focus on feminist contributions to the social sciences, the recognition of different social relations and their intersectionality, epistemological debates on "standpoint," a collective and interactive research methodology, and so on.

From this experience, in fact, I drew lessons and became very involved in developing and consolidating the ethnic relations studies program at the Université de Montréal, obtaining, in 1991, a chair, and creating an interdisciplinary centre connected with practitioners in the field and international scholars. This area of research is not unrelated to feminist studies. It examines social relations previously ignored by Marxists—who only recognize one—and researchers who qualify as obsolete any approach based on social relations. I continue to be a non-Marxist materialist, interested mainly in the social relations that constitute ethnic, national, and sexual categories. In articulating these relations, I seek to escape what Stuart Hall (1986) has termed horizontal and vertical reductionism.

Two currents are to be avoided: essentialism, of course, but also a type of constructivism that floats above social relations. Defenders of this position believe social categories and identity are produced by individuals who exist outside unequal power relations and structures. The salience of a philosophical discourse that, with few exceptions, opposes equality with difference, accentuates this trend. Academics and others are interrogating difference and whether it should be managed, but never where it comes from or how it is constructed. This is sad, because the discourse praising cultural difference is used to mask the unequal relations that operate transnationally—in fact, the very ones that feminist analysis has revealed and hopes to eradicate that construct differentiated minorities and mask other power relationships.

Notes

1   *Têtes de pioche* (or "hard-headed") is a radical feminist journal founded in 1976 by a collective of six women. It was published until 1979 and gave priority to women's oppression, not wanting to subordinate the latter to class.

2   The group was founded to sensitize the Parti Québécois to gender issues and to offer, to a certain extent, its support in exchange for a feminist platform. When I arrived from Ottawa to attend the movement's founding meeting, I was told that I should go fight my own state (it was not clear if they meant the Ontario provincial government or the federal government).

3   This debate, which might seem obsolete in a world where the baby of materialism has been thrown out with the bath water of Marxism, was not yet over in 1991. At the International Sociological Association conference, Sylvia Walby, Colette Guillaumin, and I were accused of essentialism by Yuval-Davis, Anthias, and other socialist-feminists because we talked about the classes of sex.

4   The first sextet comprised—in addition to Marie-Andrée Bertrand (criminologist) and myself—Bettina Bradbury (historian), Olivette Genest (theologian), Louise Marcil-Lacoste (philosopher), and Marisa Zavalloni (psychologist).

Selected Publications by the Author

Juteau, Danielle. 1981. Visions partielles, visions partiales: Vision des minoritaires en sociologie? *Sociologie et sociétés* 13 (2): 33–47.

———. 1999. *L'ethnicité et ses frontières.* Montréal: Les Presses de l'Université de Montréal.

———, ed. 2003. *La différenciation sociale: Modèles et processus.* Edited by D. Juteau. Montréal: Les Presses de l'Université de Montréal.

Juteau, Danielle, and Nicole Laurin. 1997. *Un métier et une vocation: Le travail des religieuses au Québec de 1901 à 1971.* Montréal: Les Presses de l'Université de Montréal.

Juteau-Lee, Danielle, and B. Roberts. 1981. Ethnicity and femininity: (D')après nos expériences. *Canadian Ethnic Studies/Études ethniques au Canada* 13 (1): 1–23.

Second Wave Breaks on the Shore of U of T

🍃 *Lorna Marsden*

The Beginnings

It was not difficult in the late 1960s and early 1970s to be involved in the rising concern for the status of women. As an undergraduate at the University of Toronto in 1968, I had only one woman professor, and no questions were raised about gender issues. There was no course specifically on the sociology of women, gender, or sex and status listed in the course calendar for the department.[1] But that fall, as a graduate student at Princeton, my world was transformed both on the streets and in the classroom. While activists were engaged in key debates about abortion and women's rights, we graduate students were using the major social theories we were studying to analyze gender issues. We read Thomas Kuhn's *The Structure of Scientific Revolutions* (1962); some of us argued that a paradigm shift was occurring in the thinking about gender, that the relationship of the sexes to all forms of social structure and organization was changing, and that this would transform social science. Theories of modernization and decolonization, then dominant in social science, were used. In 1970, the politics department offered Political Modernization and the Transformation of Male–Female Relations, taught by Kay Boals.

My own interest was in economic sociology and particularly labour markets. A professor, David Featherman, now at the University of Wisconsin but previously at Princeton, required me to write a paper on the status of women academics and their careers because he thought I was being unrealistic about my future. The evidence was depressing: there was no future for most women in academia (nor in any other male-dominated profession). Jessie Bernard had published *Academic Women* (1964), and a rich crop of journal articles provided more evidence. This assignment convinced me that my future was dim and that incorporating a new field—the study of women—would not be taken seriously in the academic world. The only question was, what was I going to do about it?

The women's movement had already produced a myriad of groups from the international to the intensely personal. The politics of Vietnam and the United States civil rights movements were woven into most meetings I attended in New York or read about. Meanwhile in Canada, the Royal Commission on the Status of Women was transforming our society in a quite different fashion. This commission, established by the prime minister and led by establishment women, was revolutionizing the attitudes of ordinary women by broadcasting its public hearings on CBC radio. The leaders of women's voluntary associations were drivers of all of this. The differences between US and Canadian society were stark, and gratifying to a Canadian. Despite the Presidential Commission on the Status of Women created by President Kennedy in 1961, which had radicalized many US women participants and led to the founding of the National Organization for Women (NOW), frustration led US women into using the streets and the courts to make change. Women in Canada instead were the subject of a royal commission, and Canadians were taking it seriously. Because of these differences, I found returning to Canada very attractive for both scholarly and civic reasons.

Many individuals were already involved in both the social movements and the academic study of women when I joined the University of Toronto in 1972. There were five women on faculty, although none ranked above assistant professor (Helmes-Hayes 1988). There were interested women graduate students in the department, and many of my male colleagues supervised theses that dealt with gender issues. For example, Dennis Magill supervised the thesis of Graham Lowe, whose study of white-collar workers analyzed a gender transformation in the insurance industry (1987). By 1971–72, Janet Salaff had pioneered a third-year course, Women in Society. This and the course in the Department of History taught by Jill Ker Conway and Natalie Zemon Davis were considered path-breaking at the university (see Conway and Davis's joint essay in this volume).

Activism and Academia

Jill Ker Conway was an activist and vice-president who drew women faculty together to discuss university politics, such as the inequality of salaries, pensions, and other benefits. However, among some senior faculty there was a strong aura of disapproval about the women's movement and its incorporation into academic study. For young, untenured faculty, there was a concern that scholarship and teaching in this field, while desirable, might not be acceptable when the culling of faculty occurred at tenure time. We were told we should get down to "real" work if we were going to survive at the university. The meetings organized by Jill Ker Conway led to pressure to improve the status of women at the university by, for example, providing equity in life insurance for women faculty members. In 1972, women faculty could have only one thousand dollars worth of life insurance whereas male faculty had twice their annual salaries. Pay studies and other benefit analyses followed.

Before joining the faculty at the university, I had attended a meeting that clarified my goals in teaching in women's studies. Invited in 1971 to a meeting of the Ontario Committee on the Status of Women (ocsw) at the home of Flora McLeod Hogarth, I witnessed something new to me—two intelligent, highly educated women having a profound argument over policy priorities to improve the status of women in Canada. The two women were Naomi Black, faculty member at York University, and Lynn McDonald, then at McMaster University. By this point, I had all but defended my doctoral degree at Princeton University, had gone to many rallies and meetings in the US, and had spent years in and around universities; but such was the social convention for women that a well-argued disagreement of this sort had never been part of my experience. These days, it would be strange not to have witnessed such a discussion; then it was not usual.

I joined the ocsw, a volunteer group formed to press for the implementation of the recommendations of the Royal Commission on the Status of Women that pertained to the provincial domain. Simultaneously, a national organization was forming to press for the implementation of the federal recommendations. The national leaders were Laura Sabia, Grace Hartman, Elsie Gregory MacGill, and others. I went to the organizational meetings and was a delegate to the April 1972 convention at the King Edward Hotel in Toronto when the National Action Committee (NAC) on the Status of Women was born. In 1975, I became the third president of NAC.

All this work required the analytical skills that one acquired in the academy, so teaching and activism complemented one another. It set the tone for subsequent years of teaching in the area of women's studies. The issues had to be addressed with theory, data, and convincing scholarship—social change in Canada could only be achieved through substance.

At the university, a group had formed a Women's Studies Committee, and early on my colleague Janet Salaff persuaded me to join. By then, she and I were teaching a fourth-year seminar called Workshop on Women in Canadian Society. We were using, among other new publications, the report and studies of the Royal Commission on the Status of Women. It was in the Women's Studies Committee that I met Chaviva Hosek of the English department at Victoria College, Vi Colman from the history department, and many other interesting faculty. Our aim was to establish scholarly women's studies. One of our greatest advocates was the principal of New College, Peter Richardson. He welcomed us to the college and urged us to make our home there. Kay Armatage of film studies was instrumental in this process.

A key goal in my university work was to ensure that the subject was embedded thoroughly in scholarly theory, methods, and research. This, some of us thought, was the only way to ensure that it was not a passing fad. Quite apart from our social activism, we wanted to work with historians, economists, scientists, and, in fact, with people in all disciplines to build a serious body of scholarship on the subjects of gender, sex, and the status of women. In part, this focus came from studying sociology in the US, where most data sets were divided into Black and non-Black populations before analysis. I thought it equally important to address the inequality between men and women, as Americans did with respect to racialized groups, and therefore to examine theory, data, and methods. In teaching on the subject of labour markets and the labour force, the data were clear. Women had less opportunity than their male peers, holding constant education; women were compensated much less than men for the same work; and women had a double burden in the household and the paid labour force (Epstein 1971; Oppenheimer 1970).

How were our students to be introduced to all this complexity? We did not lack for studies from governments. Not only had the royal commission produced a series of published and unpublished papers on a wide range of subjects, but government departments, university groups (e.g., McGill University's senate report on sex discrimination), and professional associations were publishing their own studies. Statistics Canada had some reasonable data, and the Women's Bureau in the Department of Labour, under the inspired direction of Sylva Gelber (see Helen Levine's essay in this volume), had highlighted issues related to women in Canada's workplaces.

With all this, I introduced my students to the field. At first, most students were men. When I arrived in 1971, the calendar description for the Sociology of Occupations was "The relation of man to his occupations in contemporary society." I introduced gender comparisons and data analysis into the readings and assignments. By 1975, the calendar description for soc 207 Work and Occupations was "the nature and meaning of work in occupations … discussed in relation to changes in the position of the professions, unions and government, of women and other minority groups, and in industrial societies more generally." I asked my undergraduate students, "What do you see? How do you explain it?" More and more women students appeared. Two male colleagues were teaching women's studies. Over the years, students wrote papers that linked their own experience with the population data in the field and used a wide range of theories to explain what they found.

But academic research in my field required not only showing the data but explaining it at the level of theory. Economic theory was most unsatisfactory. Sociological theory was also quite limited. Socio-psychological theory seemed more promising. In 1974, I gave a paper at the Canadian Association of American Studies entitled "Academic Women: Role Models and Achievement," which asked, "Why are the genders so different with respect to academic careers, and how does one explain this?" I drew on the reference group theories of Theodore Kemper (1968; see Marsden 1984).

Within a few years of my joining the university, a women's studies colloquium was set up, composed of faculty members from U of T, York, and other institutions to try to understand what others were researching and writing about. We met over potluck suppers in New College and at York to see what could be done. Our numbers were so small at any institution that banding together gave us all confidence and led to some significant scholarly debate. Many interesting papers were given in a variety of fields. Clara Thomas, from York University in the field of Canadian literature, both kept the peace and provided impetus to the work. Naomi Black, Rusty (Ann) Shteir, and Johanna Stuckey were leaders from York; Janet Salaff, Chaviva Hošek, Phyllis Grosskurth, and Ursula Franklin were leaders at the University of Toronto.

There was much resistance at the University of Toronto to this activity. Well-meaning male colleagues lectured me on "wasting" my time and "ruining" my career; but several male and female colleagues were seriously interested in the analytic work, and many students wrote fascinating term papers on the subject. Among many others, Pam Sugiman (1994) and Vappu Tyyska

(1995) come to mind, both now professors and researchers in sociology. They and others analyzed the situation of entire occupations, or whole generations. My first graduate supervisions were Kitty Lundy and Patricia Connelly, both in economic sociology although quite different in their approaches. Pat was my first supervision and her thesis was later published (1978). Many students went on to do graduate work in this field, to work in the public service, or to take their analyses into their professions.

The librarians at the University of Toronto were not only sympathetic but acted quickly in increasing the holdings in both government documents and other areas of the libraries to support teaching and research in women's studies. Katherine Packer was interested in all equality-seeking movements, and many others were equally interested in building the collections.

All courses and their format and readings had to pass through a departmental committee, be approved by a departmental meeting, and then be supported at the faculty level. In all those years, I do not recall ever being turned down in a course proposal in the field of women's studies although I do recall some rather intense questioning of the value and significance of the courses and the readings involved. Any course seen as "too political" or "not theoretical enough" was the object of suspicion in some quarters, but most colleagues were sympathetic. With the exception of the Ontario Institute for Studies in Education, where it was believed by many members of the University of Toronto establishment that simply anything could be taught, no matter how academically dubious, women's studies struggled to advance. The silos of disciplines at the university made working together a genuine effort, so some fine scholarship on women's studies was carried forward under the headings of development studies, or human development, or immigration studies rather than through the departmental structure.

By 1975, the United Nation's International Women's Year, the pattern was set and, although many other battles were fought both in the community and in the university, the questions of women's rights, of equity, and of serious scholarship had been raised and established. If one looks at the previous waves of the women's movement, one can see the incremental change. The battle of the nineteenth century was the admission of women to the university and then to classes; in the early part of the twentieth century it was the acceptance of women as faculty members and graduate students into science and other "male fields"; in the 1970s, our role was to embed the serious study of gender, of sexuality, and of women's rights into scholarship—the literature and the social fabric of the institution (Marsden 2004; Prentice 2006). All things considered, those early years were important in setting a pattern for change and tending to the boundaries of activism, ideology, and scholarship in sociology at the University of Toronto. The women and men who took the ideas from unacceptable to the university to mainstream in scholarly life were greatly influenced by the women's movement and by legal, economic, and social changes outside the academy.

Note

1 The course calendars are found in the E. J. Pratt Library at the university; I am grateful to Karen Myers for locating and copying them for me.

Selected Publications by the Author

Jones, Charles, Lorna R. Marsden, and Lorne J. Tepperman. 1990. *Lives of their own: The individualization of adult women's lives*. Toronto: Oxford University Press.

Marsden, Lorna R. 1979. Agitating organizations: The role of the National Action Committee on the status of women in facilitating equal pay policy in Canada. In *Equal employment policy for women: Strategies for implementation in the United States, Canada and Western Europe*, edited by R. S. Ratner. Philadelphia: Temple University Press.

———. 1981. "The labour force" is an ideological structure: A guiding note to the labour economists. *Atlantis* 7 (1): 57–64.

———. 1984. Work, technical role models and the absence of women in academia. In *The sociology of work*, edited by A. Whipper. Toronto: Oxford University Press.

Marsden, Lorna R., and Edward B. Harvey. 1979. *The fragile federation: Social change in Canada*. Toronto: McGraw-Hill Ryerson.

Surviving Political Science … and Loving It

◉ *Jill Vickers*

MY PERSONAL JOURNEY into feminist scholarship was shaped by being the sole woman, or one of only two or three isolated women, in a very resistant discipline: political science. As a student in the undergraduate political science program at Carleton University during 1961–65, at the London School of Economics from 1966–69, and through my first decade of teaching, women were virtually absent from politics and political science. No woman professor taught me, and one lone woman member of Parliament (MP), Grace MacInnis, sat in the House of Commons (1964–75) throughout my student career. Carleton had two women political scientists when I was hired— Pauline Jewett, who was away trying to get elected, and Teresa Rakowska Harmstone, a Soviet specialist, who became my mentor. Historian Naomi Griffiths recruited me into the Ottawa founding group of the Canadian Research Institute for the Advancement of Women (CRIAW), which provided the infrastructure for my "women in politics" research, dismissed both by political scientists and by feminists influenced by US-style anti-statism. CRIAW activists were interested in Canadian politics. Griffiths, historian of Acadians, promoted links between anglophone and francophone feminists, which influenced my research also.

I was active in party politics in the New Democratic Party (NDP), where I worked in the women's caucus with Muriel Duckworth and Kay Macpherson for a decade and a half to insert feminist concerns into the party's policy and increase women's participation both in decision making and as candidates. Consequently, I was working at the crossroads between state and feminist politics. The lack of like-minded colleagues in political science made CRIAW and, later, women's studies, my community. CRIAW made me open to Franco-Québec and Acadian feminists, to First Nations and anti-racist women's struggles. CRIAW's practice of meeting in different parts of Canada each year, and recruiting participants from varied backgrounds, made me aware of the diversity of women's experiences and political views.

Women in Politics

My academic mentors included theorist K. D. (Ken) McRae and my PhD thesis supervisor, Michael Oakeshott. Neither encouraged me to study "women in politics," which in the 1960s and 1970s was still a virtually unthinkable topic. To succeed as a lone woman in political science, I learned its values and, like the Queen visiting Arab lands, became an honorary male. Usually the only woman in a resistant discipline, I looked for allies outside political science, finding them in CRIAW, the NDP, and the faculty association. I thought unionization was more effective than consciousness-raising for combating discrimination and getting paid maternity leave. I led the movement for faculty unionization at Carleton in the early 1970s, which earned me clout in bargaining two collective agreements and gaining protections for women in legally enforceable documents. This no doubt persuaded me that governments could also be bent to women's needs. I applied Eleanor Roosevelt's advice to women about political parties—getting into the game instead of throwing mud from the outside. If unions or parties could be transformed to serve women's needs and achieve their goals, it would happen only if women got into the game and struggled to change them. I believed activism with or in parties and governments potentially could result in benefits for women on a society-wide scale. It took me a decade of unlearning to see that working within existing political structures didn't always work for women, no matter how hard they tried, and to theorize how to open up state structures and make them more responsive to women's demands as citizens. I believed governments *should* be more open: women were half of every state's citizens. Unlike radical feminists who wrote states off as essentially patriarchal and unreformable, I was eager in political science to imitate women like Ruth Benedict and Margaret Mead in anthropology.

In 1973, Sue Findlay of the Women's Program[1] offered me resources to do research about women in politics. The Royal Commission on the Status of Women had documented women's absence as MPs. Political science naturalized this absence by arguing that women were unsuited to, or uninterested in, politics, a premise challenged by the demands of an increasingly vocal women's movement. Working from newspapers, because official statistics did not reveal a candidate's sex (fortunately reporters did), I mapped information about women candidates. In 1975, I submitted two reports—*A Preliminary Statistical Map of Female Candidacies in Federal and Provincial Elections* and *Private Lives and Public Responsibilities: Canadian Women in Politics*—outlining where women ran (close to home), and also why I thought so few ran for political parties (starting "barriers research"). The database expanded over time, was used by a generation of graduate students, and made possible Janine Brodie's benchmark survey of women candidates for her PhD thesis, later published as a book (1985). It also formed the basis for the Women in Politics course I taught for two decades, out of which other courses developed. (For example, "gender and politics" now is a degree concentration with numerous courses.) In this period, I also ran, federally, as an NDP candidate, gaining rich insights into how women were treated by party gatekeepers, the electorate, and other candidates. The impact of my candidacy on my children was also an eye-opener.

Women's Politics

Work on gendered issues in political science in the 1970s and 1980s was limited to a few women working in isolation and interacting mainly through CRIAW conferences. Political science journals wouldn't publish the results (none of my work was published by a political science journal). Interdisciplinary journals, the *CRIAW Papers*, and collaborative women's studies volumes provided the venues for the next phase. "Where are the Women in Canadian Politics?" appeared in 1978 in *Atlantis*, and "women in politics" research was explored at CRIAW and the United Nations Educational, Scientific, and Cultural Organization (UNESCO) conferences throughout the 1980s. The research remained focussed on barriers to women's participation in partisan, electoral, and legislative politics; but women's activism in the large quasi-public sector of "informal politics," which women had created while excluded from active citizenship, was increasingly important as second-wave feminism moved beyond small groups and consciousness-raising. Feminists who wanted to influence state politics organized networks and then umbrella structures like the National Action Committee on the Status of Women (NAC). My involvement in movement politics, as a parliamentarian of NAC, and in the "equality-seeking" movement around the Charter of Rights, embodied my unwillingness to abandon women's citizenship. Working in CRIAW with Franco-Québec feminists like Micheline de Sève helped me understand feminists who were also nationalists eager to shape "their" state to be "women friendly."

Working in CRIAW with Mary Two-Ax Early helped me understand why many First Nations women rejected feminism but sought allies to restore them to their rightful places within First Nations. I participated in, and wrote about, women's constitutional politics. Influenced by Scandinavian feminists who theorized that both state-focussed and autonomous feminist activism are needed to achieve change, and by Carolyn Andrew's demonstration of the roles women played in creating Canada's welfare state, I developed a "double vision" approach in which both "women in politics" and "women's politics" played a role. Funded by CRIAW and UNESCO, I led a mapping of Canadian women's diverse forms of political activism. The results appeared in 1986 in a pilot study *Women's Participation in Political Life*, and in two CRIAW papers that I co-edited with Evelyn Tardy, whose research on women's participation in Québec was particularly valuable.

I presented both the framework and our findings in Norway, the United States, and Australia, meeting other feminists working in political science. In 1988, I was invited to describe "The Political Structure of the Canadian Women's Movement" to a Ministerial Workshop on Federal Policy Development. The hostility to feminist activism displayed by most deputy ministers and ministers' political aides showed how resistant men who controlled partisan, electoral, and legislative politics were to women who demanded their rights as citizens, but who were not willing to be "integrated"/co-opted into male-dominated structures. The presence of women deputy ministers and ministers made me realize how important bridges between them and women activists could be. It also demonstrated that the more women were elected and appointed in formal politics, and the stronger women's movements became, the more likely would become competition and conflict over who really "represented" women.

Such conflict between women of the political class and in independent women's movements emerged in the constitution repatriation debates and around the Meech Lake Accord. It persuaded me that a feminist subfield of political science had to be developed to study how these branches of women's political activism interacted. Women were also becoming more visible in the legal profession, the courts, and the public service. Such women could be co-opted into male-dominated political visions, or could be conduits for projects of transformation and advancement of women's needs and goals. I also glimpsed the fact that similar developments were happening in other countries, although with different results in some cases. Clearly, a broader, comparative framework was needed.

Feminist Political Science

Many of my women's studies colleagues rejected the project of a feminist political science, believing states, parties, and mixed-sex movements like nationalisms were invariably "bad for women." Their vision was "stand-alone" feminism. My vision was a feminist approach to political science that integrated knowledge of "women in politics" and "women's politics" into a broader understanding of how gender and power interact in political systems. Some theoretical leverage had resulted from comparing "women in politics" with "women's politics," but mature theorization required conceptual bridge-building between gender-focussed analysis and mainstream political science.

Ironically, it was only possible to develop a mature framework for feminist political science outside the discipline initially. When my department opposed my promotion to full professor (granted by the university) on grounds that my work was "not of interest to political scientists," I moved to the Department of Canadian Studies as graduate supervisor and later as director. To my disciplinary colleagues, my work was not legitimate—in part because it was published in women's studies journals and considered of interest only to women.

In Canadian studies, I worked to create a master's-level Women's Studies Program working with Pat Smart, a scholar of Québec literature, with whom I shared an interest in Québec feminist nationalism. I kept teaching my Women in Politics course, while incorporating research about women's relationships with power into the graduate courses I taught in Canadian studies. This allowed me to enter into comparative, constitutional, and international politics (which I wasn't considered an "expert" in within political science) and to focus on "women's politics." We trained two new generations of scholars interested in "women's politics," some of whom were later recruited into political science. Canadian Studies also provided opportunities to be in contact with the emerging field of feminist political science in the US, Australia and New Zealand, and Scandinavia, and to develop work in interdisciplinary methodology.

It became clear that the relative openness of state politics to women depended on the relative power of different states—the more powerful, the less open to women. Feminists in the US, Britain, or France, allied with the left and alienated from nationalism, experienced their powerful, post-colonial/neo-imperial states as closed to women's influences and dangerous. Transferring that judgement to less powerful nation-states was often unjustified. In any case, what alternative did women have? Could women with relatively little power create a new "game" without states? Statelessness seemed a worse situation for women than repressive states. Creating a counterculture based on feminist values, as radical feminists envisioned, seemed dangerous for most women, if it deflected more powerful women from trying to reshape state politics. Women's politics in Canada became increasingly "radical" and anti-state; however, where state politics became more "conservative" and neo-liberal, policies reduced meaningful exchanges between governments and feminist organizations, defined now as "special interests." I was recruited to conduct research several times by public officials trying to understand women's movements (even what their language meant); but no effective bridging mechanism resulted. My academic work focussed increasingly on theoretical issues, including the nature of equality and power. Studying women's non-partisan, political activism on its own terms—assimilated neither into the mainstream, positivist paradigm, nor into the left counter-paradigm, which subordinated gender to class—also produced considerable insights.

From the mid-1980s to the mid-1990s, I was also active in equality-seeking and constitutional politics movements, which prompted my writings about sex/gender, national identities, equality issues, equality-seeking movements, and women's interests in constitutional reform and federalism. Some of my students were active in the gay/lesbian and disability rights movements, in Aboriginal and anti-racist politics. Insights from supervising their theses inspired the concept of "the new scholarship," which could underwrite a broad, equality-seeking coalition. I found myself bridging between mainstream and feminist scholars and activists: trying to persuade feminists to care about constitutional reform, while trying to persuade mainstream academics that women's rights were human rights, worthy of constitutional protection. I saw the need for many more bridges among diverse groups of people eager for recognition, but experiencing exclusion from state politics and women's movements. My publications about these issues were still in journals and books rarely read by political scientists or political theorists, but I was also increasingly influenced by work from a band of feminist political scientists who were more and more visible at disciplinary conferences.

I undertook two projects which contributed to building a feminist approach to political science. The first was a study of politics within NAC, building on Chris Appelle's MA thesis and Pauline Rankin's work, published by the University of Toronto Press as *Politics As If Women Mattered* (Vickers, Rankin, and Appelle 1993). We connected "women's politics" to feminist critiques and mainstream understandings of the Canadian political system. Along with work by Sylvia Bashevkin, Jane Arscott, Linda Trimble, and others, this study conceptualized how an excluded group as large as "women" affects a political system when it is finally allowed to enter while insisting on doing so on its own terms. The second project was *Reinventing Political Science: A Feminist Approach* (1997), a textbook to help the many young instructors teaching "women in politics" courses, or trying to add a gender dimension to mainstream courses. In it, I tried to build a conceptual platform for more theoretically demanding work by outlining key feminist approaches and concepts in the discipline's subfields. The text was greeted dismissively (or ignored) by most disciplinary colleagues, but was well received by those for whom it was written. My aims were modest because I could see that feminist political science was at the take-off point, with a new generation of graduate students eager to develop the field and an explosion of new work on the horizon.

The fragmentation disrupting "Western" feminist movements in response to globalization, as well as to claims based on "race," sexuality, class, Aboriginality, and nationality, has shaped my work in recent years. Sociologist and CRIAW colleague Vanaja Druhvarajan and I produced *Gender, Race and Nation: A Global Approach* (2002), outlining how feminist scholars can undertake comparative work that treats women's differences respectfully and with real understanding (see Druhvarajan's essay in this volume). Another textbook, *The Politics of "Race": Canada, Australia and the United States* (2002), responded to a teaching need identified first by my colleague Vince Wilson when president of the Canadian Political Science Association (CPSA). Not only did the political science paradigm render women and gender invisible, but it also excluded "race" as cultural and psychological. I argued that settler states created "race regimes" as part of the political system by treating Aboriginal peoples as a different legal category without citizenship; and then new "race" regimes build on the first to exclude or exploit Asians and Blacks. I also worked with Micheline de Sève to produce a special issue of the *Journal of Canadian Studies,* comparing women's diverse experiences with nationalism in Canada. These projects demonstrate some of the rapids of diversity that feminist political science must navigate to be a coherent field in a globalizing world in which "women" is a contested term.

Why has political science proved so resistant to change? Unlike sociology or history, where three decades of feminist scholarship have been transformative, feminist political science has had little impact on the mainstream paradigm. Feminist work in the discipline is now possible, although it remains difficult to work on feminist political theory in some places. Perhaps the closer women come to power in institutions that powerful men have dominated for millenia, the stronger the resistance grows. It will take considerable collaboration and exchange among scholars from different countries to unlock the puzzle of how to change male dominance. But the new generations don't have to build their own infrastructure, and "gender/women and politics" fields now exist at the doctoral level, as do dedicated journals, to foster ongoing recruitment. I was honoured when the CPSA named an annual award for the best "gender and politics" paper after me. Responding to the demands of young scholars, the field, albeit with its feminism removed, was legitimized. Becoming an elder in an increasingly legitimate field (despite its persisting outsider status) gives me a sense of reassurance that the project will continue to be significant.

Note

1   The Women's Program was created in 1973 in response to a recommendation of the Royal Commission on the Status of Women. The Commission called for the creation of a federal mechanism of support for the direct participation of Canadian women in the efforts to advance women's equality. The mandate of the Women's Program is to facilitate women's participation in Canadian society by addressing their economic, social, and cultural situation through Canadian organizations. The Women's Program fulfills this mandate by providing financial and non-financial (technical) assistance to organizations to carry out projects at the local, regional, and national levels in key areas, such as women's economic status and violence against women and girls, in an accountable and transparent framework. In 1995, as a result of the federal government's consolidation of women's programs, the Women's Program was transferred from the office of the Secretary of State to Status of Women Canada. See http://www.swc-cfc.gc.ca/funding/wp/wpguide_e.html.

Selected Publications by the Author

Vickers, J[ill] McCalla. 1975a. *A Preliminary Statistical Map of Female Candidacies in Federal and Provincial Elections, 1951–74*. Ottawa: Women's Programme, Secretary of State.

———. 1975b. *Private Lives and Public Responsibilities: Canadian Women in Politics*. Ottawa: Women's Programme, Secretary of State.

Vickers, Jill. 1978. Where are the women in Canadian politics? *Atlantis* 3 (2): 40–51.

———. 1997. *Reinventing political science: A feminist approach.* Halifax, NS: Fernwood.

———. 2002. *The politics of race: Canada, Australia and the United States.* Ottawa: Golden Dog Press.

Vickers, Jill, Pauline Rankin, and Christine Appelle. 1993. *Politics as if women mattered: A political analysis of the National Action Committee on the Status of Women.* Toronto: University of Toronto Press.

Blood on the Chapel Floor:
Adventures in Women's Studies

Kay Armatage

I CAN'T REMEMBER exactly how it happened.

I was a graduate student in English literature without any clear direction or career plans. I liked reading, so I just kept at it.

As an undergraduate (1960–65), I had rampaged through women's novels and poetry, and when I got to the University of Toronto, I gravitated emotionally and intellectually to women's writing. I took graduate courses on Jane Austen, the nineteenth-century novel, and a modern literature course that included Virginia Woolf and Edith Wharton. My MA thesis, supervised by Phyllis Grosskurth—one of the few women in the University of Toronto English department—was on Emily Brontë's poetry.

Then, I read Gertrude Stein's monograph *Picasso* (1938) and discovered writing that I didn't know existed. I devoured Stein and the other modernist women writers she led me to, as well as the other powerful American expatriate women of the Left Bank. Retrospectively, I recognized Jill Johnston, whose column I had read weekly in the tattered copies of the *Village Voice* passed around amongst my undergraduate friends, and who became the subject of my first documentary film, as the contemporary literary "daughter" of Stein. Somehow I came across Charlotte Perkins Gilman's autobiographical novella, *The Yellow Wallpaper* (1899), a text that would shortly become a classic of reclaimed feminist literature, and Monique Wittig's revolutionary masterpiece, *Les Guérillères* (1973). After several skirmishes, as no one in the English department at the time claimed to know anything about her, I persuaded them to accept my proposal of a dissertation on "The Woman in the Writings of Gertrude Stein."

When I first came to Toronto (after Renfrew, a small town in the heart of the Ottawa Valley, and Kingston, population less than 100,000), I discovered cinema. There were movie theatres here that showed foreign movies, as well as regular cinematheque screenings of classics and less commercial recent films at the newly opened Ontario Science Centre. The first film I saw by Jean-Luc Godard (*Une Femme Mariée*, 1964) was another modernist revelation, and I plunged into the study of film, art, and history with avidity.

As I said, I don't remember how it happened, but around 1971, a small group of women who were interested in starting a course on Women in Society contacted me. Suddenly I was an expert on women's literature. I must admit, however, that I was an expert on not much else that was pertinent. Although I had read *The Feminine Mystique* (Friedan 1963) and *The Female Eunuch* (Greer 1970), my only response had been a vow that these nightmares were not going to happen to me: I would choose my lifestyle and partners more carefully. I wasn't a feminist. I didn't really know the meaning of the word.

But there I was, somehow part of a collective of women who were not only politically active in the women's liberation movement and abreast of the latest developments in feminist thought, but also keenly knowledgeable about historically significant political theory. They had read Marx, Engels, Levi-Strauss, and Mao. As well as mainstream feminist texts such as *Sisterhood Is Powerful* (Morgan 1970), they knew the more radical texts, *The SCUM Manifesto* (Solanas 1969) and "The Myth of the Vaginal Orgasm" (Koedt 1973). The women's collective met regularly over the summer of 1971 to formulate bibliographies, discuss texts and pedagogical strategies, and debate theory. I was reading like crazy, trying to catch up.

At the end of the summer, the women's studies group spent a weekend at a farm to agree on the final course syllabus. That excursion was a trial by fire for me, raising questions of cultural heritage and class. There we were in rural Ontario in August, and the provisions included canned vegetables and a large supermarket salami in a plastic wrapper. Not that I'm a food fanatic, but in Ontario, in August, no corn, no tomatoes, no fresh vegetables at all? Small-town middle-class (which had always involved fresh garden vegetables), I nearly bailed. At one point, I just hijacked someone's car and persuaded Ceta Ramkhalawansingh to come with me to local farm stands for fresh food. As far as I was concerned, the meetings went well after that.

By the time we entered the university teaching year, the group was oper-
ating as a committed collective. Luckily for me, I was one of them. We were
teaching in pairs, with the aim of breaking down hierarchies in the classroom
and broadening the interdisciplinary knowledge base. The course was located
in a new program called interdisciplinary studies, housed in a building on
St. George Street that had once been some kind of a religious centre. Our
principal classroom was the chapel, which we all saw as ironic, especially
later when it became the scene of bloody battles over leadership and control.
Even feminist collectives aren't always smooth sailing.

In the first two years of the course (1972–74), we had enrolments
approaching two hundred. We organized a lecture series that was open to the
public, as well as to registered students. Every week, five hundred people
attended lectures by notable locals in every field, including then-lawyer (now
a Supreme Court Judge) Rosalie Abella, writer Margaret Atwood, feminist
sculptor Maryon Kantaroff, and many others. We made a poster with a
graphic illustration, a female version of the "ascent of man" (a series of
images of a creature on all fours evolving to a woman standing), giving lecture titles in wobbly Letraset. The course was a phenomenal success.

In the spring of 1974, we proposed a Women's Studies Program. Ceta
Ramkhalawansingh had already written an essay critiquing male bias in official U of T Arts and Science documents and found calendar descriptions of
other courses relevant to the study of women. We produced a brochure
detailing a Women's Studies Program (1974–75), complete with Ceta's manifesto, program requirements and courses, and the U of T crest on the front
cover (see Ramkhalawansingh's essay in this volume).

We were called on the carpet. The dean of Arts and Science told us sternly
that this was not the way we did things at U of T; but the widespread student interest was obvious. Eventually the dean informed us of the proper procedure: a committee would be constituted to consider the proposal. We were
ecstatic, and had the temerity to suggest a chair for the committee. In due
course, a committee was convened, with Joan Foley (then a professor in the
psychology department, later vice-president and provost) as the chair and
I as a member. A program in women's studies was inaugurated.

At about that time, some traumatic changes occurred in women's studies. Interdisciplinary studies was discontinued, and what was now the introductory women's studies course moved to a new location, New College. The
collective (most of them graduate students or—even worse—activists and
teachers from the community outside the university, including women's lib-
erationists and members of the Revolutionary Marxist Group) was no longer

viable: only people with a PhD would be allowed to teach. Suddenly our leading lights, including Ceta (an undergraduate at the time she entered the course), Barbara Cameron (then a graduate student, and now a professor of political science and women's studies at York University), and others were gone.

Luckily, we got Kathryn Morgan (philosophy) and Mary Nyquist (English), who have been stalwarts of the program ever since. Sylvia Van Kirk (history) joined us very soon after that. But we weren't out of trouble even then. The university was by no means convinced that a program on women could be academically respectable. We were called to account on many charges, with "consciousness-raising" as the most frequent accusation. I remember vividly a course evaluation meeting in the New College common room where Professor Peter Prangnell, then dean of architecture and instructor of a course at New College, anticipated our problem and opted to defend his course before women's studies came up. His speech rang with contempt about the conservatism of the process, and he declared that his curriculum was fundamentally a process of "consciousness-raising" about living spaces and architecture. His administrative and academic credentials, his British accent, and his disdain for the criticisms of women's studies about to come saved us that day.

Our first program director was Chaviva Hošek, a well-established member of the English department. She brought to the program not only great academic credibility but also wide administrative connections and tremendous political savvy—she was already president of the National Action Committee on the Status of Women. Very shortly thereafter, she left the university to participate in provincial and federal politics, serving as minister of Housing in the Ontario government and director of policy and pesearch for Prime Minister Jean Chrétien. She is now president and chief executive officer of the Canadian Institute for Advanced Research.

When Chaviva left, she recommended as her successor Professor Ronnie de Sousa (philosophy). Well-known on campus for his outspoken progressive views, he would bring us even more credibility, Chaviva argued. Apparently some people thought that what women's studies needed was a man. Not all of us agreed; I wrote a letter to the *Faculty Bulletin* outlining my views (including, to my shame, an error in diction, which Ronnie delighted in pointing out to me, while still making peace). Ronnie was appointed program director, and it was soon business as usual. In retrospect, I'm happy that Ronnie succeeded in allaying faculty fears about putatively man-hating feminists.

A brilliant scholar of women's history and a gifted administrator, Sylvia Van Kirk—committed to and ambitious for women's studies—became the next program director. Sylvia had specific and adamant views on the question of interdisciplinarity, a concept that was integral to women's studies from its inception but only recently recognized as a respectable and advocated pedagogy at the University of Toronto. Sylvia insisted that interdisciplinary teaching should be firmly based in the traditional disciplines. Three discipline-based humanities scholars, for example, would teach the introductory course. In our case Kathryn Morgan and Mary Nyquist came from philosophy and English, respectively; my "discipline," cinema, was still a bit iffy, but Sylvia undertook to be broad-minded about it. A biologist, an anthropologist, and a psychologist would teach the second-year social sciences course. Although this approach to interdisciplinarity is outmoded in the academic world of the present, in which an interdisciplinary studies approach has increasing cachet, it was an extremely effective strategy at the time for regularizing our partnerships with the traditional (i.e., conservative) departments. Sylvia worked hard to encourage units to launch courses that would be suitable for cross-listing with women's studies. She succeeded brilliantly.

The newly established Women's Studies Program allowed me to design a course on Women's Film and Literature (1974–76). In subsequent years, I taught Introduction to Women Writers (1975–77), Women Writers of the World (1977–80), and Women's Cinema (1976–80). I continued to teach the course that became Introduction to Women's Studies with Mary Nyquist and Kathryn Morgan until 1988, when I was appointed program director.

Meanwhile, I had been furthering my interest in cinema. After my introduction to issues related to women, one of my first questions was, "What about women filmmakers?" Had there ever been any? Where were they? I co-edited a special issue on women filmmakers for *Take One Magazine* (1972) and became involved in the Toronto International Festival of Women Filmmakers (1973). I began to publish articles on women filmmakers in journals and to make films on women's issues.

These were the exciting years of the revolution in feminist film theory that began with Laura Mulvey's groundbreaking (now classic) "Visual Pleasure and Narrative Cinema" (1975). In that article, she introduced psychoanalysis as a useful theoretical instrument for feminism. For North Americans, this was a surprising development. Freudian psychoanalysis had been severely critiqued by feminists such as Betty Friedan (1963) and Phyllis Chesler (1972): penis envy, frigidity, toilet training, and tranquillizers were women's enemies—we were sure of that. In 1972, I had attended the Women's

Cinema Event at the Edinburgh International Film Festival. I remember overhearing, during a washroom break, one knowledgeable British woman say to another, "[Her] problem is that she just won't accept the fact of her castration." I chortled silently to myself in derision.

Mulvey's article, followed shortly by *Psychoanalysis and Feminism* (Mitchell 1975), Jacqueline Rose's introduction to *Feminine Sexuality* (Lacan 1982), and the flood of publications from the "New French Feminists," Helene Cixous, Luce Irigaray, and Julia Kristeva, took us by storm. These works argued that Jacques Lacan's recasting of Freud's theories in semiotic terms was useful for feminist understanding of language and representation in all fields.

That same summer in Paris (1972), I hooked up with an acquaintance who took me to a country gathering of a group of feminists who were all being analyzed by a Lacanian woman therapist. Another series of revelations. Their discussions, first of all, were solely concerned with feminist psychoanalytic theory—an oxymoronic notion as far as North Americans were concerned. Secondly, in contrast to the army surplus garb of militant North American feminists, these French feminists dressed extravagantly, dyed their hair, and wore jewellery and make-up—even red nail polish, which a colleague once declared verboten for feminists (inspiring me to paint my nails for the next meeting). The French feminists provided not only new ways of thinking about women's bodies and femininity, but also a vestimentary freedom, even a celebration of women's history of self-adornment. I was enraptured, despite the mysterious disappearance of my vintage red silk shawl.

For me, these years were the foundations of my career as an academic. Cross-appointed to two undergraduate college programs, women's studies and cinema studies, I remain the only member of the tenured faculty at U of T without a departmental appointment. My position in the institution is anomalous to this day.

My continued professional contact and deep friendship with Ceta Ramkhalawansingh have been tremendously productive for women's studies. Through her office at Toronto City Hall, Ceta was instrumental in getting important scholarships for both undergraduate and graduate women's studies students, bringing the program to the attention of the university administration by organizing scholarship presentations at the president's residence, and enjoining City Hall officials, including mayors, to participate in women's studies functions.

Teaching in two undergraduate college programs, both under-resourced since their inception, has been unsatisfactory in other ways, however. Both women's studies and cinema studies have had to struggle inordinately for recognition as viable academic fields, and that work has often been a knocking-head-against-the-wall grind. In addition, free-standing graduate programs in both disciplines took in their first students only in September 2007. Graduate supervision, therefore, normally a sustaining element of academic research and achievement, has not been available to me.

Have these drawbacks outweighed the advantages of the experience of life-changing intellectual and political growth, freedom to design exciting courses in my chosen fields, participation in building new academic programs, and collaboration with wonderful colleagues? Not on your life. I wouldn't trade it for anything.

Selected Publications by the Author

Armatage, Kay. 1996. Ethnography and its discontents: Ulrike Ottinger's *Taiga*. *Arachne: An Interdisciplinary Journal of Language and Literature* 3 (2): 31–47.

———. 1998. Collaborating on women's studies: The University of Toronto model. *Feminist Studies* 24 (2): 347–55.

———. 1999. *Equity and how to get it: Rescuing graduate studies*. Toronto: Inanna Publications and Education.

———. 2003. *The girl from God's country: Neil Shipman and the silent cinema*. Toronto: University of Toronto Press.

Armatage, Kay, Kass Banning, Brenda Longfellow, and Janine Marchessault, eds. 1999. *Gendering the nation: Canadian women's cinema*. Toronto: University of Toronto Press.

Genesis of a Journal

Donna E. Smyth

I CAN REMEMBER exactly when and where I heard the voice. Spring 1975. I was driving to Wolfville, where I taught at Acadia University. Highway 101, heading west. On the crest of the Avonport Hill, suddenly Cape Blomidon and the Minas Basin come into view. Jutting like a whale into the Bay of Fundy, Blomidon's pink-red sandstone cliffs glisten across the blue basin. Then you descend, down, down to the marsh flats and Acadian dykes and the Gaspereau River flowing forever into the sea.

The voice said, *you're going to start a women's studies journal.* Oh yes, I said with heavy sarcasm, of course. And what are we going to call this journal?

Atlantis, the voice said. And this was how it began.

When I told my sister colleagues what we were going to do, some of them laughed; some simply stared at me and shook their heads. However, nobody said, "It can't be done."

This was 1975, and it seemed like we could do almost anything. As I mentioned in "Conversation" with Margaret Conrad, published in the May 2000 issue of *Atlantis*, at the time "there was a lot of publicity about the United Nations declaration as International Women's Year" (2000, 105). Gathered within sight of Blomidon, at one of the oldest universities in the country, was a special group of women. Many of us had already worked together on the pioneering women's studies course at Acadia. In the process, we learned how to cross discipline boundaries and started to learn how to share with younger women and men the rich, radical potential of women's studies as it was developing in North America, Britain, and Europe. Some of us had been part of women's consciousness-raising groups. Most of us worked with community-based feminist, peace, and environmental groups outside the academy. As we talked about the project, we decided that we could find a niche in Canadian women's studies, which, at the time, had no equivalent to *Signs*, the American journal edited by Catherine Stimpson. Of course, we were aware of the comparative poverty of our resources and the audacity of our design. We wanted a strong regional base but also national and international contributors and subscribers.

During those first work-filled months, we clung to the name on our masthead as if it were a real masthead and we were the crew, trying to keep the ship afloat on a rather treacherous sea. We reclaimed Atlantis from Plato and a long line of male writer/thinker/dreamers, and redefined the name for ourselves and our readers. This is the rubric that appeared in our first issue and every issue since then: "Atlantis was a legendary ancient kingdom, an island in the Atlantic which disappeared during an earthquake. Fabulous stories are told about the beauty of the people who lived there and the kind of civilization they created. We take Atlantis as a symbol of the lost realm which women are striving to rediscover by discovering themselves."

Our first crew, or editorial board, included Maureen Baker (sociology) (see Baker's essay in this volume), Margaret Conrad (history), Carrie Fredericks (English), Lethem Sutcliffe Roden (French), Lorette Toews (psychology), and Lois Vallely-Fischer (history). I was the coordinating editor. Our art and design consultants were community-based artists and friends: Suzanne Mackay and Denise Saulnier. Suzanne Mackay came up with a stunning visual image for the first cover: the mask-like picture of a woman's face with flowing hair, emerging from … from where? From the sea. From the red mud of the Bay of Fundy. From nowhere, from everywhere. An Atlantean.

Our first production team was drawn from our editorial board, with typing done by Joy Cavazzi, then-secretary of the English Department, and layout spearheaded by Gillian Thomas, who taught English at Saint Mary's University in Halifax. This was the dark ages before computers and publishing software, when everything was done by hand and eye and ruler and Letraset. The first layout was actually done at my home on a hot, late summer day when the glue stuck to everything and everybody, and tempers sometimes frayed and we knew the women at *Signs* didn't do it this way.

Securing funding for the first issue was also a challenge. In 1975, the Department of the Secretary of State had established an International Women's Year Fund, and we applied for a grant. When we were turned down, we were outraged. In retrospect, it was clear that Ottawa-based funding bodies tended not to take applications that came out of the Maritimes very seriously. We protested their decision quite loudly and effectively, ultimately getting a grant that helped us through our first year (Smyth 2000, 105). However, throughout the early years we also received funds from private donors. When reminiscing with Margaret Conrad, I explained that "there was never enough money and nearly everyone worked on *Atlantis* for the love of it, not for the pay" (106).

We also knew that, if we were going to survive, we needed the support and advice of our sisters across the country. Our first advisory board was a gathering of distinguished scholars in many fields: Margaret Andersen, Susan Clark, Muriel Duckworth, Margrit Eichler, Jean Elliott, Gabriel Fischer (our sole man), Silvia Hudson, Margaret McGuire, Melinda MacLean, Theresa MacNeill, Margaret Norrie, Sandra Oxner, Irene Poelzer, Mary Sparling, Marylee Stephenson, and Patricia Tanabe.

We decided that our interdisciplinary ideal included creative writing and visual arts, as well as the more conventional disciplines. We didn't want to be just another academic journal. Whether or not we succeeded is a matter for history to judge. Twenty years later, the journal moved from Acadia University to a new home at Mount St. Vincent University in Halifax, where it is still being published, now as a refereed journal. Not surprisingly, we keep getting many fine submissions: "Even with the appearance of other women's studies journals in Canada, we still had [and have] more than enough material for two issues a year, and if we published conference proceedings we produced a third issue" (Smyth 2000, 106).

On the cover of the twentieth anniversary issue is a reproduction of a hooked rug creation by the well-known artist Nancy Edell. In the foreground is a flying cow complete with wings. The cow is about to take flight over the Bay of Fundy. In the background is Cape Blomidon. The title is "Blomidon Cow." This amusing, arresting image conveys some of the "high-flying" times of a journal anchored in the Maritime region and yet part of the national and international third wave of the women's movement.

Along the way, we changed, technology changed, and so did women's studies in Canada. For a long time, *Atlantis* has been a vital part of the scene, and this knowledge gives all of us great pleasure.

Selected Publications by the Author

Smyth, Donna. 1979. *Giant Anna*. Toronto: Playwrights Canada.

———. 1982. *Quilt*. Toronto: Women's Press.

———. 1986. *Subversive elements*. Toronto: Women's Press.

———. 1999. *Running to paradise: A play about Elizabeth Bishop*. Wolfville, NS: Gaspereau Press.

———. 2003. *Among the saints: Selected stories*. Lockeport, NS: Roseway Publishing.

The Saga

◉ *Marylee Stephenson*

FOR ME, THE WOMEN'S movement started by word of mouth. My part-
ner and I lived in what was, quite literally, a little shack near the beach in Vancouver. We were both in graduate school at University of British Columbia
(UBC), she in anthropology, I in the sociology PhD program. We were originally from the United States, part of the wave of folks—men and women—
who were just fed up with things down there and came north. My route was
a bit more circuitous—I'd been in graduate school in England, doing my MA,
and wanted to continue my studies, but not in the States. My professor was
Dorothy Smith—soon to become a major figure in women's studies, but
then simply a respected teacher whose undergraduate class at Berkeley had
converted me from anthropology to sociology. Then it turned out Dorothy
(it's hard to think of another way of referring to Dr. Smith, since these were
very informal days) was going to be teaching at UBC next, so the choice for
me was obvious (see Smith's essay in this volume).

One day, a friend came up from San Francisco and told us about her
own "conversion," for that is what it was, to women's liberation. She
explained about the "small groups" where women sat and talked about
being women, trying to understand where they were now and what had led
them there—and where they would be going next. For my partner and
me, this was a kind of vicarious revelation, or revolution might be a better word. I immediately decided to change my PhD thesis topic to women's
liberation, and since I had this contact in San Francisco—a major centre
of activities at that time—it seemed reasonable to do a comparison between

down there and up in Vancouver. Dorothy was consulted and immediately approved the idea.

I went down for a week or so, sat with a group of women, all of us bare-chested in the sun, sipping cool drinks next to someone's pool, and listened to what were genuine struggles of women, even in an environment of evident privilege and good fortune. I know I learned the basics of the logic, rhetoric, and attitudes of the movement over that brief time.

Upon returning, as summer ended, someone began to spread the word that there would be consciousness-raising groups on the UBC campus. There was already a very active women's group downtown, working hard on employment issues. They were less "experientially" oriented and tended more toward traditional organizing, given the background of some of the women in the labour movement. This was an extremely busy time, very rich and exciting, with everyone developing new ideas, new ways of seeing what we thought we understood, but now realized we didn't. It became clear to me that I had more than enough to study if I turned to these two contrasting women's groups for my thesis—one my own university "home" group and the other the downtown one. Dorothy readily agreed. Sometimes I wonder if she thought it was really doable, or if I was such a casual student, shall we say, that there was no harm in just letting me wander along. In the long run—and it was a long run—it all worked out.

Because, by definition, women's liberation—it didn't become the feminist movement for some time—called for direct, day-to-day application of what one learned and knew, it was a natural step to generate courses in it. Once my thesis fieldwork was over and I'd worn out my welcome as a graduate student, and had taken all the classes there were to be taken, I got a job as an instructor at the University of Windsor. It was a most welcoming and supportive environment to a new teacher, still a graduate student back home. There was already a course called Sociology of Sex, which was hardly one on feminist theory, but the faculty let me teach what was my first women's studies class under that rubric. It went really well, but it immediately was apparent that teaching materials did not exactly abound.

Two things began evolving at the same time that led to my developing my edited book on women in Canada—innovatively entitled *Women in Canada* (1973). First, I applied to the organizers of the conference of the Learned Societies' sociology section to put together sessions on women. There was enough interest and support for two rather than the usual single session. At the same time, I had been talking with one of the publisher's reps—the travelling tinkers of the book trade—about putting together an edited volume on women in Canada that could be used in university. He was very enthusiastic, and I began looking for a publisher. I found one in the politically aware (and long-defunct) new press (no capitals). Shortly after the book was through its first run, new press was absorbed by General Publishing, and the book stayed with them through the second edition.

The sessions at the Learned Societies supplied the basics of several articles that eventually went into the book, and along with others included later—largely through informal contacts as the movement grew in academia—the book was fairly rapidly put together, and it became the basis of most of the early women's studies classes. There were some more specialized books, but as an edited volume, it covered a wider range of topics—overview of the history of women in Canada, women in Québec, sports, women in the women's liberation movement in Vancouver, and many other topics. Through my new and very productive working relationship with Margrit Eichler, it had a very comprehensive and extremely useful bibliography chapter.

Margrit Eichler and I had established a firm collaboration and friendship starting the *Canadian Newsletter of Research on Women*, which later became *Resources for Feminist Research*, a publication that continues to be useful to this day. It was all Margrit's idea—she never stops thinking of how to do things better and faster—and I hung on for the ride. We'd go to her home in Waterloo, cut and paste items, and string them along huge rolls of paper to get them ready for the printer. No computers, little in the way of technical assistance—and her young son tottering around on the papers now and then. Margrit and I had different ideas of child-rearing, so I spent some time biting my tongue. But it became evident that she was far more accomplished at motherhood and cutting and pasting than I, so it all worked out very well. My own stellar "parental" moment came the first time I met Margrit to work on our idea of the newsletter. I came to her home. Margrit had come down with some horrible flu, so I just took over with her son, who was about two years old at the time. Single I may have been, but I had nephews, so he and I had a great time going to the park, feeding the ducks, and just hanging out as Margrit's delicate green skin tones began returning to a more normal pink. Our friendship now of some thirty-seven years was firmly established on that weekend (see Eichler's essay in this volume).

After a couple of years at the University of Windsor, I was invited to McMaster University. There was considerable interest in the sociology department, from the students in particular, I gather, to have women's studies courses. I went up for an interview, and got the job. There I taught the first women's studies class in the university. My book was out by then, and there were more and more materials to draw from. The first class had eighty-five students, and after that each one had about two hundred or so students. The teaching assistants for the course tended to do their theses and then to go on to teach in the field. It was a very active time, with an increasingly fully developed women's studies option, with several teachers coming on board to add their own expertise and interests to the wide mix of choices the students had. There were both undergraduate and graduate courses, and students could do a major in the field. It was a very active and interesting time, and a number of the graduates went on to bring women's studies to their own jobs.

After six years teaching, from 1973 to 1978, the time period you could teach before either getting tenure or being let go, I didn't get tenure at McMaster. I have to say in my defence that only one departmental colleague voted against me, but the university tenure boards were another matter. The rationale seemed to be "great teacher, active in the field—but *what* field?"—as in, women's studies is not a real academic field. That was actually stated by at least one witness at the hearings. I went before the tenure appeal boards three years in a row, with the last series, at the sixth year, lasting three weeks, and incorporating three lawyers and a lot of time and money for all concerned. There was a great deal of support in the women's studies community, and from even further afield than that. A number of the most prominent scholars in women's studies appeared as witnesses on my behalf; there were dozens and dozens of letters of support from across the country and even a few from abroad, and there was a modest but very welcome "defence" fund raised. The hearings were very stressful, but I was very touched and strengthened by the kind of support I received. Hearing scholars I had always respected speak well of me, talk about using my work, about my contributions to the field—this was very gratifying, and it helped me live with the fact that the university ultimately turned down my application. I received legal advice that the university's review committee had in its lengthy, confidential deliberations denied me "natural justice" in that during the committee's discussions apparently there was additional "evidence" brought in to which I naturally had no chance to reply. I did win this case in the Ontario Court of Appeal, and received a very small financial settlement that covered any legal fees for the appeal, but well over a year had passed by then and I was gone. I did have a Social Sciences and Humanities Research Council (SSHRC) sabbatical leave fellowship (it was timed for the first sabbatical, after six years as a full-time professor, so the university topped that up a bit). I spent a year in the field. It was during that time that the court appeal took place, and I got the word by phone of my "win" while doing my fieldwork for the SSHRC research.

By then I was long gone from academia and had no reason to try to find a position elsewhere, so I spent a year or so doing research contracts of various sorts. My bird-watching interests turned out to be a real bonus, because I did one very interesting contract for Parks Canada, which eventually prepared me for my second opus, a visitors' guide to the National Parks of Canada. (A number of years later, the parks book paved the way for my visitors' guide to the Galapagos Islands, but those are other stories.)

During this follow-up time of research contracts, I found life interesting and exciting, if a bit stressful, but here again women's networks came into play. In 1981 or so, Jennifer Stoddart, whom I'd met through her contributing a chapter to *Women in Canada*, invited me to come to the Canadian Advisory Council on the Status of Women (CACSW), as a senior research officer. Here my really quite extensive background in hands-on research and feminist analysis could come fully into play. Jennifer eventually moved onward and upward (becoming privacy commissioner for Canada), and I was the director of research for a few years.

I loved being in Ottawa, and the CACSW had its interesting and rewarding moments, but as my fortieth birthday came and went, I decided I did not want to spend what then seemed like a person's "sunset years" in Ottawa. I decided to return to Vancouver. When it became known that I was leaving, I was immediately approached by Status of Women Canada and other departments to do contracts for them. Since I'd been contracting out research for years, I knew the system, and before I knew it I was in Vancouver, doing studies for Ottawa-based, provincial, and local governments, and community organizations. It became clear to me very quickly that this was a whole career in itself, not just a bridge to a "real" job, so I formalized my company, found offices, and joined in with colleagues, and the rest is my history as a private-sector research and program evaluator consultant.

The company is in its twentieth year as I write (2007). It's a highly competitive market, but we're surviving. We often do contracts for women's agencies and departments, but in true feminist style, my teams and I bring a gender lens (as it is now known) to all of our projects. Whether it is an evaluation of a training program for down-sized miners up north, or Aboriginal fishers, or women leaving the sex trade, or a review of the labour market for industrial electricians, our gender lens is applied. The work is local, regional, national, and occasionally international. We are a small company, but very diverse and flexible. In fact, we embody the trends in the labour market today, as the old days of guaranteed employment with one organization for a lifetime, doing one kind of thing, are rapidly disappearing. Now, at a rather tired sixty-three years old, I am actually having to start thinking about winding the company down, doing some individual contracts, paying off the home, and just doing the occasional contract to keep things alive—there's no age limit on thinking and writing. I've already got the subject matter (and title) for my next book on women: something like "Navigating the Sixties," a double entendre for being in my sixties and being a "sixties" person.

This brings my mind's eye right back to the old days in California, watching the surfers in San Diego. You have to learn to catch the wave, stay with it, and know when to bail (or what to do when you're swamped). Then you pop to the surface and start swimming again. The women's movement made that possible for me—necessary and possible. I can live with that.

Selected Publications by the Author

Hanson, R. Karl, Ian Broom, and Marylee Stephenson. 2004. Evaluating community sex offender treatment programs: A 12-year follow-up of 724 offenders. *Canadian Journal of Behavioural Sciences* 36 (2): 87–96.

Stephenson, Marylee, ed. 1973. *Women in Canada*. Toronto: New Press.

———. 1976. Being in women's liberation: A case study in social change. PhD diss., University of British Columbia.

———. 2000. *In critical demand: Social work in Canada*. Final report. Vol. 1. Ottawa: Canadian Association of Schools of Social Work. Cited November 15, 2007. Available at http://www.casw-acts.ca/canada/sectorstudyes_e.pdf. [Vol. 2 is the technical report].

Stephenson, Marylee, and Ruth Emery. 2003. *Living beyond the edge: The impact of trends in non-standard work on single/lone parent mothers*. Ottawa: Status of Women Canada.

Coming of Age with Women's Studies

Meredith M. Kimball

> It was to prove much harder to alter the whole structure of education than
> to add on new spare parts. The ideals of the late sixties survived most in
> women's studies, where, long after their broader origins had been buried,
> battles were to ensue about subjectivity, community, the role of the
> teacher, the relations between experience and theory.
>
> —Rowbotham (2000, 185)

AS A CHILD, I was aware of various things that were unfair to girls, especially my exclusion from Little League baseball and other sports. However, I had no framework within which to understand this discrimination, and none of my peers felt as I did. I first discovered that I was not alone in my sense of injustice when I read Betty Friedan's *The Feminine Mystique* (1963) in college. By the time I was in graduate school at the University of Michigan in the late 1960s, feminisms[1] were part of the public political discourse, and I discovered a political home. It was a heady awakening, a conversion experience that changed my world forever. My first involvement in feminisms came during my last year in graduate school when I joined a consciousness-raising group of students and faculty.

When I arrived at the University of British Columbia (UBC) as a junior assistant professor in the psychology department in the fall of 1970, I immediately sought out feminists to continue the explorations I had begun in graduate school. I participated in the umbrella group or caucus, a conscious-ness-raising group, and a social science study group. I participated in all three for different reasons—the larger group to change the working climate for women at UBC, the consciousness-raising group in order to continue to explore my personal life in new ways, and the social science study group to explore how I could integrate feminisms into my teaching and research. Participation in these overlapping groups of women transformed my life in two important ways during the time I was at UBC (1970–76). First, I took on a lesbian identity. This was, and by and large has remained for me, more a personal than a political identity. In my teaching, I always worked to inte-grate lesbianisms and queer genders into my courses through assigned read-ings and in lecture and discussion topics. My scholarship has been centrally guided by my feminist politics that has included, but not focussed on, les-bian/queer topics. At UBC, friends and close colleagues knew of my emerg-ing lesbian identity, although I was not "out" to the wider university. Second, I had the opportunity to participate in the development of women's stud-ies at UBC, an opportunity I eagerly embraced. In 1972–73, I helped organ-ize a non-credit women's studies course in which I gave two lectures and led a small study group.

During the same time period, I joined with Helga Jacobson (anthro-pology), Annette Kolodny (English), and Dorothy Smith (sociology) to develop and teach the first credit women's studies course at UBC. This process and the structure of the program have been described elsewhere (Jacobson 1973; Kolodny 2000a; see also the essays by Kolodny and Smith in this volume). For me, negotiating the many committees necessary to implement women's studies was both frightening and empowering. I had never before encountered such public vitriolic misogyny and would never have been able to face it alone. Critical support came from Helga, Annette, Dorothy, my women's groups, and many other colleagues and students who believed in what we were doing. Helga in particular became a friend and mentor during these times. We were persistent in the face of all the official opposition, and in the end we won, which was very empowering for me as I was new to this kind of political battle. Developing the program and team-teaching the first course with Helga, Annette, and Dorothy were challeng-ing and exhilarating. Because there were no journals, very little published information, and no national women's studies organization, the analyses we came up with were constructed by the four of us and by our students, who were also experiencing feminist scholarship for the first time. Sharing in this development of knowledge was one of the most intellectually exciting experiences of my life. We were infused with the spirit of being pioneers, a heady feeling indeed.

In teaching women's studies for the first time with an interdisciplinary team of scholars and students from a wide range of backgrounds in the university, I began both to challenge psychology as it was practised and to develop a commitment to the importance of interdisciplinary scholarship. My critiques of psychology focussed on androcentric research and the exclusion of women within the discipline. Examples of androcentric research included generalizing results from male university students to everyone, basing social theories of gender on biology alone, and privileging quantitative experimental methods over other forms of knowledge. As a discipline, psychology included women mostly at the lowest academic ranks; very few women held positions of power as journal editors or members of governing bodies.

Support for these challenges came from a number of sources. Within psychology, pivotal experimental studies that demonstrated such things as discrimination against women applying for university positions in psychology departments (Fidell 1970) or the association of masculinity and males with psychological health (Broverman et al. 1970) were critical tools that I used in lectures and discussions with colleagues. Popular feminist writers such as Phyllis Chesler (1972) and Elizabeth Janeway (1971) made important critiques of psychology and psychiatry that supported the challenges that I and others were making to these disciplines. Within the Canadian Psychological Association (CPA), the Status of Women Task Force examined discrimination against women within universities and within the organizational structure of the discipline (Wand 1977). Many of the task force recommendations were later implemented through concerted feminist activism within CPA (Pyke 2001).

Although much of my time was taken up with debates within psychology, teaching women's studies made me aware that working within disciplinary boundaries was far too limiting. I embraced a strong commitment to interdisciplinary scholarship and teaching. Working with colleagues from a range of the humanities and social sciences supported and further developed this commitment. My political involvement in feminisms also supported my growing interest in the influence of social power on individual development. To understand biological and environmental determinants of women's behaviours required pulling together knowledge of biology, psychology, sociology, history, and political science at the least. To understand the ways in which women and the feminine were devalued in society required analyses of both the symbolic hierarchies in myths, paintings, and poems, and the material hierarchies of the workplace, politics, and home. To propose models of change, it was useful to examine the advantages and disadvantages of both liberal and Marxist models of equality. Understanding women's sexualities required analyses of how biologies were constructed, a power analysis of rape, an appreciation of the range and diversity of women's sexual fantasies, the malleability of sexual identities, homophobia, and the economics of women's dependency in heterosexual relationships.

As exciting as teaching women's studies was for me intellectually, it was not validated by UBC. The interdisciplinary course was not part of a stand-alone program, but was taught by the four of us on a released-time basis, a system each of our departments was unwilling to support beyond the first year. For me this lack of support carried over to the psychology department and in 1975 I received a negative tenure decision. After a year of unsuccessful appeals, I left UBC in 1976 and took up a joint appointment in psychology and women's studies at Simon Fraser University (SFU), where I worked until I retired in 2004.

The official reason for denying me tenure at UBC was that I had not published enough. The psychology department defined psychology very narrowly, and the only publications that were taken seriously were peer-reviewed journal articles in mainstream psychology journals. I had published a few such articles, and most of my interdisciplinary feminist-based scholarship was in edited books and therefore counted for little. Although nothing was ever said to me in writing, I am sure that developing and teaching women's studies was seen by the majority of the tenure committee (all tenured faculty in the department) as a diversion, not "real" psychology, and unimportant. Furthermore, I had by that time also served as president of the Faculty Association at UBC the year we made an unsuccessful attempt to form a faculty union. The senior faculty across the university, including those in psychology, had made their opposition to the union clear.

In contrast to UBC, my career at SFU was both successful and fulfilling. I was tenured easily, and when I retired I was a full professor. The main difference between the two universities was in the institutional structures. At UBC, all departmental tenure and promotion decisions were made by the faculty who already held the rank. This led to decisions being unduly focussed on who was to enter the club of the already initiated. I was not alone in being denied tenure; it happened to a number of my colleagues and friends in the department. SFU at that point had a very different history and structure. Founded in 1965, it was a new university, and in the early years a number of faculty were fired without cause by a very conservative administration. This led to a boycott by the Canadian Association of University Teachers. In order to get the boycott lifted, the university was required to set up formal and fair tenure and promotion policies. By the time I arrived, all departmental tenure and promotion decisions were made by an elected committee consisting of two assistant, two associate, and two full professors. The department chair was required to send forward the majority decision of the committee in each case. The other main structural difference was that women's studies was a stand-alone program at sfu with its own budget, faculty positions, staff, and space (see Andrea Lebowitz, Honoree Newcombe, and Meredith M. Kimball's joint essay in this volume). This meant that my tenure and promotion decisions were based equally on the decisions of both psychology and women's studies. More generally, it provided the structure for women's studies to grow and develop in the same way as other departments. In addition to these structural factors, the psychology department at sfu validated a range of publications and the interdisciplinary work done by me and several of my colleagues in the department.

In founding the women's studies program at ubc, feminisms were central to all the scholarship we generated. This has remained true as women's studies has expanded into a discipline and a very large body of scholarship with many national and international journals and monographs. In thirty years, the field has gone from the position where those of us teaching were generating the material as we went, to a body of scholarship that no one person could even read in her lifetime. In this process, feminisms have also had an influence on the academy and scholarship more generally.

Feminisms and other politically based interdisciplinary studies, such as anti-racist, anti-colonial, queer, and disability studies, have had an impact on methodologies, methods, and subject matter of scholarship. This impact has opened up scholarship to the voices of those not heard from before and validated a wider range of ways of knowing. Over the years, an increased emphasis on diversity has been the most important development. From the beginning, women's studies at ubc emphasized that women's lives and political concerns were varied. As an anthropologist, Helga Jacobson provided an excellent induction into the cultural diversity of women's lives and an inoculation against ethnocentric and essentialist thinking about women's lives. Dorothy Smith made anti-capitalist and class-based analyses central to the understanding of women's lives. Annette Kolodny included lesbian women's literature, and I searched for social science scholarship for information that made sense of women's many sexualities. We were, as I remember, less inclusive of different racial perspectives, including Aboriginal women's issues, and there was no acknowledgement of women with disabilities. However, the assumption that one had to think, not only about gender, but also about other dimensions of women's lives was well established in my thinking, so that it was natural to expand my own scholarship and teaching to include other aspects of women's lives as feminists continued over the years to make important claims for inclusion.

In the process of writing this paper, I have looked back over some of my writing from the early 1970s. In that work, I see the seeds of my later feminist scholarship. In the talk I gave at SFU as a part of my job application in 1976, I emphasized that I was unwilling to choose between psychology and politics. I argued that both are useful to a feminist analysis, and both are problematic if used in isolation. Most of my later work has focussed on approaching dualisms as "both/and" rather than "either/or" (Kimball 1995, 2003). This "both/and" approach has led me to understand that any feminist political strategy has both strengths and limitations, and that the choice of a strategy should depend on an analysis of the context in which it will be used, not on the strategy's superior or inferior nature in isolation. This in turn led me to an appreciation of the diversity of feminisms, which is necessary if we are to honour a diversity of women. Jeanne O'Barr said it well: "Think of the feminist toolbox as having everything—master's tools, new tools, and old tools that can be deployed for new purposes. Use the toolbox: spend energy on deciding which tools to use, not only on how to equip the box" (O'Barr 2000, 1207).

The early 1970s were intoxicating years for women's studies. Those of us involved were privileged to be pioneers, and this spirit infused all that we did. For me, as well as for Helga, Annette, Dorothy, and many of our students, this was the most exciting of times (Kolodny 2000a). The moment to be pioneers is fleeting, and nothing can ever quite match up to the experience. However, the excitement of discovery, the importance of doing work that matters, and the support of like-minded people stayed with me throughout my career. For that I am truly grateful.

Note

1 Although I would have used the singular at the time, I use the plural here and throughout this paper because, through my experience in women's studies, I have come to believe that a diversity of women requires a diversity of feminisms and feminist strategies to create social change (Kimball 1995).

Selected Publications by the Author

Kimball, Meredith M. 1986. Developing a feminist psychology of women: Past and future accomplishments. *Canadian Psychology* 27 (3): 248–59.

———. 1995. *Feminist visions of gender similarities and differences.* Binghamton, NY: Haworth Press.

———. 2001. Gender similarities and differences as feminist contradictions. In *Handbook on the psychology of women and gender*, edited by R. Unger. New York: Wiley.

———. 2003. Feminists rethink gender. In *About psychology: Essays at the crossroads of history, theory, and philosophy*, edited by D. B. Hill and M. J. Krall. Albany, NY: SUNY Press.

Stark-Adamec, Cannie, and Meredith M. Kimball. 1984. Science free of sexism: A psychologist's guide to the conduct of nonsexist research. *Canadian Psychology* 25: 23–34.

Doing Women's Studies

Pat Armstrong

FOR ME, WOMEN'S studies is a continual, collaborative project. The methods and analysis necessarily change over time and with context and experiences, but the objective remains: to understand, in order to change, the conditions and forces that create and perpetuate inequalities, not only between women and men, but also among women themselves and the full spectrum of genders. These are not sequential, but rather simultaneous efforts. Theory, research, and practice are integrally intertwined, and women's studies happen within and outside the boundaries of disciplines and academics. This approach to women's studies reflects both my long-held beliefs and what I am learning as I work with others, feminist and non-feminist. I started out as a feminist political economist who still finds much to learn from Marx. I remain a feminist political economist, but the nature of feminist political economy has developed significantly over time through challenges from research, theory, and practices.

Given this understanding, it is difficult to say when I first began to do women's studies. In the mid-sixties, I was employed full-time at the students' council, University of Toronto, and the Canadian Union of Students—student organizations focussed on inequalities. We were concerned with class bias in access to universities, commissioning Robert Rabinovitch, later head of the CBC, to examine the multiple barriers to higher education that began long before kindergarten. The research was a central feature in various campaigns to demand changes throughout the education system. We were concerned with regional inequalities, especially those related to Québec.

We were concerned with what we then called Native rights, employing Harold Cardinal at the Canadian Union of Students as a full-time student organizer on this issue. All this research and action touched on women. We did distribute materials that could be clearly identified as focussed on women, although the term women's studies was not yet in use. Analysis of women's conditions and the forces that contributed to inequalities was developing around us, and many of us were engaged in women's groups. I have a vivid memory of travelling by train from Ottawa to Toronto and exchanging ideas with Peggy Morton, who was sitting there writing her groundbreaking work "Women's Work is Never Done" (1972). It remains an incredibly sophisticated analysis of data on women's work, one that should still be required reading for anyone interested in women's studies. These student organizations could not be said to have had what we would now call a gender analysis or even a feminist approach. Indeed, one of the most exciting pieces written during this period was "Sisters, Brothers, Lovers ... Listen" (Bernstein et al. 1972), a collective critique by engaged women of the young male leadership of the sixties.

While I was involved during those years in various consciousness-raising groups and read the literature being produced—often informally—by feminists, it was not until 1969 that I became engaged more formally in the scholarly study of women. An assortment of Ottawa women began meeting regularly in our lofty space above a chicken restaurant on Bank Street. It was another women's group that sparked these meetings. Several of us had been asked to join a number of women working within the Waffle—an organization of those seeking to reform the New Democratic Party. We were not ready to join party politics but were ready to consider the kinds of questions they were raising about women. Three of the women—Maureen O'Neil, Suzanne Findlay, and Cathy Moses—were working in various government offices. At least four of the rest—Barbara Cameron and Joyce Cameron, Sheilagh Hodgins Milner, and I—were students. We read and critiqued the limited number of feminist books available, books by current authors such as Simone de Beauvoir, Germaine Greer, Kate Millett, Juliet Mitchell, and Betty Friedan. It was then possible to cover the genre as we raced through newly minted texts. We also read Sigmund Freud, John Stuart Mill, Mary Wollstonecraft, and other historical figures, seeking to develop our own understanding and evaluation of their work. It felt like we were exploring entirely new territory, covering ground not travelled before or seen with these eyes. At the same time, we were aware that what was happening in that loft was happening across Europe, the United Kingdom, and North America. We did not spend much time thinking about what women were doing in the rest of the world, in part because we had little access to materials written by them. While we faced enormous opposition, we were optimistic about our collective capacity to understand women's conditions and our ability to make change. Our ignorance about the strength of that opposition was also possibly our strength. Our collective reading laid the ground for our individual futures. The students became professors in women's studies; the government employees led important initiatives focussed on women (Findlay 1988).

During those years, I was working on my master's degree in Canadian studies. My political economy approach led me to focus on work because I understood work as central, not only to survival and our individual identities, but also to the parameters of historical development. Our reading had made me particularly conscious of two things. First, we would have to produce more empirical research that could provide the kind of evidence acceptable in the public domain. Second, we needed to integrate theory and research in ways that make transparent both the links amongst various kinds of women's work, and the conditions and forces that keep women doing women's work at women's wages.

I was still working on this thesis that was to become a book called *The Double Ghetto: Canadian Women and Their Segregated Work* (1978) when I was hired to teach at Sir Sandford Fleming College in Peterborough and my husband, Hugh Armstrong, was hired to teach at Trent University. While we were living in the don's residence at Trent, I made two forays into women's studies: one at the university and the other at the college. The first of these was at the initiative of incredible young women who had just entered the university and who wanted to learn about women. They approached Hugh and me, asking if we would read with them in women's studies. They were fabulous: active, politically engaged, stimulating, and very smart. Together we learned a great deal about the burgeoning literature and explored from a feminist perspective old and new texts that were not necessarily focussed on women. They all remain activists and feminists. Debbie Field started Foodshare in Toronto; Connie Clement, along with Madeline Boscoe, Gina Jones, Diana Majury, Kathleen McDonnell, Jennifer Penney, and Susan Wortman, started the feminist magazine *Healthsharing;* Sue Genge moved from the Ontario Pay Equity Tribunal to head the equity programs at the Canadian Labour Congress.

At the same time, I worked with four women teaching at the college to start a credit course in women's studies. Sally Rex and I both taught in social science, while Mary Sharpe taught in the secretarial program, and the fourth woman, whose name I have lost, in English courses. Over lunch and late afternoon drinks, we talked over our concern for the many young women in the college who saw no alternative to secretarial work and an early marriage. We did not want to denigrate secretarial work, but we did want them to see that there were a range of possibilities for women. We drew up a proposal for a course called Alternatives for Women. We would team-teach, in keeping with both our commitment to collective work and in recognition of our own need to learn together about this whole new area. We did not know of any other courses on which to model ours. We were determined to make it a credit course and to have it count as part of our teaching load in order to establish its legitimacy. Our dean was equally determined to prevent this from happening. He wrote us a memo saying he had watched stallions bite mares' asses in order to get them to behave, and he saw this as the proper order of relations between sexes. By 1972, we had won the struggle to have the course taught as a credit course but not to have it count as part of our teaching load. We gave up our second demand and had the rewarding experience of creating a new field, at least in that place, and of watching young women develop new ways of seeing.

By 1974, I was teaching at Vanier College in Montréal with a group of activist women committed to making changes, not only in the college curriculum, but also in the whole way the place was run. We started a Women's Studies Program, with its own coordinator, and made a course called Alternatives for Women our team-taught core course. It, too, was a credit course, and at least the coordinator of the program, who also coordinated the course, received a course credit. As many as a dozen women taught in the course, with modules on such areas as art, physics, English, social science, and history. Initially, we all attended each session, learning from one another and providing feedback after classes. It was voluntary labour for most of us, because our victory here too had only been partial. It was a credit course for which most of us received no credit. The course was incredibly stimulating and offered new approaches to old disciplines. In art, for example, the students learned to overcome their ideas about not being able to draw as they developed self-portraits in class. In the physics lab, women who thought they could not do such male stuff followed a recipe they later learned was actually a university-level experiment. At the end of term, we interviewed each student and used these conversations as the basis for further developing the course. It was by far the most rewarding teaching I have ever experienced and. the most intellectually rewarding work I have done as head of a program. The daycare centre, started by women faculty such as Greta Nemiroff the year before I arrived, made it possible for me to work full-time and to influence the care my children received through serving as chair of the collective that ran it.

The course was only part of our work. After several of us heard from students about their experiences with harassment, we started a campaign to develop a sexual harassment policy and to appoint a sexual harassment officer. Initially, the reaction was either much like that of my former dean in Peterborough or simply a rejection of the notion that sexual harassment happened. But the women were articulate and organized, and used the union as a means of furthering our project. I learned years later from a presentation on sexual harassment policies that ours was the first academic policy in Canada. We did not know we were pioneers; we were simply addressing the problem as we saw it.

We also had fun. We made International Women's Day into a week of celebration, decorating the college with banners, art, and photographs. We had music in various forms. We had a champagne breakfast for the women staff and faculty; we had a large public lecture, library displays, and special editions of the union newsletter. We ran programs on self-defence. Three of the women, Judith Crawley, Shirley Pettifer, and Marilyn Bicher, were central to the collective that was the Women's Health Press, so women's health issues were often part of the week. We also supported other courses in the program. For example, a teacher in the physical education program ran a survival weekend for women, a weekend that qualified as their credit for physical education. Thirty-some years later, the program is still there.

While I was at Vanier College, I started in the graduate program at Carleton University. There were no doctoral-level courses in women's studies in the 1980s, so I initiated a reading course with one of the male professors that stimulated him to establish such a course. I also did one comprehensive examination on feminist theory, in spite of objections that such theory could not be comprehensive—it being only about women! I won that battle in part by arguing that if the requirement was to be comprehensive, then all those males doing other theory should also have to take feminist theory. Since this was not seen as acceptable, I was allowed to focus on feminists although I still had to cover Marx, Weber, and Durkheim. My thesis focussed on women's work. At the defence, attended by a crowd because it was such a new field, one faculty member demanded that I remove the claim that as many as one in ten women had experienced abuse and rejected the evidence from Linda MacLeod's published research on the topic (1987).

When I was hired at York in the late 1980s, most of the battles for women's studies had been won. I was asked by the dean to conduct the internal assessment of the existing program the year after I arrived, a nice contrast to some of my earlier dean experiences. The assessment gave me the opportunity to see just how far we had come; yet the program still depended heavily on volunteer labour and had very few independent resources. Very soon after that, in 1991, York introduced the first Canadian doctoral program in women's studies, a clear signal that women's studies had arrived.

While I retain a cross-appointment in women's studies, I now do most of my work within the health field rather than within the Women's Studies Program. In many ways, working on women in health feels like déjà vu all over again. When I challenged a quite senior colleague recently about his failure to consider gender in his analysis, he responded by saying he always takes gender into account when he is dealing with gendered populations. When I asked at a consultation on indicators for primary health care why there was no gender analysis evident in the proposal, I was told that I was invited because they thought I could add it in. Have we come a long way, baby?

Selected Publications by the Author

Armstrong, Pat. 1996. The feminization of the labour force: Harmonizing down in a global economy. In *Rethinking restructuring: Gender and change in Canada*, edited by I. Bakker. Toronto: University of Toronto Press. Original edition, 1995.

Armstrong, Pat, and Hugh Armstrong. 1987. Beyond sexless class and classless sex: Towards feminist Marxism. In *The politics of diversity*, edited by R. Hamilton and M. Barrett. Montréal; London: Book Center; Verso. Original edition, 1983.

———. 2001. *The double ghetto: Canadian women and their segregated work*. 3rd ed. Toronto: Oxford University Press.

———. 2003. *Wasting away: The undermining of Canadian health care*. Don Mills, ON: Oxford University Press.

———. 2004. Thinking it through: Women, work and caring in the new millenium. In *Caring for/caring about. Women, home care and unpaid caregiving*, edited by K. R. Grant, C. Amaratunga, M. Bosco, A. Pederson, and K. Willson. Aurora, ON: Garamond Press.

Pioneer in Feminist Political Economy: Overcoming the Disjuncture

Joan McFarland

MY EARLY INTEREST in feminist studies took place outside the university. Indeed, there was a total disjuncture between my personal interests and concerns and what I was studying, and, later, what most of my colleagues were teaching and researching. I was in my twenties during this period. From 1965–67, I was in the last two years of an honours economics program at the University of Victoria; from 1967–71, I was doing my MA and PhD in economics at McGill University, and from 1971–76, I was beginning my teaching career, as one of only two economists, in the Department of Social Sciences at St. Thomas University in Fredericton, New Brunswick.

My first feminist influence was reading Betty Friedan's *The Feminine Mystique* (1963). I was eighteen and working with other young people in British Columbia's Department of Education for the summer. We all read and discussed the book. I don't know if I had thought about these issues before then, but all of a sudden I saw life, particularly women's role, through a completely new lens. Marriage had been a very important goal of mine ("I'll kill myself if I'm not married by 21"), but after I read *The Feminine Mystique*, marriage became a very scary and unappealing prospect, a feeling I haven't got over to this day—although I have raised two daughters as a single mother.

None of this new thinking and questioning was reflected in my studies. At UVic, I was the only female honours economics student. There was no critical element of any sort in the curriculum. I had just fallen into economics and entered the honours program because I had done well in the intro course and was invited into the program. I wanted to do well but was not very ambitious and had no particular idea what I would do with my degree.

Similarly, I went to graduate school because I was accepted into the McGill program and offered a scholarship.

At McGill, I was the only female in my class. There was virtually no critical content in the program, certainly not with respect to women. Again, I worked hard in order to "do well." I remember that when my results were good, other students (all male) made comments to the effect that I was being graded by a different standard.

I can't really remember who I was reading other than Friedan, but my "new lens" persisted. I do remember that in my last year at McGill, Marlene Dixon, the radical American Marxist feminist, was in town, and I was told that a small women's liberation group was starting up. I was interested enough to go to one meeting, but I was shy and didn't continue my participation after that.

When I was finishing my PhD and entering the job market, I applied for a few jobs, including one at the United Nations in New York City. I remember my interview there, where I was told that I would never be sent on an international mission because I was a woman and so wouldn't be accepted in such a role by many countries. Also, an economist on staff told me that he hoped that they would hire a woman "because she could edit our work." I decided that I didn't want that job! Along with a few other graduate students from McGill, I applied for a teaching job at St. Thomas when an ad for it appeared on the departmental bulletin board. I was hired as the second choice after a White male, originally from New Brunswick, turned an offer down.

When I got to St. Thomas, my only other colleague in economics turned out to be a radical economist who encouraged me to teach and research in areas critical of traditional economics. His wife was very involved in the women's liberation movement. Through her, I joined a local women's liberation group. The issue of the day was the integration of a local pub where women weren't allowed in the main lounge, only in a small separate room and escorted by a male. We also formed a consciousness-raising group. In the social sciences department at St. Thomas, I found a like-minded feminist sociologist, Kate Strouch (now Driscoll). We soon began planning for the first women's studies class—not only at St. Thomas but also on the broader Fredericton campus that encompasses the University of New Brunswick.

The course, given for the first time in 1973, was called Women in Society: A Socio-Economic Perspective. Although we were questioned by curriculum committee members about whether there would be enough readings to offer such a course, we were able to convince them that there were, and we were granted approval to go ahead. The course was given in the evening but was a full credit, interdisciplinary course. It was popular—we had some forty students, all young women. We used the 1973 text *Women in a Man-Made World: A Socio-Economic Handbook*, edited by Nona Glazer-Malbin and Helen Youngelson Waehrer. It was a reader with as many women's liberation as traditional academic readings. We also used the recently published report of the Royal Commission on the Status of Women (1970) and Marylee Stephenson's book of readings, *Women in Canada* (1973). We had films, speakers, and small groups; the class was very interactive compared to most classes in those days.

Around the same time, Kate and I embarked on a small book, *Equality for Women* (Strouch and McFarland 1974) for the New Brunswick Human Rights Commission. It sought to explain, in a catchy fashion, the 1967 United Nations *Declaration on the Elimination of Discrimination Against Women*, which was precursor to the 1979 *Convention on the Elimination of All Forms of Discrimination Against Women*.[1]

The literature that I was most influenced by in that period was the radical feminist literature, much of it coming out of New York City. The writings of Kate Millett, Phyllis Chesler, Shulamith Firestone, and the reader *Sisterhood is Powerful* (1970), edited by Robin Morgan, come to mind. I also read Germaine Greer and Simone de Beauvoir in this period. As well, *Ms.* magazine appeared in 1972, and I was an early subscriber. The Canadian anthology on women's liberation *Women Unite!* was published in 1972 and included an article by a member of our Fredericton women's liberation group. There was also the now-classic paper by Canadian Margaret Benston, "The Political Economy of Women's Liberation," published in *Monthly Review* (1969a). Benston was a scientist, not a political economist, but she had been a feminist participant in a Marxist study group. Using a Marxist framework, she argued that women's inferior status is based on their work in the household, which produces use value but no exchange value, thus appearing valueless. Therefore, socialism would not bring women's liberation without the accompanying industrialization of housework. The paper was very influential at the time. Another important political economy paper—which Benston drew on in her work—was Juliet Mitchell's "Women: The Longest Revolution" (1966). Mitchell's paper was also a critique of socialist theory in that it looked to change in the economic sphere alone to bring about women's liberation. Mitchell's analysis suggested that, in fact, women's liberation would need change in four structures in society: production, reproduction, socialization, and sexuality.

During this time, I had been working on an academic paper, "Economics and Women: A Critique of the Scope of Traditional Analysis and Research" (1976). In addition to critiquing traditional economic theory, its "economic man," and its total failure to deal with the issue of women, I suggested alternative questions that needed to be asked and alternative approaches that could be used. For example, traditional economic researchers were looking at women's increasing participation in the labour force in order to improve the predictions of their macroeconomic models. I suggested that research could go beyond the status quo and look at what a post-liberation economy with universal daycare and no discrimination might look like. Both the questions and the approaches I proposed were inspired by the women's liberation literature. The paper was accepted for publication in the inaugural issue of *Atlantis: A Women's Studies Journal*. Margaret Conrad, who currently holds a Canada Research Chair at the University of New Brunswick, was one of the editors of *Atlantis* at the time and gave me a lot of support for my work.

I attended a couple of women's studies conferences in this period. At the 1973 Learneds (now the Congress of the Humanities and Social Sciences) conference, there were some sessions for feminist academics, organized by Margrit Eichler, Marylee Stephenson, and Greta Nemiroff (see the essays by Eichler, Stephenson, and Nemiroff in this volume). My colleague Kate Strouch and I attended and felt quite supported in the work that we were doing at St. Thomas. In 1975, a Women's Studies in Higher Education conference took place in Calgary, where I gave my "Economics and Women" paper. Marsha Hanen was one of the conference organizers; Jill Conroy was the keynote speaker; and Dorothy Smith, Barb Roberts, and Maureen Baker were among the many presenters.

I was also involved in some organizing of feminist academics on campus. We met with the then-premier of the province, Richard Hatfield, in 1973, to discuss discrimination against women faculty at both St. Thomas University and the University of New Brunswick. We told him of our small numbers, our under-representation at the higher ranks, and our lower pay compared to male faculty. I can still remember his visible trembling at our challenge when I read out our statement to him. However, I don't think that our meeting necessarily led to much immediate change.

Thirty years later, I can look back on a very interesting career in feminist studies. Although I was trained in mainstream economics, most of my research and writing has been in feminist political economy, and I continue to teach cross-listed women's studies/gender studies courses. Presently I teach the two courses, Political Economy of Women and Women in the Third World, in alternate years. My inspiration for the latter course came from my participation in the Nairobi (1985) and Beijing (1995) United Nations women's conferences.

We have a Women's Studies/Gender Studies Program at St. Thomas. It exists in the context of an interdisciplinary majors/honours program—a situation that, in my view, has both advantages and disadvantages. A student can complete either a major or honours in women's studies/gender studies, which is great. However, not being an independent program, it is very under-resourced. We don't have a single position in women's studies/gender studies as such.

I still find feminist scholarship to be sophisticated, leading edge, and exciting. Some of the work that has had a lot of meaning for me in my teaching and research in the last decade has been that by such Third World feminist scholars as Chandra Talpade Mohanty and Vandana Shiva (see Mohanty 1991; Mies and Shiva 1993). I have been inspired by the way they have used feminist political economy to challenge the conventional wisdom.

Note

1 The Declaration on the Elimination of Discrimination Against Women, resolution 2263(XXII), was proclaimed by the United Nations General Assembly on November 7, 1976. It is available online at http://www.unhchr.ch/html/menu3/b/21.htm (Office of the High Commissioner for Human Rights 1976). The Convention on the Elimination of All Forms of Discrimintion Against Women, resolution 34/180, was adopted by the General Assembly on December 18, 1979, and entered into force on September 3, 1981. It is online at http://www.hrweb.org/legal/cdw.html (United Nations Commission on the Status of Women 1981).

Selected Publications by the Author

McFarland, Joan. 1976. Economics and women: A critique of the scope of traditional analysis and research. *Atlantis* 1 (2): 27–41.

———. 1980. Changing modes of social control in a New Brunswick fish packing town. *Studies in Political Economy* 4: 99–113.

———. 1998. From feminism to women's human rights: The best way forward? *Atlantis* 22 (2): 50–61.

———. 2002. Call centres in New Brunswick: Maquiladoras of the north? *Canadian Woman Studies* 21/22 (4/1): 65–70.

———. 2003. Public policy and women's access to training in New Brunswick. In *Training the excluded for work*, edited by M. Cohen. Vancouver: UBC Press.

Women's Studies at Guelph

Terry Crowley

THE UNIVERSITY OF GUELPH, founded in 1964, has the distinction of being the sole university in Canada founded on veterinary and agricultural colleges—with women largely segregated in the home economics section of the latter, the Macdonald Institute. Few women had graced the halls of either the Ontario Agricultural or Ontario Veterinary colleges, which dated back to 1862, but they overflowed in the Macdonald Institute because home economics teaching was a highly attractive career option for young women in the postwar years. This scene was distinctly inauspicious to develop women's studies during the early 1970s, but the determination of female students and dedicated faculty members eventually overrode these disadvantages, many of which were inherent in the parochial nature of academic disciplines themselves.

History was one of the departments added to make the university, but history as a discipline was as male as the twentieth century was bloody in its unprecedented destruction of human lives. The historical profession was so dominated by males that, across Canada, only Margaret Ormsby, Hilda Neatby, and Jean Murray received regular tenure-track positions as assistant professors before 1960 (and Jean Murray's father was president of the University of Saskatchewan). Since the Cold War intensified misogyny by emphasizing the importance of deterrence preparedness, the male-dominated history profession in Canada concentrated almost exclusively on national political history, diplomacy, and war. The discipline hardly budged one iota in reaction to the influx of women following the phenomenal growth in Canadian university enrolments beginning in the mid 1950s. Women were handmaidens, used occasionally as part-time assistants or lecturers, but not admitted to the club. Epistemology was as male-centred as philosopher Lorraine Code later identified so brilliantly in *What Can She Know? Feminist Theory and the Construction of Knowledge* (1992).

Males dominated the teaching and writing of history to such an extent that British Columbia historian Margaret Ormsby (b. 1909) found her desk relegated to the women's washroom at McMaster University in 1940 when she became a lecturer amidst the shortages accompanying the Second World War. Women historians such as the University of Saskatchewan's Hilda Neatby, who did invaluable service on the Massey Commission (the Royal Commission on National Development in the Arts, Letters, and Sciences), and as author of *So Little for the Mind*, produced original history—but in the exacting male mode of her male colleagues and mentors. In this same era, well-known University of Toronto historian Frank Underhill referred to a woman graduate student, Margaret Banks, as "mousy" in a letter he wrote as Banks sought futilely to find a regular university teaching post in history (Wright 2005). I myself was on a committee to hire a sessional lecturer in East Asian history during the early 1970s where the same form of sexism occurred. The letter the hiring committee received from the chair of the history department at the University of Western Ontario was glowing about the woman applicant's teaching and personal attributes, but he concluded with the damning assertion that he had been one of those who had dissented from her recent decision to have her child out of wedlock.

Closed-mindedness in history was seen in outmoded attitudes, restricted subject matter, and a methodology that purported to be objective by stressing the use of archival research to overcome supposed contemporary prejudices. Things were generally not so tough for women in literature and languages departments because their presence there was longer and stronger. Sometimes English and theatre scholars were seen in couples with both partners teaching in the same department, but this was a practice almost universally shunned in history and such social science departments as political science. Women historians accepted by academic males were frequently unmarried, like Hilda Neatby, or Alice Stewart at the University of Maine; if married, they were independent scholars in the manner of Canada's Isabel Skelton, wife of political economist O. D. Skelton, or the American Mary Beard, whose husband, Charles, taught at Columbia University.

Within less than a decade, the University of Guelph emerged as a mid-sized institution of some ten to twelve thousand students imposed on a small city of just over fifty thousand people. Many new faculty members in arts, social sciences, and the physical and biological sciences believed that the creation of a new university held the possibility for greater innovation than was possible in more traditional institutions. At Guelph, four women and one man—all foreigners—were particularly instrumental in furthering academic interest in and concern for women beyond the traditional roles that had been perpetuated in Guelph's original faculties. Women wanted to teach about women and were prepared to do so by stealth in order to avoid the confrontations that might accompany seeking committee approvals for new courses. American-born Joanna Boehnert began teaching the Psychology of Women in 1970, although her course did not enter the university calendar as such until 1978. The same transpired in sociology/anthropology, where Nora Cebotarev, a Latin American, started teaching the sociology of women in the summer of 1971, in a course titled Society and the Individual, but the course on the Sociology of Sex Roles did not appear until 1976. Similarly, in the English department the Scot Leslie Marshall began teaching Women and Literature as one of a number of courses offered under a rubric called Themes and Forms (see Marshall's essay in this volume). This pattern was broken in the Department of Languages by the outspoken Marguerite Andersen, a German who specialized in French literature. After Andersen came from Loyola (Concordia) University to chair the languages department in 1973, she quickly moved to have a course devoted to women in world literature adopted; it appeared in 1975 (see Andersen's essay in this volume).

The most visible activist woman on campus was psychology professor Norma Bowen. An African-Trinidadian through birth in a family of fourteen children, Norma Bowen had emigrated to Canada in 1956, attended the universities of Toronto and Waterloo, and been appointed at Guelph in 1966. Bowen was an organizational woman par excellence, and she also had a flare for publicity as grand as her smile was wide. She worked with the Academic Women's Association on campus (see Wendy Robbins's essay in this volume), headed the Faculty Association in 1972–73, and chaired the Ontario Confederation of University Faculty Associations in 1974–75. With widespread discontent on campus about women's salaries (there was no salary scale at the time) and women's positions at all levels in the university, Norma Bowen was the driving force that led President William Winegard (later a Conservative federal cabinet minister) to forestall an immediate problem by appointing her in 1972 to head a task force on the status of women at Guelph. For three years, until its report was published in 1975, Bowen's group commissioned surveys, dug deeply, and used media creatively to expose the university's failures in regard to women as students, staff, and faculty members. Guelph mirrored the national debate that accompanied the federal Royal Commission on the Status of Women.

During the early 1970s, the University of Guelph was as much a seething cauldron in regard to women as Duke University had been about African Americans' civil rights and war resisters when I had studied in North Carolina between 1968 and 1970. As a twenty-five-year-old faculty member, I was especially attuned to the concerns of students, since my own views had seemingly been of no account in my own post-secondary education. Women students at Guelph suggested to me in the early 1970s that they would benefit from a course in women's history. The thought was novel and the timing right. Women might have been present in literature but they were largely absent from the past, and there was a pressing need to include the largest component of humanity in humanity's story. Newer approaches by French historians identified as Annalistes (from the journal *Annales: Economies—Sociétés—Civilisations*) wrote women into history in new ways. Universities were also gripped by the tremors emanating from student upheavals, as I saw most forcefully in Paris during 1968, or in the demonstrations at Sir George Williams University (Concordia) in the following year. Guelph's history department was young and its members, even those among the oldest cohort, were generally concerned about serving their student constituency. My colleague Mary Rogers, a medieval historian from the United States, and I discussed student suggestions and decided in 1974 to proceed jointly with a broadly sweeping course in Western women's history. We agreed that she would be responsible for the first part up to the Renaissance and I for the second. Other history colleagues greeted our departure more with skepticism than hostility, but doubts were overridden through invoking student requests and judiciously having the word "topics" in the course title.

Both social climate and evolving disciplinary norms helped to gain acceptance for the idea of women's history, but Mary Rogers and I still had to decide what we would actually teach in the course when it appeared in 1976. Due to the dearth of research on women by women themselves, I assumed an approach that gave greater attention to what men thought about women than would later be necessary. The course was quickly fully subscribed, and Mary Rogers and I each took our own weekly seminar with half of the course enrolment. Fortunately, a book entitled *Not in God's Image: Women in History from the Greeks to the Victorians*, had recently been edited by Julia O'Faolain and Lauro Martines and published in New York in 1973. This text provided the primary sources (documents) that historians so value, even if many of them were dry legal records conveying male views. In my lectures during the second half of the course, I tried to enliven things by emphasizing the contrasts among social classes in Western history, introducing students to the differing outlook of peasant women from their better-off counterparts, and by playing up the drama inherent in the fight for women's suffrage. Occasionally we had a male student, but in the main the classes were filled with women students.

The personal reason that I wanted to transcend history's limiting paradigms was that I am a gay man, or as was said in those days, a homosexual. My sexuality eased my relations with women. I consciously reasoned that homosexuals might never be free due to our numerical inferiority and the ferocity of the prejudices against us, but that women were a majority and their situation was capable of being radically improved. American journalist Betty Friedan's criticisms of the narrowness of women's lives relegated to domesticity struck a personal note for me as I and my sister helped my mother adjust to empty nest syndrome in the years after she turned fifty. Marguerite Andersen also edited a phenomenally successful book in 1972 that sold six thousand copies with a title that struck me forcefully, *Mother Was Not a Person* (2004). My mother was truly wonderful, but she had never emerged as a full person in the same sense as men were allowed. My sister, in the wake of the short-lived women's liberation movement of the late 1960s (historians see the liberation movement of the sixties and early seventies as distinct from the feminist movement that supplanted it), and having thrown aside an affair with a married lover, abandoned her two previous careers in banking and in nursing to return to university in 1972 to better prepare herself for a fuller life.

The varying mixtures of peoples from differing backgrounds at Guelph during the early 1970s promoted experimentation. Marguerite Andersen (she also signed "Margret"), who later established a significant reputation in francophone literary circles, was a formidable presence in academic matters, even if her abrupt, no-nonsense manner did not readily gain her allies. Born in 1924, Andersen left Germany to teach in Tunisia, gave birth to a daughter in Addis Ababa, moved to Montréal in 1958, obtained the doctorate in 1965 for a thesis that was published, taught in North Dakota, and offered one of the first interdisciplinary women's studies courses in Canada at Loyola in Montréal in 1971–72 (see Andersen's essay in this volume). Andersen wanted to promote everything related to women in the academy and managed to scrape money together to hold the first women's studies conference at Guelph in 1974. The gathering attracted well over a hundred people and centred on Canadian suffragist Nellie McClung. The day was notable for the presence of Nellie's son, Mark McClung, who told a delightful story of his mother being so chagrined at charges of maternal neglect that she taught her sons to retort mockingly, "I am a suffragist's son and I've never known a mother's love." Historian Veronica Strong-Boag was decidedly more provocative in asserting (and elaborating) that women did not need men for anything any more. With successes such as this conference, it is unsurprising that Andersen was also well connected in the emerging women's network through service on the editorial boards for *Atlantis: A Women's Studies Journal* beginning in 1973 and later for *Resources for Feminist Research*.

Psychology professor Joanna Boehnert embodied the right combination of academic commitment and organizational ability to begin knitting these diverse stands into a coherent Women's Studies Program. Educated at Lake Erie College and the universities of Iowa and Toronto, Joanna had married a Canadian academic of German extraction, come to Guelph in 1968 for her first regular faculty position, and given birth to two girls. She was motivated by genuine academic concern for the failings of her discipline in its disregard of women and for the university's deficiencies as so recently laid bare in its presidential task force. By her own admission, Joanna had determined that she would be superwoman: super mom, super prof, super advocate for women. She possessed a quiet self-assurance and was immediately open to students, but slightly diffident in faculty circles. Joanna consciously sought to associate sympathetic colleagues, whether female or male, with her project and thereby cut across faculties/colleges within the university. Beginning in 1977, she built on the initiatives already mentioned and brought in such faculty members as Brian Calvert from philosophy and Donna Lero from family studies, the latter a woman who was soon to be a major player in the national child-care debate. Creating an introductory women's course and capping the program with a fourth-year seminar, Joanna Boehnert crafted a modest women's studies offering that provided for a major in the three-year degree program or a minor in the honours program.

I happened to be chair of the BA Program Committee at the time, because the deans of the faculties of Arts and Social Sciences were fighting so badly that a mediator was needed. Recently involved in promoting rural studies and assisting a political scientist to secure approval of a new international development program, I was able to help Joanna in the smooth passage of the women's studies program early in 1978. Knowing that women's studies was likely to arouse controversy, I suggested to her that we stage a public debate one evening. Joanna and I assumed the affirmative, and philosophy professor Michel Ruse and chief librarian Margaret Beckman the negative. Beckman voiced the argument common among the few successful women of the day that, since she had made it to the top by mastering what men had to learn, women students should do the same. In the hall afterwards, Priscilla Reid, the wife of the founding chair of the history department, was so distraught at the thought of women's studies that she maintained that women's real role was, like hers, to manipulate their husband behind the scenes. The evening of debate drew media attention to herald the advent of women's studies at Guelph, but, in line with most interdisciplinary initiatives, it received few resources from the university. Joanna nevertheless assembled a large number of colleagues to voluntarily offer the first introductory course, with each of us attending all classes and taking smaller discussion groups. Joanna Boehnert remained at the helm of women's studies at Guelph over the course of three decades, but she had left the coordinating role before her untimely death in a car accident in 2001.

In retrospect, I see little in the development of women's studies at Guelph that constituted pace-setting, but the process itself taught all who were involved to think more broadly as we ventured along our own intellectual journeys. In that first women's studies class, I was pleased to learn new forms for student assessment and to be introduced to literary titans like Garcia Lorca, with his plays on the tragic life of Spanish women, such as *House of Bernarda Alba* (1945), and Virginia Woolf, who created a new literary form in *A Room of One's Own* (1929). The history of women's studies at Guelph, as I am sure it was in many places, represented new beginnings in personal terms that have not really become old as we have ourselves aged or died. Reaching out, discarding the outmoded, and embracing what is new and worthwhile should always be the hallmarks of intellectual and academic life.

Selected Publications by the Author

Crowley, Terry. 1986. Madonnas before Magdalens: Adelaide Hoodless and the making of the Canadian Gibson girl. *Canadian Historical Review* 62: 520–49.

———. 1988. *Clio's craft: A primer of historical methods.* Toronto: Copp Clark Pitman.

———. 1990. *Agnes Macphail and the politics of equality.* Toronto: Lorimer.

———. 1999. *The college on the hill: A new history of the Ontario Agricultural College, 1874–1999.* Toronto: Dundurn Press.

———. 2003. *Marriage of minds: Isabel and Oscar Skelton reinventing Canada.* Toronto: University of Toronto Press.

Women's Studies: Oppression and Liberation in the University

◉ Meg Luxton

Introduction

AS A WHITE GRADUATE of a high school in Toronto, I started university in 1965 juggling two contradictory messages. My working-class mother, who strove explicitly to produce a middle-class daughter, urged me to get a "just-in-case" education as a nurse or teacher, an occupation I could fall back on if (horror of horrors) I was unsuccessful in marriage. My (sexist and sex-blind) middle-class high school teachers swore that, if we worked hard, we could do anything we wanted and that a university education guaranteed success. Well-trained in values of hard work, respect for authority, and conformity, I assumed I would get married, become a devoted wife and mother, and have interesting work that contributed to the well-being and advancement of the world. I was too naive to know to that the two worlds of women's work were significantly incompatible. My world was too heteronormative for me to even contemplate alternatives to traditional marriage.

What Brought Me to Feminist Studies?

My first years at the University of Toronto as an anthropology student were exhilarating and confusing. I loved the scholarly environment, the pace of work, and the new world of ideas available to me. But as women we faced sexism and misogyny. My first year anthropology professor joked that his subject was "the study of man embracing woman," a joke that was hollow when everything we read was about "Man" and his place in the world. I began to sense that middle-class success for women might demand more than hard work.

In graduate school, the sexism became more personal. My first application to graduate school was rejected explicitly because, as a woman, I could not be serious about a career. My second attempt was rejected on the grounds that, as a married woman, I had a husband who would support me, while the other student applying was a man with a wife to support. When the man pointed out that his wife was a high school teacher earning good money and my husband was unemployed, they just shrugged and reiterated that married women were not serious about professional careers. I was finally accepted into graduate school—not into the MA program with my male colleagues, but into the MPhil, known popularly as the married women's degree. This degree required a year longer than the MA and entitled the holder to teach in university but was usually considered an inferior alternative to a PhD. It took four years of struggle before I finally got into the PhD program at the University of Toronto in 1973.

In my program, students writing their comprehensive exams usually withdrew for several months to prepare for the exams that were written over three eight-hour days. In 1971, I showed up visibly pregnant, and the professor monitoring the exam refused to let me in because "You can't write exams in that condition!" We fought about it for several hours and, when they finally let me in, they did not permit me to make up the time lost. That summer, when one of the professors realized I was pregnant and teaching, he launched a complaint. When asked to explain his position, he said it was "unseemly" and claimed that I would miss too many classes. Ironically, he got the flu and missed several weeks. I missed the Monday class on the day my baby was born but was in the classroom on Wednesday. The newly emerging feminist politics made sense of what was happening to me, inspired me to fight on, and gave me strategies for how to fight.

At the same time, the various socialist revolutions and national liberation struggles provided both compelling critiques of imperialism and examples of people mobilizing together to change their world. In Canada, anti-poverty activists, Aboriginal movements, Québec nationalists, student protest mobilizations, a growing left-wing critique of the social democracy of the CCF-NDP (Co-operative Commonwealth Federation and New Democratic Party), and the opposition to the United States invasion of Vietnam combined to create a climate in which the women's liberation movement was born. My favourite button proclaimed "Question Authority!" It was a heady time, when those of us building such movements believed there was a possibility of changing the old world, based on a politics that assumed that our own liberation depended on the liberation of all (Rowbotham 1972a, 11). We dreamed that the liberation struggles going on around the world might produce a new world for us, too. I came to understand the need for, and value of, collective political action.

Who Were My Allies?

In the university, our allies were varied. A few sympathetic and visionary administrators and faculty members agreed to facilitate our new course proposals or supported our actions (see the essays by Ramkhalawansingh and Armatage in this volume). A passionate and enthusiastic group of students kept us inspired and mobilized. We were also lucky at the University of Toronto to have a collective of women committed to creating a new field of study and to learning new ways of understanding the world. As feminist activists, we were also part of a larger community of left-wing activists in the city who validated our politics and celebrated our endeavours.

Liberation was a dynamic that mobilized the delight, exhilaration, and limitless capacities that intellectual life had promised into a broader commitment to winning freedom and self-determination through working collectively. It also demanded a rigorous dedication to activism on all fronts. Self-determination for the new left activists of the late 1960s and early 1970s challenged us to examine every aspect of our lives as thoroughly as possible using as many resources as possible. We read widely, we debated endlessly, and we used our new insights into psychoanalysis to probe our own psyches and our newly acquired marxism[1] to probe both what we knew about the world and what the world might actually be like. Most importantly, we tried to practise our new ways of knowing the world. In just a few short years (1969–75), the women's liberation movement in Toronto was instrumental in setting up and maintaining a wide range of institutions and service-providing organizations, typically run on a non-profit, collective basis. These included radical daycare centres, which aspired to raise socialist, non-sexist children and succeeded in providing excellent care for several generations; the Women's Press, which published socialist feminist material no other press would touch; rape crisis and battered women's centres, to both care for women after attacks and challenge the way the legal system treated such crimes; and the Women's Bookstore. The women's liberation movement also developed a network of interpersonal care and support for activists such as communal housing, consciousness-raising groups, and women's dances. Our involvement in all those activities and in the debates surrounding them gave us a chance to put into practice some of our political visions, and those experiences tempered our theories. For example, 1971 activists occupied a U of T building for over six months, demanding the university provide child-care services. As a new mother, I learned about child-rearing as part of a live-in community with over 150 adults helping me think about progressive ways to care for children.

What Was the Scholarship We Challenged?

One of the most important lessons to emerge from this activism was the power of collective knowledge production as opposed to the individual performance conventionally valued. Coming together collectively to assess our experiences, we moved from the personal to the social and even the political. We developed new ideas and were able to transform personal complaints into political demands. For example, individual women resented the way many men paid little attention to the ideas woman expressed, prevented women from speaking in public meetings, and publicly declared women unfit intellectually. When women compared their own experience with other women's, they began to recognize a social problem and came up with strategies to deal with it. Some women challenged their exclusion from public events, forcing the men in power to begin recognizing women (Kerans 1996; MacPherson 1994). Others employed direct action, such as the women who attended a public lecture by anthropologist Robin Fox on the natural inferiority of women. Presenting themselves as adoring groupies, the women disrupted his talk, made a mockery of his sexist ideas, and created a space for a public discussion of sexism. Once they gave the problem a different name with new political and moral meanings, such as sexism, the focus shifted from something humiliating to women to something shameful for men to do. The new way of thinking made political organizing possible— educating other women and men, negotiating new ways of holding meetings to ensure women had a chance to speak, or lobbying for affirmative action measures to overcome entrenched sexism.

For those of us who came to women's liberation and academia simultaneously, the two projects were integrally interconnected. What we learned in and about the university shaped our politics; our politics provided the inspiration and questions with which we challenged both the formal knowledge legitimated in the universities and the prevailing structures of the academy. In 1970, a collective of thirteen women's liberation activists at the University of Toronto forced the administration to let them offer a course under the auspices of the Interdisciplinary Studies Program called, in the first year, Women in the Twentieth Century. This was revamped the next year as Women: Oppression and Liberation. I learned more in a few years of teaching this course than I had in my undergraduate studies. Wildly popular, this course offered evening lectures open to the public that drew audiences of five hundred or more, women and men eager to learn about women's history, present situations, and dreams for the future.

This course, and the growing feminist scholarship it drew on and inspired, challenged university knowledge and institutional practices in a variety of ways. First, it offered a critique of, and a corrective to, the androcentrism of formal knowledge by focussing on the women "hidden from history" (Rowbotham 1977). Second, it identified new objects of study, such as the sex/gender system (Rubin 1975), and laid a basis for what became the new field of feminist theory (Maroney and Luxton 1987). Third, it challenged the existing accreditation and hiring practices of universities by revealing the inability of existing departments and faculty members to analyze and revise their curriculum and research in light of feminist critiques. The teachers in this course were there because, as activists in the women's liberation movement, we were knowledgeable in ways that long-time faculty were not. Finally, and this explains its ability to survive inside the university, because the course offered a way of explaining women's lives to make sense of their experiences, while offering strategies for changing their lives and a vision of better ways of living, it was popular. Fee-paying students attended in droves and threatened widespread opposition to any efforts to eliminate it. Instead, they demanded more.

The Major Challenges We Faced

The biggest challenges, of course, came from the sexism of individuals and the institution. Every time we spoke publicly, every time we raised feminist issues in a classroom or in the university at large, we had to expect ridicule, opposition, and contempt from some. The professor who had tried to prevent me from teaching when I was pregnant told me two years later what a terrible mother I was for abandoning my child to the horrors of daycare so I could "indulge" myself by "playing" at teaching. When I proposed to do my PhD research on women's work in the home, I was told that, if I really insisted on studying women, I should at least study "real" work, like that of nurses or teachers. One of my committee members told me there was nothing to learn about women's work in the home because "women don't do anything but lie around the house all day." The week before my thesis defence, another professor in my department told me my work was on a vacuous topic, and told several colleagues in a loud voice what a silly fool I was for arguing that women's work in the home contributed to the well-being of society and the economy. He went on to say that he was embarrassed to be part of a department that would even consider such work suitable for a doctorate.[2]

I remember going before a committee in 1973 that approved new course proposals. The request before ours was for a full-year course on Man in the Middle East. It passed with murmurs of approval. I presented our proposal for a full-year course on Women in the World. It was rejected as having "too narrow" a focus. I was encouraged to redo the proposal as a half course. While some men took our courses because they wanted to learn, there was often at least one man who tried systematically to undermine our teaching or who said he was in the class to see "how many chicks he could lay in the year."

The feminist scholarship that led to, and developed out of, our early efforts, and out of thousands of similar initiatives across the country and internationally, had at its heart a commitment to generating knowledge in order to understand oppression, to mobilize effective opposition to that oppression, and to fight for the liberation of all human beings. It was strongly based in an activist movement committed to the struggles of working-class and the most oppressed women. We faced explicit sexist hostility and outrage from many who valued the existing knowledge and institutional structures of the academy and decried our scholarship as partisan. But the most important challenges came from the difficulties we faced in trying to reconcile our lives, with all our anxieties, hesitations, and deferences, with the vision we aspired to as strong, indomitable women. Our formal commitment to the liberation of all was challenged, too, by lesbian, working-class, Aboriginal, Black, and immigrant women, who readily pointed out the discrepancies between our declared politics and our failure to adequately take up issues of sexual orientation, racism, and class inequality. Our comrades in Québec challenged us on the national question and on our linguistic chauvinism.

We also had to invent almost everything we needed to teach, and, while that was usually exciting, it was also time-consuming, hard work. For example, as there was no suitable material in print on Aboriginal women, I researched and wrote a twelve-page handout on "Indian and Inuit Women of Canada" in 1972.[3] We needed guest speakers who could tell our classes about issues when there was nothing to read, so we relied on volunteers to prepare and present classes on lesbianism, on racism, and on working-class women's struggles. What made it all worthwhile was our sense that we were changing the way formal knowledge was produced and taught—by taking women seriously and producing knowledge by, for, and about women.

Notes

1 One convention of the new left uses marxism (lower case) as a way of indicating a distinction from the Marxism of the Third International and the Comitern.

2 The thesis became my book *More Than a Labour of Love: Three Generations of Women's Work in the Home* (Luxton 1980). It has become a classic text and is still in print; I have won awards based on its success.

3 A copy of this paper is available on request from Meg Luxton, School of Women's Studies, York University.

Selected Publications by the Author

Cheal, David, Frances Wooley, and Meg Luxton. 1998. *Families and the labour market: Coping strategies from a sociological perspective.* Ottawa: Canadian Policy Research Networks.

Luxton, Meg. 1980. *More than a labour of love: Three generations of women's work in the home.* Toronto: Canadian Women's Educational Press.

———. 2001a. Family responsibilities: The politics of love and care. Paper read at 32nd Annual Sorokin Lecture, at University of Saskatchewan, Saskatoon.

———. 2001b. Feminism as a class act: Working class feminism and the women's movement in Canada. *Labour/le Travail* 48: 63–88.

Luxton, Meg, and June Corman. 2001. *Getting by in hard times: Gendered labour at home and on the job.* Toronto: University of Toronto Press.

Reflections on Teaching and Writing
Feminist Philosophy in the 1970s

🖋 *Susan Sherwin*

THROUGH A COMBINATION of good luck and good timing, my experiences in teaching feminist studies at Dalhousie University have been unusually positive. Since my arrival in 1974, I have been encouraged and supported in my efforts at teaching feminist philosophy. Many feminist philosophy colleagues who began their careers at different sites or different times, where the constellation of stars and players was tilted at a different angle, have had very different experiences. I describe my own extraordinarily good fortune in awareness that my experience, while not unique, was also far from typical.

Let me backtrack a little. I began university in 1965, headed for a career in mathematics. Though I had little idea of what philosophy actually was, I believed it to be something one ought to study in university; hence, I pursued a degree in mathematics and philosophy. As graduation approached, I found myself with many intellectual questions but no firm life plan and no clear strategy for moving away from my parents' home other than marriage or graduate school. Happily, the second option won.

I received plenty of warnings against my decision to pursue a doctorate: my undergraduate professors told me that I would be wasting my time since no one hired women in philosophy (a fact I had little reason to doubt: there were no women faculty members in the philosophy departments in which I did my degrees), and my parents worried that no one would want to marry a woman with a PhD (again, no contrary examples in my direct experience). More troubling to me was the fact that my principal mentor, a male philosophy professor who specialized in logic and philosophy of mathematics, committed suicide during my last year of undergraduate training. This event left me deeply shaken about the virtues of an academic life. Nonetheless, when offered scholarship support, I headed off to Stanford in 1969 to specialize in the philosophy of mathematics and logic. Quickly, I discovered that formal philosophy at the graduate level was now more drudge than fun, so I veered towards philosophy of language (along with nearly half of the philosophy PhDs in the United States at the time).

Arriving in the US in 1969 meant that I, like so many others, was caught up in anti-war activism. The Vietnam War was not the only political issue to affect me, however. I also joined a women's consciousness-raising group. This I did out of a sense of responsibility for others. I considered myself already liberated; after all, I was pursuing a doctorate in a field with no women role models anywhere in sight. I felt a strong obligation to use my privilege and influence (such as it was) to help those less fortunate women (whoever they were).

Well, they don't call them consciousness-raising groups for nothing. I quickly learned that I was a lot less liberated than I imagined myself to be and that feminism was about changing myself as well as the world. I have been "under construction" ever since. I am still inclined to believe my efforts should primarily be directed at assisting others—I still consider myself to be unusually privileged—but I have learned that I must not mistake privilege for insight nor assume that I have no need for personal work and growth. I know that honesty in my work requires honesty in my life; both are best pursued with the insight that comes from self-reflection while trying to avoid self-indulgence. Change, like charity, really does begin at home. Feminism makes it very clear that neither one ends there.

Feminism grabbed my attention and my passion in a profound way. It made the abstract areas of philosophy seem far less interesting to me than they had to that point; in particular, it caused me to reorient my energies towards finding ways to connect my philosophical training with the world around me. I began at Stanford planning to work in the most abstract area of philosophy (logic and philosophy of mathematics) and soon discovered that my interests were actually in the areas of philosophy best described as the most engaged or applied. When it came time to choose a dissertation topic, I wanted to write about feminist thought since it was, at that time, the principal area of personal and intellectual excitement for me. I decided to explore what I then called, rather unfortunately, "the moral foundations of feminism"—today, I am skeptical of foundational approaches (since they imply a single, true version of feminism rather than the possibility of overlapping approaches with a variety of core commitments) though my interest in moral dimensions of feminism remains strong. In the thesis, I pursued a modification of Aristotle's virtue theory, which allowed me to discuss the possibility of developing the skills (virtues) for living a good life, "thriving," independently of preconceived gender stereotypes.

Writing in the early 1970s, I could find very little feminist philosophical scholarship to work from—John Stuart Mill was the principal feminist philosopher I discussed. Non-philosophers will wonder why I did not refer to Simone de Beauvoir's *The Second Sex* (1953). In the twentieth century, a sharp divide occurred within the realm of Western philosophy: most philosophers in England and the United States pursued an analytic approach centred on logic and theories of language, while most philosophers in France, Italy, and other parts of Europe followed the lead of important German philosophers (especially Hegel, Heidegger, and Kirkegaard) and engaged in a "Continental" approach to philosophy. In analytic circles, de Beauvoir was generally dismissed as the common-law wife (and, hence, follower) of the existentialist Jean-Paul Sartre, and little attention was paid to her work. Stanford's philosophy department was squarely situated within the analytic tradition; as such, no French theorists beyond Descartes were taught. I was simply ignorant of de Beauvoir's work; I knew only enough to adopt the snobbish, dismissive attitude of my teachers and colleagues, despite the fact that she had written the most important book on feminist philosophy to have been published. It sounds very odd to me now, but at the time, it seemed quite natural.

In my years at Stanford, there were no women, let alone any feminists, on faculty in the philosophy department, so it was not obvious who would be able to supervise my project. Thankfully, Thomas Schwartz agreed to take me on and helped me through the process despite his own lack of knowledge of (or interest in) feminist philosophy. I am convinced that I was allowed to pursue this thesis topic primarily because none of the faculty at the time took women philosophers or feminist philosophy seriously enough to challenge me; in other words, there was little motivation either to engage with me or get in my way. This is a lesson worth noting: sometimes feminist work can thrive when the scholar is just left alone. My timing was impeccable: too soon to be threatening, so I faced no active opposition, yet late enough to find a few kindred spirits beginning to publish their work.[1]

I was very grateful for the few philosophy articles within the analytic tradition that I did manage to find (nearly all published since 1970). Most of my feminist sources came from other disciplines, mainly psychology. My inspiration and support during the dissertation came primarily from the other members of my consciousness-raising group; though none was in philosophy and only one was on an academic track, they all believed in the importance of the project and helped me feel confident about its value.

My good fortune and good timing continued in that I began to attend the national meetings of the American Philosophical Association (the largest national professional association of philosophers in the world and the primary site for initial job contacts) in 1972, a time that coincided with the formation of the Society for Women in Philosophy (SWIP), an organization created to promote and support women in philosophy. Since that time, SWIP has grown and evolved into three regional organizations in the US, as well as other national organizations including c-SWIP in Canada and UK SWIP. All hold annual meetings, maintain websites, and publish newsletters.[2] Its meetings, held in conjunction with those of the larger organization, helped me identify and network with other feminist philosophers as I hit the job market.

In 1973–74, I took up a post-doctoral fellowship in the Moral Problems in Medicine project at Case Western Reserve University, which allowed me to continue to use philosophy to make a difference in the world. For the first time in my career, I actually had a woman as a mentor: Ruth Macklin, the sole woman philosopher in that department and the first woman philosophy professor I encountered in the three departments I had been associated with to that point (York, Stanford, and Case Western). Ruth was an excellent mentor and role model despite her (continuing) determination to avoid being labelled a feminist. In addition to being a single mother of two teenage daughters, she was one of the most productive members of the department—showing leadership in teaching, research, and administration—and she was unfailingly supportive of me.

The post-doctoral year helped position me to face a very competitive job market, and, here, too, I was remarkably lucky. After five years of study in the United States, I was eager to return to Canada, so I was delighted to be offered a job at Dalhousie University; despite periodic tempting offers, I have chosen to stay at Dal for my entire career. My colleagues-to-be had decided that it would be good to offer classes in feminist philosophy and in biomedical ethics, my two areas of specialization. This was in sharp contrast to most of the other philosophy departments with whom I interviewed, where the faculty tended to dismiss my practical orientation as not "real" philosophy—one person called it "no better than *Ms.* magazine." (I was flattered by this.) Dal actually *wanted* me to teach exactly what excited me. In the three and a half decades I have spent here, it has been, with a few notable exceptions, a very supportive environment in which to pursue feminist philosophy. Although I was the sole woman faculty member in the department for close to twenty years, I am happy to report that at present, in a department of fourteen full-time faculty members, we now have six people who consider feminist philosophy a principal area of research, including four women. Lesson number two is: feminist philosophy *really* thrives when done within a supportive department.

My biggest problem in teaching feminist philosophy in those early years was finding enough resources to teach a full-year class. There was so little feminist philosophy published until the late 1970s that it was difficult to piece together a reader that would keep the students engaged for two semesters. In a course titled Philosophical Issues in Feminism, I assigned readings dealing with different approaches to feminism, as well as with specific topics such as abortion, affirmative action, pornography, language use, and discrimination; I also had students look closely at the various conceptions of women offered by key figures in the history of philosophy. Fortunately, adding a feminist lens makes nearly any topic worthy of exploration, so it was always possible to adapt interesting philosophical essays even though few of the readings could be described as explicitly feminist philosophy. Students were asked to reflect on a range of questions, including how insights from feminism might extend to treatment of other disadvantaged groups (e.g., the mentally ill, or the elderly), the significance of biological differences between men and women, how to understand the ideal of equality between men and women, and the nature of personhood. The most notable gap in the early years was a failure to address issues of racialization except as a parallel form of discrimination.

Almost immediately in arriving at Dalhousie, I discovered a feminist colleague, Toni Laidlaw, in the Department of Education. We made a pact to try to meet weekly to provide support for each other within an institution that made room for, but had little understanding of, the significance of feminist studies. My friendship with Toni has deepened over the last three decades, and we still meet regularly for supportive lunches. Within a couple of years, we identified others interested in feminist ideas and values, and we helped to launch the Dalhousie Women Faculty Organization. For many years, the Dalhousie Women Faculty Organization was an important voice on campus, playing a major role in key university policies (including sexual harassment, employment equity, maternity and paternity leaves, and child care), supporting various incarnations of student-run women's groups, and providing input on the selection of all senior administrators. In 1984, we hosted the Dorothy Killam Lecture Series on Feminist Thought and brought Mary Daly, Marge Piercey, and Sheila Rowbotham to campus over the course of three exciting weeks. This was the most successful Killam lecture series ever held at Dalhousie, and it certainly raised the profile of feminist work on campus.

Efforts to launch a program in women's studies at Dalhousie in the early 1980s sailed through the various levels of university committees, but got bogged down at the Maritime Provinces Higher Education Committee, an interprovincial agency responsible for reducing "duplication" within the Maritime provinces. For many years, this committee thought it sufficient to teach women's studies at one university (Mount St. Vincent University); eventually, it was persuaded that this was a subject that belonged in every university.

For many years, I went along my merry way, doing what I was hired to do: teaching and research primarily in the areas of feminist philosophy and health care ethics. I was quite content to be working in these two areas in the 1970s and even into the early years of the 1980s. And then, the great *aha* moment: I would combine the fields and look for their overlap. I was actually surprised to find that there wasn't very much overlap since bioethicists spoke as if gender equality was a given. Feminist work in the area of women's health was making it very clear that gender equality in health and health care was by no means the norm. My own book, *No Longer Patient: Feminist Ethics and Health Care* (1992), was the first monograph published in the area of feminist health ethics.

My work since that revelation has continued to be situated primarily within the emerging field of feminist health ethics, now a well-recognized subject of broad international interest and activity. Feminism has been accepted as one of the most significant areas of health ethics, and it has provided me with the opportunity to be directly involved with government policy-makers on many subjects (including reproductive and genetic technologies, research involving humans, privacy, and even tobacco control). The most important source of inspiration and enlightenment for me over the past decade has been my participation at the biannual meetings of the International Network of Feminist Approaches to Bioethics. The opportunity to discuss and exchange ideas with colleagues from around the globe has stretched my understanding of feminism and of health ethics. I feel very fortunate indeed to be able to pursue questions I believe to be important and interesting, and to receive a salary and travel grants to do so. Feminist research continues to define my academic identity and career, though my understanding of what it means has evolved significantly over the years.

Notes

1 Joan Callahan, who acts as archivist for the Society of Women in Philosophy, believes that mine was the first philosophy dissertation explicitly on feminism ever written in the United States.

2 See SWIP's website at http://www.uh.edu/~cfreelan/SWIP/index.html.

Selected Publications by the Author

Sherwin, Susan Bernice. 1973. Moral Foundations of Feminism. PhD diss., Stanford University.

———. 1992. *No longer patient: Feminist ethics and health care*. Philadelphia: Temple University Press.

———, ed. 1998. *The politics of women's health: Exploring agency and autonomy*. Philadelphia: Temple University Press.

———. 2001. Feminist reflections on the role of theories in a global bioethics. In *Globalizing feminist bioethics*, edited by R. Tong, G. Anderson, and A. Santos. Boulder, CO: Westview Press.

———. 2003. The importance of ontology for feminist policy-making in the realm of reproductive technology. *Canadian Journal of Philosophy* 28: 273–95.

From Marginalized to "Establishment": Doing Feminist Sociology in Canada, Australia, and New Zealand

Maureen Baker

WITH HINDSIGHT, MANY of us can identify pivotal experiences that shaped our future careers. I recall one such experience in the late 1960s while preparing an undergraduate essay in sociology at the University of Toronto. I discovered some official statistics comparing average earnings by educational attainment, showing that women with a master's degree earned the same amount as men with elementary school education. These findings startled and enraged me but also reinforced my decision to obtain postgraduate qualifications.

My parents and teachers had encouraged me to attend university, but employment options remained murky. My mother thought I should teach high school, but my father encouraged me to continue studying. After assisting several sociologists with their research, and reading Jessie Bernard's American study, *Academic Women* (1964), I decided to complete a doctorate in sociology and study women university professors. I chose the University of Alberta because it was one of the few sociology departments in Canada with a doctoral program, it was a large department with diverse courses, and one of my professors spoke highly of it. The decision to study women professors related to my growing interest in the status of women and gender-based employment discrimination. I also wanted to meet some women who could become role models because all of my sociology professors at the University of Toronto had been men.

My first year as a doctoral student at the University of Alberta (1972) was challenging, and I felt marginalized in every respect. I saw myself as a left-leaning feminist in a politically and socially conservative province. All thirty professors in the sociology department were White men,[1] and only four doctoral students out of seventy-four were women. I worked part-time as a research assistant for a senior male professor who asked me to file his newspaper clippings while he published with his male doctoral students. The doctoral courses barely mentioned women, and feminist analysis was belittled and called "fashionable ideology." By the end of my first year, I had successfully completed the coursework and comprehensive exams but felt like quitting. Fortunately, my sister and a professor talked me into finishing.

In 1973, I met Dr. Rosalind Sydie who had been employed by the University of Alberta on numerous temporary contracts but was still fighting for a permanent position in sociology (see the joint essay by Sydie, Patricia Prestwich, and Dallas Cullen in this volume). She graciously agreed to supervise my thesis even though she was not officially permitted to do so as a short-term employee. A male professor served as temporary chair of my thesis committee until Rosalind was given a tenure-stream position in 1974, upon the insistence of the university's Status of Women Committee. As her first doctoral student, I am sure that I provided Rosalind with numerous problems, but she generously gave me the intellectual guidance and emotional support I required to complete my thesis. Around the same time, I was inspired by the early career of American anthropologist Margaret Mead, after reading her autobiography.

During my doctorate, I was asked to teach a course at the University of Alberta called The Sociology of Women. I eagerly accepted this position and developed a feminist course that focussed on "sex differences" in socialization, education, work, and politics, and examined research relating to gender differences in attitudes and behaviour, as well as structural barriers to women's equality. Ironically, the same professor who encouraged me to finish my doctorate actively discouraged students from taking this course, arguing that it would hinder their employment opportunities. Nevertheless, over one hundred students enrolled, and my first teaching experience encouraged me to pursue an academic career.

My doctoral dissertation, titled "Women as a Minority Group in the Academic Profession," focussed on the discrepancies between ideologies of professionalism and merit, and the realities of academic particularism. Based on qualitative interviews, it examined women's decisions to become a professor, their career progression, experiences as teachers and researchers in male-dominated departments, and feelings of belonging in the profession, arguing that the organization of academia marginalized women. Feminist theory was not well developed at the time, but my research drew on theoretical insights from liberal feminism, such as Jessie Bernard (1964) and Cynthia Epstein (1971), general studies of inequality, and the structure of the academic profession. Some of the women I interviewed had a heightened awareness of their disadvantage, but a few acted like queen bees, denying that any barriers existed for "committed" women scholars. In August 1974, I successfully defended the thesis with Dr. Margrit Eichler as the external examiner. A few weeks later, I left Alberta for my first "real" job.

Finding an academic position had been more difficult than I had anticipated, even though there were thirty vacancies in Canada for which I could realistically apply, and I had completed my doctorate in record time. In retrospect, I now realize that I should have sought some mentoring about my CV and interview preparation. However, I soon found a tenure-stream position as assistant professor at Acadia University, and in September 1974, I left for Nova Scotia.

At Acadia, I was the only woman in the sociology department and the only PhD except for the near-retirement head, who called me "my dear" as he smiled wistfully and patted me on the head when I made feminist comments. Nevertheless, my experiences there were generally positive. In the first year, I expanded my feminist understanding by teaching in the interdisciplinary women's studies program and attending colleagues' lectures. In 1975, I became the coordinator of the women's studies program, familiarizing myself with feminist material from several academic subjects.[2]

In 1975, I also became one of the founding members of the editorial committee for *Atlantis: A Women's Studies Journal*. With Donna Smyth (English department) as founding editor and Margaret Conrad (history department) as associate editor, a group of us from the women's studies program started this journal because all of us had experienced problems getting our work accepted in mainstream journals. We decided to expand publishing options for the growing amount of feminist research and writing, using a local printing firm. Because the university would not give us any space or resources for this journal, we prepared the camera-ready copy for each issue on someone's living-room floor in our spare time. However, this experience brought us together and reinforced our commitment to feminist publishing (see Smyth's essay in this volume).

During my two years at Acadia, I developed and taught five sociology courses, and lobbied to hire another woman in sociology (Dianne Looker). I also wrote a women's studies textbook that was never published because the publisher went bankrupt and failed to honour my contract. In addition, I joined a women's centre in town. Although my first academic position was satisfying in many respects, I had always yearned to travel and live in other places. I also craved a more satisfying personal life as my commuter relationship became more committed. My then-partner wanted to complete a doctorate in demography, and, when I encouraged him to enrol at the Australian National University in Canberra, he persuaded me to accompany him. Although I had a doctorate and two years teaching experience, the Australian immigration officials would not give me a visa in my own right but only as a "fiancée," which meant that I had to agree to marry within three months or leave the country. Although I had qualms, we decided to go ahead with this arrangement. Against the advice of feminist colleagues, I quit my job, sold most of my possessions, and prepared to leave Canada.

Migrating to Australia in 1976 represented several personal ambitions, including my desire to travel and a potential marriage. I was also becoming disillusioned with sociology as a discipline, feeling that it was too heavily into quantitative methodology. Family sociology seemed to have reached an intellectual impasse, and feminist scholarship was not academically accepted. This made it easier for me to quit my job. After the teaching year ended in 1976, I flew to Canberra where my fiancé had enrolled as a doctoral student four months earlier. To my horror, I soon discovered that he had found a more suitable partner and wanted to end our relationship. Returning to Canada was not feasible, and I was eager to see some of Australia, so I accepted a teaching job at a provincial college in small-town Victoria and was granted a temporary work permit.

This migration experience confirmed all that I had intellectually known about the risk of romantic ventures but also confirmed how difficult it was to secure a university job in Australia as a female foreigner. In those days, the head of department selected his own candidates, often with little staff consultation. However, in 1977, I improved my situation by accepting a position at what is now Sydney University of Technology, teaching mainly older male students organizational sociology. In the second semester of 1977, I persuaded the department head to allow me to develop a new course called Sex Roles and Sexism, which I taught to mainly female students.

Although Macquarie University had previously introduced a women's studies course, the Australian media still perceived mine as dangerously subversive. The national newspaper (the *Australian*) ran a large article with the caption "Maureen Sets Out to Fight Sexist Ockers."[3] The accompanying photograph showed a poster behind my head of a chick lying on its back, with a caption of "Women are not chicks!" In this article, my course was mildly ridiculed, and I was accused of inciting discontent among Australian women, who were happy caring for husbands and children at home. Despite the negative publicity, numerous students enjoyed this "revolutionary" course.

My experiences in 1970s Australia were both personally rewarding and deeply disturbing. The women's liberation movement focussed on state support for mothering at home, as well as issues around sexuality and reproduction. Intellectually, I became interested in women and trade unions, as the union movement in Australia was still very strong at that time. In my personal life, I began singing with the Sydney Philharmonia Choir, which performed in the famous Sydney Opera House. However, as a woman in my late twenties, I continually fought to be taken seriously as a scholar and teacher in a society that seemed more gendered than Canada.

In 1978, one of my older male students held me hostage at gunpoint in the college cafeteria. He had previously flirted with me, and when he was unsuccessful, he challenged my academic authority. After asking my advice on his term paper for my course, he repeatedly taunted me by saying that my (male) colleagues had given him different advice. After some discussion, I foolishly and angrily told him to "piss off." Several days later he returned, enticed me into the college cafeteria to discuss his term paper "on neutral ground," and then threatened to blow my head off, shaking while he held a gun under his jacket (so no one else could see it). He repeatedly said that no woman had ever sworn at him before and I was going to "pay a price."

When I later escaped and reported my experience to college authorities, they refused to call the police, telling me that I was "making too much" of this incident. However, I defined it as a dangerous form of sexual harassment, and it became another turning point in my life. I asked myself why I remained in Australia when my career was not progressing and my father was ailing. In February 1978, at the age of thirty, I set off for Canada, travelling across Asia to Europe on the Trans-Siberian Railway and returning to Toronto.

For the next four years, I taught sociology at the University of Toronto, but my positions were contractually limited with little hope of permanency. In 1982, Lorne Tepperman (then sociology editor for McGraw-Hill Ryerson) invited me to prepare a Canadian family textbook; the fifth edition of this edited book—*Families: Changing Trends in Canada*—was published in 2005. When my new partner (now my husband of over twenty-five years) left academia to work for the government in Ottawa, I decided to search for a research position there, as neither of us saw our future in academia.

The Canadian Advisory Council on the Status of Women was looking for someone to research the aspirations of adolescent women. With the help of Lorna Marsden from the University of Toronto, I managed to secure this one-year contract and settled in Ottawa in 1983, completing my family book and a monograph from the adolescent study. The next year, when Lorna became a senator, she wrote me a reference for a research position in Canada's Parliament, where I specialized in family and women's issues (see Marsden's essay in this volume). Ironically, this was my first legitimate opportunity to do feminist research, although my work had to be framed in the language of family policy. In this position, I also found time to write scholarly articles, deliver conference papers, and publish several books, always with a feminist slant.

In 1990, I was recruited to McGill University, initially to direct a research centre. In my seven years there as a professor, I taught family and social policy, coordinated the women's studies program, and continued my cross-national feminist research on family policies. In 1997, a former student from McGill (Myra Hird) urged me to apply for a job at the University of Auckland in New Zealand, where she worked. Although I was initially convinced that I would not be hired, I accepted their offer and became the first female full professor of sociology and first female head of a sociology department in that country in 1998, where I remain today. After several administrative positions, numerous publications, and a career spanning more than thirty years, I now feel more comfortable with academic practices and increasingly enjoy teaching and research. My own analysis has been influenced by the work of Pat Armstrong, Sylvia Bashevkin, Margrit Eichler, Linda Hantrais, Jane Lewis, Meg Luxton, Ann Orloff, Diane Sainsbury, and Jane Ursel.

I realize that my occupational story is somewhat atypical, but it highlights several gendered themes. Although I had no children, my career trajectory for years represented one step forward and two steps back. It was clearly influenced by relationships and sex discrimination, as well as by my own occupational goals and achievements. I continued for years to feel marginalized. Although much of this was lack of confidence, there were definitely personal and structural barriers that challenged the comfort zone of women academics.

Since the 1970s, I believe that the feminist movement has made a noticeable impact on scholarship. Gender is now routinely included as a variable in social inquiries and feminist analysis is widely respected, although not by all our colleagues. Women students outnumber men in many disciplines, and academic women are better represented in the profession even though we still face barriers. Those of us who tenaciously pursued our research and teaching in women's studies against considerable opposition have come to enjoy relative legitimacy as senior professors. As puzzling as it now seems after years of struggle, some of our younger colleagues even view us as members of "the establishment."

Notes

1 Only one of these men was Canadian. The rest were American, British, or other European.
2 I am afraid that I cannot accurately elaborate on the women's studies program at Acadia. I think that it started in 1973 before I arrived, and that I was the second coordinator.
3 *Ocker* is Australian slang for a male chauvinist. The article, by Lyndall Crisp, appeared around March or April, 1977.

Selected Publications by the Author

Baker, Maureen. 1995. *Canadian family policies: Cross-national comparisons.* Toronto: University of Toronto Press.

———. 2001. *Families, labour and love: Family diversity in a changing world.* Vancouver: UBC Press.

———. 2002. Child poverty, maternal health and social benefits. *Current Sociology* 50 (6): 827–42.

———, ed. 2005. *Families: Changing trends in Canada.* 5th ed. Toronto: McGraw-Hill Ryerson.

———. 2006. *Restructuring family policies: Convergences and divergences.* Toronto: University of Toronto Press.

"To Ring True and Stand for Something"

◉ Wendy Robbins

The Making of a Feminist

SOME SAY THAT feminists are made, not born. In my case, it was a bit of both. I grew up in the repressive Duplessis era in Québec; I may also have inherited a gene for feminism. I lived in a "Father Knows Best" family, yet also had strong women, the stuff of legend, behind me. One great-grandmother was headmistress of a girls' school in England; one grandmother jointly ran a small "mom 'n' pop" dairy in Québec; my mother was a gold medalist at McGill University in 1945.

My father, an engineer, worked; my mother, a housewife, allegedly didn't. For a quarter century, she cooked, sewed, cleaned house, managed finances, helped my brother and me with our homework, and volunteered in the church and the community. I remember putting my arms around her and asking why she didn't go back to school or go out to "work" (she did both, in mid-life). I cringe at that recollection now, of course, but, at the time, I cringed at her isolation and dependence on my father's paycheque.

The "click!" experience came in my teenage years when I realized that my mother, as a married woman, by law could not have her own bank account and was even barred from buying, without my father's signature, the $4.00 annual licence for the small utility trailer that we pulled behind our car on camping trips. I had this epiphany about the time that Betty Friedan's *The Feminine Mystique* (1963) helped set off the second wave of the women's movement.

Role Models, Real and Imaginary

Important role models included the smattering of great women and spirited girls I learned about. In history, these included Boadicea in her war chariot, Joan of Arc, and Elizabeth I (about whom I wrote an elementary school play), and, in literature, Shakespeare's Cordelia, Anouilh's Antigone, and author Pearl Buck herself who ventured to China. Closer to home were Jeanne Mance, a founder of Montréal; Laura Secord, a symbol of bravery in the War of 1812; and L. M. Montgomery's Anne of Green Gables, cheerfully determined to prove that she is as good as any boy. I later discovered Harriet Tubman, conductor of the underground railway for escaping slaves; Pauline Johnson, activist Mohawk poet; Charlotte Whitten, Canada's first woman mayor, whom my father always referred to as "that battle-axe," spurring my curiosity; and Doris Anderson, editor of *Chatelaine*, a magazine as paradoxical as our lives, dispensing recipes, beauty tips, and calls to action about the Royal Commission on the Status of Women or the repeal of the law criminalizing abortion.

As an undergraduate in the 1960s at Bishop's University, I had one woman professor, Kathleen Harper (an "old maid," in the language of the day), who herself had had no women professors at all. During my junior year abroad at l'Université de Rennes, France, I had two more. One taught French (married, dowdy, with children); the other, art history (single, sexy, childless). During my graduate student years in the early 1970s at Queen's, I had no women professors, but I served as a teaching assistant to one who taught part time, Elisabeth Gerver (married and pregnant). Who might I become? Could I have it all—career, family, adventure, romance?

Irritants, Which Yielded the Pearl

Queen's University had caps that limited the number of women students to a token few in programs ranging from medicine to graduate studies in English. The English curriculum was focussed on the so-called "Great Tradition" of dead White men of Britain and the United States. In eight years at university, I had one course on Canadian and none on women's literature. With an MA thesis on W. B. Yeats (Irish) and a PhD on Ralph Gustafson (Canadian), I discovered Margaret Laurence, Marian Engel, and Margaret Atwood on my own, and had that thrill of a real, visceral connection. In my PhD dissertation, I forayed into feminist criticism when I looked at some of the female characters (typically minor) in Ralph Gustafson's short stories, suggesting that their plight needed elucidation, too (Keitner 1973, 1979). I also broke the rules when I insisted that, if we could refer to a male author by his surname only, there was no reason to put a "Miss" before Atwood. I eventually became a self-taught specialist in women's writing and feminist criticism.

My first feminist acts also included reading *Ms.* magazine, writing letters to decriminalize abortion in a campaign led by CARAL (Canadian Association for the Repeal of the Abortion Law was its name then), and sending ten dollars to the legal defence fund of a complete stranger, Annette Kolodny, a Jewish-American feminist professor fighting against sex discrimination and anti-Semitism in the Department of English at the University of New Hampshire, where she had been denied tenure. Years later, I nominated her for an honourary degree, awarded at the University of New Brunswick in 2000.

In 1975, International Women's Year, I was asked by Margret (later Marguerite) Andersen, chair of the modern languages department at the University of Guelph, to make a presentation on "Great Women's Poems." The truth was, I hardly knew any, given my misogynist education. *The World Split Open*, a pioneering anthology edited by Louise Berkinow, had only just appeared, with its shattering revelation to our discipline that "literary history is actually a record of choices" (1974, 3). English studies, until then, had been permeated by notions of the "timelessness" and "universality" of judgements about beauty and truth, thought to be some sort of Platonic absolutes.

In 1975, too, I gave birth to my first child, a daughter, Chimène, an extraordinarily empowering experience, which connected me with Corinne Devlin, a professor of obstetrics and gynecology at McMaster University, and later a "founding mother" of its Women's Health Clinic. Shortly after Chimène's birth, I organized a reception for Germaine Greer, who gave a public lecture on the Guelph campus. I also went, baby in arms, to negotiate a promotion and pay raise with my dean, the way men traditionally did when they took on new family responsibilities. I raised my rank from lecturer to assistant professor, with a concomitant increase in salary from $12,000 to $15,000, by pointing out that a male colleague, who did not yet have a PhD, had been appointed at the higher rank, while I, PhD and three publications in hand, had been hired at the lower rank. I had found my calling: academic, mother, feminist activist.

My best friend and ally was Lois Gottlieb, hired, like me, on a limited-term contract at the University of Guelph in 1974. We went through our first pregnancies one after the other, and we collaborated on several early feminist research projects. Influenced by the literary criticism and methodologies of Germaine Greer, Kate Millett, and Adrienne Rich—all trained in English studies—we turned a feminist lens on everything we read. Lois and I published the first of a series of articles exploring fiction by Canadian women writers, "Mothers and Daughters in Four Recent Canadian Novels," in 1975. We asked "what shapes women's lives when they are no longer defined only in terms of their satellite roles to the male sun?" We predicted that "As women write more out of fidelity to their own experience and judgment and less as inheritors of male-identified appropriate subjects, themes, and styles, they will inevitably contribute to a new aesthetic, and this will require a new critical perspective so that we may treat new works intelligently, and re-read in an entirely fresh light, works which have already been definitively analyzed" (Gottlieb and Keitner 1975, 21).[1] We became contributing editors of the *Women's Studies Newsletter* produced by Florence Howe at the Feminist Press in New York. One of our "Books from Canada" reviews (Gottlieb and Keitner 1976, 13) focussed on Margret Andersen's *Mother Was Not a Person* (1972) and Marylee Stephenson's *Women in Canada* (1973).

Lois and I, working together with many others under the leadership of Joanna Boehnert in psychology and Norma Bowen, the only Black woman professor I knew (who, like Joanna, died tragically young), grouped ourselves into an Academic Women's Association for faculty, staff, and students. I still have a blue, mimeographed version of its constitution, which I was largely responsible for drafting. Some of us unabashedly championed women's rights; some preferred the presumably generic term "human" rights. We did not yet have a good analysis of how much of "human" was taken up by "man." We tried to persuade ourselves and others that "women's rights *are* human rights" (two decades before Hillary Clinton stated it as fact at the 1995 United Nations Women's Conference in Beijing), but we were as yet unable to conceptualize "women's human rights" as neither an oxymoron nor a redundancy.

Social activism was the grounding theory; women's studies became the practice. That's how I experienced the revolution. It touched my life—body, family, and friends; it touched my work—academic discipline, profession, institution; and it touched society—both here and around the world. It coalesced in interdisciplinary women's studies. Lois and I were amongst the pioneers of feminist scholarship and women's studies at Guelph, but, with our limited-term contracts, neither of us was still there when an official program opened in 1979. Lois decided to change her career to the practice of law, and I moved to the US as a "private scholar."

In the mid 1970s, a male professor, Leslie Marshall, initiated the University of Guelph's first course on women in literature, which he invited both me and Lois to teach subsequently, and I initiated its first course on Commonwealth literature, all of us enlarging our field to include more than just White men (see Marshall's essay in this volume). In fiction from Africa and India, male authors not uncommonly portrayed violence against women as a fact of life. Few of us had any idea at the time just how widespread a problem such violence was in Canada, too; even the *Report of the Royal Commission on the Status of Women in Canada* (1970) was silent on the issue. Resources by and for women in Canada were scarce; for minority groups, they were almost non-existent. I had to type up handouts on Native Canadian material since no published collections existed.

So, in English literature departments everywhere, curriculum reform became a major undertaking, and "canon wars" were waged so that we could teach the work of writers who were marginalized as not British or American, not male, and not White. It was a renaissance and, as Adrienne Rich so movingly said at the time, it was, for many of us, no less than "an act of survival" (1996, 1982).

Making Waves

In 1977, at an international literature conference in New Delhi, India, distressed at the general neglect or sexist treatment of women's work, I persuaded Robert McDowell, the editor of a key journal, *World Literature Written in English* (WLWE), to let me guest-edit a special issue devoted to "Women Writers of the Commonwealth." The conversation took place in a motorized rickshaw, so I remember it well. In truth, at the time, I could name only a handful of women authors who were deemed important. Several key entries in that special issue are bibliographies as, around the world, women professors (and some men) struggled to lay the foundations for a new curriculum based on a gender-balanced and inclusive canon and body of criticism. This special issue of WLWE (April 1978), which Lois Gottlieb and I guest-edited, was its most successful; it charted new territory in our field, which subsequently became known as post-colonial literary studies.

By then I had lost my series of limited-term contracts at Guelph over a dispute about maternity leave. (I won the battle, but lost the war.) I moved with my husband to Brown University in Providence, Rhode Island, where I was loosely associated with the Pembroke Center and witnessed the laying of the groundwork of its massive, computerized Brown University Women

Writers Project. Within five years, I moved home again to Canada with my children but not my husband, becoming in 1988 (the year of our divorce), through sheer tenacity, the first woman tenured full professor of English in the two-hundred-year history of UNB. In 1986, I became one of a handful of "founding mothers" of UNB's interdisciplinary Women's Studies Program—but that's a story for another day.

With our moxie, many women of my generation created exciting careers, raised feminist daughters and sons, and fought for such things as reproductive freedom, pay equity, and, most recently, the legal right for gays and lesbians to marry their same-sex partner. We can point with pride to centres for excellence in women's health, family violence research centres, campus child care, safety audits, women university presidents, women's presses and bookstores, and women's studies programs from coast to coast. The majority of university degrees awarded in Canada today are earned by women, and the body of knowledge that is being passed on has been, at least to some degree, "re-visioned" (Rich 1996) through a feminist and anti-racist lens. These are some of the impacts that we have had in the course of just one generation.

Back to the Future?

We cannot ignore the backlash and the tragedies, most particularly the Montréal Massacre of December 6, 1989. It is a haunting part of the story of the second wave of the women's movement in Canada. We cannot forget the injustices meted out to some of our strong women colleagues, including Marylee Stephenson (denied tenure); Sheila McIntyre (harassed in a law faculty); Phyllis Grosskurth, Ursula Franklin, et al. (paid unjust wages and pensions); and Nancy Olivieri and her "gang of five" (forced to defend their academic freedom against a big pharmaceutical company). The list also includes less well-known women, most of whom belong to minority groups as Aboriginal women, women of colour, women with disabilities, and lesbians, whose stories are narrated in recent publications, such as *Women in the Canadian Academic Tundra* (Hannah, Paul, and Vethamany-Globus 2002) and *The Madwoman in the Academy* (Keahey and Schnitzer 2003). Each of us knows talented and vibrant women who left the academy altogether, judging that the precarious contracts, isolation, fiercely competitive and often petty departmental politics, and the time demands of an academic career are "just not worth it."

The institution that, arguably, has undergone the most profound change in the same period as the rise of women's studies on campus is the Supreme

Court of Canada. It is now the most gender-balanced high court in the world: four of nine judges are women. That my daughter, Chimène Robbins Keitner, born in International Women's Year, was able to win a Rhodes Scholarship (open only to men until 1977), and then to clerk with Canada's first female chief justice, Beverley McLaughlan, are luminous realities that I never dreamed possible.

However, the millennium Canada Research Chairs Program is but one symptom of how, in the blinking of an eye, hard-fought human rights can start to slip away. Women are only 24% of the chairholders to date (Canada Research Chairs 2007), though we are 33.9% of the professoriate in Canada—and more than that in many other countries (Canada Research Chairs 2006; Canadian Federation for the Humanities and Social Sciences 2006). The Canada Research Chairs Program did not even collect data for other equity groups, which prompted me and seven other women across Canada in 2003 to launch a complaint with the Canadian Human Rights Commission, where, laboriously, we reached a mediated settlement in 2006 (see Side and Robbins 2007).

I am proud to have contributed in a small way, beginning in the 1970s at the University of Guelph, and, since the 1980s, in larger ways at the University of New Brunswick and in national organizations, to the ongoing narrative of women's education and women's human rights in Canada. Ultimately, I think there is no higher purpose in human life than, in the words of early educational activist Agnes Cameron, "to ring true and stand for something" (qtd. in Forster 2004, 57).

Note

1 The editor of the *Sphinx*, Aydon Charlton, praised our work for demonstrating "how qualities of intelligent engagement with issues facing women in Canadian society today can result in original and provocative criticism" (1975, 7).

Selected Publications by the Author

Gottlieb, Lois C., and Wendy Keitner [Robbins]. 1977. Demeter's daughters: The mother-daughter motif in fiction by Canadian women. *Atlantis* 3 (1): 130–42.

Robbins, Wendy Keitner. 1984. Canadian women writers and the syndrome of the female man: A note on the poetry of Audrey Alexandra Brown and Anne Wilkinson. *Tessera* 8 (4): 76–81.

———. 2001. 'Breasting body': The beginnings of maternity poetry by women in Canada. *Canadian Poetry Studies, Documents, Reviews* 49: 74–93.

Robbins, Wendy, and Laurie McLaughlan. 2002. *A chronology of the development of women's studies in Canada.* Cited July 11, 2007. Available from http://www.unb.ca/PAR-L/chronology1.htm.

Robbins Keitner, Wendy. 1989. Anglophone Canada. In *Longman anthology of world literature by women 1875–1975,* edited by M. Arkin and B. Shollar. New York: Longman.

Socialist Feminist and Activist Educator

● *Linda Briskin*

> Feminists thought that simply exposing the extent of this oppression
> would itself create change ... It seemed obvious that, once revealed, the
> oppression of women would no longer be tolerated. All things were pos-
> sible; change would result from recognizing the need for it.
>
> —Adamson, Briskin, and McPhail (1988, 256)

AFTER SOME HEADY YEARS organizing in the women's movement in
Montréal in the late 1960s and early 1970s, it became increasingly clear that
the exhilarating optimism of those years was naive—in fact, shockingly
innocent. With the growing understanding of the depth and breadth of
women's oppression, the question of how to organize for change no longer
seemed straightforward. The belief that reason, knowledge, and justice would,
in and of themselves, support change was clearly misplaced.

Although, at the time, I assumed that there was a set of truths to be discovered which would help ground the women's movement strategically, as
an undergraduate at McGill University (1966–70), I quickly discovered the
androcentrism of scholarship, the absence of concern for women's experience, and the ridicule attached to even asking questions about women. In
1969–70, when I was in the fourth year of my BA, a few of us fought for permission to take a reading course on women with Marlene Dixon who was

then a visiting professor at McGill.[1] It was a considerable battle, but we did eventually succeed.

Although the course gave us some space to study "women," there were few scholarly books on the subject. I do remember devouring the newsprint collection of *Notes from the Second Year* (Radical Feminists 1970), and mimeographed articles from the *New England Free Press*, which came up from the United States and circulated almost underground. Then there was an explosion of writing: *Sisterhood Is Powerful* (Morgan 1970), *Sexual Politics* (Millett 1970), *Women's Estate* (Mitchell 1970), *The Dialectic of Sex* (Firestone 1972), and the Canadian anthology *Women Unite!* (Discussion Collective No. 6 1972). Perhaps for me the most compelling was Sheila Rowbotham's *Women, Resistance and Revolution* (1972b).[2] I was stunned by the extent and complexity of women's organizing. The past was astounding—certainly not as I had imagined it.

At the same time that I was discovering women's past, it was apparent in the Montréal women's movement that, even as we organized in the 1970s, the histories of our own organizing were vanishing. It was "ironic that at the same time we were discovering 'herstory,' we were often ignoring the history that we ourselves had made" (Adamson, Briskin, and McPhail 1988, 28). This concern for disappearing histories inspired a lifelong dedication to documenting women's organizing. Ironically, it was some time before I would see documenting and analyzing second-wave women's organizing as a relevant project in the academy. In fact, the first two books in which I was involved were conceived, inspired, and largely completed outside of the academic realm. *Union Sisters: Women in the Labour Movement*, co-edited with Lynda Yanz (1983), focussed on stories from the emerging movement of union women, told by union women themselves. In the early stages of *Feminist Organizing for Change: The Contemporary Women's Movement in Canada*, co-authored with Nancy Adamson and Margaret McPhail (Adamson, Briskin, and McPhail 1988), our goal was to map out, in what we imagined would be a pamphlet, a strategic vision for Canadian socialist feminism. Although our audience widened, we held to the emphatically political purpose of demonstrating "the viability of socialist feminism as a world view and profil[ing] its contribution to the women's movement" (1988, 19–20). In recent years, I have turned to theorizing the practice of women's organizing in unions, in the community-based women's movement, and in the classroom (Briskin 1990; 2004).

Socialist Feminism

Undoubtedly, it is significant that my undergraduate years at McGill University coincided with the student movement and the movement against the Vietnam War. Although the energy of people coming together to speak out and resist was inspirational, not surprisingly, women were marginalized in these movements—a troubled reality that led to my first consciousness-raising group, which included many women both active in and silenced by the student movement. During the 1970 War Measures Act, soldiers carrying machine guns and tanks positioned around the university crystallized a new understanding of the state. I also discovered Marxism in those years and thus came to the women's movement already identifying as a Marxist.

One of my compelling intellectual "discoveries" during this period was the importance of family-household systems to shaping women's oppression, and the interwoven character of households and workplaces, later to be the topic of my PhD thesis. The early articles of Margaret Benston (1969a) and Peggy Morton (1972) (originally published in 1970) and the 1971 Maria Rosa Dalla Costa pamphlet on the Italian movement that came to be known as "Wages for Housework" stimulated this thinking. Selma James and Dalla Costa visited Montréal in 1972 (or 1973) and undoubtedly provided critical input into the emerging socialist feminist perspective in Canada, one that recognized the significance of the private sphere and the realm of reproduction, disputed the privileging of waged work, and struggled with the complex intersection between patriarchies and capitalism. Out of these discussions, the strategic and theoretical "domestic labour debate" crystallized (Briskin 1980).

In 1974, I wrote "Toward a Socialist Feminist Movement" for *Our Generation*, an independent radical journal published in Montréal, my first entry into more "academic" or theoretical writing. Although scholarly, this piece maintained a distinctly polemical edge. In this text, now more than thirty years old, I can see the resonance of two sometimes competing desires: to dig deeply into theoretical study to understand the complex roots of women's oppression, on the one hand; and to document contemporary women's organizing, to preserve it, and to support the building of a mass movement, on the other.[3] In the article, I start out with the claim that despite the "vast changes" occurring as a result of the decade-old women's movement, the "most manifest failure" was "the unsuccessful attempt to create a mass structure," a failure that I suggested was due, in part, to "an inadequate understanding of women's oppression" (Briskin 1974, 23).

Activist Educator in the Making

My sense of urgency about the need to understand the "origin" of women's oppression encouraged me to set up and facilitate various study groups at a number of women's centres (the preferred organizational structure in Montréal in the early years of the English-speaking women's movement). At the same time, I was teaching high school English in Montréal's "inner city," working with poor, immigrant, and working-class students, a career I began in 1971 and continued until 1975. In fact, teaching was what I imagined I would do into the foreseeable future. In the contexts of both community and school, I was already developing an interest in politicized pedagogical practices and a commitment to incorporating issues of power and discrimination into whatever subject matter I was teaching. For example, in my English classrooms we talked about women's roles, and students wrote about these issues; we also read *Good Times Bad Times* (Kirkwood 1968), a novel in which the central character is gay. I had persuaded the English department to order copies of this book without really saying what it was about. The book circulated through the school in an underground way, and, although I always expected to be challenged by angry parents or school administrators, I never was. I suspect the students understood the subversive nature of our discussion and cooperated in maintaining a degree of secrecy. These experiences outside the university critically affected how I later entered into the project of university women's studies.

In 1972, Mary Porter, then teaching American history at Loyola College (now part of Concordia University), who had come to Canada with her draft-dodger husband and whom I met in a consciousness-raising group, suggested that I apply to teach a new third-year course on the History of Women. At the time, I was teaching high school English, and had no university-level history courses. Surprisingly, I got the job. Apparently I had more ideas about what might be included in such a course than anyone else who was interviewed. I taught this early women's studies course in 1972–73.

Pack rat that I am (or perhaps I should say "archivist"), I still have my course file. Many of the old dittoed handouts, some on newsprint, are too faded to read, but the first page of the course outline says, "The study of history is our aim, but we should not separate this from our own experience. The ideal is to *change* through our insights." I remember how little historical material I could find and most of it on the suffrage movement. I myself knew so little, perhaps only some of the questions to ask. In my suggested topics for papers and presentations, I included, not only the suffrage movement, but also women's role in the French Revolution, the Paris Commune, and the Russian and Chinese revolutions; women's relation to unions; the effect of the Industrial Revolution on women and family structures; the history of prostitution; the marriage contract, and so on.

Up to this point, the *idea* of graduate school had not registered on my radar. I had not really enjoyed my undergraduate years and had spent most of my time organizing outside the university. Increasingly, however, a compelling reason to go to graduate school emerged: to study history and understand better the roots of women's oppression. I believed that if we were going to change the world, we had to understand it, to paraphrase Marx. Alas, with one university-level history course (which I took at Sir George Williams, now also part of Concordia, as a preparation for applying to graduate school), and the one university history course that I had taught, I could not get into any graduate program in history. I ended up doing a degree in social and political thought at York University, which I began in 1975—International Women's Year.

In 1978, I was offered a job (for which I had not actually applied) to teach women's studies and English at Sheridan College. Rumour had it that the universities would never again hire full-time faculty, and I needed to support myself. I remained at the college until 1986, when I completed my PhD and was the first person hired in the tenure stream to teach women's studies in the Faculty of Arts at York University. I remember being stunned that York hired me, given my background. I came to the project of university teaching and research as a socialist feminist activist, and an activist educator.

Difference and Power in the 1970s

In my view, the image of Canadian second-wave feminism as a middle-class, White movement needs considerable revisioning. This image was as much a product of the left and the student movements, both of which used such a view to dismiss feminisms, as it was a result of the dominance of liberal feminism in the public imagination. In fact, *within* the women's liberation movement, intense struggles over class, "race," and sexuality were already occurring. I can recall with painful clarity some of the 1970s conflicts and controversies in Montréal women's centres about the lack of inclusiveness, particularly for lesbians, as well as sustained and difficult discussions about Québec's right to self-determination and organizing across the language barrier.[4] In the 1974 *Our Generation* article, I recognized this struggle and claimed that "the ideology of Sisterhood" was "intrinsically apolitical" and suggested that "energy was expended in maintaining the delusion [of] a basic commonality of experience ... Working class women and Black women, for example, had never found a meaningful relation to the movement ... This sisterhood was itself essentially middle class" (1974, 26). This comment was directed at both liberal and radical feminists, who, each for their own reasons, had a commitment to the notion of an uncontested sisterhood. It highlights how early the issues of difference and power were on the feminist agenda, albeit not with great sophistication nor with an adequate understanding of privilege. It is also an important reminder of the ongoing debates among and across a multiplicity of feminisms, even in the 1970s. Furthermore, outside of the explicitly feminist women's liberation movement, women were organizing around a multitude of issues, increasingly with a gender consciousness, for example, in the Voice of Women (Macpherson and Sears 1976; Macpherson 1987) and in the unions (Sugiman 1993). These instances of organizing also need to be understood as part of women's movements.

Since the 1970s, along with many others, I have been struggling with issues of difference and power—politically, theoretically, strategically, and pedagogically. In fact, I have argued that such struggles have shaped a unique Canadian women's movement and help to explain the significance of socialist feminism in this country (Briskin 1989). Recuperating this history is important to contemporary struggles to reinvigorate women's movements.

The Trajectory of Women's Studies

I remember the early discussions about how women's studies would be the educational arm of the women's movement. Alas, this too was naïve. Such a perspective did not take account of the institutional pressures on the emergent programs in women's studies, and the difficulties finding the resources and the political will to maintain active links with community-based women's movements. Nevertheless, I continue to believe that women's studies can offer a vehicle to promote not only consciousness, but also activism. In fact, I have argued that women's agency should be central to the vision for women's studies in the twenty-first century (2004).

Notes

1   Marlene Dixon was a controversial figure. A Marxist and feminist activist, she was fired by the University of Chicago in 1969, which prompted a student sit-in. Although it did not stop Dixon's firing, the sit-in helped to galvanize the women's liberation movement in Chicago (cwlu Herstory 2005; Freeman 1969). See http://www.cwlu herstory.com/index.html and http://www.jofreeman.com/sixtiesprotest/styles.htm.

Dixon then obtained a position in the sociology department at McGill University, where she also met great opposition. Although not fired, she was eventually harassed out of the university. For her account of the events, see Dixon (1976).

2 Although I can't quite remember, I think this book was the inspiration for *Women in Revolution*—a thirty-minute video documentary on women in history that I made for Montréal's educational TV in 1972.

3 It is interesting that I was finishing my thesis on the capitalist family-household system at the same time as I was collaborating on the writing of *Feminist Organizing for Change*.

4 Cara Banks's thesis on Saskatchewan Working Women, an organization of unionized, non-unionized, and unpaid working women that existed from 1978 to the early 1990s challenges "the common belief that the women's movement in Canada has been concerned mainly with middle-class, white women's issues" (2001, iv). Banks concludes that "sww's strong links to unions and its class and race analysis of women's circumstances demonstrated a working-class perspective and a concern with the issues of marginalized women" (2001, iv).

Selected Publications by the Author

Briskin, Linda. 1972. *Women in revolution*. Montréal. Video Documentary.

————. 1974. Toward a socialist feminist movement. *Our Generation* 10 (3): 23–34.

————. 1980. Domestic labour: A methodological discussion. In *Hidden in the household*, edited by B. Fox. Toronto: Women's Press.

————. 1989. Socialist feminism: From the standpoint of practice. *Studies in Political Economy: A Socialist Review* 30: 87–114.

————. 1990. *Feminist pedagogy: Teaching and learning liberation*. Feminist Perspectives Monograph Series. Ottawa: Canadian Research Institute on the Advancement of Women (CRIAW).

————. 2004. Privileging agency and organizing: A new approach to women's studies. In *Feminisms and womanisms: Foundations, theories and praxis of the women's movement*, edited by A. Prince and S. Silva-Wayne. Toronto: Women's Press.

Briskin, Linda, and Lynda Yanz, eds. 1983. *Union sisters: Women in the labour movement*. Toronto: Women's Press.

My Path to Feminist Philosophy, 1970–76

Christine Overall

IN 1970, WHEN I HAD just finished my third year of an undergraduate program in philosophy at the University of Toronto, I discovered feminism.

It happened because I finally read Betty Friedan's *The Feminine Mystique* (1963). I had heard about the book some years earlier, around the age of fifteen, from a friend's mother, who had discussed it in a flirtatious manner with our music teacher. The music teacher, male, scoffed at it, and since I admired him, I felt no interest in reading the book. However, in 1970 I had learned the phrase "male chauvinist pig"—from my boyfriend, of all people—and my experiences of being one of the few women in philosophy were starting to awaken a nascent feminist consciousness.

Just as so many other women told Friedan, reading her book changed my life (Friedan 1976). I had been on the point of giving up my intellectual aspirations and my love of philosophy. I'd been thinking of going to library school to get what I thought would be an easy job. Most important of all, I was engaged to my boyfriend, and we were planning to marry in the following summer. I already had an engagement ring.

After reading Friedan, I immediately broke my engagement and spent the money I'd been saving for our wedding on a plane ticket to England, where I experienced four frightening but heady weeks of freedom. When I returned, I decided to continue in philosophy. I finished my fourth year and was admitted first to the MA program and then to the PhD program in philosophy at the University of Toronto. I was looking for liberation, both intellectual and personal, though I lacked the courage to apply to a different university.

Almost nowhere was there any formal opportunity to study women and their texts. Several of my instructors, including professors David Savan and Jack Stevenson, were supportive of my situation as one of very few women students in philosophy, but they were unable to help me study women's issues. (Indeed, Jack used to say that I educated him about feminism.) However, one of my instructors, Professor Danny Goldstick, was a Marxist. He regarded as quite reasonable my interest in what was then called women's liberation, and guided me to Friedrich Engels's *The Origin of the Family, Private Property, and the State* (1884).

Certainly there were no university women's studies courses in the early seventies, although by 1971 the University of Toronto had offered its first self-described women's studies course, a team-taught cornucopia of topics about women. By then a master's student, I sat in on some of the classes, which were packed, and carried away amazing mimeographed notes about the hidden lives of women. I had hoped to incorporate into my own studies some of the fascinating literature that was just coming out of the women's movement. I suspect it is no coincidence that the process by which I became a feminist philosopher started in a year when several feminist classics were published. From 1970 to 1975, I studied feminist texts mostly on my own. They were not available in the university library and so, poor student though I was, I bought them for myself.

The most interesting issue for me at the time was how to describe, understand, and explain women's oppression and women's relationship to men as a group. Should women be understood as constituting something like a class, a caste, or a minority group? There were useful similarities and disconcerting differences in each case. Another issue I investigated was the differences and similarities among various forms of feminism, which to my knowledge at that time included Marxist or socialist feminism, existentialist feminism, liberal feminism, and radical feminism. (I knew nothing about Black feminism or cultural feminism, and very little about lesbian feminism.) When I read Shulamith Firestone's *The Dialectic of Sex* (1972), I immediately identified myself as a radical feminist, convinced that "biology itself—procreation—is at the origin" (8) of all dualisms of inequality and oppression, that "the sexual imbalance of power is biologically based" (9), and that feminists should "attempt to develop a materialist view of history based on sex itself" (5).

I was also fortunate that, around 1973, sociology professor Janet Salaff began offering a graduate course in the Sociology of Women. I had never before studied sociology except in a one-hour-a-week, one-term elementary sociology course as a first-year undergraduate. Nonetheless, I was permitted to enrol in the course. In terms of my PhD program, Sociology of Women was categorized as my "complementary" course, although arguably it had no connection whatever to my doctoral research. However, I had by now had my first experience with sexual harassment, by a male graduate student, and although I had no name for the experience and did not even blame him for it, I needed a better framework for understanding my situation. Fortunately for me, my advisors recognized the legitimacy of that need.

I had never had a female philosophy professor, either as an undergraduate or as a graduate student, so it was a relief to take a graduate-level course taught by a woman. We met each week at the home of the professor, and sometimes she even nursed her young baby during our discussions. This was an almost revolutionary demonstration, for the time, of the possibility of combining motherhood and the academic profession. We read a variety of sociological literature on women. Taking this course made me wonder, for the first time, if there might be such a thing as women's knowledge. This was my first inkling of what later came to be called feminist epistemology, but at the time I made little progress in thinking about it because there was literally nothing available to read on that topic. Indeed, there seemed to be no possibility of doing feminist work in any area of philosophy at the PhD level, and I ended up working on a very traditional thesis in analytic philosophy of religion, which bore no indication whatever that I had acquired a feminist consciousness.

With my sparse but nonetheless exciting knowledge of feminist theory, I went on the job market in 1974. Although my PhD course work was done, my thesis was at a standstill. Nevertheless, I could see the professional writing on the wall: jobs were drying up, and if I wanted to be an academic, I realized I should apply immediately rather than risk missing the opportunity.

I was shortlisted for both of the positions for which I applied. At one of them, at a major university in Ontario, I had the job interview from hell. I was subjected to intellectual bullying by male professors and graduate students, who made no secret of their contempt for me during my job talk. It happened to be near the beginning of International Women's Year (1975), and at lunch one of the interviewers (they were all male) asked me, in the most unctuous way possible, what I was doing for International Women's Year. I was speechless, this being a question I had not thought to prepare for. Only afterward did my feminist mother point out the obvious answer: "I'm trying to find a job!"

I didn't get the position.

I was also interviewed for a job at Marianopolis College, an excellent anglophone CEGEP (Collège d'enseignement général et professionnel, meaning "College of General and Vocational Education") in Montréal. The appointments committee, which included women as well as men, wanted to hire me to teach both philosophy and humanities. At my interview, I was asked which courses I might teach. Within philosophy, my answers were quite conventional. I could teach a "problems of philosophy" course and an ethics course. The humanities category, however, offered me a unique opportunity. All CEGEP students were required to take four humanities courses, one in each term of their two-year program.

I proposed to teach a course that I called Theories of Women's Liberation. At that time, "women's liberation" was a more widely used term than "feminism." I met no resistance to this proposal. Indeed, the intellectual support I received at the college was remarkable. Marianopolis was a former private girls' school, run by the sisters of the Congregation de Notre Dame. When I was hired in 1975, the sisters were still the administrators of the college, and some of them were also teaching. The college had become an "institution in the public interest" and admitted male students. Even so, unusually, the majority of the lay instructors also were female. At the time, the college had the highest entrance standards of all the anglophone CEGEPs. The students were a wonderful mix of Greek, Italian, Jewish, Québecois, and English ethnicities, virtually all of them impeccably bilingual, and some trilingual or quadrilingual.

At Marianopolis, I had my work cut out for me. I had never taught an entire course before. The most advanced teaching position I'd held was a teaching assistantship, and I wasn't very good at that. I was hired to teach two sections of each of two courses per term. Despite my severe lack of experience, in addition to my philosophy courses I taught two sections of Humanities 101, Theories of Women's Liberation, in the fall term of 1975 and again in the winter term of 1976. The underlying goal of my humanities course was to reveal, describe, and account for women's oppression in the Western world. I assigned *The Feminine Mystique* (Friedan 1963), *The Second Sex* (de Beauvoir 1953), *The Origin of the Family, Private Property, and the State* (Engels 1884), and *The Dialectic of Sex* (Firestone 1972). The course consisted both of lectures and discussions. I also made use of a series of wonderfully creative short films about women that were coming out of the National Film Board's Studio D.

I had two challenges specific to the course. First, I had to teach the students enough about liberalism, existentialism, and Marxism to enable them to understand the books. In retrospect, I realize that most students—who would have been aged sixteen to nineteen—were seriously underprepared by their high school education to plough through texts as difficult as those I had assigned.

Second, although most students seemed interested in the material and were surprisingly willing to sit through what would have been the earliest, and only, feminist theory course at the college at that time, I also had to deal with a certain amount of skepticism about and resistance to the course material on the part of a handful of students, both male and female. One young woman, for example, informed the class contemptuously that there could be no such thing as rape in marriage, because by getting married a woman agrees to sex anywhere and at any time. I also got tired of the cockiness and condescension of some of the young men who were happy to exert their social power over the female students and me. As a result of these pressures, for a few years in the late seventies I actually designated the course as "intended primarily for women students"—and got away with it.

On the whole, the course was a success, although in subsequent years I gradually modified it away from its highly theoretical beginnings into a vehicle that handled much more down-to-earth issues, including sexual assault, women's employment, and motherhood. Karen Wood, the then–area coordinator for the Liberal Arts at Marianopolis, also urged me to change the title to something more attractive to students. In the late seventies, Theories of Women's Liberation ceased to be a wholly theoretical feminist course, and became the more pragmatic and policy-oriented Feminism in the Eighties.

As I look back on that course in its first incarnation in 1975, it seems both naive and brave. Naive, because I had no understanding of the significance of racialization, sexual orientation, age, or disability, and only the most superficial notions of class. And brave because I was more or less alone. I was the only woman teaching philosophy at Marianopolis College. The only other person whom I knew well who was covering any feminist material was Beverley Kennedy, an English professor, who taught women's literature from a feminist standpoint.

Moreover, because I was raising two young babies and finishing my PhD thesis while working full-time at the college, I had very little time or opportunity to network. I do remember attending one meeting of some women instructors at nearby anglophone CEGEPs, where we discussed the difficulty of engaging women students in feminist issues. One of those present was Greta Hoffman Nemiroff, who sagely remarked, "They won't recognize their oppression until they're married."

Finally, I think I was both naive *and* brave in first teaching my Women's Liberation course, because I didn't really know what I was doing, yet I offered a feminist theory course nonetheless. That course was the beginning, for me, of a career in feminist philosophical teaching and scholarship that is ongoing today. In 1984, I began working at Queen's University, where I was tenured in 1990 and promoted to full professor in 1992. Almost all of the books and articles that I have published (with the exception of a few in my original field, philosophy of religion) are explicitly feminist, and several of my courses, undergraduate and graduate, are in feminist philosophy.

I am happy to be a feminist philosopher. No other academic identity would even be possible for me. I no longer characterize myself as a radical feminist in the sense used by Firestone—that is, as a feminist who takes sex to be the most fundamental organizing category of society and the origin of all forms of oppression. Firestone wrote, "Nature produced the fundamental inequality—half the human race must bear and rear the children of all of them—which was later consolidated, institutionalised, in the interests of men.... Women were the slave class that maintained the species in order to free the other half for the business of the world" (1972, 205).

I realized that it is not women's biology itself that disadvantages women; rather it is the social interpretation and evaluation of our biological characteristics that creates systemic injustices, social and economic. I am no longer so naive as to think that other forms of oppression originate from sexism, although they are certainly connected. Nonetheless, I have remained primarily interested in issues related to women's embodiment, and have published widely on reproductive ethics and social policy, on sexuality and sexual orientations, and on sex, gender, age, and disability. For me, what has been key to the development of feminist philosophy is the shift from talking about women as individuals and groups to talking about social categories, especially gender but also sex, sexual orientation, racialized groups, ethnicity, class, age, and (dis)ability.

Selected Publications by the Author

Overall, Christine. 1987. *Ethics and human reproduction: A feminist analysis*. Boston: Allan and Unwin.

———. 1993. *Human reproduction: Principles, practices, policies*. Toronto: Oxford University Press.

———. 1998. *A feminist I: Reflections from academia*. Peterborough, ON: Broadview Press.

————. 2001. *Thinking like a woman: Personal life and political ideas*. Toronto: Sumach Press.

————. 2003. *Aging, death, and human longevity: A philosophical inquiry*. Berkeley: University of California Press.

Women's Sight: Looking Backwards into Women's Studies in Toronto

Ceta Ramkhalawansingh

"HERSTORY" OF THE women's studies program at the University of Toronto is set within the context of university reform underway during the 1960s, and it is one of many about women's struggles to gain admission and equal treatment at the University of Toronto. Thirty-five years ago, when we proclaimed that there was gender bias within the academy, we were not fully aware of the extent to which previous generations of women had faced greater barriers and that we were part of a very long journey for equality rights. I am keenly aware that this "herstory" contains its own perspective—mine.

In *A Path Not Strewn with Roses* (1985), Anne Rochon Ford traced the battle for equality at the University of Toronto from the nineteenth century.[1] Prior to 1877, when the first woman student was admitted to Victoria College, there were many attempts to gain entry. Questions were raised: Were women capable of coping with the challenges of learning presented by higher education? Would it be a waste of resources to admit women if their main role in society was that of mother and wife? Would women's presence distract men? Should separate schools be established for women? Should women be admitted but receive private tutoring rather than permitted to attend classes? And so on. Direct intervention by the provincial legislature in 1884 was required to force the hand of Daniel Wilson, president of Victoria College and the university, who opposed women's entry to the university.

When I arrived on campus in 1968, little did I realize that within a year I would become completely immersed in the institutional changes and become that part of the movement to establish one of the first courses on women studies to be offered at a major university in Canada.

My parents and the rest of the family moved to Canada in 1967. I attended one year of high school in Toronto after five years attending an all-girl faith-oriented high school in Trinidad and Tobago, where my academic focus was mathematics and sciences. At my new high school, I was introduced to the new math, Gabrielle Roy and other Canadian writers—a far cry from Shakespeare—and to coeducation. I did not have to wear a school uniform. New College was my undergraduate college of choice as I did not expect it to be steeped in tradition or religious affiliation. My interest in my science program was soon overtaken by campus politics and learning about the new country in which I was living.

One of the first campus meetings I attended in the fall of my first year, 1968, concerned the differential treatment in the requirements for physical education for male and female students. Physical education was compulsory for first-year female students, who would fail their term for non-attendance. Male students had no such requirement because insufficient athletic facilities for male students made it impossible to enforce compulsory attendance. It was ironic that this meeting about compulsory physical education for women was held at Hart House, which was built to provide a social, cultural, and athletic meeting place for *men* only. Hart House was completed in 1919, but women did not gain full admission to this facility until 1972, after many attempts by women students to "storm" the building.

Across the entire university, students wanted campus reform. They wanted a role in decision making, they challenged the image of the university as an "ivory tower" and its role in conducting war research, and they lobbied for course evaluations, credited part-time degree programs, student housing, and better bursary programs. The Students Administrative Council (SAC), the central student government, waded into gender equity issues by flaunting the prohibition against the distribution of birth control information. First published in 1968 by a group of feminists at McGill who set up the Montréal Health Press, thousands of copies of the *Birth Control Handbook* were distributed by SAC—a practice that continued for several years. SAC also rented busses to enable students to join the abortion caravan that went to Ottawa in the spring of 1970. The first sit-in that took place on campus was over the retention of a building that was being used by parents as a cooperative daycare centre. Student leaders also addressed rampant misogyny in the engineering student newspaper, whose funding was stripped from the student government budget, along with funding for cheerleaders' costumes and football team banquets.

Racism was largely invisible. Few racial minorities could be observed among the student body and not in sufficient numbers to document incidents or patterns of racism. Sexism was more evident than racism. Women faculty were very few, held junior positions, and were paid badly. Meanwhile, the student body was changing as girls were enrolling alongside boys. At the national level, the Royal Commission on the Status of Women had raised important issues about women's role in Canada in its 1970 groundbreaking report.

It was within this context that the demand for women's studies arose. New academic programs began to be introduced within the Faculty of Arts and Sciences, including an Interdisciplinary Studies Department. Its first chair was Professor Geoffrey Payzant, a progressive philosopher and Glenn Gould scholar. This department became the first home for women's studies when, in 1970, it convened an open meeting for members of the university community to bring forward ideas about the department's program. Led by Charnie Cunningham (née Guettel), some members of the campus women's liberation movement proposed that a course be established to address women's equality issues. Filled with progressive types, the department committee, of which I was a member, accepted this proposal for a course that became, in 1971, FSW (Faculty Studies: Women) 200: Women in the Twentieth Century. Also in 1971, two of the university's brightest scholars, Jill Ker Conway and Natalie Zemon Davis, introduced a course on the history of women in early modern Europe (see Conway and Davis's joint essay in this volume). Other feminist scholars were teaching under the radar.

Given the times and the origin of the proposal, planning proceeded on the basis of having a "teaching collective."[2] Work collectives were in vogue at the time and did not fit the hierarchical structure of the university, which required that courses be headed by appointed faculty. After much, much, much searching, Professor Barbara Martineau, an American scholar in English and film, agreed to be the faculty lead. My recollection is that for the rest of 1970 and 1971, especially the summer of 1971, the group held many study sessions to develop a course outline and a syllabus that was interdisciplinary and cross-cultural. The study sessions reviewed lengthy bibliographies prepared by women in the teaching collective on Canadian women's literature, historical feminism, economic history, and cinema studies (see Kay Armatage's essay in this volume), and included books and articles on women in Africa, China, and Japan, and by significant women writers of the twentieth century. We became one another's teachers.

By the start of the school year in 1971, FSW 200: Women in the Twentieth Century was offered with a syllabus built around themes of women's
images, health and sexuality, the family, the economy, and revolution. A
public lecture series partially funded by the Students' Administrative Council had a weekly attendance of over 350 people, including nearly 250 students. Well-known personalities such as June Callwood, Margaret Atwood,
Maryon Kantaroff, Marion Powell, and Rosalie Abella were invited to give
lectures, as were important activists such as Sandra Lovelace and Jeanette
Lavell, who were fighting for rights for First Nations women. Given the nov-
elty of women's studies, several articles were written in local papers and
national magazines, as well as campus papers.

An ongoing agenda item for the teaching group was the course pedagogy. The teaching method and content were interdisciplinary and experimental. Sections of about twenty students were taught by teaching teams.
Students were asked to write journals about their involvement in action
projects within the community.

During this period, new feminist women's groups were being established, such as the Rape Crisis Centre, the Immigrant Women's Health
Centre, and the Toronto Women's Bookstore. The Women's Press was set
up when a group of women could not find a publisher for *Women Unite!*
(1972), one of the early Canadian anthologies. I joined the labour history
collective, which wrote an essay in the award-winning book on women's
labour history in Ontario, *Women at Work: Ontario 1850–1930* (Acton,
Goldsmith, and Shepard 1974). To prepare this manuscript, I spent countless hours looking at primary sources in the national archives in Ottawa
and local public libraries. It soon became apparent that women's invisibility meant that their contributions and efforts were not part of the
record. I used the research to illustrate the types of biases that can arise
from relying on census data on women's labour force participation. The
1911 census recorded paid agricultural workers and heads of family farms
or male farm workers but no women. We projected that if women's agricultural labour were counted, their representation in the workforce would
be close to levels achieved in the paid labour force of the 1970s. Other
chapters of the book provided analyses of women's work, including that
of domestic workers, women in the trade union movement, women's professions such as nursing, and women's work in the sex trades. Hindsight
provides vision; today such a publication would have addressed questions
of the intersectionality of gender, racialization, sexual orientation, Aboriginal issues, and so on.

The *Canadian Newsletter of Research on Women*, which evolved into *Resources for Feminist Research*, was founded by Margrit Eichler and Marylee Stephenson and provided an important point of connection among women academics and feminist researchers of all genders (see the essays by Eichler and Stephenson in this volume). Using the vehicle of the Learned Societies, a network of women scholars convened a series of national conferences on women in colleges and universities. The first meeting was convened in Montréal in 1972 by Margret Andersen and Katherine Waters of Loyola University, and the second at Queen's University in Kingston in 1973 by Evelyn Reid, dean of women. In the summer of 1973, the women's studies teaching collective at the University of Toronto threw its weight behind plans for the third national conference, held at York University, which was followed by the fourth, held in 1975 at Hart House, University of Toronto.

Unlike the Learned Societies, these meetings addressed issues concerning all women who were part of the university and college system. The minds behind this strategy belonged to Johanna Stuckey, a scholar at York University who was the national coordinator of the organization, and to Marion Boyd, the conference convenor, who eventually became an attorney general of Ontario in the Rae government. Strength in numbers propels movements forward. Nearly two hundred women from across Canada attended this 1974 meeting of women in colleges and universities at York University, clearly signalling the priority that women were giving to their status in higher education, and, more importantly, signalling their intention to be vocal activists.

Part of the drama of getting women's studies permanently established at the University of Toronto was the publication of an unofficial women's studies program calendar. By cutting, pasting, and borrowing photocopy machines, a women's studies calendar was printed using much of the format of existing brochures. Official statements from university publications were reproduced and all the sexist terms were highlighted and cross-references were given to courses that would complement women's studies. I might have been the moving force here—but it couldn't have happened without Kay Armatage being there doing it with me, side by side—nor would I have done it alone (see Armatage's essay in this volume). The response from some quarters was to attack the program by saying that women's studies was "political" and "anti-intellectual." Kay responded to these attacks by stating, "To be effective, women's studies should offer students a perspective from which they could question the bases and methods of all the other forms of knowledge generated by centuries of *scholarship*" (1979).

One upshot of our "theatre" was the establishment of a formal university committee to give recommendations for the future. One perspective offered by Kay Armatage was that the university had to find a way of "defusing and containing" the women's studies approach that was underway. It had taken a few years to reach this stage, and many of us who were originally involved had graduated or were ready to move on.

After finishing the credits for my first degree in 1972, I continued to teach part-time and continued on to graduate studies also at the University of Toronto, first in child studies and—after a period working as a research and policy analyst in education—then in a doctoral program in 1978 at the Ontario Institute for Studies in Education (OISE). My classmates there were also engaged in feminist studies, as OISE had hired several feminist scholars. By the time I finished my residency for a doctoral degree focussed on equality theory and specifically on women's employment issues, I had a mixed career as a part-time university teacher, a community organizer on housing and land-use issues, and a policy analyst on "race" relations and immigration, and I had published many articles on a range of issues. I was ready to move on. I began full-time work at Toronto City Hall to address equality issues, which led to opportunities to establish linkages between the city and the Women's Studies Program. One of these links was the establishment of scholarships in women's studies to commemorate the centenary in 1977 of women's admission to the university.

Although I played a role in the effort to establish women's studies at the University of Toronto, this success required at least three conditions. First, there were allies and supporters who were willing to acknowledge that gender had not been included as a subject of study or that women scholars were not included in curriculum. Second, there were resources for teaching stipends and other support, such as office space and telephones. Third, there was passion and commitment among the teachers—all of whom, except one, was a student—to implement what we set out to do, despite any obstacle that we would face. While our persistence some thirty-five years ago may have advanced the start date for women's studies at the University of Toronto, its inclusion in all educational institutions since then suggests that women's studies would have taken root sooner or later. Its time had come.

Notes

1 This book contains an excellent history of women's equality struggles until 1985, which are still ongoing but not yet documented.

2 The members of the planning and teaching collective of FSW (Faculty Studies: Women) 200: Women in the Twentieth century included the following women: Kay Armatage, Barbara Cameron, Connie Chapman, Robin Endres, Ruth McKeown, Professor Barbara Martineau (the one faculty member), Kathryn Peterson, Ceta Ramkhalawansingh, Lyba Spring, Bonnie Ward, Karen Webster, and Jane Wingate. In 1972, the course was renamed Women: Oppression and Liberation and was transferred to Innis College, where the teachers included Kay Armatage, Barbara Cameron, Debra Curties, Meg Luxton, Ruth McKeown, Kathryn Petersen, Ceta Ramkhalawansingh, and Sandra Foster. A few years later, the course was again transferred, this time to its permanent home at New College.

Selected Publications by the Author

Ramkhalawansingh, Ceta. 1973. Women's courses: Tough problems, far-reaching aims. *Varsity*, March.

————. 1974. Women during the Great War. In *Women at work: Ontario 1850–1930*, edited by J. Acton, P. Goldsmith, and B. Shepard. Toronto: Women's Educational Press.

◉ Personal and Intellectual Revolutions: Some Reflections

THE ESSAYS IN THIS book represent a multiplicity of experiences and voices that do not always agree with one another. We consider such contradictions a strength rather than a weakness of the book.[1] They emerge out of the different interests, concerns, disciplines, timing, and social and geographic locations that characterize the various authors; and they demonstrate that things unfolded differently not only in Canada and in Québec, but also in the various anglophone provinces—and sometimes even in different departments at the same university, as the essay by Rosalind Sydie, Patricia Prestwich, and Dallas Cullen demonstrates.

For some of the general trends that we can identify, there are also contrary examples. While all of the authors shared in an overall social structure that was generally patriarchal and sexist, as well as racist, heterosexist, and ableist, some authors spent significant parts of their lives in countries other than Canada: e.g., in Australia, France, Germany, Great Britain, and the United States. Many studied abroad—primarily in the United States, Great Britain, and France—and were thus exposed to somewhat different contexts. In addition, local and individual factors varied greatly.

Most of the authors are from the social sciences and humanities—the disciplines within which women's studies started.[2] Reflecting the general make-up of the faculty at the time, all but two are White; Vanaja Dhruvarajan and Ceta Ramkhalawansingh are women of colour. All but two are female; Terry Crowley and Leslie Marshall are the two males, which somewhat under-represents the proportion of men who actually taught women's studies in the beginning, namely 13% (Eichler and Vandelac 1990, 70), but slightly over-represents the proportion of male academics who had a lasting impact on the development of the field.

The essays variably address the questions we editors posed to the authors; this chapter draws on those aspects that are descriptive of the 1966–76 period. Together, the essays can be read as something more than merely the sum of their parts: they offer a kind of group biography or collective snapshot. They provide some insights into the social roots of feminist activism on college and university campuses across Canada and Québec in the late 1960s and early 1970s—the period in which women's studies first emerged—and they demonstrate some of the struggles and the exhilaration involved in creating a new way of looking at the world, and the many hurdles that had to be overcome in the process.

The Patriarchal Context

The context within which the women's movement and women's studies emerged is patriarchy. Experiencing and coping with patriarchy in their own lives is one of the unifying themes in the essays to which there is no exception. Benokraitis (1997) has identified nine different types of subtle sex discrimination: condescending chivalry, supportive discouragement, friendly harassment, subjective objectification, radiant devaluation, liberated sexism, benevolent exploitation, considerate domination, and collegial exclusion; we find examples of most of these in the essays. However, beyond such more subtle forms of sexism, we encounter again and again examples of blatant and atrocious sexism of a type that is no longer permissible in Canada but was part of the daily experience of women at the time. It took various forms.

Open Legal and Policy Discrimination against Women

This was the time before the Charter of Rights and Freedoms was even thought of. Treating women and men by different standards was a regular—and widely accepted—practice. For instance, there was open discrimination in immigration policy: Margrit Eichler received her immigration visa on the basis on her husband's potential to obtain a job in Canada, although she had a contract in her pocket and he did not. Maureen Baker obtained a visa to Australia only because of her status as a fiancée in spite of two years of teaching experience (her fiancé subsequently refused to marry her). There was also perfectly legal discrimination with respect to banking and credit. Wendy Robbins realized that her mother, a married woman, by law could not have her own bank account and was barred from buying, without her husband's signature, the $4.00 annual licence for the small utility trailer that the family pulled behind their car on camping trips. Sandra Pyke had to fight hard to get a credit card in her own name rather than her husband's. She adds, "It was an incredible, demeaning experience, which still has the power to evoke anger, bewilderment, and shame, and it marked a turning point in my life." Universities had anti-nepotism rules—meaning that spouses could not be employed at the same university (Eichler).

The prevailing ideology was one of sex differentiation rather than gender equality, and discrimination on the basis of sex was widely practised and accepted in law, as well as in a wide array of policies. Married women were treated as their husband's dependent; splitting of family property upon divorce was almost unthinkable.

Married women were supposed to look after the family, while husbands brought in the money; if a married woman chose to pursue a career, it was supposed to be kept subordinate to the career needs of her husband. Micheline Dumont followed her husband to Paris so that he could complete his PhD while she taught school. Alison Prentice tailored her PhD work around her husband's career. Deborah Gorham struggled, like her mother, "to balance marriage, motherhood, and career." As Dumont notes, "today it's hard for people to imagine the powerful hold of social and religious dictums on the young women of that era."

Discrimination in pay on the basis of sex was legal—laws on equal pay for equal work and equal pay for work of equal value were yet to be enacted nationally. When Linda Christiansen-Ruffman tried to find a job with her honours BA, potential employers asked if she could type (to become a secretary).[3] She mused that she could be hired at two-thirds the advertised rate and with better qualifications than any man. Later, when she did get an academic job, she was hired at a lower salary than a male counterpart.

Violence against women was not seen as a political issue, and sexual harassment was often seen as trivial. When Christine Overall was harassed by a male graduate student, she had "no name for the experience and did not even blame him for it." Maureen Baker was held up at gunpoint by a student who had tried unsuccessfully to flirt with her, but when she reported the incident to the college authorities, they refused to call the police, telling her that she was "making too much" of it.

Openly and Blatantly Sexist Attitudes Towards Women as Students and Faculty

Openly and blatantly sexist attitudes towards women were pervasive in the university system. Examples abound. Here are a few: Pat Armstrong and her colleagues received a memo from their dean, in response to a request to start a credit course on women, in which he wrote that he had watched stallions bite mares' asses in order to get them to behave and he saw this as the proper order of relations between the sexes. When Meg Luxton attempted to write her comprehensive exams while pregnant, the monitoring professor first denied her entry on the grounds that "You can't write exams in that condition!" and, after she was finally permitted entry to the exams hours later, refused to allow her the full time. Alison Prentice was asked what she would do with her PhD after she got it and who would look after her children. A colleague of her husband's noted that if *his* wife wanted to do a PhD, he would kill her. She also reports her dean's words on seeing her lunching with four women colleagues: "'Aha,' crowed the dean as he looked in the door. 'If I shot all of you, that would finish the women's movement at Atkinson, wouldn't it?'" Meredith Kimball recalls that, at a meeting at which she and her colleagues were putting forward a proposal for a women's studies course, a senior professor compared the faculty advancing this proposal, and the students who supported it, to Nazis, "because women's studies would separate and segregate women, as the Nazis had once separated out and segregated Jews."

Clara Thomas writes glowingly about a close male friend, Brandy Conron. Nonetheless, when she applied to the University of Toronto's PhD program in 1949, he sent her a "scathing letter" threatening to withdraw his support; she put off her doctoral work for seven years. This, of course, happened significantly earlier than other events. However, about twenty years later, Meg Luxton's experience was not all that different: the University of Toronto rejected her application to the MA program on the grounds that a woman "could not be serious about a career"; her second application was refused because she "had a husband who would support [her]," while another (male) candidate "had a wife to support." Luxton finally entered the master of philosophy (MPhil) program, known as "the married women's degree"; she did not begin her PhD for another four years. Similarly, Linda Christiansen-Ruffman reports that she was "initially rejected as a Columbia Fellow because females were not considered to be serious scholars."

Given that women were often seen as unsuitable candidates for academic jobs, many report difficulties in getting hired. Non-academic criteria were applied to denigrate women, such as the decision to have a child "out of wedlock," as Terry Crowley reports. Margrit Eichler was told by St. Francis Xavier, a Roman Catholic university, that they would consider her application only if her husband would accompany her. During a job interview, Christine Overall "was subjected to intellectual bullying by male professors and graduate students, who made no secret of their contempt for me during my job talk." At this time hiring largely followed the old boys' network—male professors wanted to place their students in jobs at universities—and was a lot less formal than it is today. Occasionally, this worked to the benefit of women. Micheline Dumont, for instance, received a telephone call offering her a job in the Department of History at Sherbrooke University, if she would send in her CV.

Given this overall situation, it is not surprising that many of the authors recount that they themselves had had no, or very few, female professors. For instance, Jill Vickers notes that "women were virtually absent from politics and political science: no woman professor taught me, and one lone woman MP ... sat in the House of Commons ... throughout my student career." Many others echo this experience (Baker, Christiansen-Ruffman, Davis, Gillett, Overall, Robbins, Sherwin). When the English department secretary at York needed to be away, she requested of Dr. Thomas (who was a professor), "Mrs. Thomas, please try to make Professor MacLean a good cup of tea." By the time Lorna Marsden joined the University of Toronto in 1972, there were five women on faculty; none ranked above assistant professor. In addition to there being no or very few female professors, in some disciplines there were also few or no other female students. Joan McFarland, for instance, was the only female student in her class in economics. When she worked hard and was demonstrably able to "do well," her male co-students observed that she "was being graded by a different standard."

Intellectual Discrimination

Intellectual discrimination took two major forms: exclusion and denigration. Exclusion manifested itself in the almost complete absence of women in what the authors themselves were taught, the ignoring or derogation of women in accepted textbooks, and the omission of women's concerns in models, theories, and intellectual frameworks. This was, of course, related to the lack of women on faculty. All this meant that those who were to teach women's studies courses had themselves not had an education that prepared them for it. There are two notable exceptions to this general rule:

Maïr Verthuy writes about the education she received in Great Britain, where her female professors ensured that women were included in their subject matter, and Danielle Juteau commends her education at the Collège Marguerite-Bourgeois, a classical college for girls in Montréal, where the nuns "encouraged us to become doctors, not marry them."

Generally, however, women simply did not fit—and several of the authors speak of behaving as honourary males (Christiansen-Ruffman, Vickers) in order to be able to survive academically. As Dorothy Smith notes, women "weren't wanted in sociology faculties; we weren't mentioned in sociological writing and research; and we were excluded conceptually in the order of sociological discourse ... We were never the subjects, never the knowers of sociological discourse."

.The second way in which intellectual discrimination manifested itself was a sometimes vicious, sometimes simply dismissive attitude that the authors encountered when they tried to deal with women's issues. Lorna Marsden recounts that "there was a strong aura of disapproval" about incorporating issues raised by the women's movement into academic studies: "For young, untenured faculty there was a concern that scholarship and teaching in this field, while desirable, might not be acceptable when the culling of faculty occurred at tenure time. We were told we should get down to 'real' work if we were going to survive at the university."

Indeed, a number of authors were denied tenure or promotion because of their involvement in women's studies: Meredith Kimball was denied tenure at the University of British Columbia and Marylee Stephenson was denied tenure at McMaster. Stephenson sums up: "The rationale seemed to be, 'great teacher, active in the field—but *what* field?'—as in, women's studies is not a real academic field." Jill Vickers's department refused to promote her to full professor because, it argued, her research " was 'not of interest to political scientists.'"

Those who wrote their PhD theses at this time also ran into outright denigration: when Meg Luxton proposed women's work in the home for her doctoral research, she was told by one of her committee members that "women don't do anything but lie around the house all day." Another professor in her department "told several colleagues in a loud voice what a silly fool I was for arguing that women's work in the home contributed to the well-being of society and the economy. He went on to say he was embarrassed to be part of a department that would even consider such work suitable for a doctorate." In fact, her PhD about housework has become a classic that is still in print after more than a quarter century (Luxton 1980).

At Pat Armstrong's thesis defence, one faculty member demanded that she "remove the claim that as many as one in ten women had experienced abuse," which was based on Linda McLeod's published work (1980). Today we know that her early estimate was too low, not too high. Vanaja Dhruvarajan was told that she could study Hindu families but not the lives of Hindu women, because "the latter are not considered a legitimate research topic."

The evidence concerning the introduction of new courses and programs on women is contradictory, demonstrating the importance of local factors—for instance, a single dean or chair who was either sympathetic or antagonistic towards such courses. Many of the authors had to fight hard to get their first course on the books. Pat Armstrong and her group were, after an epic struggle, able to offer a credit course on women—but it did not count as part of their teaching load. Meg Luxton presented a proposal for a full-year course entitled Women in the World that was rejected "as having 'too narrow' a focus." The group at Simon Fraser University did a slow march through eleven committees before they could launch their program. In the process, Andrea Lebowitz reports, one committee member suggested that "giving us a program was tantamount to allowing the prisoners to create a prison education program."

By contrast, when Patricia Prestwich informed her chair that she wanted to start a course on women's history, he not only agreed but gave her a half-course teaching release to prepare a course in this new area. Dallas Cullen was asked by the dean of business to teach a course on women and leadership. At the same time, Rosalind Sydie encountered difficulties in teaching her course in sociology. Yet Sydie, Prestwich, and Cullen were all at the University of Alberta, although in different departments and faculties, which demonstrates that there could be major differences even within the same university.

Regardless of how hard they had to fight for their first course, or whether it was offered to them, everybody had to deal with an almost complete absence of materials. There were no specialized journals and no organizations, unless they were created by the professors themselves. The very scarcity of resources led to the invention of new scholarship and the creation of many different structures: formal and informal groups, associations, journals, publishers, and new courses and programs. Before further considering the new scholarship and new structures, we will briefly look at the social movements that were important at the time, and how racialization, gender, class, and sexual orientation intersected.

Countervailing Social Movements

While patriarchy constituted the overall context, there were a number of social and political movements that were very active at the time and that, together, created counterpoints to the prevailing hierarchical order. While the women's movement was important to all of the authors, many of them were also influenced by the anti–Vietnam War, peace, and gay and lesbian rights movements; the nationalist movement in Québec; the Native rights movement; left-wing, anti-racist, anti-poverty, and environmental movements; the labour movement; the movement for reproductive control; and, within the academy, the Canadianization movement.

The Canadianization movement worked in sync with the feminist movement on campus, in the experience of Clara Thomas, Dorothy Smith, and Andrea Lebowitz. A main issue was the large number of foreign academics teaching in Canadian universities, particularly in the culturally sensitive fields of the social sciences and humanities. English departments were shifting from an almost exclusive focus on British and American literature to include writers from Canada and other English-speaking former colonies, as Wendy Robbins observes. Margaret Atwood's *Survival: A Thematic Guide to Canadian Literature* (1972b), a book of literary criticism, became a bestseller. It gave an anatomy of victimization that had resonance for women as well as for Canada with its lingering "colonial mentality" and persistent economic and political control from the US. Clara Thomas records that in 1972, Beth Appeldoorn and Susan Sandler opened the Longhouse Bookshop in Toronto, the first bookshop to stock exclusively Canadian books, another important landmark for Canadian writing.

The impact of the Canadianization movement was felt not only on research and the curriculum but also on hiring. The objection was not so much the foreign country of origin of people teaching in Canada, but three other concerns: Had they familiarized themselves with the issues important for Canada? Were they teaching from Canadian or foreign (mostly American) texts? And were they doing research about Canada? The Symons report noted that "the result of the Commission's examination of about fifty areas of academic work, teaching, and research is that there is no area … in which a reasonable balance and attention is being given to Canadian matters" (Symons 1978, 13). Another concern was that Canadians were discriminated against in hiring even though Canada had started to produce larger numbers of PhDs capable of filling the positions. There was much evidence that these issues were genuine problems in Canada at that time.

There was thus a parallel between the academic women's movement and the Canadianization movement, in terms of both knowledge creation and the experience of outright discrimination. Symons's report includes a short section on women's studies, in which he suggests that women's studies "can provide valuable new insights into our society and assist with the sharpening of critical scholarly analysis in Canada" (1978, 77)—an oblique acknowledgement that women's studies in the 1970s on our campuses was largely oriented towards Canadian issues.

In Québec, *la Révolution tranquille* (the Quiet Revolution)—a major force with transformative political, economic, social, and cultural power—was intimately linked to the feminist movement, a point too little appreciated in the rest of Canada, as Nadia Fahmy-Eid observes. Nationalism did not steer women away from feminism and its issues. On the contrary, the call to equality and independence resonated doubly for many women in Québec.

The women's movement was a vital force for all of the authors. It has often been said that women's studies began as the academic arm of the women's movement, and this is largely confirmed by what these stories reveal. Many of the authors (e.g., Armstrong, Briskin, Eichler, Forman, Kolodny, Levine, McFarland, Sherwin, and Stephenson) trace their personal transformation to their participation in the consciousness-raising groups that sprang up in the late 1960s and early 1970s. Many of the women working to transform the academy were also shaking things up in their families and communities. They were invigorated, challenged, nourished, and occasionally criticized; Margaret Gillett even felt betrayed by the movement. They were intensely involved, debating issues hotly, putting themselves on the line, becoming a vital part of the women's movement, not only through their teaching and research, but also by participating in demonstrations, public educational events, and grassroots groups (e.g., Andersen, Caron). Beyond inventing a new scholarship, they pushed for new policies on campus, in the region, and nationally (e.g., Andersen, Armstrong, Pyke).

Intersections of Gender, Racialization, Class, and Sexual Orientation

There is a prevailing image that the second-wave women's movement was racist by failing to take racialization into account, and that the emphasis on woman's situation—in the singular—led to a false universalization of the experience of middle-class White women. The picture that emerges from the essays in this book is a more complex one. There are only two women of colour in this book—Ceta Ramkhalawansingh and Vanaja Dhruvara-jan—and they offer rather different assessments. Norma Bowen was another highly active and important Black academic involved in women's studies at this period. Hired in 1966, Norma Bowen may possibly have been Canada's first Black woman faculty member—a time lag of half a century compared to White women and half a dozen years compared to Black men, that itself speaks volumes. Bowen's career was cut short by cancer, and she died early (see Crowley).[4]

Ceta Ramkhalawansingh notes that, in her experience, "Racism was largely invisible. Few racial minorities could be observed among the student body and not in sufficient numbers to document incidents or patterns of racism. Sexism was more evident than racism." Some of the authors, such as Mere-dith Kimball and Christine Overall, acknowledge that at the time they did not pay sufficient attention to racialization (as well as class, sexual orienta-tion, and disability. Others, however, tried to integrate issues of racialization into their teaching from the very beginning. It must be remembered that everyone suffered from a lack of resources to a degree that today is almost unimaginable, and that the major anti-racist works still were to be written.

Linda Christiansen-Ruffman recalls that, in her first courses, "a focus on equality issues associated with racialization, class, and nationality had equal billing with sex or gender." Meg Luxton similarly suggests that "Our formal commitment to the liberation of all was challenged, too, by lesbian, working-class, Aboriginal, Black, and immigrant women, who readily pointed out the discrepancies between our declared politics and our failure to ade-quately take up issues of sexual orientation, racism, and class inequality. Our comrades in Québec challenged us on the national question and on our linguistic chauvinism." Luxton researched and wrote a twelve-page hand-out on "Indian and Inuit Women of Canada" in 1972 because there was no suitable material in print on Aboriginal women. Wendy Robbins also remem-bers typing up handouts of Native Canadian literature since no published collections existed. Ceta Ramkhalawansingh remembers that the University of Toronto group invited guest speakers to address some of the lacunae, among them Sandra Lovelace and Jeanette Lavell, who were fighting for First Nations women's rights. Linda Briskin recalls "with painful clarity" struggles over class, racialization, sexuality, and linguistic barriers in Mon-tréal. Jill Vickers recounts how working with Mary Two-Ax Early in the Canadian Research Institute for the Advancement of Women (CRIAW) helped her "understand why many First Nations women rejected feminism but sought allies to restore them to their rightful places within First Nations."

There was also the issue of appropriation, recognized as a problem even then. Andrea Lebowitz reports that, when the Corrective Collective (1971) in Vancouver worked on the book *She Named It Canada,* they invited several local Native activists to contribute to the project: "They couldn't do this as they were already too committed and busy with their own projects. When we asked them what we as non-Native women should do, they told us not to presume to talk about them, but to write what we knew. Therefore, on the title page ... we included a statement acknowledging this situation."

In contrast, Vanaja Dhruvarajan's experience speaks to the racism that did exist among White feminists. She describes her alienation from and uneasy relationship with her White colleagues. For instance, when they celebrated the accomplishments of Nellie McClung, she could not celebrate with them, due to McClung's explicit racism; and when she organized a colloquium on visible minorities in Canada, her White colleagues found it irrelevant to them. She adds sadly, "I often wondered whether I could truly belong anywhere."

To sum up, then, the image of the complete neglect of racialization and racism during the early years of the second-wave feminist movement is too simplistic, but certainly racism did exist, then as well as now. Like sexism, which has generally tended to become less blatant and more subtle over time, racism in Canada has been changing. The blatant racism that Clara Thomas describes when she joined a sorority in 1937—"Jewish and Chinese girls were not eligible, and Blacks were unthinkable"—may be turning into what Henry et al. (2000) describe as "democratic racism,"[5] the kind of racism that allows a "democratic" society to be committed in principle to egalitarian ideals while engaging in behaviour that actually sabotages them.

The oppressions that were talked about the most in the sixties and seventies were class, "race," and gender. Sexual orientation was less overtly addressed even in the women's studies classroom, as many lesbians did not feel conditions were yet safe to be "out." Amongst our authors, only Meredith M. Kimball, Marylee Stephenson, and Terry Crowley identify as lesbian or gay; Kimball and Stephenson are two of only three contributors who report receiving negative tenure decisions, though ostensibly for grounds other than their sexual orientation. Annette Kolodny records discovering lesbian writers outside, not inside, the classroom in the 1950s. Linda Briskin comments on including gay and lesbian material in her course, successfully, if somewhat surreptitiously: "I had persuaded the English department to order copies of this book [*Good Times Bad Times*] without really saying what it was about. The book circulated through the school in an underground way, and, although I always expected to be challenged by angry parents or school administrators, I never was. I suspect the students understood the subversive nature of our discussion and cooperated in maintaining a degree of secrecy." Even further below the radar were disability issues until the 1980s, and an integrated, intersectional analysis of all these issues together did not emerge until the 1990s.

Inventing a New Scholarship and New Structures

The overall patriarchal system, with its intense sexism, racism, and homophobia, was the context within which the new scholarship developed. Because women were either completely disregarded or else denigrated in the existing scholarship, these pioneers developed—out of their own experiences and with enormous courage—their own theories, models, methods, and empirical studies. The evolving women's movement was the context of these endeavours, serving as both inspiration and backup. Both on campus and off, there were blind spots and lacunae, as there are undoubtedly still today, which will be revealed in their turn by activists in the future. The fact that students flocked to the new courses not only made them progressively more acceptable to the administration, but also provided the intellectual and emotional support that was mostly missing within the academy—notwithstanding the fact that some of the pioneers forged deep and lifelong friendships with some of their colleagues (e.g., Nemiroff and Allen, Sherwin and Laidlaw, Armatage and Ramkhalawansingh, and Davis and Conway).

New viewpoints created new visions of reality, for which the existing concepts and language were inadequate. New concepts had to be created, or old ones redefined. As Smith recalls, "We began to name 'oppression,' 'rape,' 'harassment,' 'sexism,' 'violence,' and others. These were terms that did more than name. They gave shared experiences a political presence." One must remember that "marital rape" was considered an oxymoron at the time. Overall recalls a young female student who "informed the class contemptuously that there could be no such thing as rape in marriage, because by getting married a woman agrees to sex anywhere and at any time."

Marie-Andrée Bertrand recognized, without being able to explain it at the time, the double standard that condemned women who had sexual relations outside of marriage while considering such behaviour normal in men. Micheline Dumont describes her struggle in writing the history of women in Québec in the absence of any information on the subject. Given that there were no archival sources, she decided to interview women. Because she needed to fill the gap, in the process she started developing a new epistemology for history. As Andrea Lebowitz states wryly, "When you asked about which theorists we relied upon, my answer would have to be—ourselves."

This is typical for the group as a whole. Because feminist scholars were embattled, they devised new structures to provide some support: local formal and informal groups and networks, national associations, new publishing houses, journals. Some of these new groups included the Groupe interdisciplinaire pour l'enseignement et la recherche sur les femmes (GIERF) at Université du Québec à Montréal (Fahmy-Eid, Caron); the Academic Women's Association at the University of Alberta (Sydie, Prestwich, and Cullen); the Professors'/ Professionals' Action Committee on Education at the University of Winnipeg (Dhruvarajan); GROW, the Group for Research on Women at OISE (Eichler); city-wide dinner meetings between feminists at York University, the University of Toronto, and OISE (Eichler); the Academic Women's Association for faculty, staff, and students at the University of Guelph (Robbins); and the Dalhousie Women Faculty Association (Sherwin). Some of the organizations were inclusive of women from outside of the university, such as the Montréal Women's Liberation Movement, founded by anglophones connected with McGill and Sir George Williams University (now Concordia) in support of Henry Morgentaler's crusade to decriminalize abortion, and the Front de libération des femmes, founded by francophone Québécoises a few months later (Fahmy-Eid). The latter "framed its rhetoric in the discourse of 'total liberation,' believing that women's emancipation was inextricably linked to the goal of creating an independent and socialist Québec" (S. Mills 2004, 184). This approach is expressed by its first slogan "Pas de libération des femmes sans libération du Québec! Pas de libération du Québec sans libération des femmes!" (No women's liberation without the liberation of Québec! No liberation of Québec without women's liberation!) By the mid-1970s, however, its successor, the Centre des femmes, abandoned Québec nationalism and began to look to working-class emancipation as the necessary condition for women's liberation. This is, of course, by no stretch of the imagination an exhaustive list; it represents merely a few of the organizations mentioned by the authors in their essays.

The new structures went beyond lending support, however. Scholarship is a collective endeavour, not an individual one. The give and take between scholars engaged in a collective search for understanding the world is a necessary aspect of being able to work fruitfully. This may involve personal interactions in symposia, conferences, seminars, and the like, or less direct interactions via publishing. Since mainstream conferences and association meetings usually failed to include women's issues, we had to organize our own. For instance, Sandra Pyke describes how, when the Canadian Psychological Association failed to welcome submissions with feminist content, a group of untenured faculty and graduate students decided to mount their own symposium. At least two hundred convention delegates attended this unsanctioned event, which received unprecedented press coverage. When Linda Christiansen-Ruffman, Susan Clark, and Lynn McDonald failed to get funding for a major research project/book designed to make the many invisible women in history and contemporary times visible, on the grounds that "no research on women existed on which to base the book," they organized a Canada-wide conference, Research on Women: Current Projects and Future Directions, that drew hundreds of participants. Since mainstream publication outlets—journals and existing publishers—usually rejected our work, we had to create our own. For instance, as Ceta Ramkhalawansingh points out, the Women's Press was set up when a group of women could not find a publisher for *Women Unite!* (1972), one of the important early Canadian anthologies. Andrea Lebowitz remembers that, in Vancouver, the Corrective Collective published materials that were used in women's studies courses because other materials were not available. Jill Vickers published most of her work in interdisciplinary journals and outlets such as the CRIAW Papers, because the mainstream journals would not accept it. The Women's Educational Resources Centre at OISE served as a resource to many researchers. Both Marylee Stephenson and Margrit Eichler write of how the *Canadian Newsletter of Research on Women* (now *Resources for Feminist Research*) served as the first medium to pull information together from across Canada. Donna Smyth describes the founding of *Atlantis* to give Canadian women's studies scholars our own scholarly journal.

Beyond creating a new scholarship, then, the authors were involved in creating new structures through which the scholarship could be disseminated. Teaching and writing went hand in hand. Since materials were generally lacking, teachers had to devise their own resources, many of which would eventually become publications. There were no models to follow in constructing a course, no pre-existing syllabi, so everyone had to struggle to devise a suitable vehicle for instruction. As Natalie Davis and Jill Ker Conway state, "We had to decide on our topics, our ordering of themes, our explanations, our ways of seeing connections between gender relations—relations between 'the sexes' as we called them—and other forms of social life and historical changes."

Because it is difficult to teach without resources, authors had to be inventive, not just in *what* to teach, but also in *how* to teach. We experimented with new strategies, which included journal writing (Levine, Marshall), agitprop theatre (Lebowitz), posters with graphic illustrations (Armatage), and team-teaching (Kimball, Armatage, Nemiroff, Davis, and Conway). Activities went beyond the classroom, and included public lectures of various types (Andersen and Armatage), library displays, programs on self-defence and music (Armstrong), and efforts to reform university policies (Sherwin).

Disciplinarity and/or Interdisciplinarity

From day one, there were different ways of looking at the ultimate goal of women's studies or *études féministes*. One approach was firmly committed to interdisciplinarity, ironically seeing as its end goal the creation of a new discipline of women's studies; the other saw as its final goal the eradication of sexism from all knowledge, and hence the integration of women's perspectives into all disciplines. This played out in terms of courses being lodged firmly as interdisciplinary or disciplinary courses. At OISE and a few other places, the decision was to change the individual disciplines by working together across disciplines to stretch each department beyond the borders that contained its ways of knowing. Elsewhere, the explicit goal was to create interdisciplinary women's studies. Disciplinary scholars worried about ghettoizing women's studies; interdisciplinary scholars pointed to the need to shed all disciplinary restrictions (e.g., Caron, Fahmy-Eid, Kimball, Sydie, Prestwich, Cullen, Nemiroff); still others proposed that both were necessary.

However, this distinction was more philosophical than real. In the essays, it becomes abundantly clear that scholars from very diverse disciplines all used the same early resources, regardless of the discipline(s) that generated them. Simone de Beauvoir, Betty Friedan, Kate Millett, Germaine Greer, and the report of the Royal Commission on the Status of Women (1970) are cited by many authors, both francophone and anglophone, as influential, as are the early Canadian books *Women Unite!* (1972), Marguerite Andersen's *Mother Was Not a Person* (1972), and Marylee Stephenson's *Women in Canada* (1973). Sociologists used novels; literary scholars used social science studies; a natural scientist—Maggie Benston (1969a)—wrote one of the most influential social science papers. In Québec, women read, in addition, the periodicals *Partisans* and the *Cahiers du Grif*. Christine Delphy, Colette Guillaumin, and Nicole Claude Mathieu were becoming influential thinkers

(Fahmy-Eid), while essays and novels by Benoîte Groult, Annie Leclerc, and Marie Cardinal were the first French feminist bestsellers to reach Québec. Nearly all the early pioneers in women's studies (with the sole exception of Ceta Ramkhalawansingh, who was an undergraduate student at the time) came out of some other discipline, since women's studies did not yet exist. How things developed later on was also shaped by the response of each administration and the varying circumstances in which academics could find a niche for engaging in this intellectually revolutionary practice.

Student–Teacher Relations

The role of students was extremely significant in the development of women's studies. Some of the authors were themselves students while teaching and publishing their first papers (including Armstrong, Baker, Briskin, Luxton, and Ramkhalawansingh). Students often pushed faculty to develop courses on women (e.g., Armstrong, Crowley, Marshall) and helped faculty teach them. Fahmy-Eid, for instance, credits the contributions of Marie Lavigne and Jennifer Stoddart as her teaching assistants. Both of them went on to become important figures in feminist scholarship in their own right. Honoree Newcombe describes student pressure to develop the women's studies program at Simon Fraser University.

When they started teaching women's studies courses, many of the faculty were on sessional contracts—a bridging position, for some, between being a student and becoming a tenured professor—and hence they were still close to their own student experiences. Some of the authors—Frieda Forman, Greta Nemiroff, Leslie Marshall, and Dorothy Smith—explicitly note that they were co-learners along with their students. The difference in knowledge between professors and students was relatively small, and students co-generated knowledge in a variety of ways: by drawing on their experiences in the women's movement; by writing weekly journals that the professor would then use to prepare for the next class; or by going out, observing, and analyzing manifestations of the gender structure, and writing papers about it that would later on be used as reading materials for subsequent classes. Margrit Eichler reports choosing the best papers from among her students' work and copying them for use in later years.

This is very different from today—there is a wealth of very diverse materials available. While it makes preparing courses considerably easier, it takes away the excitement of being in the forefront of creating new knowledge through teaching: "The moment to be pioneers is fleeting, and nothing can ever quite match up to the experience," Meredith M. Kimball observes. It means that students, particularly undergraduate students, are less likely to find themselves in the role of co-creators of knowledge, and more likely to be relegated to the role of recipients of knowledge.

Personal Impacts

Besides the external battles that had to be fought, we had to face internal challenges; Meg Luxton describes the dilemma of "trying to reconcile our lives, with all our anxieties, hesitations, and deferences, with the vision we aspired to as strong, indomitable women." The personal costs were sometimes high; some academic careers were made, others broken, because of women's studies. Regardless of career outcomes, all the authors in this volume agree that this "intellectual and educational adventure that was at once extraordinary and perilous" (Fahmy-Eid) was "exciting but demanding" (Sydie), "incredibly stimulating" (Armstrong), and "the most exciting of times" (Kimball). "Nothing I've experienced before or since was like this," Dorothy Smith asserts.

For all, it was a life-changing period that "altered the whole course of my life," as Honoree Newcombe puts it—both "professionally and personally," Lebowitz agrees. It was an experience from which, as Greta Hofmann Nemiroff observes, "you 'can't go home again'; you cannot unlearn feminism or enjoy a life unexamined through a feminist lens. When I recall the intense feeling of those early years, what I remember most is a continual sense of exploration and newness. As you headed for the next corner, you did not know what you would find as you turned it. There were painful discoveries and deeply uncomfortable moments, but it was also a period of unprecedented intellectual collaboration among women. Participating in the 'invention' of women's studies changed my life forever."

Interesting Times

When the women in this volume reflect upon where we have come from, where we are today, and where we are going, the mood is ambivalent. There is no question that there have been gains. There is much to celebrate in terms of what we have achieved—but it usually falls short of the exuberant expectations and hopes we had when we started the process of inventing feminist scholarship (e.g., Nemiroff, Kolodny). Most authors agree that there have also been setbacks, and that many of the original problems that feminist scholarship was developed to confront, remain. While women's studies professors cannot be simply divided into two generations, some early "pioneers" tend to regret the greater emphasis nowadays on individual empowerment rather than on finding power through group action.

Like some of the contributors, we, the editors, worry about the depoliticization of many women's studies courses and a lack of leadership and coordination in anglophone Canada. Much of the highly specialized language of current women's studies is more suited to a conversation among academics than a conversation with society at large. Today, most women's studies students come to feminism through the classroom, and they often have difficulty making links to an activist women's movement. However, their family backgrounds are more diverse, which means that they do not have the same monolithic vision of gender roles that many of our authors report having held: many come from one-parent or step-families, some from gay or lesbian families; their parents, whether female or male, are very likely to be in the paid labour force; some have fathers who participated actively in child care; and some had feminist mothers.

Women's studies was born out of a deeply felt need for change at all levels. Today, the challenge that is posed by a commitment to improve the world for all remains great. Since the 1980s, corporate power has increased, which has led to a growth in precarious jobs without benefits and security. Structural adjustment programs in many countries and restructuring in welfare states have led to increased costs for health care and education, and a reduction in social services (Bezanson 2006). The increasing disparity between rich and poor, both in the world at large and in Canada, has made the lives of millions of women and children, as well as those of men, a struggle for survival (Yalnizian 2007). The growing strength of religious fundamentalism has undermined many of women's equality struggles. The devastating effects of environmental deterioration and climate change are beginning to be seen, and will certainly be experienced more dramatically and sooner by those who are at the bottom than those at the top of society; in the long haul, environmental damage may render our planet uninhabitable for human beings, unless we change our way of life, decisively and soon.

Feminist scholarship plays a vital role in documenting the impact of these changes on women globally and in assessing women's status around the world. The United Nations estimates that between 20% and 50% of all women are abused. Economically, women make up 45% of the paid labour force around the world, but their wages range from 20% to 50% less than men's. Fewer than 2% of top executive positions are held by women. Over a billion people live in absolute poverty, which means they live on less than

US$1.00 per day; 70% of them are women. One in four adults today is illiterate; that is, they cannot read or write. Two-thirds of them are women (United Nations Development Fund for Women 2005).

The women's movement in Canada has succeeded in winning improvements in women's status here. Formal legal equality between the sexes is enshrined in the Charter of Rights and Freedoms, and the Supreme Court of Canada is one of the most gender-balanced in the world. In sharp contrast to the 1970s, more female than male students graduate from university today. Most women, including most mothers, have paying jobs. However, the neo-conservative/neo-liberal agenda has made times difficult, and there have been major setbacks and failures on the political and social fronts. Violence against women remains endemic; the greatest job growth is in precarious positions, with women, particularly racialized minority women, most prone to fall through its "trap door"; finding child care continues to be an ongoing struggle; women are seriously under-represented in governments and at senior levels of teaching and administration in universities, and in the prestigious new millennial Canada Research Chairs Program (Robbins and Ollivier 2007), leading some women to identify the barriers to top decision-making ranks as a "second glass ceiling" (Mason and Ekman 2007).

Women's groups have lost government funding, which has undermined their capacities and led to the implosion of Canada's largest umbrella feminist organization, the National Action Committee on the Status of Women, as well as to closures and layoffs in many of their former member organizations. In October 2006, the Conservative federal government removed the word "equality" from the mandate of Status of Women Canada and withdrew funding from the Law Commission of Canada, as well as from the Court Challenges Program, which had enabled equality-seeking groups to mount legal challenges against discrimination. The United Nations Committee on Economic, Social, and Cultural Rights, in its concluding observations a few months earlier, in the spring of 2006, had called on Canada to do more to alleviate persistent poverty for women, Aboriginal peoples, African Canadians, people with disabilities, youth, and single mothers (Feminist Alliance for International Action 2006; United Nations Committee on Economic Social and Cultural Rights 2006).

This collection of personal, retrospective essays documents feminist activism from the founding of groups such as Voice of Women and the Committee for the Equality of Women in Canada in the 1960s, through the Royal Commission on the Status of Women and the abortion caravan that travelled from Vancouver to Ottawa, the "first unified action of the women's movement" in Canada (Rebick 2005, 36), to the founding of women's studies in our universities in the early 1970s. In spite of the setbacks that the women's movement has suffered, there continue to be hopeful signs of collective action as well—at home, internationally, and transnationally—that connect "then" with "now."

Consider, for example, the Native women's march from Oka to Ottawa to change the Indian Act in the 1970s; the groundbreaking Canadian feminist research that first documented the shocking extent of male violence against women; the establishment of the five federally funded regional chairs in women's studies in the 1980s; the creation of centres of excellence for women's health; new networks of women in science and engineering; the diversification of women's studies to include more Aboriginal women, women of colour, out lesbians, and women with disabilities; and the extraordinary successes of the Bread and Roses march by women against poverty in 1995. Other important changes include the creation of online activist organizations by women in Canada, including the Policy Action Research List (PAR-L), Womenspace, Netfemmes, and Cybersolidaires; the recognition of rape as a war crime and the concomitant creation by the United Nations in 1994 of a Special Rapporteur on violence against women; and, organized largely by women in Québec, the World March of Women 2000 against poverty and violence. All of these actions and mobilizations have insisted that feminist scholarship is vital to their success, and have called for ongoing feminist research.

In this context, women's studies continues to monitor what is happening to women, develop new feminist theory, and engage new generations of students. Women's studies programs exist on campuses all across the country. We have our own scholarly organization, the Canadian Women's Studies Association. In May 2006, a Consortium of the French-speaking feminist studies programs in Québec and Canada was launched. This was a joint initiative of the Institut de recherches et d'études féministes at Université du Québec à Montréal, the Institut d'études des femmes of the University of Ottawa, the Chaire d'étude Claire-Bonenfant sur la condition des femmes at Université Laval, and the École d'études des femmes du Collège universitaire of Glendon at York University. Four universities—York, UBC, Simon Fraser, and Toronto—grant a PhD in the field, and more than forty scholars have earned PhDs in women's studies. Feminist scholarship and women's studies are well established as a legitimate field.

Women's studies faculty and students, along with feminist researchers in all domains, continue to develop the knowledge and the tools of analysis that we need to change ourselves and our world. But knowledge alone is not enough. As feminist scholarship and women's studies programs have become an indisputable part of the academy, new generations of students grapple with the questions of how to make their academic studies relevant to the issues of their lives, and how to create new feminist scholarship and politics that understand their history while responding to the present climate. The task remains, now as then, to create, in Ursula Franklin's words, progress *by* women, *through* women, *for* all.[6]

Notes

1   We, the editors, struggled with the choice of pronoun. We use "we" in three ways: first, the "we" of us, the editors. The context makes it clear when "we" is used in this way. However, we also use "we" to mean the women involved in the feminist struggle, and to refer to the authors of the essays (since three editors are also authors). The other options would have been either to use a passive construction, which we did not like, or to use "they" when talking about the authors or activists, thus distancing us from two groups of which we consider ourselves a part. We therefore eventually decided to include ourselves by using "we" for this final chapter when talking about the situation of the early pioneers.

2   The Canadian Women's Studies Professors Project found that by 1976 the following number of people had taught courses in their respective disciplines: anthropology 7, education 6, history 31, languages 29, philosophy 8, political science 4, psychology 14, religious studies 5, social work 4, sociology 44, women's studies 6, other humanities 4, other social sciences 12, other disciplines 14. See Eichler (1992b, 90, t. 12).

3   This was so prevalent that Jill Vickers and June Adams actually wrote a book with the title *But Can You Type? Canadian Universities and the Status of Women* (1977).

4   Howard D. McCurdy, who in 1959 was hired at the University of Windsor (becoming a full professor ten years later), was Canada's first Black male faculty member.

5   Henry et al. stipulate that democratic racism "results from the retention of racist beliefs and behaviours in a 'democratic' society. The obfuscation and justificatory arguments of democratic racism are deployed to demonstrate continuing faith in the principles of an egalitarian society while at the same time undermining and sabotaging those ideals" (2000, 19).

6   Ursula Franklin has expressed the view many times that "the women's movement does not create changes by women for women, but through women for all." The original source seems to be Franklin's opening address at the "Made to Measure" conference in Halifax in October 1999 (qtd. in Eichler 2001, 397).

Appendices

Appendix A: Alphabetical List of Authors

Appendix B: List of Authors by Discipline

Notes on Contributors

MARGUERITE ANDERSEN has lived and taught in Germany, France, Tunisia, Ethiopia, the United States, and Canada. She obtained a PhD from the Université de Montréal in 1965. In Canada, she taught French studies at Loyola (now Concordia) and the University of Guelph, where she was chair of the Department of Languages and Literatures. She has held the Nancy Ruth Chair at Mount Saint Vincent University and received a doctorate, h.c., from that university in 1999. She was a founding member of the Canadian Association of University Teachers Committee on the Status of Women in the early 1970s.

KAY ARMATAGE is a professor at the University of Toronto, cross-appointed to Cinema Studies, Innis College, and the Women and Gender Studies Institute. She is the author of *The Girl from God's Country: Nell Shipman and the Silent Cinema* (2003), co-editor of *Gendering the Nation: Canadian Women's Cinema* (1999), and editor of *Equity and How to Get It* (1999); author of articles on women filmmakers, feminist theory and Canadian cinema; and producer/director of documentary and experimental narrative films. At U of T, she was director of the Undergraduate Women's Studies Program 1987–92 and founding director of the Graduate Collaborative Program in Women's Studies 1994–2000.

PAT ARMSTRONG has served as chair of the Department of Sociology at York University and director of the School of Canadian Studies at Carleton University. Currently, she is a partner in the National Network on Environments and Women's Health, and she chairs a working group on health reform that crosses the Centres of Excellence for Women's Health. She holds a Canadian Health Services Research Foundation/Canadian Institutes of Health Research Chair in Health Services. She is co-author or editor of several books on health care, including *Exposing Privatization: Women and Health Reform in Canada* (2001), *Heal Thyself: Managing Health Care Reform* (2000), and *Universal Health Care: What the United States Can Learn from Canada* (1998).

MAUREEN BAKER is a professor in the Department of Sociology at the University of Auckland, New Zealand. She has taught in Canada, Australia, and New Zealand, and worked as a researcher in Ottawa for Canada's Parliament. Her main areas of teaching and research are changing families and comparative policies for families with children. She is the author of fifteen books and over ninety scholarly articles.

MARIE-ANDRÉE BERTRAND received her D. Criminology from the University of California at Berkeley (1967) and is currently professor emeritus at the Université de Montréal (1996). She has taught and conducted research at the universities of Hamburg, Oslo, and Berkeley; at the Centre d'études sociologiques sur le droit et les institutions pénales in Guyancourt, France; and at the International Institute for the Sociology of Law in Onati, Spain. She was a member of the Law Commission of Canada Advisory Council until its abolition on September 29, 2006, and is an officier de l'Ordre national du Québec.

LINDA BRISKIN, a professor in the Social Science Division and the School of Women's Studies at York University, has both an activist and a scholarly interest in the documentation and development of feminist strategies for change. She has published widely on women and unions, women's organizing, and inclusive pedagogies, and has been involved in union and university activism for many decades.

ANITA CARON Professor emeritus at the Université du Québec à Montréal, Anita Caron retired from the Department of Religious Sciences in June 1993. Her main areas of teaching and research were feminist studies, moral and religious education, ethics, and teacher training. Much of her research concerned the question of women and religion. Co-founder of the Institut de recherches et d'études féministes, she was also its first director, from 1990 to 1993.

LINDA CHRISTIANSEN-RUFFMAN is professor of sociology at Saint Mary's University, where she helped to initiate women's studies, including the interuniversity graduate program. As a feminist, she has led both sociology and women's organizations locally, nationally, and globally. She increasingly trusts women's wisdom to resist patriarchal forms and to find alternative ways.

JILL KER CONWAY taught American social and intellectual history at the University of Toronto (1964–75) and served as vice-president of Internal Affairs (1973–75)—the first woman to hold vice-presidential rank. In 1975, she became the first woman president of Smith College, and, a decade later, visiting professor in MIT's Program in Science, Technology, and Society. She holds thirty-eight honorary degrees and currently writes about autobiography and biography. She retains ties to Canada through her late husband, John J. Conway, the founding master of Founders College at York University, and as the 2007 recipient of the Sarah Shorten Award from the Canadian Association of University Teachers.

TERRY CROWLEY is chair of the Department of History at the University of Guelph. The author of a dozen books, his most recent, *Marriage of Minds: Isabel and Oscar Skelton Reinventing Canada* (2003), won the Floyd S. Chalmers Award of the Champlain Society, the Clio Award, and an Honorable Mention for the Sir John A. Macdonald Award of the Canadian Historical Association.

DALLAS CULLEN has a BA in history from the University of Alberta, an MSc in psychology from Iowa State University, and a PhD in experimental social psychology from Ohio State University. She is Professor Emerita in the Department of Strategic Management and Organization in the School of Business at the University of Alberta, where she also served an eight-year term as chair of the Women's Studies Program. She was a founding member of Women in Scholarship, Engineering, Science, and Technology (WISEST), and was awarded a lifetime membership in the Academic Women's Association of the University of Alberta.

NATALIE ZEMON DAVIS has been an innovator in the social and cultural history of early modern Europe, especially its working people and peasants. Over her years of teaching, she has been a founder of courses in the history of women at the University of Toronto, the University of California at Berkeley, and Princeton University. She is the author of eight books, all of them appearing in translations in Europe and Asia. In 1987 she became the second woman president of the American Historical Association (the only previous one was forty-four years earlier). Retired as Henry Charles Lea Professor of History at Princeton, she is now adjunct professor of history and professor of medieval studies at the University of Toronto.

FRANCINE DESCARRIES is a professor in the Department of Sociology at l'Université du Québec à Montréal and scientific director of the alliance Institute de recherches et d'études féministes/Relais-femmes, which does research on the Québec women's movement. In the early 1980s, she authored one of the first Québec books on women and "pink collar" work, *L'école rose … et les cols roses* (1980). Jointly with Christine Corbeil, she published a reader on maternity entitled *Espaces et temps de la maternité* (2002). She has also recently edited volume 6 of the electronic journal *Labrys* (Québec–Brazil), which gives a picture of the research in partnership currently being done in Québec.

VANAJA DHRUVARAJAN is currently an adjunct professor at Carleton University, Ottawa. She completed her undergraduate education at the University of Mysore, India, and her graduate education at the University of Chicago. Her teaching and research interests include globalization, family and socialization, gender, anti-racism, and knowledge monopolies. She has done research in India and Canada, and has published several articles and books. She has served as president of the Canadian Sociology and Anthropology Association and the Canadian Women's Studies Association, as well as the Ruth Wynn Woodward Endowed Chair in Women's Studies at Simon Fraser University, Vancouver.

MICHELINE DUMONT is a pioneer of women's history in Québec, having taught in that area at the Université de Sherbrooke from 1970 to 1999. As a member of the Clio Collective, she published *L'histoire des femmes au Québec* (1982) and *Québec Women: A History* (Women's Press, 1987). She is the author of many works, including *Les couventines* (1986) with Nadia Fahmy-Eid; *Les religieuses sont-elles féministes?* (1995); *Découvrir la mémoire des femmes* (2001); *La pensée féministe au Québec* (2003) with Louise Toupin; and *Brève histoire des institutrices au Québec* (2004) with Andrée Dufour.

MARGRIT EICHLER is professor of sociology and equity studies at the Ontario Institute for Studies in Education at the University of Toronto. All of her research is feminist in orientation. Over her career, her major areas of interest have been family policy, reproductive technologies, sexist and other biases in research, eco-sociology, and the history of women's studies in Canada. At present, she is engaged in two large-scale research projects: on unpaid housework and lifelong learning, and on the BIAS FREE Framework (Building an Integrative Analytical System for Recognizing and Eliminating InEquities in Research and Policies).

NADIA FAHMY-EID began her career as a professor of history at the Université du Québec à Montréal in 1970. She retired in 1997. Recipient of the Société Saint Jean-Baptiste's Prix Esdras-Minville for human sciences, she taught and researched in the history of ideas, the history of the education of girls and women's work, and the epistemology of history. In 2001, she and colleagues from various disciplines founded the Centre d'aide pédagogique aux étudiantes et aux étudiants as a means to support students in the methodology of intellectual work.

FRIEDA JOHLES FORMAN was born in Vienna and spent her early childhood as a refugee in Switzerland. At City College and City University of New York, she specialized in philosophy and German literature. She married, had two children, and was active in the anti-war movement before immigrating to Toronto in 1970. She introduced the first women's studies course while teaching at the Ontario College of Art, and subsequently established and coordinated the Women's Educational Resources Centre at the Ontario Institute for Studies in Education. She is currently a visiting scholar at the Centre for Women's Studies in Education, and writing a memoir of her childhood.

MARGARET GILLETT, a lifelong feminist, is retired now from teaching in the Faculty of Education at McGill, but never from the fray. She was involved in the creation of the McGill Centre for Teaching and Research on Women. Her portrait was painted by distinguished Australian artist Judy Cassab. Recent work includes *Traf: A History of Trafalgar Schools for Girls* (2000) and a profile on Maude Elizabeth Seymour Abbott for the *Dictionary of Canadian Biography*.

DEBORAH GORHAM was a full-time member of the Department of History at Carleton University in Ottawa from 1969 to 2002, where she was active in teaching women's history and women's studies beginning in 1971. In retirement, she continues her affiliation with Carleton as a distinguished research professor. Her current research interests include gender and progressive education in the early twentieth century. She is the author of *Vera Brittain: A Feminist Life* (1996).

DANIELLE JUTEAU received her PhD in sociology from the University of Toronto in 1974 and is currently professor emeritus in the Department of Sociology at the Université de Montréal. She was a pioneer of teaching and research on the *rapports sociaux de sexe* (relations constituting sex categories), which she has expanded to apply to ethnic relations, the construction of ethnic and national boundaries, and citizenship. Ethnic Relations Chair at the Université de Montréal from 1991 to 2003, she went on to become a Pierre Elliott Trudeau Foundation Fellow from 2003 to 2006. Named to the Royal Society of Canada in 1996, she was the winner, in 2001, of the Prix Marcel-Vincent, awarded by the Association canadienne-française pour l'avancement des sciences.

MEREDITH M. KIMBALL taught in the Department of Psychology at the University of British Columbia from 1970 to 1976. During that time, she was a founder of women's studies at UBC. In 1976, she moved to Simon Fraser University in a joint appointment with women's studies and psychology. She has served as chair of the Department of Women's Studies at SFU several times and as associate dean in the Faculty of Interdisciplinary Studies. She retired from SFU in 2004.

ANNETTE KOLODNY is the College of Humanities Professor Emerita of American Literature and Culture at the University of Arizona, Tucson. Her scholarly and critical works include *The Lay of the Land: Metaphor as Experience and History in American Life and Letters* (1975); *The Land Before Her: Fantasy and Experience of the American Frontiers, 1630–1860* (1984); and the groundbreaking essay "Dancing Through the Minefield: Some Observations on the Theory, Practice, and Politics of a Feminist Literary Criticism." She was formerly dean of the College of Humanities at the University of Arizona and, based on her experiences as a feminist administrator, she published *Failing the Future: A Dean Looks at Higher Education in the Twenty-first Century* (1998).

ANDREA LEBOWITZ joined Simon Fraser University as a charter faculty member in 1965. She was a founder of the Department of Women's Studies and served as its first chair. She taught in English and women's studies, and served as associate dean of arts. She retired from SFU in 2001. She has published several books on women's nature writing.

HELEN LEVINE is a pioneer of feminist counselling and taught women's studies at Carleton University's School of Social Work until her retirement in 1988. Helen received the Governor General's Persons Award in 1989. She is a founding member of Interval House of Ottawa–Carleton, a shelter for battered women and their children; and of the Crones, a self-help group for older women. She is a member of the Women's Envisioning Group in Ottawa, concerned with local and global feminist issues. She was a major participant in the film *Motherland: Tales of Wonder*, produced by the National Film Board's Studio D.

MEG LUXTON is professor of women's studies and social sciences and director of the graduate program in women's studies at York University. Her main research interests are women's paid and unpaid work, the Canadian women's movement, and family and social policy. Her current research project investigates how personal caregiving responsibilities and social policies and programs designed to help people manage the demands of paid employment play out in the lives of the people affected by them.

LORNA MARSDEN is president emerita and professor, York University. Prior to joining York in 1997, she was on faculty at the University of Toronto (1972–92), president and vice-chancellor of Wilfrid Laurier University (1992–97), and a senator in the Parliament of Canada (1982–92). She was president of the National Action Committee on the Status of Women during 1975–77.

LESLIE MARSHALL taught for many years in the Department of English at the University of Guelph. His main interest was dramatic literature. In 1974, he introduced the first course at Guelph on women's literature. With his wife, Linda, he is now living in retirement in Guelph.

JOAN MCFARLAND is a professor of economics and women's studies/gender studies at St. Thomas University in Fredericton, New Brunswick, where she has taught since 1971. Her research, which takes a feminist political economy approach, has been on various aspects of women and the economy—in the Maritimes, in Canada, and across the globe. She is also a community activist and was the national president of the Canadian Congress for Learning Opportunities for Women in the late 1980s.

GRETA HOFMANN NEMIROFF taught at Concordia University (formerly Sir George Williams University) from 1963–79, in the Department of English and as a founding member of the Women's Studies Program and the Simone de Beauvoir Institute. Since 1973, she has taught at Dawson College, where she is currently the coordinator of the Creative Arts, Literature and Language, and Women's Studies programs. From 1991–96, she held the joint chair of Women's Studies at Carleton University and the University of Ottawa, and from 1999–2004 she was the president of the Sisterhood Is Global Institute, an international feminist non-governmental organization.

HONOREE NEWCOMBE joined the Simon Fraser University library staff in 1971 while still a student. She has worked in graduate studies and as departmental administrator in the English department. She was a founder of the Department of Women's Studies and has served as the staff representative on the Women's Studies Coordinating Committee.

CHRISTINE OVERALL is a professor of philosophy at Queen's University, Kingston, where she served as an associate dean in the Faculty of Arts and Science (1997–2005). In 1998, she was elected to the Royal Society of Canada, and in 2005, she was appointed to a Queen's Research Chair, Queen's internal equivalent of the Canada Research Chairs. During 1993–2006, she authored a weekly feminist column, "In Other Words," in the *Kingston Whig-Standard.* Her 2003 book, *Aging, Death, and Human Longevity*, won awards from the Canadian Philosophical Association and the Royal Society of Canada. Married for thirty-five years, she is the mother of two adult children.

ALISON PRENTICE taught at two secondary schools in Toronto, and at Atkinson College, York University, and the Ontario Institute for Studies in Education. Her publications range over the history of education and women's history, with special attention to women's work in education. She is currently an adjunct professor at the University of Victoria, attends a Quaker meeting, and tries to juggle continuing family and household work with choral singing, yoga, and belonging to various groups devoted to discussions of history, books, and dreams, and the creation of an intentional community.

PATRICIA PRESTWICH was born in Toronto and completed her undergraduate and master's degrees at the University of Toronto. She received her PhD in modern French history from Stanford University in 1973. From 1970 to 2007, she taught courses in modern French history, women's history, and medical history at the University of Alberta, where she is now a professor emerita. She helped to found the Women's Studies Program at the University of Alberta and was its chair for three years. She was also president of the Academic Women's Association and in 2006 was very touched to be made a lifetime member of that organization.

SANDRA PYKE (PhD, McGill, 1964) spent most of her academic life at York University where she is currently a professor emerita. Very active in the Canadian Psychological Association, she served many years as a member of the board of directors and was president of the association in 1982, as well as a member of the Task Force on the Status of Women in Canadian Psychology and the first coordinator of the Section on Women and Psychology. At York, she held a series of administrative positions, including director of the Graduate Program in Women's Studies, chair of the Department of Psychology, and dean of the Faculty of Graduate Studies.

CETA RAMKHALAWANSINGH, who immigrated from Trinidad with her family in 1967, is a co-founder of women's studies at the University of Toronto, where, in 1970, she and others formed a teaching collective. Her contributions to feminist scholarship include joining the writing collective of *Women at Work in Ontario, 1850–1930* (winner of the 1975 City of Toronto Book Award) and serving as guest editor of various feminist journals. Appointed in 1983 to the Ontario government's Advisory Council on Women's Issues, she was a formidable advocate for legislative change. Since 1981, Ceta has been introducing leading-edge policies on equity and human rights at Toronto City Hall.

WENDY ROBBINS taught at the University of Guelph and Brown University before moving to the University of New Brunswick, becoming UNB's first female full professor of English in 1988 and co-founding its Women's Studies Program. She is co-founder of the PAR-L feminist discussion list and has served as chair of the Women's Committee of the Canadian

Association of University Teachers and vice-president of Women's and Equity Issues for the Canadian Federation for the Humanities and Social Sciences. She is a mother of two and a grandmother of one, and in 2007 she received a Governor General's Award in Commemoration of the Persons Case.

SUSAN SHERWIN is a Fellow of the Royal Society of Canada and a university research professor at Dalhousie University, where she has taught since 1974. Her principal appointment is in philosophy, with honorary cross-appointments to gender and women's studies, bioethics, and nursing. Her academic training was at York University (Hons BA) and Stanford University (PhD). Her principal area of research and teaching is feminist health-care ethics.

DOROTHY E. SMITH In 1955, Dorothy Smith graduated from London University (BSc in sociology), got married, and, with her husband, entered the University of California at Berkeley). They had two children, a divorce, and a doctorate apiece. Moving to Canada with her children in 1968, she soon started writing papers proposing an alternative feminist sociology. These have been published in *The Everyday World as Problematic* (1987) and elsewhere. Since retirement in 1996, she has continued to write. The first book that she had time to conceive and write as a whole, rather than assemble from various papers, is *Institutional Ethnography: A Sociology for People* (2005).

DONNA E. SMYTH is a poet, short-story writer, playwright, and novelist. While teaching English and creative writing at Acadia University, she was the founding editor of the women's studies journal *Atlantis*. She has published two novels—*Quilt* (1982) and *Subversive Elements* (1986)—as well as a novel for children, *Loyalist Runaway* (1991), and two plays on the poet Elizabeth Bishop, *Running to Paradise* (1999) and *Sole Survivors* (2003). She is co-author of *No Place like Home: Diaries and Letters of Nova Scotian Women, 1771–1938* (1988). Her latest work, *Among the Saints* (2003), is a collection of Maritime-based short stories.

MARYLEE STEPHENSON lives in Vancouver, in an innovative "co-housing" complex. She has her own firm for doing social policy research and program evaluation. She also has a parallel business drawing on her experience as an amateur naturalist, nature writer, and photographer. Marylee has wended her way through academia, and the private sector, and now is working on developing ways to "age gracefully" while still doing research projects, leading tours to the Galapagos Islands (as the author of a guidebook for the islands and travel in Ecuador), appearing as a stand-up comic in clubs and at conferences, visiting the grandnieces and -nephews, and walking her dog.

ROSALIND SYDIE With a PhD from the University of Alberta, Rosalind Sydie was appointed assistant professor at the University of Waterloo. She returned to the University of Alberta in 1969 as a sessional instructor, becoming an assistant professor in 1974. She became the first female chair of the Department of Sociology in 2000. Rosalind has been an editor of the *Canadian Review of Sociology and Anthropology*, president of the Academic Women's Association, and president of the Western Sociological Association.

CLARA THOMAS is a specialist in Canadian literature and professor emerita at York University. She began at York in 1961, when Glendon College opened, and now has an office in York's archives, which were recently named The Clara Thomas Archives in her honour. She taught her first university course for the University of Western Ontario in 1942–43 at the air force station in Dauphin, Manitoba. She now enjoys reviewing for *Books in Canada* and *Canadian Woman Studies*.

MAÏR VERTHUY A professor of literary studies at Concordia University, now retired, Maïr Verthuy devoted a major part of her research to multiculturalism and the writings of immigrant women in Québec and France. Co-founder of Concordia University's Simone de Beauvoir Institute, she was, and continues to be, active in several feminist groups. She has held numerous positions in professional associations, including serving as president of the Association des professeures de Français des universités et collèges Canadiens. Recently, she was appointed Chevalière de l'ordre des palmes académiques by order of the prime minister of France in recognition of her remarkable career teaching and conducting research on French language and culture.

JILL VICKERS is Chancellor's Professor of Political Science at Carleton University, where, as director of Canadian Studies, she established a graduate women's studies program. She was president of the Canadian Research Institute for the Advancement of Women and the Canadian Association of University Teachers, secretary-treasurer of the Canadian Women's

Studies Association and the Association of Canadian Studies, and parliamentarian of the National Action Committee on the Status of Women. The Jill Vickers Prize, an award for the best "gender and politics" paper, was established by the Canadian Political Science Association in her honour.

LINDA WALLACE is an artist and feminist. She graduated with a BFA from the Alberta College of Art. Before devoting herself full-time to her art, she worked as a nurse and an entrepreneur on the islands of the Canadian High Arctic. Her drawings and tapestries have been exhibited nationally and internationally, and her work is in public and private collections in Canada, the United States, Australia, and the United Kingdom. Currently a co-director of the American Tapestry Alliance, she lives on Vancouver Island, where she devotes her time to research, advocacy, and the creation of art based in issues of bioethics, biotechnology, and women's health.

Cumulative Bibliography

Acton, Janice, Penny Goldsmith, and Bonnie Shepard, eds. 1974. *Women at work: Ontario 1850–1930*. Toronto: Women's Educational Press.

Adams, Bert N., and Rosalind A. Sydie. 2001. *Sociological theory*. Thousand Oaks, CA: Pine Forge Press.

Adamson, Nancy, Linda Briskin, and Margaret McPhail. 1988. *Feminist organizing for change: The contemporary women's movement in Canada*. Toronto: Oxford University Press.

Afkhami, Mahnaz, Greta Hofmann Nemiroff, and Haleh Vaziri. 1998. *Safe and secure: Eliminating violence against women and girls in Muslim societies*. Bethesda, MD: Sisterhood Is Global Institute.

Aikau, Hokulani K., Karla A. Erickson, and Jennifer L. Pierce, eds. 2007. *Feminist waves, feminist generations: Life stories from the academy*. Minneapolis: University of Minnesota Press.

Akyeampong, Ernest B. 1998. Increase in the rate of unionization among women. In *Perspectives on labour and income*. Ottawa: Statistics Canada.

Allen, Christine Garside. 1975. Conceptual history as a methodology for women's studies. *McGill Journal of Education* 10 (1): 49–58.

Allen, Prudence. 1985. *The concept of woman: The Aristotelian revolution, 750 BC–AD 1250*. Montréal: Eden Press.

Andersen, Margret. 1972. *Mother was not a person*. Montréal: Black Rose Books; Content Publishing.

———. *See also* Andersen, Marguerite.

Andersen, Marguerite. 1995. *La soupe*. Sudbury, ON: Prise de parole.

———. 2002. *De mémoire de femme*. Montréal: Quinze. Original edition, 1982.

———. 2004a. *Marguerite Andersen* [home page]. Cited July 11, 2007. Available from http://margueriteandersen.franco.ca/.

———. 2004b. *Parallèles*. Sudbury, ON: Prise de parole.

———. *See also* Andersen, Margaret.

Andersen, Marguerite, and Christine Klein-Lataud, ed. 1992. *Paroles rebelles*. Montréal: Éditions du Remue-ménage.

Anonymous. 1969. The witch manifesto. In *Masculine/feminine: Readings in sexual mythology and the liberation of women*, edited by B. Roszak and T. Roszak. New York: Harper and Row.

Antrobus, Peggy. 2004. *The global women's movement: Origins, issues and strategies*. London: Zed Books.

Anzaldua, Gloria. 1997. La conciencia de la mestiza: Towards a new consciousness. In *Through the prism of difference: Readings on sex and gender*, edited by M. B. Zinn, P. A. Hondagneu-Sotelo, and M. A. Messner. Toronto: Allyn and Bacon.

Archibald, Kathleen. 1970. *Sex and the public service: A Report to the public service commission of Canada*. Ottawa: Queen's Printer.

Armatage, Kay. 1979. Why women's studies? *University of Toronto Bulletin*, February.

———. 1996. Ethnography and its discontents: Ulrike Ottinger's *Taiga*. *Arachne: An Interdisciplinary Journal of Language and Literature* 3 (2): 31–47.

———. 1998. Collaborating on women's studies: The University of Toronto model. *Feminist Studies* 24 (2): 347–55.

———. 1999. *Equity and how to get it: Rescuing graduate studies*. Toronto: Inanna Publications and Education.

———. 2003. *The girl from God's country: Neil Shipman and the silent cinema*. Toronto: University of Toronto Press.

Armatage, Kay, Kass Banning, Brenda Longfellow, and Janine Marchessault, eds. 1999. *Gendering the nation: Canadian women's cinema*. Toronto: University of Toronto Press.

Armstrong, Pat. 1996. The feminization of the labour force: Harmonizing down in a global economy. In *Rethinking restructuring: Gender and change in Canada*, edited by I. Bakker. Toronto: University of Toronto Press. Original edition, 1995.

Armstrong, Pat, and Hugh Armstrong. 1978. *The double ghetto: Canadian women and their segregated work*. Toronto: McClelland and Stewart. (3rd ed., Toronto: McClelland and Stewart, 1994).

———. 1987. Beyond sexless class and classless sex: Towards feminist Marxism. In *The politics of diversity: Feminism, Marxism, and nationalism*, edited by R. Hamilton and M. Barrett. Montréal: Montreal Book Center; London: Verso. Original edition, 1983.

———. 2003. *Wasting away: The undermining of Canadian health care*. Don Mills, ON: Oxford University Press.

———. 2004. Thinking it through: Women, work and caring in the new millenium. In *Caring for/caring about: Women, home care and unpaid caregiving*, edited by K. R. Grant, C. Amaratunga, M. Bosco, A. Pederson, and K. Willson. Aurora, ON: Garamond Press.

Atwood, Margaret. 1966. *The circle game*. Toronto: Contact Press.

———. 1969. *The edible woman*. London: A. Deutsch.

———. 1971. *Power politics.* Toronto: Anansi.

———. 1972a. *Surfacing.* Toronto: McClelland and Stewart.

———. 1972b. *Survival: A thematic guide to Canadian literature.* Toronto: Anansi.

———. 1976. *Selected poems.* Toronto: Oxford University Press.

Austen, Jane. 2002. *Pride and prejudice.* In *The Complete Works and Letters of Jane Austen.* Oxford, UK: Oxford University Press.

Backhouse, Constance. 1988. Women faculty at UWO: Reflections on the employment equity award. University of Western Ontario, London, ON.

Bakan, David. 1966. *The duality of human existence.* Boston: Beacon.

Baker, Maureen. 1975. Women as a minority group in the academic profession. PhD diss., University of Alberta.

———. 1995. *Canadian family policies: Cross-national comparisons.* Toronto: University of Toronto Press.

———. 2001. *Families, labour and love: Family diversity in a changing world.* Vancouver: UBC Press.

———. 2002. Child poverty, maternal health and social benefits. *Current Sociology* 50 (6): 827–42.

———, ed. 2005. *Families: Changing trends in Canada.* 5th ed. Toronto: McGraw-Hill Ryerson.

———. 2006. *Restructuring family policies: Convergences and divergences.* Toronto: University of Toronto Press.

Baker, Maureen, and David Tippin. 1999. *Poverty, social assistance and the employability of mothers: Restructuring welfare states.* Toronto: University of Toronto Press.

Banks, Cara. 2001. Saskatchewan working women: Socialist feminist struggles with inclusivity and diversity in the 1980s. MA thesis, York University.

Bannerji, Himani. 1991. But who speaks for us? Experience and agency in conventional feminist paradigms. In *Unsettling relations: The university as a site of feminist struggle*, edited by H. Bannerji. Toronto: Women's Press.

———, ed. 1993. *Returning the gaze: Essays on racism, feminism and politics.* Toronto: Sister Vision Press.

Bashevkin, Sylvia. 1998. *Women on the defensive: Living through conservative times.* Toronto: University of Toronto Press.

Beard, Mary Ritter. 1946. *Woman as force in history: A study in traditions and realities.* New York: Macmillan.

Bello, Walden. 2001. *The future in balance: Essays on globalization and resistance.* Oakland, CA: Food First Books.

Bem, Sandra L. 1974. The measurement of psychological androgyny. *Journal of Consulting and Clinical Psychology* 42: 155–62.

———. 1975a. Androgyny vs. the tight little lives of fluffy women and chesty men. *Psychology Today* 9: 58–62.

———. 1975b. Sex role adaptability: One consequence of psychological androgyny. *Journal of Personality and Social Psychology* 31: 634–43.

Benokraitis, Nijole V., ed. 1997. *Subtle sexism: Current practice and prospects for change.* Thousand Oaks, CA: Sage.

Benson, Mary Sumner. 1935. *Women in eighteenth century America: A study of opinion and social usage.* New York: Columbia University Press.

Benston, Margaret. 1969. The political economy of women's liberation. *Monthly Review* 21 (4): 13–27.

———. 1969. *The political economy of women's liberation.* Toronto: Hogtown Press.

Berkinow, Louise, ed. 1974. *The world split open: Four centuries of women poets in England and America, 1552–1950.* New York: Vintage.

Bernard, Jessie. 1964. *Academic women.* University Park: Pennsylvania State University Press.

Bernstein, Judy, Peggy Morton, Linda Seese, and Myrna Wood. 1972. Sister, brother, lovers … listen. In *Women unite! An anthology of the Canadian women's movement,* edited by the Discussion Collective No. 6, 31–39. Toronto: Canadian Women's Educational Press.

Berry, Oonagh, and Helen Levine. 2005. *Between friends: A year in letters.* Toronto: Second Story Press.

Bersianik, Louky. 1976. *L'Euguélionne.* Québec: Stanké.

Bertrand, Marie-Andrée. 1967a. The myth of sexual equality before the law. In *Actes de la Société de criminologie du Québec,* edited by Société de criminologie du Québec. Montréal: Centre de psychologie et de pédagogie.

———. 1967b. Self image and social representations of female offenders. PhD diss., School of Criminology, University of California at Berkeley.

———. 1973a. Dialogue with Marie-Andrée Bertrand. Interview by Virginie Enquist Grabiner. *Issues in Criminology* 8 (2): 31–49.

———. 1973b. The hegemonic conception of criminal law and criminal policies. Paper presented at the 1st conference of the European Group for the Study of Deviance and Social Control, Florence, Italy.

———. 1978. Penal interventions against women: An illustration of male hegemony in the making and application of penal law. In *The New Criminologies in Canada,* edited by T. O. R. Fleming. Toronto: Oxford University Press.

———. 1992. La critique féministe des connaissances en criminologie. Conference proceedings. *ACFAS: Association canadienne-française pour l'avancement des sciences.* Montréal: École de criminologie, Université de Montréal, 26 pp.

———. 1994a. From "La Donna delinquente" to a postmodern deconstruction of the woman question in social control theory. *Journal of Human Justice* 5 (2): 43–57.

———. 1994b. Le pouvoir des théories féministes dans la reconsidération radicale des théories du contrôle social. In *Theoretical discourse/Discours théoriques,* edited by T. Goldie, C. Lambert, and R. Lorimer. Montréal: Association des études canadiennes.

———. 1995a. Eine Gegenuberstelung postmoderner und radikaler feministischer Theorien und Strategien. *Kriminologisches Journal* 25 (4): 276–86.

———. 1995b. The place and status of feminist criminology in Germany, Denmark, Norway and Finland. In *International feminist perspectives in Criminology,* edited by N. H. Rafter and F. Heidensohn. Philadelphia: Open University Press.

———. 2001. Incarceration as a gendering strategy. *Revue canadienne de sociologie du droit/Canadian Journal on Law and Society* 14 (1): 45–60.

———. 2003. *Les femmes et la criminalité*. Outremont, QC: Athéna. Original edition, *La femme et le crime*, 1979.

———. 2004. Les effets du genre et de la couleur du droit pénal sur l'intégration sociale des femmes autochtones judiciarisées. In *Au-delà du système pénal: L'intégration sociale et professionnelle des groupes judiciarisés et marginalisés*, edited by J. Poupart, S. Arcand, and J. Cantin. Sainte-Foy: Presses de l'Université du Québec.

———. 2005. Féminisme, perspective épistémologique. In *Études sémiotiques, féministes et sotériologiques en l'honneur d'Olivette Genest*, edited by France Fortin and Alain Gignaca. Montréal: Mediaspaul, 215–33.

Bertrand, Marie-Andrée, Louise L. Biron, Andrée B. Fagnan, Julia McLean, and Concetta di Pisa. 1998. *Prisons pour femmes*. Montréal: Éditions du Méridien.

Bertrand, Marie-Andrée, and André Payette. 1970. *Étude de la criminalité féminine comparée, 1968–1970: Canada, Europe de l'Ouest et de l'Est et Amérique du Sud*. Montréal: Centre international de criminologie comparée.

Bertrand-Ferretti, Andrée, and Gaston Miron (comp). 1992. *Les Grands textes indépendantistes: Écrits, discours et manifestes Québécois, 1774–1992*. Montréal: L'Hexagone.

Bezanson, Kate. 2006. *Gender, the state and social reproduction: Household insecurity in neo-liberal times*. Toronto: University of Toronto Press.

Birth Control Handbook. 1968. Montreal: Montréal Health Press.

Blais, Marie Claire. 1965. *Une saison dans la vie d'Émmanuel*. Paris: B. Grasset.

———. 1968. *Manuscrits de Pauline Archange*. Paris: B. Grasset.

———. 1990. *Les nuits de l'underground*. Montréal: Boréal.

Bliss, Karen. 2007. "Mitchell, Joni." *The Canadian Encyclopedia*. Historical Foundation. Cited July 24, 2007. Available from http://www.thecanadianencyclopedia .com.

Bosco, Monique. 1970. *La femme de Loth*. Paris: R. Laffont.

———. 1975. *Lot's wife*. Translated by J. Glassco. Toronto: McClelland and Stewart.

Boucher, Jacques. 1970. L'histoire de la condition juridique et sociale de la femme au Canada français. In *Le droit dans la vie familiale: Le livre du centenaire du code civil*, edited by J. Boucher and A. Morel. Montréal: Presses de l'Université de Montréal.

Bourgeault, Ron. 1983. The development of capitalism and the subjugation of native women in northern Canada. *Alternate Routes* 6:109–40.

Bourne, Paula, ed. *Women's Paid and Unpaid Work*. Toronto: New Hogtown Press, 1985.

Bowen, Norma V. 1973. Symposium: On women, by women. *Ontario Psychologist* 5 (2): 16–20.

Briskin, Linda. 1974. Toward a socialist feminist movement. *Our Generation* 10 (3): 23–34.

———. 1980. Domestic labour: A methodological discussion. In *Hidden in the household*, edited by B. Fox. Toronto: Women's Press.

———. 1989. Socialist feminism: From the standpoint of practice. *Studies in Political Economy: A Socialist Review* 30: 87–114.

———. 1999. Autonomy, diversity and integration: Union women's separate organizing in North America and Western Europe in the context of restructuring and globalization. *Women's Studies International Forum* 22 (5): 543–54.

———. 2004. Privileging agency and organizing: A new approach to women's studies. In *Feminisms and womanisms: Foundations, theories and praxis of the women's movement*, edited by Althea Prince and Susan Silva-Wayne. Toronto: Women's Press.

Briskin, Linda, and Lynda Yanz, eds. 1983. *Union sisters: Women in the labour movement*. Toronto: Women's Press.

Brittain, Vera. 1978. *Testament of youth: An autobiographical study of the years 1900–1925*. London: Virago. Original edition, 1933.

Brodie, Janine. 1985. *Women and politics in Canada*. Toronto: McGraw-Hill Ryerson.

Brontë, Charlotte. *Jane Eyre*. Ed. Margaret Smith. Oxford, UK: Oxford University Press, 1998.

Brossard, Nicole. 1974. *French kiss: Étreinte-exploration*. Montréal: Éditions du jour.

———. 1986. *French kiss; or, A pang's progress*. Translated by P. Claxton. Toronto: Coach House Press.

Broverman, I. K., D. M. Broverman, R. E. Clarkson, P. S. Rosenkratz, and S. B. Vogel. 1970. Sex role stereotypes and clinical judgements of mental health. *Journal of Consulting and Clinical Psychology* 64: 1–7.

Brown, George Williams. 1945. *Dictionnaire biographique du Canada*. Québec: Presses de l'Université Laval.

Brown, Rosemary. 1989. *Being brown*. Toronto: Ballantine Books.

Brown, Wendy. 2003. Gender in counterpoint. *Feminist Theory* 43 (3): 365–68.

Brownmiller, Susan. 1975. *Against our will: Men, women and rape*. New York: Bantam Books.

Campbell, Douglas F. 2000. Annie Marion MacLean: The first Canadian-born sociologist. *Society/Societé* 24 (1): 5–6.

Campbell, Mildred. 1968. *The English yeoman under Elizabeth to the early Stuarts*. New York: Kelley. Original edition, 1942.

Campbell, Robert. 1987. *Grand illusions: The politics of the Keynesian experience in Canada 1945–1975*. Peterborough, ON: Broadview Press.

Canada Research Chairs. 2007. *Program Statistics*. Cited January 12, 2008. Available from http://www.chairs.gc.ca/web/media/statistics_e.asp.

———. 2006. *General Statistics of Current Chairholders*. December 6. Cited July 11, 2007. Available from http://www.chaires.gc.ca/web/about/stats/dec2006.pdf.

Canadian Association of University Teachers. 2006. *Women in the academic work force* (8.1). Cited July 15, 2007. Available from http://www.caut.ca/en/publications/educationreview/education-review8–1.pdf.

Canadian Federation for the Humanities and Social Sciences. 2006. *Ivory towers: Feminist and Equity Audits 2006*. Cited July 11, 2007. Available from http://www.fedcan.ca/english/issues/issues/audit/.

Canadian Labour Congress. 1968. CLC adopts changes in structure. *Canadian Labour* 13:5.

Caplan, Paula J. 1973. The role of classroom conduct in the promotion and retention of elementary school children. *Journal of Experimental Education* 41: 8–11.

———. 1975. Sex differences in antisocial behavior: Does research methodology produce or abolish them? *Human Development* 18 (6): 444–60.

Cardinal, Harold. 1969. *The unjust society: The tragedy of Canada's Indians.* Edmonton: Hurtig.

Caron, Anita. 1984. *Les parents et le statut confessionnel de l'école au Québec.* Sillery: Presses de l'Université du Québec.

———. 1985. *La famille québécoise, institution en mutation? Analyse de discours et de pratiques de groupes intervenant auprès des couples.* Montréal: Fides.

———. 1987. *L'éducation morale en milieu scolaire: Analyse de situation et perspectives.* Montréal: Fides.

———. 1991. *Femmes et pouvoir dans l'Église.* Montréal: Agenda de distribution populaire.

Caron, Anita , and Lorraine Archambault. 1993. *Thérèse Casgrain: Une femme tenace et engagée.* Sainte-Foy: Presses de l'Université du Québec.

Carroll, Berenice A., ed. 1976. *Liberating Women's History.* Chicago: University of Illinois Press.

Carty, Linda E. 1993. Combining our efforts: Making feminism relevant to the changing society. In *And still we rise: Feminist political mobilizing in contemporary Canada,* edited by L. E. Carty. Toronto: Women's Press.

Centrale de l'enseignement du Québec (CEQ). 1974. Le travail salarié de la femme. In *Condition féminine, Travaux colligés: années 1973–1974.* Comité Laure Gaudreault. D-5699–2. Montréal: CEQ.

Cheal, David, Frances Wooley, and Meg Luxton. 1998. *Families and the labour market: Coping strategies from a sociological perspective.* Ottawa: Canadian Policy Research Networks.

Chesler, Phyllis. 1971. Patient and patriarch. In *Women in sexist society: Studies in power and powerlessness,* edited by V. Gornick and B. K. Moran. New York: Basic Books.

———. 1972. *Women and madness.* New York: Doubleday.

Chicago Women's Liberation Union. 2005. *Chicago women's liberation union herstory project.* Cited July 11, 2007. Available from http://www.cwluherstory.com/index.html.

Cholmondeley, Tom. 2005. *Big ideas that changed the world.* United Kingdom: Channel 5 Television.

Chomsky, Noam. 1967. A special supplement: The responsibility of intellectuals. *New York Review of Books,* 23 February, 16–26. Online at www.nybooks.com/articles/12172. Retrieved 4 February 2008.

———. 1997. *Perspectives on Power: Reflections on Human Nature and the Social Order.* London: Black Rose Books.

Chopin, Kate. 1976. *The awakening.* New York: Norton. Original edition, 1899.

Christiansen-Ruffman, Linda. 1976. Newcomer careers: An exploratory study of migrants in Halifax. PhD diss., Columbia University.

———, ed. 1977. *Research on women: Current projects and future directions.* Special issue of *Atlantis* 2 (2): pt. 2.

———. 1980. Women as persons in Atlantic Canadian communities. *Resources for Feminist Research* 8 (Special Publication): 55–57.

———. 1989. Inherited biases within feminism: The "patricentric syndrome" and the "either/or syndrome" in sociology. In *Feminism: From pressure to politics*, edited by A. R. Miles and G. Finn. Montréal: Black Rose Books.

———. 1998. Developing feminist sociological knowledge: Processes of discovery. In *Feminist perspectives: The global feminist enlightenment; Women and social knowledge*, edited by L. Christiansen-Ruffman. Madrid: International Sociological Association.

Christiansen-Ruffman, Linda, Ruth Hafter, Faith Chao, Wendy Katz, and Helen Ralston. 1975. *Women's concerns about the quality of life in the Halifax metropolitan area.* Halifax, NS: Saint Mary's University.

Churchill, Caryl. 1982. *Top girls.* London: Methuen in association with the Royal Court Theatre.

Clark, Alice. 1992. *Working life of women in the seventeenth century.* London: Routledge. Original edition, 1919.

Cleverdon, Catherine L. 1950. *The woman suffrage movement in Canada.* Toronto: University of Toronto Press.

Clippingdale, Linda. 1996. *Memories and visions: Celebrating 20 years of feminist research with CRIAW/ICREF, 1976–1996.* Ottawa: Canadian Research Institute for the Advancement of Women.

Code, Lorraine. 1992. *What can she know? Feminist theory and the construction of knowledge.* Ithaca, NY: Cornell University Press.

Collectif Clio. 1992. *L'histoire des femmes au Québec depuis quatre siècles.* Montréal: Le jour éditeur.

Commission royale d'enquête sur l'enseignement dans la province de Québec. 1966. L'administration de l'enseignement: Diversité religieuse, culturelle, et unité de l'administration. In rapport, tome 3. Chair Alphonse-Marie Parent. Québec: Government of Québec.

Committee on the Status of Women in India. 1975. Report. New Delhi: Ministry of Education and Welfare.

Confédération des syndicats nationaux. 1976. La lutte des femmes, combat de tous les travailleurs. In *Rapport du comité de la condition féminine, 47e Congrès.* Québec, juin: Document 4.

Connelly, Patricia M. 1978. *Last hired, first fired: Women and the Canadian work force.* Toronto: Women's Press.

Connelly, Patricia M., and Linda Christiansen-Ruffman. 1977. Women's problems: Private troubles or public issues? *Canadian Journal of Sociology* 2 (2): 167–78.

Conway, Jill Ker. 1982. *The female experience in 18th and 19th century America: A guide to the history of American women.* New York: Garland Publishers.

————. 1989. *The road from Coorain*. New York: Alfred A. Knopf.

————. 1992. *Written by herself: Autobiographies of American women; An anthology*. New York: Vintage.

————. 1994. *True north: A memoir*. 1st Canadian ed. Toronto: A. A. Knopf Canada.

————. 1996. *Written by herself*. Vol. 2, *Women's memoirs from Britain, Africa, Asia and the United States*. New York: Vintage.

————. 2002. *A woman's education*. New York: Alfred A. Knopf.

————. 2003. *In her own words: Women's memoirs from Australia, New Zealand, Canada and the United States*. New York: Vintage.

Corrective Collective. 1971. *She named it Canada: Because that's what it was called*. Vancouver: Press Gang Publishers.

————. 1974. *Never done: Three centuries of women's work in Canada*. Toronto: Canadian Women's Educational Press.

Costa, Dalla Maria Rosa. 1972. *The power of women and the subversion of the community*. Nottingham: Falling Wall Press.

Crean, Susan. 1995. *Grace Hartman: A woman for her time*. Vancouver: New Star Books.

Crisp, Lyndall. 1977. Maureen sets out to fight sexist Ockers. *The Australian*, c. March–April.

Cross, Suzanne D. 1973. The neglected majority: The changing role of women in 19th century Montréal. *Social History/Histoire sociale* 6 (12): 202–23.

Crowley, Terry. 1986. Madonnas before Magdalens: Adelaide Hoodless and the making of the Canadian Gibson girl. *Canadian Historical Review* 62: 520–49.

————. 1988. *Clio's craft: A primer of historical methods*. Toronto: Copp Clark Pitman.

————. 1990. *Agnes Macphail and the politics of equality*. Toronto: Lorimer.

————. 1999. *The college on the hill: A new history of the Ontario Agricultural College, 1874–1999*. Toronto: Dundurn Press.

————. 2003. *Marriage of minds: Isabel and Oscar Skelton reinventing Canada*. Toronto: University of Toronto Press.

Cullen, Dallas. 1994. Feminism, management and self-actualization. *Gender, Work and Organization* 1: 127–37.

————. 1997. Maslow, monkeys, and motivation theory. *Organization* 4: 355–73.

Cullen, Dallas, and Lise Gotell. 2002. From orgasms to organizations: Maslow, women's sexuality and the gendered foundations of the needs hierarchy. *Gender, Work and Organization* 9: 537–55.

Dagg, Anne Innis, and Patricia J. Thompson. 1988. *MisEducation: Women and Canadian universities*. Toronto: OISE Press.

Daly, Mary. 1973. *Beyond god the father: Toward a philosophy of women's liberation*. Boston: Beacon Press.

Danis, Aimée. 1973. *Souris tu m'inquiètes*. Canada: National Film Board of Canada.

Dansereau, Mireille. 1974. *J'me marie, j'me marie pas*. Canada: National Film Board of Canada.

Darsigny, Maryse, Francine Descarries, Lyne Kurtzman, and Evelyne Tardy. 1994. *Ces femmes qui ont bâti Montréal: 350 ans de vie de femmes*. Montréal: Éditions remue ménage.

Davis, Natalie Zemon. 1975. *Society and culture in early modern France*. Stanford: Stanford University Press.

———. 1976. "Women's history" in transition: The European case. *Feminist Studies* 3: 83–93.

———. 1983. *The return of Martin Guerre*. Cambridge, MA: Harvard University Press.

———. 1995. *Women on the margins: Three seventeenth century lives*. Cambridge, MA: Harvard University Press.

———. 2000. *The gift in sixteenth-century France*. Madison: University of Wisconsin Press.

Davis, Natalie Zemon, Josephine Grimshaw, Alison Smith Prentice, and Germaine Warkentin. 1966. Preliminary report: A study of 42 women who have children and who are in graduate programmes at the University of Toronto. Toronto: University of Toronto.

de Beauvoir, Simone. 1949. *Le deuxième sexe*. 2 vols. Paris: Gallimard.

———. 1953. *The second sex*. London: J. Cape.

de Beauvoir, Simone, and Jean-Paul Sartre. 1975. Simone de Beauvoir interroge Jean-Paul Sartre. *L'Arc*.

de Pizan, Christine. 1998. *The book of the city of ladies*. Translated by E. J. Richards. New York: Persea Books.

Delphy, Christine. 1970. L'ennemi principal. *Partisans: "Libération des femmes année zéro"* (54/55): 157–72.

Descarries, Francine. 1980. *L'école rose … et les cols roses. La reproduction de la divison sociale des sexes*. 2nd ed. Montréal: Les éditions cooperatives: Albert Saint-Martin et Centrale de l'enseignement du Québec.

———. 1998. Le projet féministe à l'aube du 21e siècle. Un projet de libération et de solidarité qui fait toujours sens. *Cahiers de Recherche Sociologique* 30: 179–210.

———. 2003. The hegemony of the English language in the academy. The damaging impact of the socio-cultural and linguistic barriers on the development of feminist sociological knowledge, theories and strategies. *Current Sociology* 51 (6): 625–36.

———. 2005a. *Émergence et développement des études féministes au Québec*. Cited July 15, 2007. Available from http://www.unb.br/ih/his/gefem/labrys7/fem/francine .htm.

———. 2005b. Le mouvement des femmes québécois. État des lieux. *Cités* 23: 125–36.

Descarries, Francine, and Christine Corbeil. 1989. Un espace éclaté. Figures de la famille au Québec. In *Le courrier de l'Unesco*, juillet, 42–46

———, ed. 2002. *Espaces et temps de la maternité*. Montréal: Éditions remue-ménage.

Dhruvarajan, Vanaja. 1989. *Hindu women and the power of ideology*. Granby, MA: Bergin and Garvey.

———. 1997. Chilly climate in B. C. universities. In *Equity and justice*, edited by D. Hearne and M. L. Lefebvre. Montréal: CWSA.

———. 2000. People of colour and national identity in Canada. *Journal of Canadian Studies* 35 (2): 166–75.

————. 2002. Feminism and resistance to globalization of capitalism. In *Global shaping and its alternatives*, edited by Y. Atasoy and W. Carroll. Aurora, ON: Garamond Press.

————. 2005. Colonialism and capitalism: Continuities and variations in strategies of domination and oppression. In *Teaching as activism: Equity meets environmentalism*, edited by P. Tripp and L. Muzzin. Montréal: McGill-Queen's University Press.

Dhruvarajan, Vanaja, and Jill Vickers. 2002. *Gender, race, and nation: A global perspective*. Toronto: University of Toronto Press.

Discussion Collective No. 6. 1972. *Women unite! An anthology of the Canadian women's movement*. Toronto: Canadian Women's Educational Press.

Dixon, Marlene. 1969. *The future of women*. San Francisco: Synthesis Publications.

————. 1976. *Things which are done in secret*. Montréal: Black Rose Books.

Dobrowolsky, Alexandra. 2000. *The politics of pragmatism: Women, representation, and constitutionalism in Canada*. Don Mills, ON: Oxford University Press.

Dufebvre, Bernard. 1950. *Cinq femmes et nous*. Montréal: Belisle.

Dumas, Jean, and Yves Péron. 1992. *Mariage et vie conjugale au Canada: La conjoncture démographique*. Ottawa: Statistique Canada.

Dumont, Micheline. 1989. The influence of feminist perspectives on historical research methodology. In *The effects of feminist approaches on research methodologies*, edited by W. Tomm. Waterloo: Wilfrid Laurier University Press.

————. 2001. *Découvrir la mémoire des femmes. Une historienne face à l'histoire des femmes*. Montréal: éditions du remue-ménage.

————. *See also* Johnson, Micheline.

Dumont-Johnson, Micheline, Michèle Jean, Marie Lavigne, and Jennifer Stoddard, eds. 1982. *L'Histoire des femmes au Québec depuis quatre siècles. Collection Idéelles*, edited by Collectif Clio. Montréal: Quinze Collection.

Dumont, Micheline, and Louise Toupin, eds. 2003. *La pensée féministe au Québec. Anthologie 1900–1985*. Montréal: éditions du remue-ménage.

Egan, Carolyn. 1987. Toronto international women's day committee: Socialist feminist politics. In *Feminism and political economy: Women's work, women's struggles*, edited by H. J. Maroney, H. Jon, and M. Luxton. Toronto: Methuen.

Eichler, Margrit. 1980. *The double standard: A feminist critique of feminist social science*. London: Croom Helm; New York: St. Martin's Press.

————. 1983. Introduction. In *As things stand: Ten years of recommendations*. Ottawa: Canadian Advisory Council on the Status of Women.

————. 1988. *Canadian families today: Recent changes and their policy consequences*. 2nd ed. Toronto: Gage.

————, ed. 1990. Reports from the Canadian women's studies project. Special issue of *Atlantis* 16 (1): 69–91.

————. 1991. *Nonsexist research methods: A practical guide*. New York: Routledge.

————. 1992a. Not always an easy alliance. In *Challenging times: The women's movement in Canada and the United States*, edited by C. Backhouse and D. H. Flaherty. Montréal: McGill-Queen's University Press.

———. 1992b. The unfinished transformation: Women and feminist approaches in sociology and anthropology. In *Fragile truths: Twenty-five years of sociology and anthropology in Canada*, edited by W. K. Carroll, L. Christiansen-Ruffman, R. F. Currie, and D. Harrison. Ottawa: Carleton University Press.

———. 1997. *Family shifts: Families, policies and gender equality*. Toronto: Oxford University Press.

———. 2001. Women pioneers in Canadian sociology: The effects of a politics of gender and a politics of knowledge. *Canadian Journal of Sociology* 26: 375–403.

Eichler, Margrit, and Mary Anne Burke. 2006. *The BIAS FREE framework: A practical tool for identifying and eliminating social biases in health research*. Geneva: Social Forum for Health Research.

Eichler, Margrit, and Meg Luxton. 2006. Feminist challenges to knowledge. *Atlantis* 31 (1): 76–82.

Eichler, Margrit, with the assistance of Louise Vandelac. 1990. An awkward situation: Men in Women's Studies—Part 1. Reports from the Canadian women's studies project. Special issue of *Atlantis* 16 (1): 69–91.

Engel, Marian. 1974. *Sarah Bastard's notebook*. Don Mills, ON: PaperJacks. Original edition, 1968.

———. 1976. *Bear: A novel*. Toronto: McClelland and Stewart.

Engels, Friedrich. 1884. *The origin of the family, private property, and the state in the light of researches of Lewis H. Morgan*. New York: International Publishers, 1972.

Epstein, Cynthia. 1971. *Women's place: Options and limits in professional careers*. Berkeley: University of California Press.

Essed, Philomena. 1991. *Understanding everyday racism: An interdisciplinary theory*. London: Sage.

Fahmy-Eid, Nadia. 1991. Histoire, objectivité et scientificité. Jalons pour une reprise du débat épistémologique. *Histoire sociale/Social history* 24 (47): 9–34.

———, ed. 1997. *Femmes, santé et professions. Histoire des diététistes et des physiothérapeutes au Québec et en Ontario (1930–1980)*. Montréal: Fides.

———. 1997. L'histoire des femmes. Construction et déconstruction d'une mémoire sociale. *Sociologie et sociétés* 29 (2): 21–30.

Fahmy-Eid, Nadia, and Micheline Dumont. 1983. *Maîtresses de maison, maîtresses d'école. Le rapport femmes/famille/éducation au Québec*. Montréal: Boréal Express.

———. 1986. *Les couventines. L'éducation des filles au Québec dans les communautés religieuses enseignantes (1840–1960)*. Montréal: Boréal Express.

Fédération des travailleurs et des travailleuses du Québec. 1973. *Travailleuses et syndiquées: Rapport du comité FTQ sur la situation de la femme*. Montréal: Fédération des travailleurs et des travailleuses du Québec (FTQ).

Feminist Alliance for International Action and National Association of Women and the Law. 2006. UN committee criticizes Canada for persistent poverty in the midst of wealth: Notes discriminatory impact on women. Press release, 23 May. Ottawa. Available from http://dawn.thot.net/fafia7.html. Accessed 5 February 2008.

La femme canadienne française. Almanach de la langue française. 1936. Montréal: Éditions Albert Lévesque.

Fernie, Lynne, and Aerlyn Weissman. 1982. *Forbidden love: The unashamed stories of lesbian lives.* Canada: National Film Board of Canada.

Fidell, Linda S. 1970. Empirical verification of sex discrimination in hiring practices in psychology. *American Psychologist* 25: 1094–98.

Findlay, Sue. 1988. Feminist struggles with the Canadian state, 1966–1988. *Resources for Feminist Research* 17 (3): 5–9.

Firestone, Shulamith. 1972. *The dialectic of sex.* St. Albans: Paladin.

Ford, Anne Rochon. 1985. *A path not strewn with roses: One hundred years of women at the University of Toronto, 1884–1984.* Toronto: Governing Council, University of Toronto.

Forman, Frieda, ed. 1989. *Taking our time: Feminist perspectives on temporality.* Oxford: Pergamon Press.

———. 1996. Sister voyager: The feminist ticket to Yiddish culture. Paper read at Di Froyen: Women and Yiddish, New York, NY.

———. Forthcoming 2008. *We escaped: Jewish refugees in Switzerland during World War II.* London: Valentine Mitchell.

Forman, Frieda, and Mary O'Brien, eds. 1990. *Feminism and education: A Canadian perspective.* Toronto: Centre for Women's Studies in Education, Ontario Institute for Studies in Education.

Forman, Frieda, Ethel Raicus, Sarah Silberstein-Swartz, and Margie Wolfe, eds. 1994. *Found treasures: Stories by Yiddish women writers.* Toronto: Second Story Press.

Forster, Merna. 2004. *100 Canadian heroines: Famous and forgotten faces.* Toronto: Dundurn Press.

Freeman, Jo. 1969. The changing styles of student protests. *Moderator* 8 (3): 17–19. Cited July 11, 2007. Available from http://www.jofreeman.com/sixtiesprotest/styles.htm.

———. *See also* Joreen.

Friedan, Betty. 1963. *The feminine mystique.* London: Gollancz.

———. 1976. *It changed my life: Writings on the women's movement.* New York: Random House.

Gagnon, Madeleine. 1979. *Lueur.* Montréal-Nord: VLB.

Gaudet, Bérengère. 1971. Étude sur certains aspects du droit familial au Canada. In *Étude préparée pour la Commission royale d'enquête sur la situation des femmes au Canada,* edited by the Commission. Ottawa: Imprimeur de la reine.

Gazette. November 1973. Report of the president's committee on equal rights for women and men at the University of Waterloo. In *Special Supplement.*

Gelber, Sylva. 1969. *The rights of man and the status of women.* Ottawa: Labour Canada, Women's Bureau.

———. 1973a. *The new role of women.* Ottawa: Women's Bureau.

———. 1973b. Social work and the status of women. *Social Worker* 41 (3): 193–97.

Gignac, Alain, and Anne Fortin, eds. 2005. *Études sémiotiques, féministes et sotériologiques en l'honneur d'Olivette Genest.* Paris: Mediaspaul.

Gilbert, Sandra M., and Susan Gubar. 1979. *The madwoman in the attic: The woman writer and the nineteenth-century literary imagination.* New Haven, CT: Yale University Press.

Gillett, Margaret. 1963. *A history of education: Thought and practice.* Toronto: McGraw-Hill of Canada.

———. 1973. Women in the Montréal area. Paper read at Women in the University, Queen's University, Kingston, ON.

———, ed. 1975. *Women and education.* Special issue of *McGill Journal of Education* 10 (1).

———. 1981. *We walked very warily: A history of women at McGill.* Montréal: Eden Press.

Gillett, Margaret, and Ann Beer, eds. 1995. *Our own agendas: Autobiographical essays by women associated with McGill University.* Montréal: McGill-Queen's University Press.

Gillett, Margaret, Janet Donald, Erin Malloy, and Andrea Vabalis. 1976. A survey of teaching and research on women at McGill: Report to Principal Bell. McGill University, Montréal, QC.

Gillett, Margaret, and Kay Sibbald, eds. 1984. *A fair shake: Autobiographical essays by McGill women.* Montréal: Eden Press.

Gillett, Margaret, Kay Sibbald, and Elizabeth Rowlinson, eds. 1996. *A fair shake revisited.* Montréal: McGill Printing Services.

Gilman, Charlotte Perkins. 1899. *The yellow wallpaper.* Boston: Small and Maynard.

Glazer-Malbin, Nona, and Helen Youngelson Waehrer, eds. 1972. *Woman in a man-made world: A socioeconomic handbook.* Chicago: Rand McNally.

Godard, Jean-Luc. 1964. *Une Femme Mariée.* France: Anouchka/Orsay.

Gordon, Linda. 1986. What's new in women's history. In *Feminist studies, critical studies,* edited by T. de Lauretis. Bloomington: Indiana University Press.

Gorham, Deborah. 1996. In defense of discipline-based feminist scholarship. In *Graduate women's studies: Visions and realities,* edited by A. B. Shteir. Toronto: Inanna Publications.

———. 1997. Women's history: Founding a new field. In *Creating historical memory: English-Canadian women and the work of history,* edited by B. Boutilier and A. Prentice. Vancouver: UBC Press.

Gornick, Vivian, and Barbara K. Moran, eds. 1972. *Women in sexist society.* New York: Significant Books.

Gottlieb, Lois C., and Wendy Keitner [Robbins]. 1975. Mothers and daughters in four recent Canadian novels. *Sphinx* 4:21.

———. 1976. Books from Canada. *Women's Studies Newsletter* 4 (3): 13.

———. 1977. Demeter's daughters: The mother–daughter motif in fiction by Canadian women. *Atlantis* 3 (1): 130–42.

Graham, Mayo. 1975. *Some Canadian women artists/Quelques artistes canadiennes.* Ottawa: National Gallery of Canada.

Granatstein, J. L. 1982. *The Ottawa men: The civil service mandarins, 1935–1957.* Toronto: Oxford University Press.

Greenglass, Esther. 1972. Attitudes toward abortion. *New Feminist* 3: 2–12.

———. 1975. Therapeutic abortion and its psychological implications. *Canadian Medical Association Journal* 113: 754–57.

————. 1976. *After abortion*. Toronto: Longman.

Greer, Germaine. 1970. *The female eunuch*. London: MacGibbon and Kee.

Gripton, James. 1974. Sexism in social work: Male takeover of a female profession. *Social Worker* 42: 78–89.

Gripton, James, and Mary Valentich, eds. 1986. *Social work practice in sexual problems*. New York: Haworth Press.

Groult, Benoîte. 1975. *Ainsi soit-elle*. Paris: B. Grasset.

Groupe de femmes de Montréal. 1971. *Manifeste des femmes québécoises*. Montréal: Etincelle.

Guettel, Charnie. 1974. *Marxism and feminism*. Toronto: Women's Press.

Guèvremont, Germaine. 1945. *Le survenant*. Paris: Plon.

Guillaumin, Colette. 1978. Pratique du pouvoir et idée de nature: (1) L'appropriation des femmes; (2) Le discours de la nature. *Questions féministes* 2: 5–30; 3: 3–30.

Habermas, Jürgen. 1970. Toward a theory of communicative competance. *Inquiry* 13: 114.

Hall, M. Ann, Dallas Cullen, and Trevor Slack. 1989. Organizational elites recreating themselves: The gender structure of national sport organizations. *Quest* 41: 28–45.

Hall, Radclyffe. 1990. *The well of loneliness*. New York: Anchor. Original edition, 1928.

Hall, Stuart. 1986. Gramsci's relevance for the study of race and ethnicity. *Journal of Communication Inquiry* 10 (2): 5–27.

Hamilton, Roberta, and Michele Barrett, eds. 1986. *The politics of diversity: Feminism, Marxism, and nationalism*. London: Verso.

Hannah, Elena, Linda Paul, and Sawni Vethamany-Globus, eds. 2002. *Women in the Canadian academic tundra: Challenging the chill*. Montréal: McGill-Queen's University Press.

Hansberry, Lorraine. 1994. *A raisin in the sun*. New York: Vintage. Original edition, 1959.

Hanson, R. Karl, Ian Broom, and Marylee Stephenson. 2004. Evaluating community sex offender treatment programs: A 12-year follow-up of 724 offenders. *Canadian Journal of Behavioural Sciences* 36 (2): 87–96.

Hébert, Anne. 1970. *Kamouraska*. Paris: Éditions du Seuil.

————. 1975. *Les enfants du sabbat*. Paris: Éditions du Seuil.

Heidensohn, Frances. 1968. The deviance of women: A critique and an inquiry. *British Journal of Sociology* 19 (2): 160–76.

Heilbrun, Carolyn G. 1973. *Toward a recognition of androgyny*. New York: Alfred A. Knopf.

Helmes-Hayes, Rick, ed. 1988. *A quarter-century of sociology at the University of Toronto, 1938–88*. Toronto: Canadian Scholars' Press.

Henry, Frances, Carol Tator, Winston Mattis, and Tim Rees. 2000. The ideology of racism. In *The colour of democracy: Racism in Canadian society*, edited by F. Henry, C. Tator, W. Mattis, and T. Rees. Toronto: Harcourt and Brace Canada.

Hesoid. 1966. *Theogony*. Oxford: Clarendon Press.

Hill Collins, Patricia. 1990. *Black feminist thought: Knowledge, consciousness and the politics of empowerment*. Boston: Unwin Hyman.

hooks, bell. 1994. *Outlaw culture: Resisting representations.* London: Routledge.

Howe, Florence. 2000. *The politics of women's studies: Testimony from 30 founding mothers.* New York: Feminist Press.

Iacovetta, Franca, and Wendy Mitchison, eds. 1998. *On the case: Explorations in social history.* Toronto: University of Toronto Press.

Institoris, Heinrich. 1485. *Malleus maleficarum.* Translated by M. Summers. 1928 ed. London: J. Rodker.

Institut de la statistique du Québec. 2007a. *Naissances et taux de natalité, Québec, 1900–2006.* Cited July 15, 2007. Available from http://www.stat.gouv.qc.ca/donstat/societe/demographie/naisn_deces/naissance/401.htm.

———. 2007b. *Proportion des mariages rompus par un divorce à certaines durées depuis le mariage Québec.* Cited July 15, 2007. Available from http://www.stat.gouv .qc.ca/donstat/societe/demographie/etat_matrm_marg/512.htm.

———. 2007c. *Taux d'activité des femmes selon certains groupes d'âge, moyennes annuelles à tous les cinq ans, Québec, Ontario, Canada, 1976–2001.* Cited July 15, 2007. Available from http://www.stat.gouv.qc.ca/donstat/societe/march_travl _remnr/parnt_etudn_march_travl/pop_active/indicat_activite/taux_act_fage_76 .htm.

Institut d'histoire de l'Amérique française. 1947. *Revue d'histoire de l'Amérique française.* Montréal: Institut d'histoire de l'Amérique française.

Iverson, Lucille, and Kathryn Ruby, eds. 1975. *We become new: Poems by contemporary American women.* New York: Bantam Books.

Jacobson, Helga E. 1973. Organizing women's studies at the University of British Columbia. *Canadian Newsletter of Research on Women* 2 (October): 19–24.

Jameson, Anna. 1832. *Characteristics of women, moral, poetical and historical: With fifty vignette etchings.* London: Saunders and Otley.

———. 1944. *Winter studies and summer ramblings in Canada.* Edited by J. J. Talman and E. M. Murray. Toronto: T. Nelson. Original edition, *Winter Studies and Summer Rambles in Canada,* 1838.

Jamieson, Kathleen. 1979. Multiple jeopardy: The evolution of a Native women's movement. *Atlantis* 4 (2): 157–77.

Janeway, Elizabeth. 1971. *Man's world woman's place: A study in social mythology.* New York: Delta.

Johnson, Micheline Dumont. 1971. Histoire de la situation de la femme dans la province de Québec. In *Tradition culturelle et histoire politique de la femme au Canada. Étude préparée pour la Commission royale d'enquête sur la situation de la femme au Canada,* edited by the Commission. Ottawa: Imprimeur de la Reine.

———. *See also* Dumont, Micheline.

Jones, Charles, Lorna R. Marsden, and Lorne J. Tepperman. 1990. *Lives of their own: The individualization of adult women's lives.* Toronto: Oxford University Press.

Joreen. 1969. The bitch manifesto. In *Masculine/feminine: Readings in sexual mythology and the liberation of women,* edited by B. Roszak and T. Roszak. New York: Harper and Row.

————. 1973. The tyranny of structurelessness. In *Radical feminism*, edited by A. Koedt, E. Levine and A. Rapone. New York: Quadrangle Books.

————. *See also* Freeman, Jo.

Joseph, Joe. 2005. Who knows what women want? *Times*, June 8, 27.

Joyce, Arthur. 2001. Abortion in Canada. *Human Quest* 215 (2): 3–5.

Juteau, Danielle. 1981. Visions partielles, visions partiales: Vision des minoritaires en sociologie? *Sociologie et sociétés* 13 (2): 33–47.

————. 1999. *L'ethnicité et ses frontières*. Montréal: Les Presses de l'Université de Montréal.

————, ed. 2003. *La différenciation sociale: Modèles et processus*. Montréal: Les Presses de l'Université de Montréal.

Juteau, Danielle, and Nicole Laurin. 1988. L'évolution des formes de l'appropriation des femmes: Des religieuses aux "mères porteuses." *Revue canadienne de sociologie et d'anthropologie* 25 (2): 183–207.

————. 1997. *Un métier et une vocation: Le travail des religieuses au Québec de 1901 à 1971*. Montréal: Les Presses de l'Université de Montréal.

Juteau-Lee, Danielle, and B. Roberts. 1981. Ethnicity and femininity: (D')après nos experiences. *Canadian Ethnic Studies/Études ethniques au Canada* 13 (1): 1–23.

————. *See also* Juteau, Danielle.

Kaite, Berkeley. 2005. Letter to the editor. *Globe and Mail*, April 16.

Keahey, Deborah, and Deborah Schnitzer, eds. 2003. *The madwoman in the academy: 43 women boldly take on the ivory tower*. Calgary: University of Calgary Press.

Keitner [Robbins], Wendy. 1973. Ralph Gustafson: Heir of centuries in a country without myths. PhD diss., Queen's University.

————. 1979. *Ralph Gustafson*. Boston: Twayne Publications.

————. *See also* Robbins, Wendy.

Keitner [Robbins], Wendy, and Lois C. Gottlieb, eds. 1978. *Women writers of the commonwealth*. Special issue of *World Literature Written in English* 17 (1).

Kelly, Joan. 1984. *Women, history and theory: The essays of Joan Kelly*. Chicago: University of Chicago Press.

Kemper, Theodore D. 1968. Reference groups, socialization and achievement. *American Sociological Review* 33 (1): 31–45.

Kerans, Marion Douglas. 1996. *Muriel Duckworth: A very active pacifist; A biography*. Halifax: Fernwood.

Kimball, Meredith M. 1973. Mothers, children, work and guilt. *Ontario Psychologist* 5 (2): 36–47.

————. 1986. Developing a feminist psychology of women: Past and future accomplishments. *Canadian Psychology* 27 (3): 248–59.

————. 1995. *Feminist visions of gender similarities and differences*. Binghamton, NY: Haworth Press.

————. 2001. Gender similarities and differences as feminist contradictions. In *Handbook on the psychology of women and gender*, edited by R. Unger. New York: Wiley.

————. 2003. Feminists rethink gender. In *About psychology: Essays at the crossroads of history, theory, and philosophy*, edited by D. B. Hill and M. J. Krall. Albany, NY: SUNY Press.

Kirkwood, James. 1968. *Good times bad times*. New York: Simon and Schuster.

Klein, Bonnie Sherr. 1981. *Not a love story: A film about pornography*. Canada: National Film Board of Canada.

Koedt, Anne. 1973. The myth of the vaginal orgasm. In *Radical feminism*, edited by A. Koedt, E. Levine, and A. Rapone. New York: Quadrangle Books.

Kolodny, Annette. 1975. *The lay of the land: Metaphor as experience and history in American life and letters*. Chapel Hill: University of North Carolina Press.

———. 1989. I dreamt again that I was drowning. In *Women's writing in exile*, edited by M. L. Broe and A. Ingram. Chapel Hill: University of North Carolina Press.

———. 1998. *Failing the future: A dean looks at higher education in the twenty-first century*. Durham, NC: Duke University Press.

———. 2000a. "A sense of discovery, mixed with a sense of justice": Creating the first women's studies program in Canada. *NWSA Journal* 12 (1): 143–64.

———. 2000b. "A sense of discovery, mixed with a sense of justice": Creating the first women's studies program in Canada. In *The politics of women's studies: Testimony from thirty founding mothers*, edited by F. Howe. New York: Feminist Press.

Kuhn, Thomas S. 1962. *The structure of scientific revolutions*. Chicago: University of Chicago Press.

Labarge, Margaret Wade. 1971a. The cultural tradition of Canadian women: The historical background. In *Cultural tradition and political history of women in Canada*. Study presented to the Royal Commission on the Status of Women in Canada. Ottawa: Information Canada.

———. 1971b. Historique des traditions culturelles de la femme canadienne. In *Tradition culturelle et histoire politique de la femme au Canada: Étude préparée pour Commission royale d'enquête sur la situation de la femme au Canada*, edited by the Commission. Ottawa: Imprimeur de la reine.

Ladner, Joyce. 1971. *Tomorrow's tomorrow: The black woman*. New York: Doubleday.

Laurence, Margaret. 1965. *The stone angel*. Toronto: McClelland and Stewart.

———. 1966. *A jest of God*. Toronto: Macmillan.

———. 1974. *The diviners*. Toronto: McClelland and Stewart. Rpt. Toronto: Bantam, 1975.

Lebowitz, Andrea. 1991. *Star gazing: Charting feminist literary criticism*. Ottawa: Canadian Research Institute for the Advancement of Women.

———. 1996. *Living in harmony: Nature writing by women in Canada*. Victoria: Orca Book Publishers.

Lebowitz, Andrea, Gillian Milton, and Gilean Douglas. 1999. *Gilean Douglas: Writing nature, finding home*. Victoria: Sono Nis Press.

Le Moyne, Jean. 1961. *Convergences*. Montréal: Éditions HMH.

Lerner, Gerda. 1997. *Why history matters: Life and thought*. New York: Oxford University Press.

Leslie, Pat. 1992. "Pat Leslie." In *Faces of feminism: Portraits of women across Canada*, edited by P. Harris. Toronto: Second Storey Press, 72–73.

Lessing, Doris. 1964. *Martha quest and a proper marriage*. New York: Simon and Schuster.

————. 1967. *The golden notebook*. New York: Simon and Schuster.

————. 1996. *Play with a tiger and other plays*. London: Flamingo. Original edition, 1962.

Levine, Helen. 1976a. Feminist counselling: A look at new possibilities. *'76 and Beyond*. Special issue of *The Social Worker* 44: 12–15.

————. 1976b. On women and on one woman. In *Women: Their use of alcohol and other legal drugs*, edited by A. MacLennan. Toronto: Addiction Research Foundation of Ontario, 21–43.

————. 1989. Feminist counselling: A woman-centred approach. In *Women, work and wellness*, edited by Virginia Carver and Charles Ponee. Toronto: Addiction Research Foundation of Ontario, 227–52.

Levine, Helen, and Alma Estable. 1981. *The power politics of motherhood: A feminist critique of theory and practice*. Occasional paper. Ottawa: Centre for Social Welfare Studies, Carleton University.

Light, Beth, and Alison Prentice, eds. 1980. *Pioneer and gentlewomen of British North America, 1713–1867*. Toronto: New Hogtown Press.

Light, Beth, and Joy Parr, eds. 1983. *Canadian women on the move, 1867–1920*. Toronto: New Hogtown Press.

Light, Beth, and Ruth Roach Pierson, eds. 1990. *No easy road: Women in Canada, 1920s to 1960s*. Toronto: New Hogtown Press.

Loranger, Françoise. 1967. *Encore cinq minutes: Suivi de un cri qui vient de loin*. Ottawa: Cercle du livre de France.

Lorca, Frederico Garcia. 1945. *House of Bernarda Alba*. In *Three tragedies*. London: Folio Society, 1977. Buenos Aires: Losada.

Lorde, Audrey. 1984. *Sister outsider*. Freedom, CA: Freedom Press.

Lowe, Graham. 1987. *Women in the administrative revolution: The feminization of clerical work*. Toronto: University of Toronto Press.

Lumby, Catharine. 2005. Germaine Greer: The Michael Jackson of feminism. *Age*, January 14.

Luxton, Meg. 1980. *More than a labour of love: Three generations of women's work in the home*. Toronto: Canadian Women's Educational Press.

————. 1984. Conceptualizing "women" in anthropology and sociology. In *Knowledge reconsidered: A feminist overview*, edited by U. M. Franklin. Ottawa: Canadian Research Institute for the Advancement of Women.

————. 2001a. Family responsibilities: The politics of love and care. Paper read at 32nd Annual Sorokin Lecture, at University of Saskatchewan, Saskatoon.

————. 2001b. Feminism as a class act: Working class feminism and the women's movement in Canada. *Labour/le Travail* 48: 63–88.

————. 2006. Feminist political economy and the politics of social reproduction. In *Rethinking social reproduction: Critical debates in feminist political economy*, edited by K. Bezanson and M. Luxton. Montréal: McGill-Queen's University Press.

Luxton, Meg, and June Corman. 2001. *Getting by in hard times: Gendered labour at home and on the job*. Toronto: University of Toronto Press.

Luxton, Meg, and Heather Jon Maroney. 1987. *Feminism and political economy: Women's work, women's struggles.* Toronto: Methuen.

———. 1992. Begetting babies, raising children: The politics of parenting. In *Socialism in crisis? Canadian perspectives,* edited by J. Robert and J. Vorst. Halifax, NS: Fernwood.

MacEwen, Gwendolyn. 1963. *The rising fire.* Toronto: Toronto Contact Press.

———. 1969. *The shadow-maker.* Toronto: Macmillan.

MacLellan, Margaret E. 1971. Histoire des droits de la femme au Canada. In *Tradition culturelle et histoire politique de la femme au Canada: Étude préparée pour la Commission royale d'enquête sur la situation de la femme au Canada,* edited by the Commission. Ottawa: Imprimeur de la reine.

MacLeod, Linda. 1987. *Battered but not beaten: Preventing wife battering in Canada.* Ottawa: Canadian Advisory Council on the Status of Women.

Macpherson, Kay. 1987. Persistent voice: Twenty-five years with voice of women. *Atlantis* 12 (3): 60–72.

———. 1994. *When in doubt, do both: The times of my life.* Toronto: University of Toronto Press.

Macpherson, Kay, and Meg Sears. 1976. The voice of women: A history. In *Women in the Canadian Mosaic,* edited by G. Matheson. Toronto: Peter Martin.

MacRae, Marion, and Anthony Adamson. 1975. *Hallowed walls: Church architecture of Upper Canada.* Toronto: Clarke, Irwin.

Maheux-Forcier, Louise. 1969. *Une forêt pour Zoé.* Montréal: Cercle du livre de France.

Maillet, Antonine. 1971a. *La Sagouine: Pièce pour une femme seule.* Montréal: Leméac.

———. 1971b. *The tale of Don l'Orignal.* Toronto: Clarke.

———. 1979. *Pélagie-la-Charrette.* Paris: B. Grasset.

Mandel, Miriam. 1973. *Lions at her face.* Edmonton: White Pelican.

Maroney, Heather Jon, and Meg Luxton, eds. 1987. *Feminism and political economy: Women's work, women's struggle.* Toronto: Methuen.

Marsden, Lorna R. 1979. Agitating organizations: The role of the National Action Committee on the Status of Women in facilitating equal pay policy in Canada. In *Equal employment policy for women: Strategies for implementation in the United States, Canada and Western Europe,* edited by R. S. Ratner. Philadelphia: Temple University Press.

———. 1981. "The labour force" is an ideological structure: A guiding note to the labour economists. *Atlantis* 7 (1): 57–64.

———. 1984. Work, technical role models and the absence of women in academia. In *The sociology of work,* edited by A. Whipper. Toronto: Oxford University Press.

———. 2004. Women, universities and the Canadian tradition. Paper read at The Canada Seminar, February 20, 2004, at Lady Margaret Hall, Oxford University, UK.

Marsden, Lorna R., and Joan Busby. 1989. Feminist influence through the Senate: The case of divorce. *Atlantis* 14 (2): 72–81.

Marsden, Lorna R., and Edward B. Harvey. 1979. *The fragile federation: Social change in Canada.* Toronto: McGraw-Hill Ryerson.

Marshall, Leslie. 1980. Review of *The novelistic vision of Doris Lessing: Breaking the forms of consciousness*, by Roberta Rubenstein. *WLWE* 19 (2): 178–81.

Martin, Claire. 1966. *La joue droite*. Montréal: Cercle du livre de France.

Martineau, Harriet. 1838. *How to observe manners and morals*. London: Charles Knight and Co. rpt. New Brunswick, NJ: Transaction Publishers. Sesquicentennial ed., 1838–1988.

Mason, Mary Ann, and Eve Mason Ekman. 2007. *Mothers on the fast track: How a new generation can balance family and careers*. London: Open University Press.

Mathieu, Nicole-Claude. 1971. Notes pour une définition sociologique des catégories de sexe. *Épistémologie sociologique* 11: 19–39.

McDaniel, Susan A. 1991. Feminist scholarship in sociology: Transformation from within? *Canadian Journal of Sociology* 16 (3): 303–12.

McFarland, Joan. 1976. Economics and women: A critique of the scope of traditional analysis and research. *Atlantis* 1 (2): 27–41.

———. 1980. Changing modes of social control in a New Brunswick fish packing town. *Studies in Political Economy* 4: 99–113.

———. 1998. From feminism to women's human rights: The best way forward? *Atlantis* 22 (2): 50–61.

———. 2002. Call centres in New Brunswick: Maquiladoras of the north? *Canadian Woman Studies* 21/22 (4/1): 65–70.

———. 2003. Public policy and women's access to training in New Brunswick. In *Training the excluded for work*, edited by M. Cohen. Vancouver: UBC Press.

McPherson, Kay. 1994. *When in doubt, do both: The times of my life*. Toronto: University of Toronto Press.

Mead, Margaret. 1935. *Sex and temperament in three primitive societies*. London: Routledge.

———. 1949. *Male and female: A study of the sexes in a changing world*. New York: W. Morrow.

Michel, Andrée, and Geneviève Texier. 1964. *La condition de la Française d'aujourd'hui*. 2 vols. Paris: Plon.

Mies, Maria, and Vandana Shiva. 1993. *Ecofeminism*. Halifax, NS: Fernwood; London: Zed Books.

Millett, Kate. 1970. *Sexual politics*. New York: Doubleday.

Mill, John Stuart. 1869. *On the subjection of women*. rpt. *The subjection of women*. Peterborough, ON: Broadview Press, 2000.

Mills, Charles Wright. 1959. *The sociological imagination*. New York: Oxford University Press.

Mills, Sean. 2004. Québécoises debutte! Le front de libération des femmes, le centre des femmes et le nationalisme. *Mens: Revue de l'histoire intellectuelle de l'Amérique française* 4 (2): 183–210. Available online at http://www.hst.ulaval.ca/revuemens/Quebecoises.html, accessed July 2007.

Milton, John. 1968. *Paradise lost*. Menston, UK: Scolar Press. Original edition, 1667.

Miron, John. 1985. *Demographic change, household formation and housing demand: Canada's postwar experience*. Toronto: Centre for Urban and Community Studies, University of Toronto.

Mitchell, Joni. 1982. "Chinese café." *Wild Things Run Fast*. Geffen.

————. 1971. "Little green." *Blue*. WEA/Rhino.

Mitchell, Juliet. 1966. Women: The longest revolution. *New Left Review* 40: 11–37.

————. 1970. *Women's estate*. London: Penguin.

————. 1975. *Psychoanalysis and feminism*. New York: Vintage.

Moers, Ellen. 1976. *Literary women*. New York: Doubleday.

Mohanty, Chandra Talpade. 1991. Under western eyes: Feminist scholarship and colonial discourses. In *Third world women and the politics of feminism*, edited by C. T. Mohanty, A. Russo, and L. Torres. Bloomington: Indiana University Press.

Molière. 2001. *The bourgeois gentleman*. Mineola, NY: Dover. Original edition, 1732.

Morgan, Robin, ed. 1970. *Sisterhood is powerful: An anthology of writings from the women's liberation movement*. New York: Vintage.

————. 2004. The proper study of womankind: On women's studies. In *Women's studies in the academy: Origins and impact*, edited by R. Rosen. Upper Saddle River, NJ: Pearson Education. Original edition, 1973.

Morton, Peggy. 1972. Women's work is never done. In *Women unite! An anthology of the Canadian women's movement*, edited by Discussion Collective No. 6, 46–68. Toronto: Canadian Women's Educational Press.

Mount Saint Vincent University Archives. 2007. MSVU Archives: Former presidents of MSVU. *Mount St. Vincent University Library*. Cited July 24, 2007. Available from http://www.msvu.ca/library/archives/apres.asp.

Mulvey, Laura. 1975. Visual pleasure and narrative cinema. *Screen* 16 (3): 6–18.

Munro, Alice. 1968a. *Dance of the happy shades: Stories*. Toronto: Ryerson Press.

————. 1968b. The office. In *Dance of the happy shades*. Toronto: McGraw-Hill Ryerson.

————. 1972. Interview with Graeme Gibson. In *Eleven Canadian novelists*. Toronto: Anansi.

————. 1974. *The lives of girls and women: A novel*. New York: New American Library.

Nakamura, Masao, Alice Nakamura, and Dallas Cullen. 1979. Job opportunities, the offered wage and the labour supply of married women. *American Economic Review* 69 (5): 787–805.

Nash, Terre. 1982. *If you love this planet*. Canada: National Film Board of Canada.

National Council of Women of Canada. 1900. *Les femmes du Canada, leurs vies et leurs oeuvres*. Paris: Exposition Universelle.

Neatby, Hilda. 1953. *So little for the mind*. Toronto: Clarke, Irwin.

Nemiroff, Greta Hofmann. 1987. *Women and men: Interdisciplinary readings on gender*. Markham, ON: Fitzhenry and Whiteside.

————. 1989. *Celebrating Canadian women: Prose and poetry by and about Canadian women*. Markham, ON: Fitzhenry and Whiteside.

————. 1993. *Reconstructing education: Towards a pedagogy of critical humanism*. New York: Praeger; Toronto: OISE Press.

————. 1999. *Women's changing landscapes: Life stories from three generations*. Toronto: Second Story Press.

Neuman, Shirley, and Smaro Kamboureli, eds. 1986. *A mazing space: Writing Canadian women writing*. Edmonton: Longspoon/NeWest.

Nochlin, Linda. 1971. Why are there no great women artists? In *Woman in sexist society: Studies in power and powerlessness*, edited by V. Gornick and B. K. Moran. New York: Basic Books.

Nolan, Stephanie. 2005. Equality a paradox for African women. *Globe and Mail*, May 26.

Nourbese Philip, Marlene. 1992. *Frontiers: Essays and writings on racism and culture.* Stratford, ON: Mercury Press.

O'Barr, Jeanne F. 2000. My master list for millennium. *Signs* 25 (4): 1205–7.

O'Brien, Mary. 1989. *Reproducing the world: Essays in feminist theory.* Boulder, CO: Westview Press.

O'Faolain, Julia, and Lauro Martines, eds. 1973. *Not in god's image: Women in history from the Greeks to the Victorians.* New York: Harper and Row.

Office of the High Commissioner for Human Rights. 1976. *Declaration on the elimination of discrimination against women.* Last revised 2002. Cited July 11, 2007. Available from http://www.unhchr.ch/html/menu3/b/21.htm.

O'Neill, Brenda. 2003. *The royal commission on the status of women: Looking back, looking forward.* University of Manitoba. Cited July 15, 2007. Available from http://www.uwc-wpg.mb.ca/royal_commission_talk.pdf.

Ontario Women's Bureau. 1977. *Women and labour unions.* Toronto.

Oppenheimer, Valerie Kincade. 1970. *The female labor force in the United States.* Berkeley: University of California Press.

Ornstein, Michael, and Michael Stephenson. 1999. *Politics and ideology in Canada elite and public opinion in the transformation of a welfare state.* Montréal: McGill-Queen's University Press.

Overall, Christine. 1987. *Ethics and human reproduction: A feminist analysis.* Boston: Allan and Unwin.

———. 1993. *Human reproduction: Principles, practices, policies.* Toronto: Oxford University Press.

———. 1998. *A feminist I: Reflections from academia.* Peterborough, ON: Broadview Press.

———. 2001. *Thinking like a woman: Personal life and political ideas.* Toronto: Sumach Press.

———. 2003. *Aging, death, and human longevity: A philosophical inquiry.* Berkeley: University of California Press.

Ozick, Cynthia. 1971. Women and creativity: The demise of the dancing dog. In *Women in sexist society: Studies in power and powerlessness*, edited by V. Gornick and B. K. Moran. New York: Basic Books.

Pederson, Diane. *Changing women, changing history.* Ottawa: Carleton University Press, 1996.

Pelletier-Rowan, Renée. 1962. "La régulation des naissances." *La Revue populaire*, septembre: 32–37.

Peters, Daniel. 1978. *Border crossings.* New York: Harper and Row.

Pike, Douglas, ed. 1967. *Australian dictionary of biography.* Vol. 2, 1788–1850. Melbourne: Melbourne University Press.

Pinchbeck, Ivy. 1969. *Women workers and the Industrial Revolution, 1750–1850*. London: Frank Cass. Original edition, 1930.

Plath, Sylvia. 1971. *The bell jar*. New York: Harper and Row.

Pope, Alexander. 1961–69. The rape of the lock. *Poems*. Vol. 2. Twickenham Edition, ed. John Butt. New Haven, CT: Yale University Press.

Porter, Gene Stratton. 1993. *A girl of the limberlost*. Charlottesville, VA: University of Virginia Library. Original edition, 1909.

Power, Eileen Edna. 1922. *Medieval English nunneries*. New York: Cambridge University Press.

———. 1924. *Medieval people*. London: Methuen.

———. 1975. *Medieval women*. New York: Cambridge University Press.

Prentice, Alison. 1975. The feminization of teaching in British North America and Canada, 1845–1875. *Social history/Histoire sociale* 8: 5–20.

———. 1977. *The school promoters: Education and social class in mid-nineteenth century Upper Canada*. Toronto: McClelland and Stewart.

———. 1999. Workers, professionals, pilgrims: Tracing Canadian women teachers' histories. In *Telling women's lives: Narrative inquiries in the history of women's education*, edited by K. Weiler and S. Middleton. Buckingham: Open University Press.

———. 2006. "A blackboard in her kitchen": Women and physics at the University of Toronto, 1890–1990. *Scientia Canadensis* 29 (1): 17–44.

Prentice, Alison, Naomi Black, Gail Brandt, Paula Bourne, Beth Light, and Wendy Mitchinson. 1988. *Canadian women: A history*. Toronto: Harcourt Brace.

———. 1996. *Canadian women: A history*. 2nd ed. Toronto: Harcourt Brace.

Prentice, Alison, and Marjorie R. Theobald, eds. 1991. *Women who taught: Perspectives on the history of women and teaching*. Toronto: University of Toronto Press.

Prestwich, Patricia E. 1993. Women and madness in a nineteenth-century Parisian asylum. In *ReImagining Women*, edited by S. Neuman and G. Stephenson. Toronto: University of Toronto Press.

———. 1994. Family strategies and medical power: "Voluntary" committal in a Parisian asylum, 1876–1914. *Journal of Social History* 27 (4): 797–816.

———. 1998. Germaine Poinso-Chapuis et les femmes du MRP. In *Germain Poinso-Chapuis, Femme d'Etat (1901–1981)*. Aix-en-Provence: Edisud.

———. 2002. Modernizing politics in the Fourth Republic: Women in the Movement Républican Populaire, 1944–58. In *Crisis and renewal in modern France, 1918–1962*, edited by K. Mouré and M. Alexander. New York: Berghahn Books.

———. 2003. Female alcoholism in Paris, 1870–1920: The response of psychiatrists and of families. *History of Psychiatry* 14 (3): 321–36.

Pyke, Sandra W. 1971. Sugar 'n' Spice. *The Velvet Fist* 1 (8): 8.

———. 1974a. Sex and the *Ontario Psychologist*. *Ontario Psychologist* 6 (4): 42–44.

———. 1974b. Counselling and the feminist. *Ontario Psychologist* 6 (1): 45–48.

———. 1975. Children's literature: Conceptions of sex roles. In *Socialization and values in Canadian society*, edited by R. M. Pike and E. Zureik. Ottawa: Carleton Library Series, Vol. 2, 51–73.

———. 1975b. Feminist counselling: The new frontier. *Ontario Psychologist* 7 (1): 43–47.

———. 1977. Sex-role socialization in the school system. In *Education, change and society*, edited by R. Calton, L. A. Colley, and N. J. MacKinnon. Toronto: Gage.

———. 1980. Androgyny: A dead end or a promise. In *Sex roles: Origins, influences and implications for women*, edited by C. Stark-Adamec. Montréal: Eden Press.

———. 1982. Confessions of a reluctant ideologist. *Canadian Psychology* 23 (3): 125–34.

———. 1997. Education and the "woman question." *Canadian Psychology* 38 (3): 154–63.

———. 2001. Feminist psychology in Canada: Early days. *Canadian Psychology* 42 (4): 268–75.

Pyke, Sandra W., and F. Ricks. 1973. The counselor and the female client. *School Counselor* 20 (4): 280–84.

Pyke, Sandra W., and Cannie Stark-Adamec. 1981. Canadian feminism and psychology: The first decade. *Canadian Psychology* 22 (1): 35–54.

Pyke, Sandra W., and J. C. Stewart. 1974. Women and television. *Ontario Psychologist* 6 (5): 66–69.

Québec. Rapport Parent. [Commission royale d'enquête sur l'enseignement dans la province de Québec]. 1966. L'administration de l'enseignement: Diversité religieuse, culturelle, et unité de l'administration. In rapport, tome 3. Chair Alphonse-Marie Parent. Québec: Government of Québec.

Radical Feminists. 1970. *Notes from the second year*. New York: Radical Feminism.

Ramkhalawansingh, Ceta. 1973. Women's courses: Tough problems, far-reaching aims. *Varsity*, March.

———. 1974. Women during the Great War. In *Women at work: Ontario 1850–1930*, edited by J. Acton, P. Goldsmith, and B. Shepard. Toronto: Women's Educational Press.

Rebick, Judy. 2004. We've come part way, baby. *Globe and Mail*, March 11, A21.

———. 2005. *Ten thousand roses: The making of a feminist revolution*. Toronto: Penguin Canada.

Research Collective. 1975. *Women on welfare*. Ottawa: Carleton University School of Social Work.

Ricciutelli, Luciana, Angela Miles, and Margaret H. McFadden, eds. 2004. *Feminist politics, activism, and vision: Local and global challenges*. Toronto: Inanna Publications and Education.

Rich, Adrienne. 1976. *Of woman born*. New York: Norton.

———. 1996. "When we dead awaken": Writing as re-vision. In *The Norton anthology of literature by women: The traditions in English*, edited by S. M. Gilbert and S. Gubar. New York: Norton. Original edition, 1972.

Ricks, Frances A., George Matheson, and Sandra W. Pyke. 1972. Women's liberation: A case study of organizations for social change. *Canadian Psychologist* 13 (1): 30–39.

Ricks, Frances A., and Sandra W. Pyke. 1973. Teacher perceptions and attitudes that foster or maintain sex role differences. *Interchange* 4 (1): 26–33.

Ringuet, Philippe Panneton. 1938. *Trente arpents*. Paris: Flammarion.

Robinson, B. A. 2002. Rape of women during wartime: Before, during, and since World War II." December 20. *ReligiousTolerance.org: Ontario Consultants on Religious Tolerance*. Cited November 15, 2007. Available at http://www.religioustolerance .org/war_rape.htm.

Robbins, Wendy. 2001a. "Breasting body": The beginnings of maternity poetry by women in Canada. *Canadian Poetry Studies, Documents, Reviews* 49: 74–93.

———. 2001b. Rev. Florence Howe: The politics of women's studies. *CAUT Bulletin, Status of Women Supplement* 8 (8): n. pag.

———. *See also* Keitner, Wendy; Robbins Keitner, Wendy.

Robbins, Wendy, Karen-Jean Braun, June Colwell, Anne Compton, Jennie Hornosty, Sheila Laidlaw, Marie MacBeath, and Nancy Nason-Clark. 1991. Milestones for women at UNB. In *Of more than academic interest: Women at UNB; A progress review of the decade since the 1979 The status of women at UNB: Task force report to the President and discussion of priorities for the 1990s*. Fredericton: President's Advisory Committee on the Status of Women.

Robbins, Wendy, and Laurie McLaughlan. 2002. *A chronology of the development of women's studies in Canada*. PAR-L: A Canadian Electronic Feminist Network/Un réseau électronique féministe canadien. Cited July 11, 2007. Available from http:// www.unb.ca/PAR-L/chronology1.htm.

Robbins, Wendy, and Michèle Ollivier. 2007. *Post secondary pyramid: Equity audit 2007*. Canadian Federation for the Humanities and Social Sciences. Cited July 24, 2007. Available from http://www.fedcan.ca/english/pdf/issues/Pyramid2007.pdf.

Robbins, Wendy, Michèle Ollivier, John Hollingsworth, and Rosemary Morgan. 2005. *Ivory towers: Feminist and equity audits 2005*. PAR-L, CFHSS, and CAUT. Canadian Federation for the Humanities and Social Sciences. Cited July 15, 2007. Available from http://www.fedcan.ca/english/pdf/issues/indicators2005eng.pdf.

Robbins, Wendy, Michèle Ollivier, and Rosemary Morgan. 2001. *Ivory towers: Feminist audits*. PAR-L, CFHSS, and CAUT. Canadian Federation for the Humanities and Social Sciences. Cited July 11, 2007. Available from http://www.fedcan .ca/english/issues/issues/audit/.

Robbins, Wendy Keitner. 1984. Canadian women writers and the syndrome of the female man: A note on the poetry of Audrey Alexandra Brown and Anne Wilkinson. *Tessera* 8 (4): 76–81.

Robbins Keitner, Wendy. 1989. Anglophone Canada. In *Longman anthology of world literature by women, 1875–1975*, edited by M. Arkin and B. Shollar. New York: Longman.

Rose, Jacqueline. 1982. Introduction. In *Feminine Sexuality: Jacques Lacan and the école freudienne*, by Jacques Lacan, edited by Juliet Mitchell and Jacqueline Rose. London: MacMillan.

Rossi, Alice, ed. 1973. *The feminist papers: From Adams to de Beauvoir*. New York: Bantam Books.

Roszak, Betty, and Theodore Roszak, eds. 1969. *Masculine/feminine: Readings in sexual mythology and the liberation of women*. New York: Harper and Row.

Rousseau, Jean-Jacques. 1762. *Emile ou De l'éducation.* Amsterdam: Chez Jean Néaulme.

Rowbotham, Sheila. 1972a. *Oppression and liberation.* London: Penguin.

———. 1972b. *Women: Resistance and revolution.* Harmondsworth: Penguin.

———. 1977. *Hidden from history: 300 years of women's oppression and the fight against it.* 3rd ed. London: Pluto Press.

———. 1992. *Women in movement: Feminism and social action.* New York: Routledge.

———. 2000. *Promise of a dream: Remembering the sixties.* London: Penguin Books.

Roy, Gabrielle. 1945. *Bonheur d'occasion.* Paris: Flammarion.

Royal Commission on the Status of Women in Canada. 1970. *Report.* Chair Florence Bird. Ottawa: Supply and Services Canada.

Rubin, Gayle. 1975. The traffic in women: Notes on the "political economy" of sex. In *Toward an anthropology of women*, edited by R. Reiter. New York: Monthly Review Press.

Sabia, Laura. 1985. Interview by Penney Kome. In Penney Kome, *Women of influence: Canadian women and politics.* Toronto: Doubleday Canada.

Sainte-Marie, Buffy. 1964. *It's My Way.* Vanguard Records.

San Francisco Redstockings. 1969. Our politics begin with our feelings. In *Masculine/feminine: Readings in sexual mythology and the liberation of women*, edited by B. Roszak and T. Roszak. New York: Harper and Row.

Schwendinger, Julia R., and Herman Schwendinger. 2002. Critical criminology in the United States: The Berkeley school of criminology and theoretical trajectories. In *Critical Criminology: Issues, debates, challenges*, edited by R. Hogg and K. Carrington. Devon, UK: Willan Publishing.

Scott, Joan Wallach. 1996. *Only paradoxes to offer: French feminists and the rights of man.* Cambridge, MA: Harvard University Press.

Segnitz, Barbara, and Carol Rainey, eds. 1973. *Psyche. The feminine poetic consciousness: An anthology of modern American women poets.* New York: Dell.

Senate Task Force on the Status of Women. 1975. Senate task force on the status of women: Report on academic women. Edmonton: University of Alberta.

Serbin, Lisa A., K. D. O'Leary, R. N. Kent, and I. J. Tonick. 1973. A comparison of teacher response to the pre-academic and problem behavior of boys and girls. *Child Development* 44:796–804.

Shaffer, Beverly. 1977. *I'll find a way.* Canada: National Film Board of Canada.

Shannon, Kathleen. 1974. *Would I ever like to work.* Canada: National Film Board of Canada.

Sheinen, Rose. 1998. The changing space of women in academe: The "en-gender-ing" of knowledge. In *The illusion of inclusion: Women in post-secondary education*, edited by J. Stalker and S. Prentice. Halifax, NS: Fernwood.

Sherwin, Susan Bernice. 1973. Moral Foundations of Feminism. PhD diss., Stanford University.

———. 1992. *No longer patient: Feminist ethics and health care.* Philadelphia: Temple University Press.

————, ed. 1998. *The politics of women's health: Exploring agency and autonomy.* Philadelphia: Temple University Press.

————. 2001. Feminist reflections on the role of theories in a global bioethics. In *Globalizing feminist bioethics,* edited by R. Tong, G. Anderson, and A. Santos. Boulder, CO: Westview Press.

————. 2003. The importance of ontology for feminist policy-making in the realm of reproductive technology. *Canadian Journal of Philosophy* 28: 273–95.

Shiva, Vandana. 1997. *Biopiracy: The plunder of nature and knowledge.* Toronto: Between the Lines.

Showalter, Elaine. 1971. *Women's liberation and literature.* New York: Harcourt Brace Jovanovich.

Shulman, Alix Kates. 1995. *Drinking the rain: A memoir.* New York: Farrar Straus Giroux.

Side, Katherine, and Wendy Robbins. 2007. Institutionalizing inequalities in Canadian universities: The Canadian Research Chairs Program. *NWSA Journal.* Special issue: Women, Tenure, and Promotion 19 (3) (2007): 163–81.

Simmons, Alan B. 1990. New wave immigrants: Origins and characteristics. In *Ethnic demography: Canadian immigrant, racial and cultural variations,* edited by S. S. Halli, F. Trovato, and L. Driedger. Ottawa: Carleton University Press.

Smart, Carol. 1976. *Crime and criminology: A feminist critique.* London: Routledge.

Smith, Dorothy E. 1977. *Feminism and Marxism: A place to begin, a way to go.* Vancouver: New Star Books.

————. 1978. A peculiar eclipsing: Women's exclusion from men's culture. *Women's Studies International Quarterly* 1 (4): 281–96.

————. 1987. *The everyday world as problematic: A feminist sociology.* Toronto: University of Toronto Press.

————. 1990. *The conceptual practices of power: A feminist sociology of knowledge.* Toronto: University of Toronto Press.

————. 2005. *Institutional ethnography: A sociology for people.* Lanham, MD: Altamira Press.

Smyth, Donna. 1979. *Giant Anna.* Toronto: Playwrights Canada.

————. 1982. *Quilt.* Toronto: Women's Press.

————. 1986. *Subversive elements.* Toronto: Women's Press.

————. 1999. *Running to paradise: A play about Elizabeth Bishop.* Wolfville, NS: Gaspereau Press.

————. 2000. Margaret Conrad in conversation with Donna Smyth, founding editor of *Atlantis.* Interviewer: M. Conrad. *Atlantis* 25 (2): 105–6.

————. 2003. *Among the saints: Selected stories.* Lockeport, NS: Roseway Publishing.

Solanas, Valerie. 1969. The SCUM manifesto. In *Masculine/feminine: Readings in sexual mythology and the liberation of women,* edited by B. Roszak and T. Roszak. New York: Harper and Row.

Sommers, Christina Hoff. 1994. *Who stole feminism? How women have betrayed women.* New York: Simon and Shuster.

Spock, Benjamin. 1946. *The common sense book of baby and child care.* New York: Duell, Sloan, and Pearce.

Spruill, Julia Cherry. 1938. *Women's life and work in the Southern colonies*. New York: Russell and Russell, 1969.

Stacey, Judith, and Barrie Thorne. 1985. The missing feminist revolution in sociology. *Social Problems* 32 (4): 301–16.

Stainsby, Jill, Honoree Newcombe, Jacqui Parker-Snedler, and Paul Reniers. 1993. *AUCE and TSSU: Memoirs of a feminist union, 1972–1993*. Burnaby, BC: Teaching Support Staff Union Publisher.

Stark-Adamec, Cannie, ed. 1980. *Sex roles: Origins, influences, and implications for women*. Montréal: Eden Press.

Stark-Adamec, Cannie, and Meredith M. Kimball. 1984. Science free of sexism: A psychologist's guide to the conduct of nonsexist research. *Canadian Psychology* 25: 23–34.

Stasiulis, Diva. 1997. The political economy of race, ethnicity, and migration. In *Understanding Canada: Building on the new Canadian political economy*, edited by W. Clement. Montréal: McGill-Queens.

Statistics Canada. 1977. *Canada year book, 1976–1977*. Ottawa: Statistics Canada.

———. 1975–93. *Education in Canada: A statistical review*. Ottawa: Statistics Canada.

———. 1996. *Historical labour force statistics*. Catalogue no. 71–220–XPB 1995 B–8. Ottawa: Statistics Canada.

———. 2000. *Women in Canada 2000. A gender-based statistical report*. Ottawa: Industry Canada.

Staton, Pat, and Beth Light. 1987. *Speak with their own voices: A documentary history of the Federation of Women Teachers' Associations of Ontario and the Elementary Public School Teachers of Ontario*. Toronto: Federation of Women Teachers' Associations of Ontario.

Stein, Gertrude. 1938. *Picasso*. Paris: Floury.

Stephenson, Marylee, ed. 1973. *Women in Canada*. Toronto: New Press.

———. 1976. Being in women's liberation: A case study in social change. PhD diss., University of British Columbia.

———. 2000. *In critical demand: Social work in Canada*. Final report. Vol. 1. Ottawa: Canadian Association of Schools of Social Work. Cited November 15, 2007. Available at http://www.casw-acts.ca/canada/sectorstudyes_e.pdf.

Stephenson, Marylee, and Ruth Emery. 2003. *Living beyond the edge: The impact of trends in non-standard work on single/lone parent mothers*. Ottawa: Status of Women Canada.

Stimpson, Catherine. 1971. Women's liberation and black civil rights. In *Women in sexist society: Studies in power and powerlessness*, edited by V. Gornick and B. K. Moran. New York: Basic Books.

Story, Norah. 1967. *The Oxford companion to Canadian history and literature*. Toronto: Oxford University Press.

Strategy for Change Convention. 1972. Report of strategy for change convention of women in Canada, Toronto, Ontario, April 7–9, 1972. Toronto: National Action Committee on the Status of Women in Canada.

Strong-Boag, Veronica, and Beth Light. *True daughters of the north: An annotated bibliography*. Toronto: OISE Press, 1980.

Strouch, Kathleen D, and Joan McFarland. 1974. *Equality for women? Understanding the UN declaration on the elimination of the discrimination against women*. Fredericton: New Brunswick Human Rights Commission.

Sugiman, Pamela. 1993. Unionism and feminism in the Canadian auto workers' union, 1961–1992. In *Women challenging unions: Feminism, democracy and militancy*, edited by L. Briskin and P. McDermott. Toronto: University of Toronto Press.

———. 1994. *Labour's dilemma: The gender politics of auto workers in Canada, 1937–1979*. Toronto: University of Toronto Press.

Sydie, Rosalind. 1987. *Natural women, cultured men*. Toronto: Methuen.

———. 1989. Humanism, patronage and the question of women's artistic genius. *Journal of Historical Sociology* 2 (3): 175–205.

———. 2003. Feminist challenges to sociological theory. In *Advances in sociological theory*, edited by N. Genov. Opladen: Leske and Budrich.

———. 2004. Sex and the sociological fathers. In *Engendering the social*, edited by B. Marshall and A. Witz. Maindenhead, UK: Open University Press.

Symons, Thomas. 1978. *The Symons report*. Toronto: McClelland and Stewart.

Taylor, Ian, Paul Walton, and Jock Young. 1973. *The new criminology: For a social theory of deviance*. London: Routledge and Kegan Paul.

———, eds. 1975. *Critical criminology*. London: Routledge and Kegan Paul.

Tessier, Albert. 1946. *Canadiennes*. Montréal: Éditions Fides.

Thomas, Clara Eileen. 1946. *Canadian novelists, 1920–1945*. Toronto: Longmans and Green.

———. 1962. Anna Jameson: The making of a reputation. PhD diss., University of Toronto.

———. 1967. *Love and work enough: The life of Anna Jameson*. Toronto: University of Toronto Press.

———. 1969. *Margaret Laurence*. Toronto: McClelland and Stewart.

———. 1975. *The Manawaka world of Margaret Laurence*. Toronto: McClelland and Stewart.

———. 1999. *Chapters in a lucky life*. Ottawa: Borealis.

Tiger, Lionel. 1969. *Men in groups*. Don Mills, ON: Nelson.

Tiger, Lionel, and R. Fox. 1972. The primate pilgrimage: From bananas to ballots. *Psychology Today* 5:23.

Timpson, Annis May. 2001. *Driven apart: Women's employment equality and child care in Canadian public policy*. Vancouver: UBC Press.

Travail Canada. 1973. Les femmes dans la population active: Faits et données. In *Tableau 86: Pourcentage de femmes dans la population active et taux de participation des femmes à la population active 1931–1972*. Ottawa: Bureau de la main-d'œuvre féminine.

Trimble, Linda, and Jane Arscott. 2003. *Still counting: Women in politics across Canada*. Peterborough, ON: Broadview Press.

Trofimenkoff, Susan Mann, and Alison Prentice, eds. 1985. *The neglected majority: Essays in Canadian women's history*. Vol. 2. Toronto: McClelland and Stewart.

Trudeau, Pierre. 1967. Media scrum outside the House of Commons. CBC television news. Broadcast 21 December. Online at http://archives.cbc.ca/IDC-1-73-538-2671/politics_economy/omibus/clip1. Accessed 26 January 2008.

Tyyska, Vappu. 1995. *The politics of caring and the welfare state: The impact of the women's movement on child care policy in Canada and Finland, 1960–1990.* Helsinki: Suomalainen Tiedeakatemia.

United Nations Commission on the Status of Women. 1979. *Convention on the elimination of all forms of discrimination against women.* Last edited 1997. Cited August 21, 2006, from *Human Rights Web.* Available from http://www.hrweb.org/legal/cdw.html.

United Nations Committee on Economic, Social and Cultural Rights. 2006. *Concluding observations of the United Nations committee on economic, social and cultural rights.* Cited July 18, 2007. Available from http://www.unhchr.ch/tbs/doc.nsf/(symbol)/E.C.12.CAN.CO.4%20E.C.12.CAN.CO.5.En?Opendocument, accessed 8 February 2008.

United Nations Development Fund for Women. 2005. *Progress of the world's women.* Cited July 14, 2007. Available from www.un-ngls.org/women-2005.

Vaughan, Genevieve, ed. 2007. *Women and the gift economy: A radically different worldview is possible.* Toronto: Inanna Publications and Education, 257–89.

Valentich, Mary, and James Gripton. 1985. *Feminist perspectives on social work and human sexuality.* New York: Haworth Press.

Verthuy, Maïr, ed. 1987. *Colloque international sur la recherche et l'enseignement relatif aux femmes, 26 juillet–4 août, 1982.* 2 vols. Montréal: Institut Simone de Beauvoir, Université Concordia.

———. 1988. L'expression "Maîtres chez nous" n'existe pas au féminine: *Pleure pas Germaine et La nuit; Femmes et patrie dans l'oeuvre romanesque de Laure Conan.* Montréal: Institut Simone de Beauvoir, Université Concordia.

———. 1992. *Fenêtre sur cour: Voyage dans l'oeuvre romanesque d'Hélène Parmelin; Essai.* Laval, QC: Trois.

Verthuy, Maïr, and Lucie Leguin, eds. 1996. *Multi-culture, multi-écriture: La voix migrante au féminin en France et au Canada.* Montréal: L'Harmattan.

Verthuy, Maïr, and Jennifer Waelti-Walters. 1988. *Jeanne Hyvrard.* Amsterdam: Editions Rodopi.

Vickers, J[ill] McCalla. 1975a. *A Preliminary Statistical Map of Female Candidacies in Federal and Provincial Elections, 1951–74.* Ottawa: Women's Programme, Secretary of State.

———. 1975b. *Private Lives and Public Responsibilities: Canadian Women in Politics.* Ottawa: Women's Programme, Secretary of State.

Vickers, Jill. 1978. Where are the women in Canadian politics? *Atlantis* 3 (2): 40–51.

———. 1988. The political structure of the Canadian women's movement. Paper given at Ministerial Workshop on Federal Policy Development, Gatineau, QC, convened by the Minister Responsible for the Status of Women.

———. 1997. *Reinventing political science: A feminist approach.* Halifax, NS: Fernwood.

———. 2002. *The politics of race: Canada, Australia and the United States.* Ottawa: Golden Dog Press.

Vickers, Jill, and June Adam. 1977. *But can you type? Canadian universities and the status of women.* Ottawa: Canadian Association of University Teachers.

Vickers, Jill, Pauline Rankin, and Christine Appelle. 1993. *Politics as if women mattered: A political analysis of the National Action Committee on the Status of Women.* Toronto: University of Toronto Press.

Wand, B., ed. 1977. Report on the task force on the status of women in Canadian psychology. *Canadian Psychological Review* 18 (1).

Weiler, Kathleen. 1988. *Women teaching for change: Gender, class and power.* South Hadley, MA: Bergin and Garvey.

———, and Sue Middleton, eds. 1999. *Telling women's lives. Narrative inquiries in the history of women's education.* Buckingham: Open University Press.

Weisstein, Naomi. 1971. Psychology constructs the female. In *Women in sexist society: Studies in power and powerlessness*, edited by V. Gornick and B. K. Moran. New York: Basic Books.

Weldon, Fay. 1971. *Down among the women.* London: Heinemann.

Westcott, Marcia. 1983. Women's studies as a strategy for change: Between criticism and vision. In *Theories of women's studies*, edited by G. Bowles and R. D. Klein. London: Routledge.

Wittig, Monique. 1973. *Les guérillères* Translated by D. L. Vay. New York: Avon.

WMST-L. 1996–2000. "The personal is political": Origins of the Phrase. *Women's Studies Online Resources.* Cited November 15, 2007. Available at http://userpages .umbc.edu/~korenman/wmst/pisp.html.

Wollstonecraft, Mary. 1792. *A vindication of the rights of woman: With strictures on moral and political subjects.* London: Printed for J. Johnson.

Women's Bureau. 1973. *Women in the labour force: Facts and figures.* Ottawa: Canada Department of Labour.

Woolf, Virginia. 1929. *A room of one's own.* London: Hogarth Press.

———. 1938. *Three guineas.* London: Hogarth Press.

Wordsworth, William. 1850. *The prelude, or, growth of a poet's mind: An autobiographical poem.* London: Edward Moxon.

Wright, Donald. 2005. *The professionalization of history in English Canada.* Toronto: University of Toronto Press.

Yalnizian, Armine. 2007. *The rich and the rest of us: The changing face of Canada's growing gap.* Ottawa: Canadian Centre for Policy Alternatives.

Zaremba, Eve. 1992. "Eve Zaremba." In *Faces of feminism: Portraits of women across Canada*, edited by P. Harris. Toronto: Second Storey Press, 110–11.

Zinsser, Judith P. 1993. *History and feminism: A glass half full.* New York: Twayne.

Index